D0929573

Ecological Economics of the Oceans and Coasts

Ecological Economics of the Oceans and Coasts

Edited by

Murray Patterson

New Zealand Centre for Ecological Economics
Massey University, Palmerston North, New Zealand

and

Bruce Glavovic

School of People, Environment and Planning
Massey University, Palmerston North, New Zealand

Edward Elgar
Cheltenham, UK • Northampton, MA, USA

Published by
Edward Elgar Publishing Limited
Glensanda House
Montpellier Parade
Cheltenham
Glos GL50 1UA
UK

Edward Elgar Publishing, Inc.
William Pratt House
9 Dewey Court
Northampton
Massachusetts 01060
USA

A catalogue record for this book
is available from the British Library

Library of Congress Control Number: 2007942983

ISBN 978 1 84542 319 3

Printed and bound in Great Britain by MPG Books Ltd, Bodmin, Cornwall

Contents

PART III: MARINE SUSTAINABILITY: INTEGRATING ECOLOGY, ECONOMICS AND SOCIAL DIMENSIONS

PART IV: IMPLEMENTING AN ECOLOGICAL ECONOMICS OF THE OCEANS AND COASTS

Contributors

Dr Chris Batstone is a Resource and Environmental Economist with the Sustainable Business Group at the Cawthron Institute in Nelson (NZ) and an Associate of Auckland University's Institute of Public Policy. His research interests lie in the areas of marine resource economics and management and sustainable business. He has published in the areas of fisheries economics and entrepreneurship. In recent years, he has lectured in economic development, business economics, entrepreneurship and business approaches to environmental sustainability.

Dr Anthony Cole is Co-Director of a research company called Pansophy Ltd and Director of environmental studies at Te Wānanga-o-Raukawa. He has broad research and teaching interests including: economics, ecology, complexity, mathematical modelling, philosophy and religion. His PhD is in theoretical ecology. He did his post-doctoral study at Massey University in ecological economics and has worked for the last six years as an ecological economist for Landcare Research (NZ) Ltd. Anthony co-authored Chapter 4 while working at the New Zealand Centre for Ecological Economics as an Ecological Economist.

Dr Mark Gibbs was the leader of the Sustainable Business Group at the Cawthron Institute in New Zealand when this book was compiled. Mark has expertise in the dynamics of marine systems, and coupled social-ecological systems with particular emphasis on sustainability and resilience of these systems. Mark trained as a mathematical modeller but also holds qualifications in marine resource management and business management. Mark sits on a number of marine resource management committees. His team provides strategic and tactical advice to resource managers and stakeholders both in New Zealand and internationally. Mark is now a Research Leader at CSIRO in Australia.

Dr Bruce Glavovic has worked in academia, private consulting and government, mainly in South Africa and New Zealand. He is currently the Earthquake Commission (EQC) Fellow in Natural Hazards Planning at

Massey University, New Zealand. His research focuses on the role of planning in building sustainable, hazard-resilient communities. It is clustered around several themes: natural hazards planning; negotiation, collaborative planning and consensus-building processes; integrated environmental management (with a particular focus on coastal, ocean and water resources); and understanding poverty–environment linkages and driving forces. Bruce was the Project Manager of the team that designed and facilitated South Africa's coastal policy formulation process that culminated in the Government's *White Paper for Sustainable Coastal Development*.

Derrylea Hardy is a Research Officer at the New Zealand Centre for Ecological Economics at Massey University. She has a social science background in organizational development and leadership; tourism; employment, equity and wellbeing; mental health; and sustainable development.

Shuang Liu is a PhD candidate in the Rubenstein School of Environment and Natural Resources at the University of Vermont. For her masters' thesis she used GIS to carry out an ecological risk assessment of land use change in a national wetland reserve in Tianjin. Her PhD dissertation research is exploring dynamic ecosystem service valuation by integrating ecosystem modelling and valuation at different spatial scales.

Dr Garry McDonald is a Director of Market Economics Ltd and a Principal Ecological Economist of the New Zealand Centre of Ecological Economics. Garry has particular research interests in complexity, urban metabolism, industrial ecology and integrated environmental–economic modelling. Garry's career spans 12 years as an Economic Consultant to government and private sector clients. Recent research projects include ecological footprinting of New Zealand regions, construction of a physical input–output table for New Zealand, and the dynamic modelling of complex systems.

Dr Ben McNeil is a Lecturer and Research Fellow at the Climate and Environmental Dynamics Laboratory at the University of New South Wales, Sydney, Australia. His expertise and publications cover a wide range of environmental science and policy issues, particularly with respect to ocean biogeochemistry, coral reefs, climate change impacts and international policy.

Prof Murray Patterson holds the Landcare Chair in Ecological Economics and is Director of the New Zealand Centre for Ecological Economics at

Massey University. He is widely published in a number of fields including ecological economics, energy analysis, environmental valuation, environmental policy and policy modelling. Much of this research is of an applied and interdisciplinary nature, working at the interface of policy and sustainability concerns. In recent years he has lectured in the resource and environmental planning programme at Massey University in policy analysis and evaluation.

Dr Keith Probert is a Senior Lecturer in the Department of Marine Science at the University of Otago. His main interests are in marine biology and ecology, particularly the ecology of seabed organisms, the effects of human impacts on marine systems, and marine conservation. His research in these areas extends from coastal to deep-sea environments and he has published widely, from numerous scientific articles to popular books on marine natural history. He teaches undergraduate and postgraduate courses, mainly in the areas of marine biology and ecology, marine pollution, and deep-sea biology.

Prof Matthias Ruth is Roy F. Weston Chair in Natural Economics, Director of the Center for Integrative Environmental Research at the Division of Research, Director of the Environmental Policy Program at the School of Public Policy, and Co-Director of the Engineering and Public Policy Program at the University of Maryland. His research focuses on dynamic modelling of natural resource use, complex systems analysis, and environmental economics and policy. His theoretical work draws heavily on concepts from engineering, economics and ecology, while his applied research utilizes methods of non-linear dynamic modelling as well as adaptive and anticipatory management. In the last decade, Professor Ruth has published nine books and nearly 100 papers and book chapters in the scientific literature. He collaborates extensively with scientists and policy makers in the USA, Canada, Europe, Oceania, Asia and Africa.

Dr Basil Sharp is an Economist at The University of Auckland. His research programme is focused on the application of microeconomics and econometric modelling to contemporary resource and environmental problems. He has published numerous papers in leading international journals on the design, use and outcomes of tradable rights. These research publications demonstrate the relative merits of rights-based systems of governance, including gains in economic efficiency and technological progress. He teaches courses in resource and environmental economics, microeconomics, and law and economics.

Nicola Smith is an Environment Analyst at Market Economics Ltd, Auckland, New Zealand. She has a background in law and environmental geography. Nicky has work experience in resource management and planning in local government. Her research interests include: ecological economics, the modelling of economic–environment interactions and the development of analytical tools for progressing towards sustainable development.

Dr Charlotte Šunde is currently undertaking post-doctoral study at the University of Versailles. Her research interests include: cross-cultural dialogue particularly as it relates to environmental issues, co-management of the conservation estate, epistemologies of environmental knowledge, complexity and ecosystem management, and planning for sustainable development. Charlotte wrote Chapter 8 when she was a Research Associate at the New Zealand Centre for Ecological Economics.

Dr Matthew Wilson is a Senior Economist and Business Analyst with ARCADIS, an international company providing consultancy, engineering and management services for achieving sustainable solutions in infrastructure and environment. Prior to joining Arcadis, he served as an Assistant Research Professor of Management and Strategy at the University of Vermont, School of Business Administration where he continues to participate as an Adjunct Assistant Professor. He is recognized as an international expert in the field of ecosystem service valuation and works with both private and public sectors to find innovative market solutions for protecting critical ecosystem services. Among his published research is a co-authored chapter titled 'Coastal Systems and Coastal Communities', now appearing in the United Nations-Sponsored *Millennium Ecosystem Assessment: Conditions and Trends* (2005) from Island Press.

Preface

There is no unequivocal or unitary view of what might constitute 'an ecological economics of the oceans and coasts'. However, we believe at the very least it should achieve two things. Firstly, it should be grounded in a holistic and integrative analysis of economic, ecological and social systems. Secondly, it should aim to provide insights into how to sustainably manage our oceans and coasts. Therefore this book, if it is to be successful, should move beyond standard economic analysis to present a broader vision of the economics of oceans and coasts.

The book covers four *sequential and interrelated themes* each of which addresses a fundamental question of importance to establishing an ecological economics of the oceans and coasts: (1) How do ecological processes underpin coastal and oceanic systems? (2) How can ecological economists deal with 'value conflicts' that result from human interactions with these coastal and oceanic processes and systems? (3) How can ecological economists 'integrate' our understanding of the economic, ecological and social dimensions of these coastal and oceanic systems? (4) How in the real world can we implement the ideas that emerge from this analysis, in order to achieve sustainability goals?

In developing this book we have adopted a somewhat 'catholic' editorial policy which may surprise some. We felt that it was important to include inputs from a variety of disciplines, even those that may be considered to be traditional foes of ecological economics. In this regard, we have included three chapters based on conventional neoclassical analysis. These chapters are included not only because neoclassical economics represents the 'status quo' of economic analysis, but because it forms the theoretical basis of much current marine governance thinking – as well as more generally it provides valuable insights into how to sustainably manage our oceans and coasts. Our argument is that neoclassical economics is 'a necessary but not sufficient' form of analysis in this context – an ecological economic analysis of the oceans and coasts needs to go beyond the confines of neoclassical analysis to form a much broader and integrative approach, by drawing on disciplines ranging from ecology to the political and social sciences. These neoclassical economics chapters thus present a useful point of departure for developing an ecological economics perspective on oceans and coasts.

Some readers may be frustrated by the lack of a coherent body of theory or a lack of definitive answers to the questions that we pose. We acknowledge these frustrations but point out that this is very much uncharted territory and an immature field of enquiry. Our view is that this book is as much about uncovering issues as it is about providing definitive answers to questions. Ultimately, we can only suggest what might constitute an ecological economics of the oceans and coasts. Hopefully, however, these suggestions do provide a solid starting point for the future development of this field. Furthermore, as can be anticipated in any relatively young field of endeavour, 'theory' is well ahead of practice. There are frustratingly few 'success stories' of effective implementation of an ecological economics of oceans and coasts. Sadly, most examples portray unsustainable practices. Moving beyond 'theory' to praxis constitutes a major challenge and the next frontier for an ecological economics of oceans and coasts that fosters sustainability.

This book was made possible due to the generosity and intellectual input of a number of people to whom we are indebted. Most importantly we wish to acknowledge the valuable role of a number of reviewers of this book and of the individual chapters: Peter Burbridge, Sue Cassels, Chris Cornelisen, Quentin Grafton, Janet Grieve, Phil Lawn, Anton Meister, John Peet, Kim Hang Pham Do, Anna Straton, Mike Young and Svein Jentoft. Any remaining errors or omissions are the responsibility of the book editors and individual chapter authors.

A special thanks is also due to John Proops for encouraging us to develop this book; to Catherine Elgar, Felicity Plester, Jo Betteridge, Alexandra O'Connell and Karen McCarthy of Edward Elgar for their guidance and patience in the publishing process; and to Derrylea Hardy for her editorial assistance. We are also grateful to Anne Austin, Nicolette Faville and Jemma Callaghan for their help in proof-reading, graphics, and formatting of the book.

Murray Patterson and Bruce Glavovic

1. Towards an Ecological Economics of the Oceans and Coasts

Murray Patterson

There is an emerging awareness by policy makers, resource management agencies and the general public of the importance of oceans and coasts[1] across a number of fronts. In spite of this, much of the ecology of the coasts (and more particularly the oceans) remains unknown to us. Although proceeding at a rapid pace, scientific discovery still demonstrably lags behind our terrestrial rate of discovery and knowledge acquisition. This has prompted calls for us to become more 'oceans literate' and led to an emerging array of international and national policy initiatives to deal with managing our oceans and coasts. Indeed, in recognition of the importance of the marine environment, the United Nations declared 1998 'The International Year of the Ocean'. This declaration provided individual organizations and governments with an important opportunity to raise public awareness and understanding of the oceans and related issues.

WHY AN ECOLOGICAL ECONOMICS OF THE OCEANS AND COASTS?

Ecological and Economic Importance of the Oceans and Coasts

Why are the oceans and coasts important and why is there an urgent need for ecological economists, as well as people involved in ocean and coastal management, to turn their attention to this domain of study? First, because the *oceans and coasts have a fundamental ecological and economic importance across global, national and regional scales.* It is an inescapable fact that the oceans are a critical part of the planet's ecological system, which is not surprising given that they cover 70 per cent of the earth's surface. They are the most conspicuous aspect of the global landscape, being highly visible from space – Earth has accordingly been dubbed the 'blue planet'. Oceans dominate the world's hydrological cycle with all but a very small part of the earth's water being in the ocean. In addition, the oceans dominate the earth's carbon cycle, holding 40 times more carbon than the atmosphere and absorbing perhaps half the carbon released from economic activity. The oceans are also a vital component of the earth's climate and weather systems. Ocean currents transport and redistribute heat, thereby affecting climate patterns and dynamics across the globe. For example, the oceans transport about half the heat from the tropics to the mid-latitudes, cooling the former and warming the latter. Sudden shifts in these currents and patterns of heat transfer are thought to have triggered past ice ages. Furthermore, the oceans are uniquely important for biodiversity, much of which still remains unknown to us. This is exemplified by the recent discovery of 50 completely new species (of fish, coral, shrimp) off the coast of Indonesia by Mark Erdmann's team. The importance of this biodiversity goes far beyond the aesthetic appeal of the so-called 'charismatic megafauna'. This was recently demonstrated by Worm et al. (2006), who showed strong empirical occurrence of marine biodiversity with ecosystem productivity, ecosystem stability and ecosystem service delivery.

The coastal ecosystems, although only covering a very small portion (1.2 per cent)[2] of the earth's surface, are a vitally important component of the global ecological system. They are productive ecosystems, 'punching well above their weight' by accounting for 4.1 per cent[3] of global productivity (photosynthesis). Coastal ecosystems, including estuaries, mangroves, tidal marshes, seagrass beds, kelp forests, coral reefs, intertidal areas and the beach shores, are very diverse ecosystems that provide a wide range of ecological functions, many of which are interconnected. Coastal wetlands act as a natural buffer between the land and ocean, absorbing flood waters and dissipating storm surges. For example, the loss of coastal wetlands along the Louisiana coastline has contributed significantly to making this region vulnerable to coastal erosion and hurricane-induced storm surges as happened in 2005. Coastal wetlands are also important in nutrient cycling and processing. As such, a significant proportion of the terrestrial nitrogen flux (from agricultural runoff, sewage and other sources) is intercepted, stored and processed by coastal ecosystems. These systems are major producers of detritus and provide nursery grounds for numerous commercially, recreationally and culturally important species. In addition, they can serve as filters to remove sediments and toxins from the water. Coastal ecosystems are also ecologically important for providing habitat for many species. Marine biologists have, for example, discovered coral reefs that rival tropical rainforests in their species diversity (Hinrichsen 1998).

Oceans and coasts are not only ecologically important, they are economically important as well. The oceans are increasingly becoming a source of raw materials for the economy as terrestrial sources are depleted and put under pressure. Much of the world's tourism industry is based on coastal attractions and activities, and the oceans still provide the major means of international transport for cargo. For many, the oceans are the 'new frontier' of economic development, offering seemingly endless potential for exploitation. They are already a major source of fossil fuels, providing the global economy with 50 per cent of its natural gas and 30 per cent of its crude oil. The oceans provide 16 per cent of the world population's protein, particularly being a major food source in parts of Asia, Africa and the Pacific. In total, it is estimated[4] that raw materials and food from the marine environment had a market value of $US1.6 trillion in 1994 – this represented 6.4 per cent of the global GDP of $US25 trillion. In addition to this direct use of these raw materials (which have a market value), coastal-marine ecosystems also produce so-called 'ecosystem services' that contribute to human welfare but do not have a market value. By using such an approach, Costanza et al. (1997) found the 'total economic value' (market plus non-market) of coastal and marine systems[5] to be $US22.6 trillion. This is equivalent to 68 per cent of the global GDP and significantly outweighs the 'total economic value' of terrestrial ecosystems at $US10.7 trillion.

Increasing Economic Pressures on the Oceans and Coasts

A second set of reasons why ecological economists should be concerned with the oceans and coasts relates to the *increasingly negative impacts of the economy and economic activities on the environment world-wide*. The Millennium Ecosystem Assessment leaves little doubt that coastal-marine ecosystems are among those most affected by the expanding global economy (Brown et al. 2006). The economic activities and pressures having a significant (and increasingly negative) impact on marine ecosystems include:

- *Growth in the coastal economy.* Coastal population growth has been prolific, with eight of the ten largest global megacities being coastal. About 44–48 per cent[6] of global economic activity occurs in coastal regions. The 6.3-fold expansion of the global economy from 1950 to 1998 inevitably had ever-increasing direct environmental impacts on coastal ecosystems. Much of the loss of estuaries, for example, can be directly attributed to port development, infilling and civil engineering works required to support economic activity in the coastal zone. Industries based in coastal regions release a wide array of point-source pollutants (nitrogen, phosphorus, oil/oil byproducts, heavy metals and persistent organic substances) into the near-shore environment, resulting in degradation of coastal ecosystems. Human sewage is another colossal coastal pollutant, as are agricultural and urban runoff. This 'highly concentrated' flow of water pollutants ends up in the relatively small area (1.2 per cent) of the globe that happens to be occupied by coastal ecosystems. This largely explains why the Millennium Ecosystem Assessment found that coastal (and marine) ecosystems are 'deteriorating faster than any other ecosystems' (Brown et al. 2006).

- *Accelerated growth of the coastal tourism industry.* Further exacerbating the environmental effects of the growth of the coastal-economy has been the even more rapid growth of the coastal tourism industry and associated ecosystem alteration. The environmental impacts of the coastal tourism industry include coastal erosion, increased water pollution and discharges into the sea, natural habitat loss, and increased pressure on endangered species. The coastal tourism industry also often puts a strain on water resources in arid areas such as, for example, the southern Mediterranean.

- *Increasing demand for fish products.* A critical driver of change in the marine environment is the increasing demand for fish and fish products. Demand for seafood products has doubled over the last 30 years and is projected to continue to grow at 1.5 per cent per annum to 2020 (World Bank 2005). This demand, however, is demonstrably 'unsustainable', with 24.1 per cent[7] of the world's fisheries having collapsed since 1950 mainly due to over-fishing. Pauly et al. (2003) point to an even gloomier prognosis unless the current level of fishing effort is substantially reduced. Worm et al. (2006) conclusively show how this collapse of fisheries not only curtails food supply, but leads to the overall loss and deterioration of marine ecosystem services. Fishing practices such as bottom trawling (loss of benthos habitat) and drift nets (catching non-target species) also have significant direct negative environmental impacts. Worldwide demand for fish products is increasingly being met from aquaculture, which also brings with it detrimental impacts on the marine environment such as the loss of habitat for native biodiversity and the spread of disease.

- *Increasing demand for food and agricultural products.* The ever-increasing demand for food to nourish the world's expanding population is an important economic driver of change in coastal-marine ecosystems. Runoff of nutrients (phosphorus and, more particularly, nitrogen) from agricultural land into the world's oceans has dramatically increased over the last 50 years, as agriculture has expanded and become more intensive and reliant on fertilizers. Indeed, the 'over-enrichment' of marine-coastal environments is largely, but not solely, attributable to increased agricultural runoff. This over-enrichment is known to result in the greater occurrence of hypoxic or 'dead zones', loss of habitat and biodiversity, and even indirectly impacts on climate change as marine rates of carbon sequestration are affected.

- *Increasing demand for marine minerals and energy.* Marine sources currently account for about 30 per cent of the world's oil production and about 50 per cent of the world's natural gas production. Furthermore, as terrestrial sources of oil and gas are exhausted, increasing attention is given to exploration and production from offshore basins of every continent around the world. Although currently only a very small amount of minerals are taken from the marine environment, many people see the oceans as the 'new frontier' for the exploitation of mineral resources. Thus, the marine environment is coming under ever-increasing environmental pressures that result from the offshore exploitation of energy and mineral resources.
- *Indirect impacts of economic growth on the marine environment.* There are a number of indirect effects of global economic growth on the coastal-marine environment that take place, even though such growth may be occurring in locations far away from the oceans and coasts. As already discussed, agricultural activity in non-coastal areas can significantly affect the coastal-marine environment by adding to the load of nutrients entering that environment. The indirect impact of greenhouse gas emissions resulting from economic activity all over the globe (irrespective of its location) can have a profound affect on the coastal–marine environment. For example, rising sea temperatures brought about from greenhouse-gas-induced climate change, is seen as the major cause of coral bleaching. Global warming, resulting from increased greenhouse gas emissions, also has a myriad of other effects on the coastal-marine environment ranging from sea level rise to changing ocean currents, and to the loss of biodiversity due to these changing conditions. Because of the strong inter-connectivity between the terrestrial, coastal and marine environments through biogeochemical cycles, it is almost inevitable that growth in the global economy, no matter where it is happening, will have at least some affect on coastal and marine ecosystems.

Intensifying Policy Focus on Oceanic and Coastal Management

A third set of reasons why ecological economists should be concerned with the oceans and coasts relates to the *increasingly urgent calls for robust and integrative policy to deal with the negative impact of economic activity on coastal and marine ecosystems*. Many of these problems have a strong ecological economics dimension. This move to a more integrative approach for coastal and marine policy has been made across a number of fronts: *Heightened international attention given to integrative management of the oceans and coasts over the last decade.* Chapter 17 of Agenda 21 of the UN Conference on Environment and Development (UNCED), for instance, called for new and integrated approaches to the sustainable development of coasts and oceans (UN 1992). Progress has been made post-UNCED to secure agreements and build programmes towards this end, including: the UN Convention on the Law of the Sea (1994); UNEP Global Programme of Action for Protection of the Marine Environment from Land-Based Activities; and the Convention on Biological Diversity's Jakarta Mandate relating to coastal and marine biodiversity. Coasts and oceans assumed a more prominent place on the agenda of the 2002 World Summit of Sustainable Development (WSSD) in Johannesburg, with commitments being made to, among other things: 'Type I' outcomes such as controlling illegal fishing by 2004, managing fishery capacity by 2005, applying the ecosystem approach to marine areas by 2010, and establishing a network of marine protected areas by 2012.

- *Proliferation of national-level integrated coastal management policies, programmes and plans.* Since the passage of the US Coastal Zone Management Act in 1972, many nations have established Integrated Coastal Management (ICM) initiatives. ICM has become accepted international practice since the 1990s, and the number of ICM initiatives has increased dramatically in recent times. An estimated 75 countries and organizations were involved in about 217 ICM initiatives in 1993. By 2002, some 145 countries and organizations were involved in 698 such initiatives (Sorensen 1993, 2002). ICM focuses explicit attention on the interconnections that characterize coastal systems and provides a holistic perspective that takes into account the links between inland catchments, the coastal zone and the marine environment. In particular, it focuses attention on integrating traditionally compartmentalized vertical (spheres of government) and horizontal (between sectors) planning and decision making processes.
- *Millennium Ecosystem Assessment* (Brown et al. 2006). The high profile Millennium Assessment carried out by the UNEP calls for 'an integrated approach to coastal management [that] requires a holistic view that includes land-based and freshwater influences and necessary political, economic and social conditions' (Brown et al. 2006). It recognized that the 'cause–effect' relationships in the coastal and marine environment are not straightforward, with many connections across ecological processes and systems, as well as cross-cutting political, social, economic and institutional dimensions. This inter-connectiveness and multi-

dimensionality provides the rationale for the integrated approach that was recommended by the Millennium Assessment.

In general, the literature on oceans and coasts tends to be artificially divided, with a focus on either oceans or coasts, or on either economics or ecology. Neither of these divisions is constructive in developing policy to advance the sustainability of these interconnected systems. An ecological economics perspective on oceans and coasts attempts to transcend these artificial divisions and should bring a fresh conceptual perspective to policy development.

DEFINING FEATURES OF AN ECOLOGICAL ECONOMICS OF THE OCEANS AND COASTS

An ecological economics view necessarily differs from (although overlaps with) perspectives from marine ecology, neoclassical economics, policy sciences and a number of other disciplines. It is our argument that an ecological economics view is important because it attempts to draw together strands from these other disciplines, in a way that particularly focuses on the interconnections between economic and ecological processes.

Ecological economics emerged in the late 1980s as a separate discipline that placed particular importance on economy–environment interactions. Its roots, however, can be traced to the 'visionary' work of Boulding (1966), Georgescu-Roegen (1971) and Daly (1973) in modern times, and even further back to the classical economists (particularly Malthus and Ricardo) and the French physiocrats.[8] Much of the initial impetus for ecological economics arose from the perceived failure of conventional (neoclassical) economics to deal with sustainability issues. A need was perceived for a new approach firmly grounded in an understanding of ecology and ecological processes and how this knowledge had a bearing on the economy and economic growth. Neoclassical economics was perceived to be too narrow and reductionist in its approach, and too 'mono-discipline' oriented in that it often ignored or 'assumed away' the findings from other disciplines in the biophysical and social sciences. Ecological economists have frequently argued for a more 'interdisciplinary' or a 'transdisciplinary' approach.

We suggest that there are *four cornerstones of ecological economics* that should be at the forefront of our thinking when setting about the task of defining an Ecological Economics of the Oceans and Coasts: (1) Sustainability as its Normative Goal; (2) Biophysical Approach; (3) Complex

Systems Approach; (4) Transdisciplinarity and Methodological Pluralism.

Sustainability as the Normative Goal

The primary focus of ecological economics is *achieving the policy goal of sustainability*. This could be said to be the normative goal of ecological economics, while the normative goal of neoclassical economics is usually seen to be allocative efficiency or, more broadly, economic efficiency. These different normative foci lead to differing approaches in defining policy problems and their solutions. Neoclassical economists, for example, tend to place greater faith in the market mechanism for resolving resource conflicts and policy issues. Gowdy and Erickson (2005) argue that there are signs of some tempering of this view, with recent Nobel Prize winners in economics holding beliefs that would have been considered heretical in the 1970s and 1980s. However, many neoclassical economists still fervently hold to the Walrasian general equilibrium framework and the role it plays in defining economically efficient outcomes – in spite of all of its attendant assumptions about optimizing behaviour, perfect information and so forth.

Early ecological economists set out the principles and pre-conditions for a sustainable economy. Boulding (1966) eloquently used the metaphor of a spaceship to emphasize the roles that 'matter', 'energy' and 'information' played in maintaining economic activity, and the need for 'social' rather than 'technical' solutions if economies were to become more sustainable. Georgescu-Roegen (1971), in more formal terms, analyzed the thermodynamic constraints on economic activity and provided insights into how to run an economy more sustainably, albeit not in a steady state. Daly (1973) also set out his principles for achieving sustainability in his visionary book *Toward a Steady-State Economy*. He positioned the analysis of sustainability questions in terms of his 'ends–means' spectrum. In this spectrum, 'low-entropy matter-energy' is the 'ultimate means' (or binding constraint on economic activity), and 'higher-level ends' are defined by human needs and ethics and not by the concept of economic efficiency.

In more recent times, ecological economists have drawn on ecological theory (rather than thermodynamic theory) to define sustainability principles. For example, Common and Perrings (1992) showed how ecological theory of communities and ecosystems can help define sustainable development. That is, they define sustainability in terms of Holling's concept of resilience, which is the 'propensity of the system to retain its organizational structure following a perturbation'.

Both neoclassical and ecological economists have used the concept of 'natural capital' to define and analyze sustainability, although both camps tend to have differing views in this area. The general view, however, is that sustainability can be defined in terms of maintaining a constant capital stock (manufactured capital plus natural capital) from generation to generation.[9] Neoclassical economists tend to be more optimistic about the ability of manufactured capital to substitute for natural capital, meaning that the depletion of natural capital is not necessarily unsustainable. Ecological economists, however, armed with their knowledge of ecological systems and thermodynamics, are less optimistic. Ecological economists often refer to 'critical natural capital', which Chiesura and de Groot (2003) define as 'that part of the natural environment which performs important and irreplaceable functions'. Accordingly, it is argued that, although some substitution of manufactured capital for natural capital is possible, this has its limits as, by definition, critical natural capital cannot be substituted indefinitely.

Many of the concepts of sustainability advanced by ecological economists are important in interpreting how the oceans and coasts should be sustainably managed. Oceans and coasts, as discussed in Chapter 2, are highly connected with global biogeochemical processes of energy and mass flow. Energy and mass flow accounting and modelling, advanced particularly by the early ecological economists, can be used to illuminate the connections between the oceans/coastal systems and the economy, as well as terrestrial systems. When considering sustainability of the ocean and coasts, it is important that these connections across space and time are understood. For instance, it is shown that, in many ways, terrestrial economic activity (for example, through greenhouse gas emissions and non-point source agricultural pollution) is highly relevant to the sustainability of the oceans and coasts.

The concept of 'critical natural capital' is also important when it comes to an ecological interpretation of the oceans and coasts. Ecological economists therefore need to give careful attention to defining the critical natural capital functions of marine systems as part of the process of determining how such systems can be sustainably managed. The services of the oceans in maintaining and regulating climate are a classic example of critical natural capital that needs be recognized in any ecological economic analysis purporting to be concerned about sustainability.

Biophysical Approach

A second cornerstone of ecological economics is its *biophysical approach to economics*. Indeed, ecological economics is sometimes referred to as physio-economics (van den Bergh 1996) or bioeconomics (Mayumi and Gowdy 1999).

A biophysical perspective emphasizes the materials, energy resources, technology, information flows, feedback and production processes underlying economic activity. Attention is paid to physical limits, which leads ecological economists to question, *inter alia*, the notion of indefinite economic growth. As Peet (1992) points out, 'most physical scientists would agree that (a biophysical approach) is applicable to the physical constraints and long-term *limits* to social activities, not to the day-to-day activities of people within those limits.'

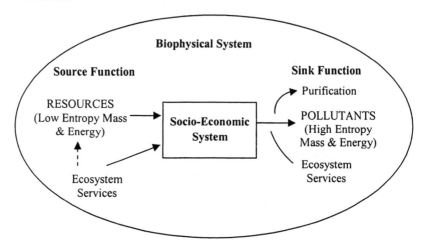

Figure 1.1   Ecological economics framework: biophysical system and its socio-economic sub-system

Ecological economists use a 'nested hierarchy model' in which the socio-economic system is a sub-system of the biophysical system – refer to Figure 1.1. Under this model, the socio-economic system is what Daly (2005) refers to as a 'wholly-owned subsidiary' of the biophysical system.

This 'biophysical model of ecological economics' has a number of important implications for sustainability:

- The extent to which the socio-economic sub-system occupies the biophysical system. Estimates by Vitousek et al. (1986) indicate that the economy has appropriated 40 per cent of the net primary productivity of the terrestrial biosphere. The ultimate physical limit cannot exceed 100 per cent, and certainly to have a safety margin it has been argued that this limit should realistically be more like 80 per cent.
- The extent to which the sustainability of the socio-economic sub-system depends on the biophysical system as a *source of resources and ecosystem*

services such as climate regulation, refugia, soil formation, and so forth. Many resources are clearly finite and depletable – for example, fossil fuels, minerals and land. Economic growth cannot be sustained indefinitely if these resources are depleted or degraded.

- The extent to which the sustainability of the economy depends on the *sink functions of the biophysical system*. For many wastes and emissions, the biophysical system can efficiently purify and absorb such pollutants. But there are critical thresholds beyond which the biophysical system cannot cope with ever increasing levels of pollutants. For instance, at a local level an estuary will become eutrophic once a certain pollution-induced nutrient threshold is reached; or on a global scale the biophysical system only has a certain capacity to absorb greenhouse gas emissions.
- There are critical limits to the ability to recycle material wastes. Despite the rhetoric of zero waste campaigns, this is a physical impossibility. The Second Law of Thermodynamics tells us that degraded energy outputs can never be recycled and there are severe limits on the degree of recycling of materials (mass).

In order to achieve a (more) sustainable situation, from a biophysical perspective, the minimization of energy and material throughput is the solution put forward by ecological economists such as Goodland and Daly (1993). An ecological economics analysis of the oceans and coasts should emphasize this biophysical approach to economics, by firstly highlighting the 'source' and 'sink' functions of the oceans and coasts. *As a source function*, they provide ecosystem services such as climate regulation and nutrient cycling as well as fossil fuels, food (fish) and other raw materials, all of which are critical inputs into the economy. Much of the current economics thinking about the exploitation of these marine resources and their ecosystem is driven by a 'frontier economics', where the biophysical limits are axiomatically assumed not to exist, or are at least not considered important. Approaches such as net energy analysis, as used by ecological economists such as Cleveland (1992), need to be used more frequently to test the true viability of energy and mineral exploitation in the seas. When it comes to fisheries, ecological models of the non-linear dynamics of fish populations need to be appreciated and integrated into any ecological economics analysis of fisheries (Mullon et al. 2005).

The *sink functions* of the oceans and coasts need to be more thoroughly analyzed than in conventional economic analysis. Again, 'frontier economics' cannot prevail, as the oceans and coasts are not the ultimate 'waste disposal unit' for economic activity – there are limits to the capacity of the oceans and coasts to continue to sustainably absorb, process and purify wastes from the terrestrial economy. Many of these limits are already showing up despite the vastness of the oceans – for example, the effects of greenhouse gas emissions on marine biota and habitat, and the effects of nitrogen enrichment on the marine environment including the greater occurrence of dead (hypoxic) zones.

In developing an ecological economics of the oceans and coasts, it is also important to recognize we are dealing with complex living systems. This is a complex picture of turbulence, surprises, and connectivity of processes across temporal and spatial scales. Ecological economists, therefore, need to be careful when taking on this ecological (biophysical) view of economics to ensure first, that they use appropriate tools of analysis such as complex systems thinking, and second, that they recommend the use of approaches such as adaptive management in attempting to sustainably manage complex marine ecosystems. All too often standard economic models assume 'idealized' smooth behaviour of living coastal-marine systems, notably with some spectacular failures, particularly in the fisheries area.

Inter-connectiveness across space and time is another important aspect of an ecological (biophysical) view of the economy and its connections with the biophysical environment. This idea is critical to an ecological economics interpretation of the oceans and coasts. As previously pointed out, marine ecosystems are part of, and connected to, global biogeochemical cycles. This means they can be affected by economic activity (farming, heavy industry) that may be situated inland and far away from the coasts. Conventional economic analysis is, however, often spatially highly compartmentalized, and rarely takes account of these spatial factors[10] and the interconnectivity of ecological processes. Redressing these shortcomings of economic analysis presents a real challenge to ecological economics when it comes to a biophysical view of the oceans and coasts.

Complex Systems Approach

A third cornerstone of ecological economics is that it is based on a complex systems approach. Both ecological economics and neoclassical economics are broadly based on a 'systems approach'. That is, the intention of both approaches is to view the *economy as a system of interdependent processes*, whether they are sectors or markets. Although, for pedagogical purposes, neoclassical economics often use 'partial equilibrium' analytics, most neoclassical economists gravitate to 'general equilibrium' ideas that see interacting markets involving a whole ensemble of producers and consumers. Ecological economics shares this view of the economy as an interdependent system, but takes it further. Ecological economics extends the systems approach to include the biophysical environment, thereby seeing the economy as a sub-system of the biophysical system, which necessarily interacts with it through inputs, outputs and feedbacks across the sub-system boundary (Peet 1992). Second, ecological economics more fully embraces the idea of complex systems, whereby the economy–environment system and its interactions are characterized by complex systems behaviour including 'emergent properties', 'irreversibility' and 'non-linear dynamics'. This is in stark contrast to neoclassical economics, based on the 'Walrasian general equilibrium system', that can only predict smooth, reversible behaviours because it is based on mechanical analogies drawn from 19th century physics (Mulder and van den Bergh 2001; Ruth 1993).

This complex systems perspective of ecological economics is critical to understanding the sustainability implications of ocean and coastal systems. Firstly, of foremost importance, is the *concept of interdependence* – a concept which is of course axiomatic to all systems approaches. In this light, we must see the oceans and coasts as systems that are strongly connected to each other as well as to the economy of the terrestrial environment.

The idea of *emergent properties* and its relationship to the *hierarchy* of complex systems is also important. 'Emergent properties' refers to the phenomenon of properties emerging as you view the system from higher hierarchical levels. For example, in marine systems when the system is studied at the level of individual organisms or even at the population level, properties such as the 'disturbance regulation' of the marine system are not apparent until you look at the entire ecosystem at a higher level.

A third important idea of complex systems thinking is that of *non-equilibrium behaviour*. In contrast, the neoclassical economic view is centred on equilibrium behaviour. The emerging view of modern ecology is that ecological systems are governed by non-equilibrium as well as equilibrium behaviour (De Angelis and Waterhouse 1987). That is, the system does not gravitate smoothly to one single general equilibrium point; rather, the behaviour is less predictable and even chaotic. Bifurcation points are critical in the development trajectories of ecological systems, whereby the system may 'flip' into a qualitatively different state or new trajectory towards an equilibrium point. Wilson et al. (1996) and Mullon et al. (2005) both argue that marine systems, such as fisheries, are characterized by this type of 'non-linear' dynamics, which implies a different approach from the conventional one that is heavily centred on predictability and system control. Instead, an ecological economics of the oceans and coasts must be based on appreciating the less predicable behaviour of such systems by adopting approaches such as adaptive management and the precautionary principle.

Transdisciplinarity and Methodological Pluralism

A fourth cornerstone of ecological economics is that it is based on ideas of transdisciplinarity and methodological pluralism. The need for methodological pluralism in ecological economics is a necessity, given the complex nature of economy–environment interactions and complexity of the related policy questions that ecological economists seek to answer. No one theory or analytical framework is in itself deemed to be sufficient. Therefore, ecological economists tend to draw on many disciplines, theoretical frameworks and methodological approaches. Norgaard (1989) established a robust rationale for this approach in ecological economics – an approach that has been broadly accepted by most ecological economists including, for example, Faber and Proops (1985), Soderbaum (1990) and Costanza (1991).

In contrast to ecological economics, neoclassical economics is firmly grounded on a single discipline approach and the idea of 'universalism', where it is assumed there is one valid framework (that is, Marshallian economics) that can be universally applied to all situations independent of context. Such ideas of universalism are not of course uncommon in other disciplines in addition to neoclassical economics, particularly in the sciences where the discovery of universal truths is seen as sign of the 'maturity' and 'rigour' of a particular discipline. But, for ecological economists, such hegemony in economic enquiry is not only unhealthy and academically stifling, it also does not reflect the reality of complex, multi-dimensional, multifaceted and often incongruous systems encountered in ecological economics enquiry.

As a consequence, ecological economists have attempted to adopt more open approaches in their research, drawing on many other disciplines as well as ecology and economics. Many ecological economists, for example, have integrated social science perspectives into their analyses, particularly when dealing with governance, and behavioural and equity questions (Hezri and Dovers 2006; Paavola and Adger 2005; Sneddon et al. 2006). Indeed, for many, ecological economics has not gone far enough in integrating social science dimensions into its thinking and there is much debate on how ecological economics can truly be transdisciplinary in its approach (van Kerkhoff 2003).

Much of this concern for transdisciplinarity and methodological pluralism is motivated by the groundswell of opinion that there needs to be a more 'integrated and holistic approach' to environmental management, an opinion also echoed in the coastal and marine governance literature (Sorensen 1997). Thus, it is clear that an ecological economics of the oceans and coasts needs to be transdisciplinary[11] (or at least interdisciplinary) in its approach. It also needs to be receptive to a variety of interpretations from other disciplines including: coastal and marine ecology; policy sciences; social sciences; and indeed neoclassical economics, which produces valuable insights into questions of optimality and efficiency, market behaviour, economic instruments for policy implementation, property rights, growth dynamics, as well as the valuation of coastal and marine goods and services.

THIS BOOK'S PERSPECTIVE ON THE ECOLOGICAL ECONOMICS OF THE OCEANS AND COASTS

This book consists of four parts, each of which addresses a key theme in developing an 'ecological economics of the oceans and coasts'. In addition to these four parts, in this introduction and a summary (Chapter 15). The main four parts of the book are:

Part I: Foundational Ecology, Complexity and Science Issues
Part II: Economic and Other Values of the Marine Environment
Part III: Marine Sustainability: Integrating Ecology, Economics and Social Dimensions
Part IV: Implementing an Ecological Economics of the Oceans and Coasts

Part I: Foundational Ecology, Complexity and Science Issues

The purpose of Part I is based on the argument that any sensible economics of the oceans and coasts must, first and foremost, understand their ecology. Otherwise, any policy prescriptions and conclusions drawn from such an economics will necessarily be misleading and unrealistic. Part I consists of three chapters that: provide an overview of the ecological processes and biophysical functioning of the oceans and coasts, and identify how this knowledge of oceanic and coastal ecology is important to an ecological economics interpretation of the oceans and coasts. Part I includes the following chapters:
    Chapter 2: Global Ecology of the Oceans and Coasts by Ben McNeil. This chapter addresses questions such as: Why are the oceans and coasts important in terms of the ecological functioning of planet Earth? What is their role in global biogeochemical cycles, climate regulation, biological productivity and habitat provision? In particular, this chapter highlights the critical role that oceans play in influencing global climate and the future impacts this will have on ocean ecology.

Chapter 3: Biodiversity of the Oceans by Murray Patterson, Garry McDonald, Keith Probert and Nicola Smith. This chapter focuses on the biodiversity of the oceans – characterization of marine species; large-scale patterns of biodiversity in the sea; biodiversity and ecosystem functioning; human (and economic) impacts on marine biodiversity; biodiversity loss and extinctions; and international legislation and initiatives aimed at preventing marine biodiversity loss.

Chapter 4: Oceans and Coasts as Complex Adaptive Systems by Mark Gibbs and Anthony Cole. Ocean and coastal systems are viewed as complex adaptive systems. Complex systems follow trajectories that are non-linear, unpredictable and thermodynamically far-from-equilibrium. This has profound implications for the way in which coastal and oceanic systems are managed for both economic and ecological purposes. The aim of this chapter is to examine oceans and coasts as complex systems, enriched by real world illustrations and particularly by drawing out the policy/management implications.

Part II: Economic and Other Values of the Marine Environment

'Value' is a core concept in economics – Cole et al. (1991) argue that fundamental tensions between opposing schools of thought often come down to how they deal with the concept. Ecological economics is therefore distinguished from other economic perspectives in terms of how it handles this conceptualization and measurement of value. Ecological economists tend to emphasize the multidimensional aspects of the value concept – beyond the anthropocentric/utilitarian focus of neoclassical economics value theory. Part II, therefore, attempts to open a broader discussion of the value of oceans and coasts based on ecological economics precepts. Part II consists of the following chapters:

Chapter 5: Neoclassical Frameworks for Optimizing the Value of Marine Resources by Basil Sharp and Chris Batstone. This chapter presents neoclassical economics frameworks for optimizing the value of both non-renewable (minerals, oil, natural gas) and renewable (fisheries, other biotic) resources of the oceans. Concepts such as Hotelling's Rule, optimal extraction pathways and maximum sustainable yield are stressed and illustrated through case study examples.

Chapter 6: Non-Market Value of Ecosystem Services Provided by Coastal and Nearshore Marine Systems by Matthew Wilson and Shuang Liu. A broader view of the economic value (than presented in Chapter 5) of oceans and coasts is put forward using the 'ecosystem services' concept. This view enables 'unpriced' ecosystem services (such as habitat provision, climate regulation, nutrient cycling, hydrological processes) to be priced and valued. This analysis draws on data from global to sub-regional levels, where such data are available.

Chapter 7: Ecological Shadow Prices and Contributory Value: A Biophysical Approach to Valuing Marine Ecosystems by Murray Patterson. This chapter focuses on the 'ecological shadow pricing' method, which is a useful emerging tool for operationalizing a more biophysical/biocentric concept, in a way that can communicate with both ecologists and economists. Its practical application has shown that it can highlight not only those species that are 'visible', but also species that are ignored or undervalued in neoclassical valuations. It is well known, for example, that the so-called 'charismatic megafauna' such as dolphins and whales receive high value in contingent valuation studies, while the inconspicuous phytoplankton, although critical in the food chain and in terms of ecosystem functioning, may not be recognized in these studies.

Chapter 8: The Open Horizon: Exploring Spiritual and Cultural Values of the Oceans and Coasts by Charlotte Šunde. For many, the oceans have spiritual and cultural values that are incommensurable with neoclassical economics concepts of value. This presents a stern challenge to ecological economists on how to approach the issue of value in the context of the oceans and coasts. Examples from oceanic peoples and their relationships with the marine environment offer a different perspective to the 'rational' approaches often used in economic analysis.

Part III: Marine Sustainability: Integrating Ecology, Economics and Social Dimensions

If oceans are to be sustainably managed, it is imperative that ecological economists have tools, methods, processes and examples of how ecological, economic and social factors can be simultaneously considered in a 'connected-up' way. On one level, we need a deeper appreciation of how the economy, the social system and the marine environment interact with each other. Sadly, this can be lacking in the literature because of the fragmented (disciplinary-based) way economists, social scientists and ecologists often investigate marine issues. On another level, we need sophisticated analytical tools that can illuminate the complex interconnections between economic and ecological processes. On yet another level, we need to understand the practice of 'integrative management' and related planning approaches if we are to have an impact in the real world. Accordingly, Part III consists of:

Chapter 9: Economic Drivers of Change and their Oceanic–Coastal Ecological Impacts by Murray Patterson and Derrylea Hardy. Economic factors drive much of the development pressures imposed on coastal and oceanic environments. Demand for food resources, exploitation of mineral and oil resources, the growing attraction of coastal properties, and so forth, are key drivers of change. This chapter describes and analyzes the economic drivers of such development and the consequential environmental impacts, including biodiversity loss, near-shore pollution and unintended oil spills.

Chapter 10: Integrative Economy–Ecology Models for Marine Management by Matthias Ruth. This chapter features and reviews a number of systems dynamics models that can be used to model the interconnections between marine economic activity and ecological processes. These models provide valuable tools for sustainably managing ocean-coastal resources and in addressing key policy questions. Such models are important as they enable us to get a better grasp of the complexity of ocean-coastal systems.

Chapter 11: Poverty and Inequity at Sea: Challenges for Ecological Economics by Bruce Glavovic. This chapter explores 'poverty' and 'inequity' in the marine context – two issues that are recognized as important in ecological economics, but which have received little attention to date. The meaning of sustainable human development and its antithesis, 'poverty and inequity coupled with environmental degradation' are explored. The chapter discusses how these issues of poverty and inequity present a serious challenge for ecological economics, and uses a South African case study to illustrate key points.

Part IV: Implementing an Ecological Economics of the Oceans and Coasts

It has been asserted that ecological economics should have a 'practical problem solving' focus that 'makes a difference in the real world'. This implies that ecological economics must move beyond just evaluating policy options, to a consideration of how to implement the preferred policy options and to think deeply about governance structures that will be required. This is the focus of Part IV, which looks at how polices can actually be implemented in order to achieve the goal of sustainable management of the oceans and coasts. Part IV consists of the following chapters:

Chapter 12: Minimum Information Management: Harvesting the Harvesters' Assessment of Dynamic Fisheries Systems by Chris Batstone and Basil Sharp. As concluded elsewhere in this book, the 'complex system properties' of fisheries make the scientific prediction of stock numbers problematical. The authors argue that one practical way to deal with such problems is to use a Minimum Information Management (MIM) system. MIM is based on the idea that the market mechanism that underlies rights trading can mitigate scientific uncertainty by providing additional information.

Chapter 13: Designing Property Rights for Achieving Sustainable Development of the Oceans by Basil Sharp. A microeconomics approach is used to analyze property rights regimes that can be used to sustainably manage 'common property' marine resources. A case study of New Zealand's fisheries management regime is used to demonstrate the operation of a tradable property rights system. This case study shows that since its introduction in 1986 the system has achieved both sustainability outcomes and the economic efficiency gains. Other case study material is also presented and discussed.

Chapter 14: Ocean and Coastal Governance for Sustainability: Imperatives for Integrating Ecology and Economics by Bruce Glavovic. This chapter outlines why prevailing ocean and coastal governance often fails to advance sustainability. It argues that this is because prevailing governance efforts remain fundamentally mismatched to the distinguishing *ecological, economic and social* characteristics of ocean and coastal systems. This gives rise to a number of governance challenges and imperatives that are specific to the coasts and oceans. The chapter concludes by identifying those 'priority actions' that are needed to translate these 'imperatives' into practical reality.

The book concludes in Chapter 15 with a discussion of our ecological economics interpretation of the ocean and coasts, and how this approach could help identify how the coasts and oceans can be managed more sustainably. A number of cross-cutting thematic conclusions are also identified, as well as areas for further research and analysis.

NOTES

1. For convenience and ease of reference, the following definitions are used throughout this book: (1) 'Ocean/s' refer/s to the seas and oceans below the low tide mark including, and going beyond, the continental shelf; (2) 'Coast/s' refer/s to estuaries, mangroves, tidal marshes, seagrass beds, kelp forests, coral reefs and beach shores above the low tide mark; (3) 'Marine' is a collective term that is used to refer to both oceans and coasts, as defined above – it is often used in this book for sake of brevity.
2. This percentage refers to the surface area of the world's coasts as defined by note 1. If the continental shelf is included in the definition of 'coastal ecosystems', then the percentage increases to 6.3 per cent of the earth's surface (3267 × 10^6 ha) (Costanza et al. 1997).
3. The data required for these calculations were obtained from Costanza et al. (1997, 1998), Field et al. (1998), Gattuso et al. (1998) and Falkowski et al. (2003).
4. Refer to Chapter 7 of this book for estimations of the market value ($US) of oil, gas, minerals and food resources obtained from the marine environment.
5. Costanza et al. (1997) calculated the 'total economic value' of the world's marine-coastal ecosystems for 1994 to be: Open Ocean ($US8.366 trillion), Continental Shelf ($US4.283 trillion), Estuaries ($US4.110 trillion), Seagrass and Algal Beds ($US3.801 trillion), Coral

Reefs ($US0.375 trillion) and Tidal Marshs and Mangroves ($US1.648 trillion). This adds up to $US22.597 trillion for all coastal and marine-coastal ecosystems. These data are further disaggregated in Table 3.1, quantifying the value ($US) of each type of ecosystem services derived from these marine-coastal ecosystems types. People involved in ocean and coastal management have much to gain from ecological economics analysis, such as that by Costanza et al., which demonstrates the unequivocal importance and value of marine ecosystem 'goods and services'. Among other things, decision-makers are more likely to relate to and appreciate the need to manage these complex systems prudently when the predominant 'language of dollars' is used to articulate relative ecosystem values.

6. Cohen et al. (1997) state that 44 per cent of the 1994 global population lived within 150 km of the coast. Data for developed countries show that wealthier people (higher income per capita) live in coastal areas (Agardy 2004). This, however, may not necessarily be the case in developing countries. It is therefore assumed that the coastal population throughout the world has a per capita income 10 per cent higher than average. On this basis, it is concluded that the GDP of the coastal economy could be as high as 48 per cent of the world's economy (if there is a 10 per cent higher per capita income for coastal regions) or 44 per cent (if there is no difference in the per capita income between coastal and non-coastal areas).

7. Mullon et al. (2005) analyzed 1591 fisheries in the FAO database over the last 50 years, revealing 366 had collapsed.

8. Martinez-Alier (1987) also links the development of ecological economics to other theorists such as Geddes, Clausius and Soddy who came from a variety of disciplinary backgrounds ranging from town planning to thermodynamics.

9. Although it is popular amongst both neoclassical and ecological economists to use capital theory to define sustainability, this approach does have its critics (for example, Faucheux et al. 1997). Furthermore, there is a view, particularly amongst ecological economists, that there is no one way to define sustainability. Lawn (2006) provides a comprehensive account of other definitions of and sustainability indicators advocated by ecological economists, in addition to those based on capital theory.

10. Indeed, our propensity for spatial 'discounting' is even more problematic when it comes to the oceans than the more renowned 'time discounting' with which resource economists are often concerned. From a sustainability perspective, however, neither are virtuous – 'Not in My Back Yard' when it comes to disposing of wastes in the oceans (spatial discounting) is arguably just as ethically bankrupt as disregarding future generations (time discounting).

11. It is often somewhat boldly asserted that ecological economics is, or should be, a 'transdiscipline' (for example, Gill 1997; ISEE 2006). With respect, this probably isn't the point, as it is unlikely and even arrogant to think that any one discipline alone can transcend all others. Instead, it is arguably more appropriate that ecological economists attempt to be part of a 'transdisciplinary endeavour' that involves working with other disciplines and, more importantly, being prepared to be 'open-minded '.

REFERENCES

Agardy, T. (2004), 'Coastal ecosystems, industrialization, and impacts on human well-being', in *Proceedings of the World Ocean Forum*, 15–16 November 2004, New York City.

Boulding, K.E. (1966), 'The economics of the coming spaceship earth', in H. Jarrett (ed.), *Environmental Quality in a Growing Economy: Essays from the Sixth RFF Forum*, Baltimore: Johns Hopkins Press.

Brown, C., E. Corcoran, P. Hekerenrath and J. Thonell (eds) (2006), *Marine and Coastal Ecosystems and Human Wellbeing: A Synthesis Report Based on the Findings of the Millennium Ecosystem Assessment*, New York: United Nations Environment Programme, 76 pp.

Cleveland, C.J. (1992), 'Energy quality and energy surplus in the extraction of fossil fuels in the U.S.', *Ecological Economics*, **6**: 139–162.

Chiesura, A. and R. de Groot (2003), 'Critical natural capital: a socio-cultural perspective', *Ecological Economics*, **44**: 219–231.

Common, M. and C. Perrings (1992), 'Towards an ecological economics of sustainability', *Ecological Economics*, **11**(3): 213–226.

Cohen, J.F., C. Small, A. Mellinger, J. Gallup and J. Sachs (1997), 'Estimates of coastal populations', *Science*, **278**: 1211–1212.

Cole, K., J. Cameron and C. Edwards (1991), *Why Economists Disagree: The Political Economy of Economics*, Harlow: Longman.

Costanza, R. (1991), *Ecological Economics: The Science and Management of Sustainability*, New York: Columbia Unity Press.

Costanza, R., R. d'Arge, R. De Groot, S. Farber, M. Grasso, B. Hannon, K. Limburg, S. Naeem, R.V. O'Neil, J. Paruelo, R.G. Raskin, P. Sutton and M. van den Belt (1997), 'The value of the world's ecosystem services and natural capital', *Nature*, **387**: 253–260.

Costanza, R., R. d'Arge, R. De Groot, S. Farber, M. Grasso, B. Hannon, K. Limburg, S. Naeem, R.V. O'Neil, J. Paruelo, R.G. Raskin, P. Sutton and M. van den Belt (1998), 'The value of ecosystem services: putting the issues in perspective', *Ecological Economics*, **25**: 67–72.

Daly, M. (1973), *Towards a Steady State Economy*, San Francisco: W.H. Freeman.

Daly, H.E. (2005), 'Economics of a full world', *Scientific American*, **293**(3): 100–107

De Angelis, D.L. and J.C. Waterhouse (1987), 'Equilibrium and non-equilibrium concepts in ecological models', *Ecological Monographs*, **57**: 1–21.

Faber, M. and J. Proops (1985), 'Interdisciplinary research between economists and physical scientists: retrospect and prospect', *KYKLOS*, **38**: 599–616.

Faucheux, S., E. Muir and M. O'Connor (1997), 'Neoclassical natural capital theory and "weak" indicators of sustainability', *Land Economics*, **73**(4): 523–528.

Falkowski, P., E.A. Laws, R. Barber and J.W. Murray (2003), 'Phytoplankton and their role in primary, new and export production', in M.J.R. Fasham (ed.), *Ocean Biogeochemistry: The Role of the Ocean Carbon Cycle in Global Change*, New York: Springer.

Field, C.B., M.J. Behrenfeld, J.T. Randerson and P. Falkowski (1998), 'Primary production of the biosphere: integrating terrestrial and oceanic components', *Science*, **281**: 237–240.

Gattuso, J.P., M. Frankingoulle and R. Wollast (1998), 'Carbon and carbonate metabolism in coastal aquatic ecosystems', *Annual Review of Ecology and Systematics*, **29**: 405–434.

Georgescu-Roegen, N. (1971), *The Entropy Law and the Economic Process*, Cambridge: Harvard University Press.

Gill, R. (1997), 'Exploring transdisciplinary theories: the New England ecological economics focus on the meaning and application of ecological economics', *Ecological Economics Bulletin*, **2**(1): 6–10.

Goodland, R. and M.E. Daly (1993), 'Why northern income growth is not the solution to southern poverty', *Ecological Economics*, **8**: 85–101.
Gowdy, J. and J. Erickson (2005), 'Ecological economics at a crossroads', *Ecological Economics*, **53**(1): 17–20.
Hezri, A.A. and S.R. Dovers (2006), 'Sustainability indicators policy and governance: issues for ecological economics', *Ecological Economics*, **60**: 86–99.
Hinrichsen, D. (1998), *Coastal Waters of The World: Trends, Threats, and Strategies*, Washington, DC: Island Press.
International Society for Ecological Economics (2006), ISEE website http://www.ecoeco.org/about/intro.htm.
Lawn, P. (2006), *Sustainable Development Indicators in Ecological Economics*, Cheltenham, UK and Northampton, MA, USA: Edward Elgar.
Martinez-Alier, J. (1987), *Ecological Economics*, Oxford: Basil Blackwell.
Mayumi, K. and J.M. Gowdy (1999), *Bioeconomics and Sustainability*, Cheltenham, UK and Northampton, MA, USA: Edward Elgar.
Mulder, P. and Jeroem C.J.M. van den Bergh (2001), 'Evolutionary economic theories of sustainable development', *Growth and Change*, **32**(1): 110–134.
Mullon, C., P. Freon and P. Curry (2005), 'The dynamics of collapse in world fisheries', *Fish and Fisheries*, **6**(2): 111–120.
Norgaard, R.B. (1989), 'The case for methodological pluralism', *Ecological Economics*, **1**: 37–57.
Pauly, D., J. Alder, E. Bennett, V. Christensen, P. Tyedmers and R. Watson (2003), 'The future for fisheries', *Science*, **302**: 1359–1361.
Paavola, J. and W.N. Adger (2005), 'Institutional economics', *Ecological Economics*, **53**: 353–368.
Peet, N.J. (1992), *Energy and the Ecological Economics of Sustainability*, Washington, DC: Island Press.
Ruth, M. (1993), *Integrating Economics, Ecology and Thermodynamics*, The Netherlands: Kluwer Academic Publishers.
Sneddon, C., R.B. Howarth and R. Norgaard (2006), 'Sustainable development in a post-Brundtland world', *Ecological Economics*, **57**: 253–268.
Soderbaum, P. (1990), 'Neoclassical and institutional approaches to environmental economics', *Journal of Economic Issues*, **XXIV**: 481–492.
Sorensen, J. (1993), 'The international proliferation of integrated coastal zone management efforts', *Ocean and Coastal Management*, **21**(1–3): 45–80.
Sorensen, J. (1997), 'National and international efforts at integrated coastal management: definitions, achievements and lessons', *Coastal Management*, **25**(1): 3–41.
Sorensen, J. (2002), Baseline 2000 Background Report: The Status of Integrated Coastal Management as an International Practice, Second Iteration, 26 August 2002, Urban Harbors Institute, University of Massachusetts, Massachusetts, USA.
UN (1992), *Agenda 21*, New York: United Nations.
van den Bergh, J. (1996), *Ecological Economics and Sustainable Development*, Cheltenham, UK and Brookfield, US: Edward Elgar.

van Kerkhoff, L. (2003), 'Beyond disciplines: exploratory research as a framework for integration', in S. Dovers, D.I. Stern and M.D. Young (eds), *New Dimensions in Ecological Economics: Integrated Approaches to People and Nature*, Cheltenham, UK and Northampton, MA, USA: Edward Elgar, pp. 35–50.

Vitousek, P.M., P.R. Erlich, A.H. Erlich and P. A. Matson (1986), 'Human appropriation of the products of photosynthesis', *BioScience*, **36**(6): 368–373.

Wilson, J.A., J. Acheson and P. Kleban (1996), 'Chaos and parametric management', *Marine Policy*, **20**(5): 429–438.

World Bank (2005), *World Bank and Partners Launch Initiative to 'Turn the Tide' of Fisheries Depletion*, Retrieved 29 Sept 2005: http://web.worldbank.org/WEBSITE/EXTERNAL/NEWS/0,,contentMDK:20624610~pagePK:34370~piPK:34424~theSitePK:4607,00.html.

Worm, B., E.B. Barbier, N. Beaumont, J.E. Duffy, C. Folke, B.S. Halpern, J.B.C. Jackson, H.K. Lotze, F. Micheli, S.R. Palumbi, E. Sola, K.A. Silkoe, J.J. Stachowiscz and R. Watson (2006), 'Impacts of biodiversity loss of ocean ecosystem services', *Science*, **314**: 787–790.

PART I

Foundational Ecology, Complexity and Science Issues

Understanding 'the ecology' should be a fundamental part of any ecological economics endeavour. An ecological economics of the oceans and coasts must therefore be respectful and mindful of the ecological processes that operate in the marine environment. Accordingly, Part I of this book provides an overview of the ecological processes and biophysical functioning of the oceans and coasts, and identifies how this knowledge of marine ecology is important to an ecological economics interpretation of the oceans and coasts.

Chapter 2 provides an overview of the *global ecology* of the oceans and coasts. It specifically addresses questions such as: Why are the oceans and coasts important in terms of the ecological functioning of planet Earth? What is their role in global biogeochemical cycles, climate regulation, biological productivity and habitat provision? In particular, this chapter highlights the critical role that oceans play in influencing global climate and the future impacts this will have on ocean ecology.

Chapter 3 focuses on the *biodiversity of the oceans*. It describes and analyzes: the ecological importance of marine biodiversity; the relationship between biodiversity and ecosystem functioning; human impacts on marine biodiversity; biodiversity loss and extinctions; and international legislation aimed at preventing marine biodiversity loss.

Chapter 4 puts forward the argument, based on ecological evidence, that oceanic and coastal ecosystems are *complex adaptive systems*. That is, these ecosystems follow trajectories that are non-linear, unpredictable and thermodynamically far-from-equilibrium. This type of systems behaviour has profound implications for the way in which coastal and oceanic systems are 'managed', and for the way in which we should develop a robust ecological economics of the oceans and coasts.

2. Global Ecology of the Oceans and Coasts

Ben McNeil

Over 3.5 billion years ago the oceans contained the necessary conditions for the first forms of simple life to evolve. Oceanic evolution is therefore intrinsically linked with the evolution of life on Earth, which continues today to spawn new and complex species. The physical and chemical conditions of the ocean were the precursors for existence of Earth's first forms of anaerobic bacteria and the eventual evolution of cyanobacteria, which led to the existence of atmospheric oxygen. Today the ecological and biological functioning of this vast biosphere are just as dependent on the circulation, currents and chemistry of the oceans as they were back in the days of the primordial soup. An understanding of the biological functioning of the oceans cannot exclude the processes that control the ingredients necessary for the existence of photosynthetic life (sunlight, carbon dioxide, oxygen and nutrients), which form the basis of Earth's ecological functioning and sustenance. In introducing the importance of oceanic and coastal ecology, it is inadequate to simply describe the marine life and its importance without understanding the ocean's general circulation and chemistry by which marine life itself is controlled. This chapter will therefore attempt to give a broad perspective of oceanic circulation, biogeochemistry and ecological functioning and how they are intrinsically linked to ensure the stability and sustenance of the earth's bedrock of life – the ocean.

PHYSICAL CHARACTERIZATION OF THE OCEANS AND COASTS

Zonation

The ocean extends from the territorial baseline of islands or continents to the gradually increasing depths that define different coastal and oceanic zones.

Figure 2.1 shows the most basic level of marine zonation extending from the continent. The coastal zone (commonly referred to as the neritic zone) extends from the continent boundary up to a depth of 200 m. The coastal zone covers approximately 6 per cent or 33 million km² of the earth's surface.

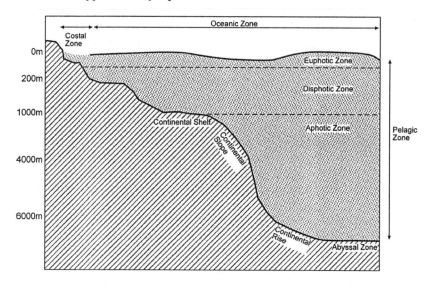

Figure 2.1   Schematic diagram of the coastal and open ocean zonations including the typical bathymetry

The oceanic covers approximately 71 per cent or 334 million km² of the earth's surface and is separated into three different ocean basins, which are mostly bound by large continents. The Pacific Ocean is the largest ocean basin, with the Indian Ocean being the smallest. The Southern Ocean circumnavigates Antarctica and is formally defined as ocean waters between Antarctica and 60°S, although many oceanographers argue the Southern Ocean extends to 40°S, that being the approximate location of the northward extent of the Antarctic Circumpolar Current. The properties within each ocean basin are quite distinct due unique geographic characteristics and adjoining seas (known as marginal seas).

Oceanic Circulation

The flow of water between the ocean basins is controlled by a number of processes including: the distribution of radiation gained from the sun, the thermodynamic properties of seawater, atmospheric winds, sea–ice dynamics, the rotation of the earth and the depth of the ocean (bathymetry). Oceanic circulation can be split into horizontal and vertical components, each playing an important role in controlling the other.

Water has a number of physical attributes that inherently influence the flow and circulation of the ocean. Water has a very high heat capacity, which means that the ocean is insensitive to sudden variations in heat. This phenomenon allows the ocean to absorb, store and transport massive amounts of heat gained from the sun. In fact, the top 2 m of the ocean holds the same amount of heat as does the entire atmosphere. Because the ocean circulates in reasonably well-defined ways, it controls to a large extent the regional climate patterns and seasonality we see on land. For example, the Gulf Stream flowing from the tropical Atlantic up the east of the US, transports water at 30–140 Sverdrups ($Sv=1\times10^6m^3/s$) into the higher latitudes of the North Atlantic. This current transports vast amounts of heat (equivalent to the energy generated by 1000 power stations) into the North Atlantic towards Europe. The Gulf Stream is therefore critical in creating relatively warm conditions for continental Europe along with the prevailing westerly winds. Furthermore, the Gulf Stream plays an important role in larval dispersal, migration of organisms and is one of the main reasons why coral reefs exist as far north as Bermuda. In the Southern Hemisphere, the Antarctic Circumpolar Current, which circumnavigates Antarctica, is the strongest current with a mean transport rate of 130Sv.

Seawater also contains dissolved minerals that have accumulated over millions of years via terrestrial runoff. The concentration of these dissolved minerals is quantified by salinity in parts per thousand (ppt), with an average seawater composition of 35ppt. The density of seawater (weight per unit volume) is highly dependent on its salinity and temperature, with denser waters being created in association with either higher salinities or colder temperatures. Density is an indicator of how likely a parcel of seawater is to sink. Variations in seawater salinity and temperature around the oceans are therefore critical in controlling the global vertical oceanic circulation, which is often referred to as the thermohaline circulation in reference to this fact.

The thermohaline circulation is controlled by warm, salty surface water and the return flow of colder deep waters. In general, most of the sun's heat enters the equatorial to mid-latitudes (20°S–20°N) and a combination of trade a winds and the earth's rotation result in poleward moving surface waters. As these waters move poleward, they lose their heat, become cooler and therefore become more dense. Eventually in the far North Atlantic and the Southern Ocean, the waters become dense enough to sink from the surface into the deep ocean, upon which a return flow towards the equator is required for mass conservation. This circulation releases huge amounts of heat across the globe; however, it does it on very long timescales as it takes about 1000 years for a parcel of water to circulate throughout the thermohaline circulation. This circulation exists via a subtle balance between variations in salinity and temperature. The first signs of changes to the thermohaline circulation are occurring and because it controls the physical dynamic of the ocean on long timescales, we are yet to understand fully the lasting repercussions on oceanic biological cycles.

BIOLOGICAL CHARACTERIZATION OF THE OCEANS AND COASTS

Fundamentals of Ocean Ecology

The marine environment contains about 250 000 known species of organisms, which represent about 14 per cent of the catalogued 1 750 000 species on earth (Trujillo and Thurman 2004). Although these estimates for the marine environment are most certainly a lower estimate especially given the difficulties of exploring the deep ocean, the ocean in general lacks the diversity of land ecosystems even though life was thought to be created in the ocean over 3.5 billion years ago. The discrepancy between the number of land and ocean species is thought to be due to the differing level of environmental extremes. The ocean is a relatively homogenous body of water in comparison with the heterogeneity of the land environment. For example, ocean temperatures range between $-1.9°C$ and about $35°C$, while on land temperatures range between $-60°C$ and $50°C$. New species are born through adaptation to differing environments. Considering the ocean environment is more stable than the land environment, the species that exist do not have to adapt as rapidly as those found on land, thereby limiting the number of species present over Earth's history.

Another important delineation in the ocean is the large difference in species diversity between the pelagic environment and the benthic environment. Organisms that live at or near the bottom of the ocean (benthic environment) comprise 98 per cent of ocean species, while the remaining 2 per cent (about 5000 species) are confined to the open ocean (pelagic environment). These marine species can be broadly classified into three differing classes – plankton, nekton and benthos – depending on where they live (habitat) and how they move (mobility).

Plankton

Plankton comes from the Greek word *planktos*, which means wandering. All organisms in the ocean that drift with ocean currents are classified as plankton. Although some planktonic organisms can swim they cannot move strongly enough to dictate their movement beyond movements from ocean currents. Planktonic organisms occur in different shapes and sizes such as some algae and bacteria at the microscopic level and some other species like typical jellyfish are easily distinguishable by the naked eye. Although their species diversity is relatively low, plankton are extremely abundant due to the vastness of the oceanic habitat. The total amount of biologically living matter (organisms) is known as biomass. Most of the ocean biomass (90%) is comprised of ocean plankton and the cycling of this material is extremely important for biogeochemical cycling and ecological functioning. Aside from the obvious importance of plankton in the current oceanic ecosystem, their importance to human economic prosperity is often overlooked. Petroleum and gas reserves, for example, which are such an important component of our economy and prosperity, are derived from millions of years of organic matter accumulation on the seafloor within shallow marginal seas. Through diagensis and bacterial biotransformation over long periods the planktonic organic matter evolves into petroleum and natural gas.

Plankton form the foundation of the ocean ecosystem and can be further segregated into phytoplankton and zooplankton based on how they obtain their food. Phytoplankton are autotrophic organisms meaning that they can produce their own food via photosynthesis. Zooplankton are heterotrophic organisms, meaning that they cannot produce their own food, but rather consume other organisms for their food. Zooplankton also include larval stages of many invertebrate and fish species.

Phytoplankton are mostly single celled photosynthetic (plantlike) marine organisms that evolved from one class of photosynthetic bacteria over 2.8 billion years ago, namely the cyanobacteria. The evolution of the bacterioplankton was essential in the formation of oxygen, carbon and nitrogen cycles that are necessary for higher forms of life to have evolved. There are approximately 10^{24} cyanobacteria cells in the ocean, which is two orders of magnitude greater than the number of stars in the universe. The cyanobacteria have diameters less than a micrometer (10^{-6}m) and have recently been estimated to comprise about half of the total photosynthetic biomass in the ocean (Falkowski et al. 2003).

The most important of today's evolved species of phytoplankton can be classified broadly into diatoms, dinoflagellates, haptophytes (which include coccolithophores) and the crysphytes. The diatoms are single celled organisms that are encapsulated by a shell composed of opaline silica (SiO_2). These phytoplankton dominate in the polar regions where there is an abundance of dissolved silicate in the ocean. Diatoms are important geologically through the production of diatomaceous ooze that accumulates on the seafloor. Diatomaceous ooze is also important economically as it is mined and used for additives to reflective paints, polishing materials and abrasives. Another type of one-celled phytoplankton are dinoflagellates, which are predominantly located in the tropical oceans. Sometimes environmental conditions promote a rapid bloom of certain types of dinoflagellates which produce a reddish color to the waters sometime referred to as *red tide*, but more accurately described as a harmful algal bloom (HAB). An outbreak of the toxic dinoflagellate species known as *Pfisteria piscicida* killed an estimated 15 million fish (Atlantic Menhaden) in a North Carolina estuary in 1995 and outbreaks continue to kill coastal fish all over the world. *Pfisteria* undergoes numerous transformations during its life cycle. It is during the toxic zoospore stage that they attach to fish, destroy their skin and undermine their ability to resist bacterial disease. These outbreaks generally occur due to an excess amount of nutrients entering the coastal environment. Coccolithophores are phytoplankton that excrete calcium carbonate ($CaCO_3$) plates called coccoliths. Upon death and settling to the ocean floor, these calcareous deposits are used to measure particular chemical or isotopic compositions so as to understand past environmental conditions.

Zooplankton are small microscopic animals with many being larval forms of benthis and nektonic organisms. Crustaceans make up about 70 per cent of zooplankton and are a large group of inverterbrates, meaning they have no backbone. Tiny zooplankton known as copepods are the most abundant crustaceans. Zooplankton also include gelatinous organisms like jelly-fish – outbreaks of which are of recent concern due to their predation on larval fishes (e.g. in the Gulf of Mexico).

Nekton

Nekton comes from the Greek word *nektos*, meaning swimming. Nekton is a group of marine organisms that move freely and independently of the ocean currents and include adult krill, adult fish, sharks and whales. It is relatively rare for nekton to freely move throughout all stages of its life cycle. For example, squid or fish are planktonic larvae at some point without the ability to swim, and as such are at the mercy of the ocean currents until they develop into adults and become independent of the current movements. For humans, nekton are the most important and well-known of the marine ecosystem, with nektonic fisheries one of the largest industries in the global economy.

Benthos

Benthos refers to organisms living on or near the bottom of the ocean. The diversity and composition of the benthic environment change markedly between shallow and deep water habitats. Shallow benthic organisms such as seaweeds and corals require sunlight and are found within the euphotic zone while some sponges and sea lilies (crinoids) live at the very depths of the deep ocean floor. Due to the presence of sunlight, the coastal benthic communities are significantly more productive than in the deeper benthic habitat. Near-shore benthic habitats like estuaries are particularly important: for providing shelter and food for higher trophic level species, for the recycling of nutrients, and for providing natural bioremediation capabilities for the ecosystem. Other important near-shore benthic habitats include mangroves (which are inter-tidal communities), seagrass meadows and kelp forests, coral reefs and soft sediment habitats.

Marine Energy Transfer

Due to energy conservation, marine ecological energy transfer can only be as great as the lowest level of the foodweb. The building block of the marine ecosystem is the phytoplankton, which is the only group not dependent directly on other trophic species for energy but rather obtains its energy from the sun via photosynthesis. The photosynthetic reaction undertaken by phytoplankton converts water, carbon dioxide and sunlight into organic matter (carbohydrates) and oxygen. This simple powerful reaction allowed for not only the adequate evolution and sustenance of the earth's ecosystem but also for the production of atmospheric oxygen needed for human life.

Energy is transferred from autotrophs ('self feeders') like phytoplankton to heterotrophs ('other feeders') like zooplankton and fish. Most zooplankton are herbivores in that they only graze on phytoplankton while other populations like sharks and dolphins are carnivores. Each of these differing levels are referred to as trophic levels and collectively comprise what is often referred to as the trophic pyramid. The transfer of energy from one trophic level to another typically has a low efficiency in the order of 10 per cent (see Figure 2.2).

The importance of primary productivity to the ecological functioning of the ocean cannot be exaggerated with 99.9 per cent of all biomass in the ocean relying directly or indirectly on primary productivity. As discussed earlier, phytoplankton production (primary productivity) supplies almost all the energy for the entire marine foodweb.

Gross primary production is defined by the total amount of organic matter produced per unit of time by photosynthetic activity. Cellular respiration is a process by which phytoplankton utilize some of this organic matter. The remaining organic matter is known as net primary production (NPP) and can be simply defined as the gross primary production minus cellular respiration. NPP is important in an ecological functioning context, as it is the total amount of organic carbon (and therefore energy) an ecosystem can utilize to support other trophic levels.

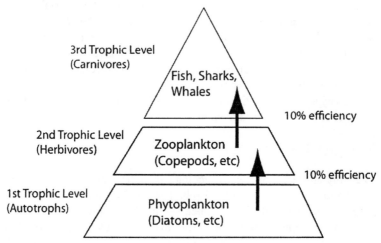

Figure 2.2 Simplified marine trophic pyramid

Primary productivity in the marine environment can be measured either by direct plankton tows (nets) that are dragged along a particular ocean depth or by analyzing the radiocarbon content of seawater that gives an indication of the amount of primary productivity in a particular area. More recently satellite measurements of ocean colour have provided a new way to understand and quantify oceanic primary productivity. Since 1997, the SeaStar satellite was launched with the SeaWIFS (Sea-viewing Wide Field-of-View Sensor) instrument which measures surface ocean colour (Figure 2.3). The photosynthetic pigment known as chlorophyll is found in all phytoplankton. Chlorophyll absorbs light at the blue-red end of the light spectrum therefore creating an intense green colour when chlorophyll concentrations are high. The concentration of chlorophyll is therefore an indicator of the ocean's productivity with a darker colour indicating low productivity up to a brighter colour indicating intense primary productivity. The global map of primary productivity (Figure 2.3) shows distinct variability and spatial patterns.

Due to the physical constraints on oceanic circulation, biologically important properties are distributed throughout the ocean in well-defined ways and, in general, levels of marine productivity vary according to their geographic location. Broad oceanic regions where marine productivity can be separated are known as biomes – the biological functioning between these biomes can vary quite significantly. Areas with high primary productivity (light areas in Figure 2.3) coincide with areas where there are more species (for example, fish) at higher trophic levels. Therefore an understanding of the underlying mechanisms driving primary production in these regions is of economic and social importance, particularly with regard to sustaining the productivity of global fisheries.

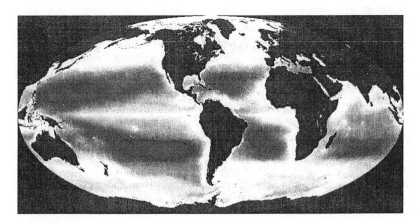

Figure 2.3 Typical ocean colour distribution in the surface ocean

Note: Lighter areas are highly productive while darker areas are unproductive.
(*Source:* National Aeronautics and Space Administration Ocean Color Program)

Southern Ocean

At around 60°S a surface divergence is formed due to a switching of the prevailing winds near Antarctica – known as the Antarctic Divergence. The Antarctic Divergence leads to large-scale upwelling of very old recirculated North Atlantic Deep Water in these surface waters. These deep waters have picked up high concentrations of nutrients and carbon in the long journey from the North Atlantic which takes up to 1000 years. This Southern Ocean upwelling introduces a large amount of nutrients (nitrate, phosphate, silicate) in comparison to the mostly nutrient depleted oceanic surface waters. The primary productivity of Southern Ocean waters is relatively low on the global scale especially considering the amount of available nutrients. The Southern Ocean habitat is therefore also known as a high-nutrient–low-chlorophyll (HNLC) regime where biological productivity is not utilizing its full potential based solely on the available nutrients. The subarctic Pacific Ocean is also characterized as an HNLC region.

Although the macro-nutrients are in high concentrations in HNLC regions, dissolved iron concentrations are very low in these isolated oceanic regions. Iron is an important limiting step for photosynthetic productivity. Most of the dissolved iron that enters the ocean is from aeolian inputs through dust transported from land. The level of dust input decreases as a function of the distance from land. Considering Antarctica is void of dust, the Southern Ocean receives little dust input due to its isolation. The hypothesis that the Southern Ocean is iron limited, and therefore has relatively low levels of phytoplankton growth, was tested in a seminal ocean experiment in 1999, known as the Southern Ocean Iron Release Experiment (SOIREE) (Boyd et al. 2000). During this experiment, iron was added to a patch of ocean near the Antarctic Divergence (~60°S) in order to determine if phytoplankton responded to this input of dissolved iron. The results of the experiment were spectacular with a pronounced phytoplankton bloom occurring and staying present up to 30 days after the iron addition. The experiment determined that the Southern Ocean productivity was indeed limited by iron. Iron limitation and the relatively low levels of sunlight received in the Southern Ocean are considered the two primary factors in producing the relatively low marine productivity in this region.

Sub-tropical Oceans

The oceanic region between about 30°S and 30°N is known as the sub-tropical region and is surprisingly low in biological productivity despite the year-round deep penetration of light. As a result, the sub-tropical ocean is sometimes referred to as the oceanic desert. The reason for this is solely due to the lack of supply of nutrients to the surface layer in the sub-tropics. The warm surface layer in the sub-tropics creates a large density gradient which inhibits the vertical mixing of nutrient-waters from the deeper ocean. Any nutrients that are supplied to the surface layer are quickly utilized by phytoplankton. Because of the limited vertical supply of nutrients, phytoplankton growth is limited in the sub-tropical oceans.

The exception to this general rule, however, is found in the equatorial region of the ocean. Higher productivity can be seen along the equator in both the Pacific and Atlantic oceans (Figure 2.3). A surface ocean divergence is created in this region via easterly trade winds and associated Ekman transport which moves surface waters towards the higher latitudes. This divergence creates upwelling that brings up older and nutrient-rich waters to the surface. As phytoplankton are limited by nutrients in the sub-tropics this added nutrient supply enhances phytoplankton production along the equator. Enhanced production in the equatorial Pacific, however, is strongly mitigated by a periodic climate event known as El Niño Southern Oscillation (ENSO).

El Niño and biological productivity
ENSO is known to impact temperature and rainfall patterns on land throughout most of the Pacific Ocean, extending into other parts of the world. The severe impacts from ENSO on the biological system especially for South America, however, are not as well publicized.

During normal conditions in the Pacific, easterly trade winds push warm equatorial surface waters to the west. Off the coast of South America this leads to a divergent surface flow, which promotes the vertical transport of deep waters to the surface in a process known as upwelling. These deep ocean waters are rich in nutrients (nitrate, phosphate, silicate, iron) in comparison to the over-utilized nutrient-poor surface ocean. Consequently this upwelling promotes marine biological productivity resulting in high yields in fisheries such as anchovies in this region. During the periodic (4–7 years) ENSO events, however, the trade winds reverse, thereby pushing warm surface waters to the east, which results in shutting off the normal upwelling conditions off the coast of South America. During ENSO there are not adequate levels of re-supply of nutrients, which leads to a reduction in the biological productivity and low yields for the fisheries that are an important part of the economy for a large proportion of these South American coastal nations (for example, Peru). Although ENSO is a natural phenomenon, potential feedbacks on future anthropogenic climate change is currently not well known.

Temperate Oceans

The temperate oceans lie in transition between the polar oceans and the sub-tropical oceans (30° to 50°) and are known for extensive biological productivity. The mixing of warmer waters in the sub-tropics and the cold waters near the poles creates sharp gradients in water properties that are known as oceanic fronts. The temperate oceans maintain a myriad of ocean fronts and can be thought of in a similar way to atmospheric frontal systems. These fronts are influenced by the rotation of the earth and pressure differences at the sea surface and are common for the temperate oceans due to their geographic location on the earth's sphere. The physical characteristics of the ocean change rapidly on either side of the front, therefore so too does the marine productivity as illustrated in Figure 2.3.

Coastal Oceans

The coastal ocean is a shallow (<200 m) unique environment where all biospheric resevoirs (land, atmosphere and ocean) exchange and interact with each other. The coastal ocean includes a variety of differing ecosystems such as estuaries, coral reefs and mangroves/salt marshes. The discharge and exchange of energy and nutrients from land to ocean is a key component in driving coastal marine biological productivity. This land/ocean exchange will vary dramatically depending on the proximity to river/estuary outflows and groundwater exchange. The primary productivity of these coastal ocean ecosystems has been discussed and estimated by Gattuso et al. (1998) and the results are shown in Table 2.1.

The average primary productivity for these differing coastal ecosystems varies widely (260–2400 $gC/m^2/yr$), with mangroves and coral reefs displaying the highest rates of productivity. However, because of the limited aerial extent of these ecosystems, they play only a minor role in the global marine productivity inventory. Other coastal habitats such as seagrass meadows and kelp forests (not included in Table 2.1) are thought to be particularly productive. Seagrasses, for example, are estimated to have the same aerial coverage as coral reefs with a similar level of primary productivity and could potentially account for up to 15 per cent of the net global CO_2 uptake by marine biota (Duarte and Chiscano, 1999).

Figure 2.3 illustrates high concentrations of phytoplankton along western continental coastlines associated directly with strong coastal upwelling. These high phytoplankton concentrations are important for providing the necessary energy for the fisheries along these coastal regions. This high water-column productivity in coastal upwelling zones is found on the eastern side of the sub-tropical gyre circulation (known as eastern boundary currents).

For example, off the Californian coastline the prevailing southward flowing winds along the coast invoke net surface Ekman transport whereby water moves perpendicular to the right of the winds. This Ekman transport results in a divergence along the coastline which requires deeper waters to replace the offshore moving surface waters. This process known as coastal upwelling brings up nutrient–rich deep waters to the surface, which results in phytoplankton growth and relatively high primary productivity rates in these zones.

Table 2.1 Marine productivity estimates for differing ecosystems on a per unit and total global inventory basis

Environment	Ecosystem	Area (10^6 km²)	Primary Productivity Average (gC/m²/yr)	Primary Productivity Inventory (Pg C /yr)
Coastal	Estuaries	1.4	260	0.4
	Coral Reefs	0.6	1700	1.0
	Mangroves/ Salt Marshes	0.6	2400	1.4
	Continental Shelf	23.4	300	7.0
	Upwelling Zone	0.2	800	0.2
	Total	26.0	~350	10.0
Open-Ocean		334	~110	40–48
Total		361	~140	50–58

(*Source:* Adapted from Gattuso et al. 1998; Falkowski et al. 2003)

Coral Reefs

Coral reefs are spectacular oceanic ecosystems built on a mutualistic symbiosis between carbonate building corals and micro-algae. Coral reefs are located at or near sea-level and distributed generally within the tropics (32°S–32°N; see Figure 2.4) depending on the physical, chemical and geological prerequisites for sustaining a coral reef ecosystem. Although coral reefs comprise only about 0.16 per cent of the oceanic surface area, it is clear that they contribute to ecological functioning in a disproportionate manner (see Table 2.1).

There are three types of geological reef formations: fringing reefs, barrier reefs and atolls. Although there is a diverse array of coral reefs, they all share important environmental requirements for their formation and survival. Temperature is an important controller on the distribution of coral reefs with most reef-building corals being unable to survive in waters colder than about 18°C. Sunlight is another important control on reef ecosystems for phytoplankton growth and photosynthesis. Nutrients are almost always in very low concentrations in coral reefs. The recycling of essential nutrients and periodic exchange of mixing with open ocean waters is a vital part for the sustenance of a coral reef ecosystem.

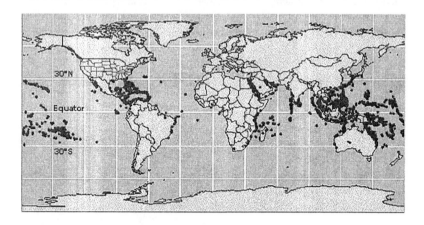

Figure 2.4 Distribution of stony coral reefs in the surface ocean

(*Source:* National Oceanic and Atmospheric Administration)

Hermatypic corals (also known as stony corals or reef-building corals) are animals that provide the building blocks for a coral reef ecosystem to exist. The geological framework is made up of calcium carbonate ($CaCO_3$), which is produced by hermatypic corals through the process of calcification. Over hundreds to thousands of years, the $CaCO_3$ skeletons accumulate in layers with living corals living on the surface layer of this $CaCO_3$ accumulation. Corals are not the only organisms to produce $CaCO_3$ with some calcifying phytoplankton known as coralline algae also playing an important role in the evolution of the coral framework by depositing within the spaces of the reef framework.

Productivity varies depending on the species composition of the reef, but on average they maintain among the highest productivity per unit area in the ocean (Table 2.1). Coral reefs house a vast variety of nekton (fish) and other colourful species including turtles, sea snakes, octopuses and sharks. Zooxanthallae are tiny single-celled algae that live symbiotically within the gut of coral polyp hosts. These micro-algae provide the colour of coral reefs and play an important role for the recycling of an already nutrient-depleted environment.

Coral reefs fundamentally enhance the biodiversity of the oceans. Aside from contributing significantly to fisheries they also provide protection for coastal environments. Overfishing and reef exploitation add stresses to the coral environment along with agricultural nutrient runoff causing potential problems with eutrophication (excess nutrients). It is important to note that coral reefs are closely linked to mangrove and seagrass systems, which are all characterized by exchange of energy and nutrients. These communities act as nurseries for many commercial species that are present on coral reefs in later stages of life.

THE OCEANIC INFLUENCE ON GLOBAL CLIMATE

The earth's atmosphere is made up of about 99 per cent gases which have no affect on the earth's climate. Most of the remaining 1 per cent of the atmosphere contains molecules that directly affect the radiation budget of the earth. Four of the most important of these gases are water (H_2O), carbon dioxide (CO_2), methane (CH_4) and nitrous oxide (N_2O) and these are commonly referred to as greenhouse gases. These greenhouse gases have the ability to absorb long-wave radiation emitted from the earth's surface. The greenhouse effect is a naturally occurring process that heats the earth's surface due to a buildup of greenhouse gases. The greenhouse effect has been critical for the existence of life on Earth. Without these greenhouse gases in the atmosphere the global average temperature would be about −18°C rather than the current temperature of about 15°C. The natural greenhouse effect therefore warms the planet by about 33°C and leads to a temperature adequate to evolve and sustain life.

Past Climate Variations

Earth's climate, however, has not always been stable and has undergone some large variations in geological time. Measurements taken within the Antarctic and Greenland ice-cores have given us the ability to peer back in time up to 500 000 years ago. Figure 2.5 shows the well-known Antarctic ice-core record illustrating the CO_2 and temperature cycles. A well-defined 100 000 year cycle was found where Earth's climate endured extensive glacial periods where the earth was between 4 and 8°C colder with glaciers extending as far south as Manhattan in New York. A brief period of warmer conditions existed between the more dominant glacial periods and is known as the inter-glacial period. These inter-glacial periods of warm conditions ranged between 5–15 000 years, which is quite brief in geological timeframes. We are currently in the middle of an inter-glacial period. The 100 000 year cycle between glacial and inter-glacial periods is known as the Milankovitch cycle. Milankovitch cycles are known to be caused mostly by changes in the earth's radiation budget due to orbital variations around the sun. However, these orbital changes cannot fully explain the global temperature range between glacial and inter-glacial periods.

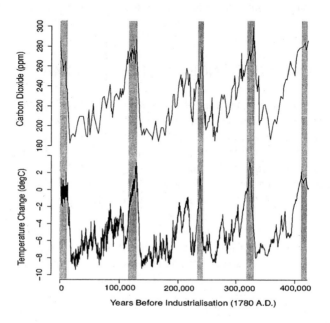

Figure 2.5 CO$_2$ (top) and temperature (bottom) record over the last 430 000 years as determined from ice-core records in Antarctica

Notes: The grey-shaded areas show the four inter-glacial periods before the current inter-glacial period, which has been present over the last 15 000 years. The x-axis shows time in 1000s of years.
(*Source:* Adapted from Petit et al. 1999)

Also shown in Figure 2.5 are the corresponding CO$_2$ concentrations on these long timescales, which range between about 200ppm during glacial times and about 280ppm during inter-glacial periods. Higher CO$_2$ concentrations during inter-glacial periods coincide with the trapping of more long-wave radiation, thereby warming the surface atmosphere of Earth. In general, paleoclimatologists accept that these CO_2 concentrations contributed to those climatic changes not explained by orbital variations.

Processes Controlling Atmospheric CO_2 Concentrations

The debate in the paleoclimatology community is over what caused these 80ppm variations in CO_2 between the glacial and inter-glacial periods. The only two biospheric reservoirs that could change the atmospheric CO_2 concentrations before pre-industrial times are the oceanic or terrestrial reservoirs. Paleoclimatologists have ruled out the terrestrial reservoir playing an important part in controlling these atmospheric CO_2 variations and now consider the oceans being the primary agent. The oceans have two differing mechanisms by which they can control atmospheric CO_2, which are also important in the context of today's global carbon cycle – the 'solubility carbon pump' and the 'biological carbon pump'.

The solubility carbon pump
The solubility of CO_2 in seawater is dependent on the ocean temperature with colder water enhancing the ability of CO_2 to dissolve. Upon dissolving, CO_2 dissociates into bicarbonate (HCO_3^-) and carbonate ions (CO_3^{2-}) as shown in following equation:

$$CO_2 + H_2O \Leftrightarrow H_2CO_3 \Leftrightarrow HCO_3^- + H^+ \Leftrightarrow CO_3^{2-} + 2H^+ \qquad (2.1)$$

The vast majority of oceanic inorganic carbon exists as either bicarbonate (~90 per cent) or carbonate (~9 per cent), with CO_2 making up only 1 per cent of the total inorganic carbon pool. The ability of inorganic carbon to be in three differing forms gives the ocean a vast ability to absorb CO_2 and influence atmospheric CO_2 on long timescales.

As described earlier, the oceans' thermohaline circulation is largely controlled by two cold water environments (North Atlantic and the Southern Ocean) through water mass formation and transport via North Atlantic Deep Water and Antarctic Bottom Water. Once at the surface, these waters exchange CO_2 with the atmosphere. As they are transferred from the surface ocean to the deep, via density transformation, large amounts of CO_2 that become sequestered (or isolated) from the atmosphere for long timescales (about 1000 years). If this transfer to the deep ocean is sped up, then the amount of CO_2 sequestered in the deeper ocean also increases which reduces the atmospheric concentration of CO_2. This process of temperature-dependent air–sea gas exchange and enhancement via water mass transfer is known as the 'oceans' solubility carbon pump' and has been suggested as one of the main contributors to atmospheric CO_2 variations between glacial and inter-glacial periods.

The biological carbon pump

The other oceanic process that can significantly alter the atmospheric CO_2 concentrations is via the biological carbon pump (Figure 2.6). Phytoplankton utilizes CO_2 through the process of photosynthesis, to form biomass. Primary productivity therefore has the effect of reducing the concentration of CO_2 in the surface ocean by creating a concentration gradient that drives an air to sea flux of CO_2 in the attempt to re-equilibrate. With a huge amount of primary productivity in the ocean (50–58 PgC/yr), it would seem that this process has the potential to significantly alter the concentration of atmospheric CO_2. However respiration has not been taken into account, which produces CO_2 in the surface ocean, thereby driving a counter-flowing flux of CO_2 from sea to air. This biological productivity therefore drives very large *gross* CO_2 fluxes across the air–sea interface – however, they are largely in balance resulting in little influence on the net changes in atmospheric CO_2.

The process that can drive significant changes to atmospheric CO_2 is the process of 'biological carbon export'. When phytoplankton utilizes CO_2 to create organic material, a portion of this organic material is grazed on by zooplankton. Via death or aggregate formation, this organic material sinks from the surface ocean into the deeper ocean. This process, known as carbon export, is an efficient way of sequestering CO_2 from the atmosphere. If the rate of carbon export is equal to the physical supply of carbon by upwelling or mixing, then the net change on atmospheric CO_2 is again negated. However, in periods when biological carbon export is increased, and/or periods where the vertical resupply of carbon is decreased, this biological carbon pump has a large potential for decreasing the atmospheric CO_2 concentrations. The biological carbon pump has been in a relatively steady state for 10 000 years because the concentration of atmospheric CO_2 has been constant for this period (Figure 2.6). However, variations in the strength of the oceans' biological carbon pump are another important factor in controlling CO_2 variations between glacial and inter-glacial periods.

Future Climate Change

Anthropogenic global carbon budget

The Industrial Revolution during the late 18th and early 19th centuries led to the wide-scale use of internal combustion engines that used fossil fuels (primarily coal and oil). Fossil fuels continue to be the dominant source of energy for the industrialized world. The combustion of fossil fuels results in the formation of gaseous carbon dioxide (CO_2). Very detailed records of energy use give us the ability to determine the amount of carbon dioxide emitted globally from anthropogenic fossil fuel use. Since the Industrial Revolution about 244±20 billion tonnes of carbon has been emitted into the atmosphere, with annual emissions of the order of 7 billion tonnes per year in recent years (Sabine et al. 2004). The question then arises: how does this CO_2 get distributed into each of the three biospheric reservoirs (atmosphere, ocean and terrestrial)?

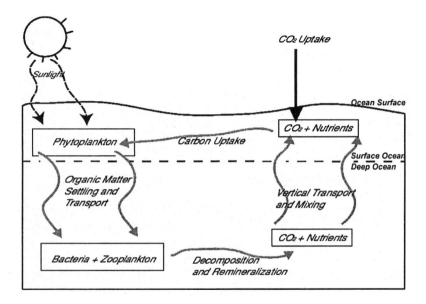

Figure 2.6 Biological carbon processes in the ocean

The role of the open ocean

Atmospheric CO_2 measuring stations are located all across the world and have accurately determined the *in situ* concentrations of CO_2 in the atmosphere over the last 60 years. Comparing the estimated concentration of CO_2 solely from fossil fuel emissions and the actual concentration in the atmosphere shows a large difference (refer to Figure 2.7). It shows that atmospheric CO_2 concentrations should be considerably higher than the actual atmospheric measurements have observed. With only three biospheric reservoirs on Earth (ocean, terrestrial and atmosphere), the 'missing' CO_2 must therefore have been absorbed by the ocean and the terrestrial reservoirs as shown by the shaded area between the dotted lines in Figure 2.7.

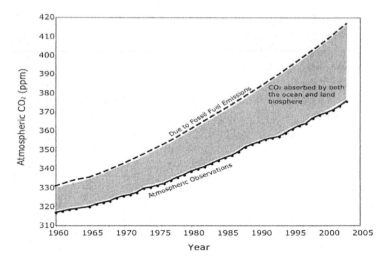

Figure 2.7   Average annual atmospheric CO₂ concentrations (dotted line) and the atmospheric CO₂ concentrations that should be in the atmosphere solely due to fossil fuel emissions (dashed line)

Note: Grey shading is the CO_2 absorbed by the oceanic and land biospheric reservoirs.

As discussed earlier, the ocean has a very large capacity to absorb atmospheric CO_2 due to both its volume and ability to redistribute CO_2 into other inorganic forms of carbon. There is, however, more doubt to what extent the terrestrial reservoir is a sink for anthropogenic CO_2 emissions. Sabine et al.'s (2004) research indicates the terrestrial reservoir actually has been a source of CO_2 of the order of 39±28 billion tonnes over the industrial era – this was mainly due to the large-scale land-use changes that emitted carbon into the atmosphere. So, in fact, the ocean was found to be the only true anthropogenic CO_2 sink over this period. However, the extent to which land is either a source or sink in recent decades is under considerable uncertainty due to the complicating effects of: (1) regrowth (where land was cleared historically); (2) CO_2 fertilization where experiments have shown plants and trees grow faster with a higher atmospheric CO_2 concentration, which has led to the belief that the terrestrial CO_2 uptake will increase in the future. In order to reduce the 'uncertainty' concerning the relative magnitude of these ocean and terrestrial reservoir CO_2 sinks, a wide variety of measuring programmes and methods have accurately determined the anthropogenic CO_2 sink over both the last two decades and the post-Industrial Revolution period (McNeil et al. 2003; Sabine et al. 2004).

The role of the coastal zone ocean
Although the coastal zone ocean represents about 6 per cent of the earth's surface, it maintains a disproportionate amount of biogeochemical fluxes for its size, since it is on the boundary between the terrestrial and oceanic reservoirs. Organic carbon and nutrient flow from land coupled with active oceanic exchanges result in one of the most biologically dynamic areas on Earth. Variations to the biological productivity in the coastal ocean are large which result in CO_2 fluxes across the air–sea interface, being some of the largest in the ocean. Despite this, an understanding of the significance of the coastal ocean for global carbon budgets is lacking due to the heterogeneity and scarcity of measurements. A recent study that synthesizes all coastal carbon budgets for air–sea CO_2 fluxes shows some significant results. The range in partial pressure of CO_2 (pCO_2) in the coastal ocean was shown to vary from 50ppm to several thousand ppm (~9000) and shows the extreme variations found in the coastal habitat (Borges 2005). In general, estuaries, mangroves and salt marshes are significant sources of CO_2 on a per unit area basis. Due to their relatively small area globally, these ecosystems represent a source of about 0.12 billion tonnes of carbon per year, or about 6 per cent of the total oceanic carbon budget (ibid.). However, taking into account the significant CO_2 sink within the coastal ocean shelf region, the most recent estimate for the entire coastal ocean is an annual CO_2 sink of 0.37 PgC/yr, which represents nearly 20 per cent of the total oceanic CO_2 sink (ibid.). Given the uncertainty and variability in the coastal carbon budget however, it will be important for future global initiatives to improve our understanding of coastal carbon cycling.

FUTURE CLIMATE CHANGE IMPACTS ON OCEAN ECOLOGY

Global Biological Productivity

Marine biological productivity requires adequate light, CO_2 and nutrients for primary producers to form biomass via photosynthesis. As discussed earlier, impacts on the productivity of primary producers will have detrimental flow-on effects to higher trophic levels in the marine ecosystem. Light and CO_2

will be in plentiful supply in the foreseeable future. However, the nutrient supply in the upper ocean is likely to change quite dramatically due to climate change. The oceanic thermohaline circulation is the primary global supplier of nutrients to the surface waters in the Southern Ocean where deep waters are transported to the surface ocean. The ensuing horizontal mixing supplies the necessary nutrients for most of the ocean. However, with climate change the upper ocean will warm to some extent. Warmer waters are lighter, which sets up a large density gradient in the ocean that limits the vertical mixing between the surface ocean and deep ocean. If the vertical circulation is retarded by a warmer ocean, the supply of nutrients to the upper ocean is shut off. Without nutrients in the upper ocean, marine biological productivity is expected to decrease significantly due to climate change impacts on the thermophaline circulation. Ocean models predict a 10–30 per cent reduction in this nutrient supply to the upper ocean due to climate change (Matear and Hirst 1999).

Ocean Acidification

In addition to its pivotal role in the atmosphere in the regulation of global climate, CO_2 and its sister chemical species, HCO_3^- and CO_3^{2-} comprise the carbonate system that regulates the acidity of seawater. The acidity or pH of an aqueous solution is a measure of the concentration of H^+ ions in the solution, with low pH meaning high H^+ concentration. The uptake of atmospheric CO_2 lowers the pH and increases the 'acidification' of seawater. Although the oceans are not predicted to become acidic in the near future, projections suggest the pH level is to drop from 8.1 to 7.6 units by the year 2100 (Orr et al. 2005; McNeil and Matear 2006). Acidifying the ocean is particularly detrimental to organisms that secrete shell material made of $CaCO_3$, such as coral reefs and a type of phytoplankton called coccolithophorids. The full effects of oceanic acidification are unknown and the subject of intense study (Raven 2005).

Coral Reefs

Climate change will most likely have a disproportionate impact on coral reef ecosystems due to the delicate physio-chemical balance for such diverse ecosystems to have evolved. Coral bleaching is a process whereby the micro-algae that live symbiotically with the coral become displaced or killed and result in the reef exposing the white $CaCO_3$ framework. Coral bleaching is known to occur when the ocean warms beyond a critical threshold. Although there is much debate about the temperature threshold to which corals 'bleach', it is usually when waters become 2°C warmer than average. The existence of a 'permanent' bleaching threshold assumes that corals will not adapt to the changed conditions. Current models suggest that the oceans will warm by 2°C over a 50-year period. With these changes, coral bleaching will become more and more frequent if the coral communities do not have the ability to adapt to the warmer ocean temperatures. Although the adaptive potential of corals to future warming is unclear, climate change has the potential to cause dramatic impacts on the functioning of this vital coastal marine habitat. Due to the important link between corals and other near-shore communities (mangroves and seagrasses) further degradation would most likely lead to knock-on impacts for these other near-shore communities that are vital for sustaining marine fisheries.

CONCLUSION

Although not well publicized, the role of the oceans and coasts in today's society is critical and it is hoped that this brief introductory chapter has touched on some of those more important aspects. From controlling regional weather patterns via the distribution of heat through its currents or by supplying the nutrients that creates the building blocks for our fisheries, the oceans and coasts are intimately part of our way of life. They have not only been critical to Earth's biological functioning today, but have been crucial in the evolution of higher life forms along with being a primary driver of past climatic variations. There is no doubt the future presents a number of global challenges to the oceans in the form of anthropogenic climate change and an ever increasing coastal population surge. The stability and sustainability of this biosphere is at risk, but an understanding of the economic, social and environmental dimensions of the issues should lead to better policy decisions to ensure its survival.

REFERENCES

Borges, A.V. (2005), 'Do we have enough pieces of the jigsaw to integrate CO_2 fluxes in the coastal ocean?' *Estuaries*, **28**: 3–27.

Boyd, P.W., A.J. Watson, C.S. Law, E.R. Abraham, T. Trull, R. Murdoch, D.C.E. Bakker, A.R. Bowie, K.O. Buesseler, H. Chang, M. Charette, P. Croot, K. Downing, R. Frew, M. Gall, M. Hadfield, J. Hall, M. Harvey, G. Jameson, J. LaRoche, M. Liddicoat, R. Ling, M.T. Maldonado, R.M. McKay, S. Nodder, S. Pickmere, R. Pridmore, S. Rintoul, K. Safi, P. Sutton, R. Strzepek, K.

Tanneberger, S. Turner, A. Waite and J. Zeldis (2000), 'A mesoscale phytoplankton bloom in the polar Southern Ocean stimulated by iron fertilization', *Nature*, **407**: 695–702.

Duarte C.M. and C.L. Chiscano (1999), 'Seagrass biomass and production: a reassessment', *Aquatic Botany*, **65**(1): 159–174(16).

Falkowski, P., E.A. Laws, R. Barber and J.W. Murray (2003), 'Phytoplankton and their role in primary, new and export production', in M.J.R. Fasham (ed.), *Ocean Biogeochemistry: The Role of the Ocean Carbon Cycle in Global Change*, New York: Springer.

Gattuso, J.P., M. Frankignoulle and R. Wollast (1998), 'Carbon and carbonate metabolism in coastal aquatic ecosystems', *Annual Review of Ecology and Systematics*, **29**: 405–434.

Matear, R.J. and A.C. Hirst (1999), 'Climate change feedback on the future oceanic CO^2 uptake', *Tellus Series B-Chemical and Physical Meteorology*, **51**: 722–733.

McNeil, B.I. and R.J. Matear (2006), 'Projected climate change impact on oceanic acidification', *Carbon Balance & Management*, 1(2) (27 June 2006). Available at: http://www.cbmjournal.com/content/1/1/2.

McNeil, B.I., R.J. Matear, R.M. Key, J.L. Bullister and J.L. Sarmiento (2003), 'Anthropogenic CO^2 uptake by the ocean based on the global chlorofluorocarbon data set', *Science*, **299**: 235–239.

Orr, J.C., V.J. Fabry, O. Aumont, L. Bopp, S.C. Doney, R.A. Feely, A. Gnanadesikan, N. Gruber, A. Ishida, F. Joos, R.M. Key, K. Lindsay, E. Maier-Reimer, R. Matear, P. Monfray, A. Mouchet, R.G. Najjar, G.K. Plattner, K.B. Rodgers, C.L. Sabine, J.L. Sarmiento, R. Schlitzer, R.D. Slater, I.J. Totterdell, M.F. Weirig, Y. Yamanaka and A. Yool (2005), 'Anthropogenic ocean acidification over the twenty-first century and its impact on calcifying organisms', *Nature*, **437**: 681–686.

Petit, J.R., J. Jouzel, D. Raynaud, N.I. Barkov, J.-M. Barnola, I. Basile, M. Bender, J. Chappellaz, M. Davis, G. Delayque, M. Delmotte, V.M. Kotlyakov, M. Legrand, V.Y. Lipenkov, C. Lorius, L. Pépin, C. Ritz, E. Saltzman and M. Stievenard (1999), 'Climate and atmospheric history of the past 420,000 years from the Vostok ice core', *Nature*, **399**: 429–436.

Raven, J. (2005), *Ocean Acidification due to Increasing Atmospheric Carbon Dioxide*, London: The Royal Society.

Sabine, C., M. Heimann, D. Artaxo, D.C.E. Bakker, C.H. Chen, C.B. Field, N. Gruber, C. LeQuere, R.G. Prinn, P. Richey, J. Romero, J. Sathaye and R. Valentint (2004), 'Current status and past trends of the global carbon cycle', in C.B. Field and M.R. Raupach (eds), *The Global Carbon Cycle: Integrating Humans, Climate, and the Natural World*, Washington, DC: Island Press.

Trujillo, A.P. and H.V. Thurman (2004), *Essentials of Oceanography*, Upper Saddle River: Pearson-Prentice Hall.

3. Biodiversity of the Oceans

Murray Patterson, Garry McDonald, Keith Probert and Nicola Smith

Marine biodiversity is an integral aspect of the global biogeochemical cycles and processes that maintain life on Earth. Compared with terrestrial biodiversity, however, relatively little is known about marine biodiversity and the exact role that it plays in many vital ecological processes. For example, an entirely new group of planktonic, photosynthetic bacteria was discovered only as recently as the mid-1980s (Chisholm et al. 1988), yet these are now recognized to be among the most abundant organisms on Earth and responsible for a significant proportion of the primary production of the oceans. The rate of discovery of marine species is indeed astounding, and scientists are only just beginning to unravel the role that marine biodiversity plays in regulating many ecological processes and the impact that it has on global climate change.

WHAT IS BIODIVERSITY?

The term biodiversity, a contraction of biological diversity (Gray 1997), emerged from relative obscurity largely through the pioneering efforts of Myers (1979), Wilson (1988) and Raven (1980). Before attaining its current international prominence, it was almost zealously associated with species protection and conservation of tropical rainforest. The pivotal moment in this transition arguably occurred at the 1992 Rio Earth Summit when the Bush Administration failed to ratify the Convention on Biological Diversity.

Article 2 of the Convention offers perhaps the most widely cited definition of biodiversity: 'the variability among living organisms from all sources including *inter alia* terrestrial, marine and other aquatic ecosystems and the ecological complexes of which they are part; this includes diversity within species, between species and of ecosystems'. The 'within species' refers to the genetic diversity contained in the genes of a species or population. The 'between species' refers to the variety of living organisms, including all the taxa of bacteria, algae, fungi, animals and plants.

By many accounts the above definition is ill-defined and contentious. Lévêque and Mounolou (2001), for example, argue that the term typically refers to diversity of life for a given taxon (that is, for species, genus, family, order, and phylum, in ascending order); nevertheless, the exact definition of the relations between, and across, taxa is very unclear. Species biodiversity, from a purist viewpoint, warrants special attention as species are the fundamental unit of evolutionary investigation (Thorne-Miller 1999). Taxonomic classification is, however, not the sole organizational principle of the biological world. In this way, many scientists now recognize at least six broad categories of biodiversity:

Species diversity refers to the number of species found in a given area. Also important is the distribution of individuals among species – whether the individuals in a community are relatively equitably distributed among the various species or unequally distributed so that certain species dominate numerically. The distinction is often made between simply the number of species in an area (species' richness) and measures that take into account the distribution of individuals among species (species diversity). A further critical aspect of species diversity is endemism.[1] Endemic species may play pivotal roles in the structure and function of their ecosystems.

Taxonomic diversity refers to the diversity that exists within other taxa. In the case of phyletic diversity, for example, the number of marine phyla is significantly greater than that recorded for the terrestrial environment (Angel 1993; Briggs 1994; Ray and Grassle 1991).

Community and ecosystem diversity encompasses diversity that occurs at other levels of ecological organization. This includes interactions between species (for example, symbiotic, predator–prey relationships) as witnessed in communities. Similarly, ecosystem diversity captures the interconnections between species and their abiotic environment.

Habitat diversity refers to diversity within a given habitat (Whittaker 1967). Habitats, unlike ecosystems, tend to have clear boundaries and are often employed as 'templates' for study (Southwood 1977). At larger scales, community boundaries may cross several habitats, in which case the study of diversity is aptly referred to as 'between-habitat diversity'. At even larger scales, 'landscape' and 'seascape' diversity may exist. It is therefore important that scale be clearly stated when studying habitat diversity.

Genetic diversity refers to the genetic makeup and variation that occurs among individuals within a species (Thorne-Miller 1999). Each species consists of one or more populations of individuals. A population is usually defined as a group of individuals which may, if sexually reproducing, interchange genetic material. Different populations tend to diverge genetically due to limited genetic mixing, mutations and genetic drift. Populations with higher genetic diversity are more likely to withstand environmental change and, in turn, pass on their genes to the next generation.

Functional diversity refers to the variety of biogeochemical functions occurring within an ecosystem (O'Neill et al. 1986; Thorne-Miller 1999). Some scientists assert that protection of functional diversity may be the most useful way of conserving biodiversity. Contention surrounds the degree of redundancy within ecosystems – that is, whether species are unique in their particular functions (Thorne-Miller 1999). Others contest that any redundancy may add to the ability of the system to absorb shocks, adapt and evolve (Naeem et al. 1994).

WHY IS MARINE BIODIVERSITY IMPORTANT?

Ecological Importance

Marine biodiversity plays an integral part in global biogeochemical cycles, in regulating ecosystem stability and change and in maintaining a rich 'gene pool' for evolutionary processes.

The role of marine biodiversity in biogeochemical cycles
Marine biodiversity plays a critical and irreplaceable role in all the global biogeochemical cycles that support life on Earth – both human and non-human. Often it is the 'inconspicuous' micro-organisms that are most important in these cycles, rather than the so called 'charismatic megafauna' such as dolphins and whales.

Marine biodiversity captures external energy sources and converts inorganic into organic compounds. Indeed, oceanic and coastal biodiversity account for 46 per cent of the solar energy captured by global photosynthetic processes (Field et al. 1998). Many species of phytoplankton contribute to about 95 per cent of marine primary production (photosynthesis). This importance of phytoplankton is due to the large area of the Earth's surface that is covered by open sea. Marine biodiversity near the shore (including single-cell algae, larger multi-cell algae and vascular plants) also plays an important role in photosynthesis.

Marine biota is also important in other biogeochemical cycles apart from carbon. For example, Capone (2001) argues that biological fixation is a far more important process in the nitrogen cycle than previously thought and may have a direct influence on the upper ocean's ability to sequester CO_2. He found the 'most conspicuous' oceanic nitrogen fixer was the cyanobacterium *Trichodesmium*, although there was a greater diversity of marine nitrogen fixers than previously thought.

The role of marine biodiversity is often subtle, intricate and critical from an ecological perspective. Planktonic uptake of some essential metals, for example, results in extraordinarily low concentration of these essential metals in surface sea water. As a consequence, Morel and Price (2003) show that this low availability of some metals controls the rate of photosynthesis and the uptake of other major nutrients such as nitrogen. Similarly, evidence from Tortell et al. (1999) demonstrates the role of marine biota in the biogeochemical cycling of iron and how this is inextricably linked to nitrogen fixing and photosynthesis.

Marine biodiversity also has important influence on climate dynamics. For example, dimethyl sulphide from plant plankton influences climate by changing the numbers of cloud condensation nuclei available in remote regions (Watson and Liss 1998).

The role of marine biodiversity in ecosystem stability

It is often suggested that higher biodiversity (variety of species) enhances ecosystem stability. This then presents a powerful rationale for preserving the biodiversity of the oceans and coasts. However, a causative link between 'more biodiversity' and 'ecosystem stability' is not as clear-cut as it may seem. For example, highly productive but low diversity ecosystems, such as estuaries, typically populated by a few species with wide niches, tend to be more resilient and 'stable'.

This 'diversity–stability' debate in ecology is a longstanding one. Before the 1970s, ecologists (Elton 1958; Odum 1953) generally believed that more diverse communities were more stable. This thinking was strongly challenged by the theoretic-mathematical research of May (1972 a, b), who showed that more complex communities are not necessarily stable. For a randomly assembled model of a multi-species community, he found that 'too rich a web connectance … or too large an average interaction strength … leads to instability' (May 1972b). In more recent years, the debate has matured, with ecologists now generally agreed that the link between '(bio)diversity' and 'stability' is dependent on the ecological context and timescale of the analysis. McCann (2000) concludes, for example, that 'diversity is not the driver of this [diversity–stability] relationship; rather, ecosystem stability depends on the ability of communities to contain species, or functional groups, that are capable of a differential response'.

It is even more unclear what the role of marine biodiversity is in maintaining community and ecosystem stability, as most of the research has had a terrestrial focus. The marine environment does, however, provide a valuable arena for resolving this 'diversity–stability' debate, because it is more diverse at higher taxonomic levels than terrestrial ecosystems and has higher levels of functional diversity.

The role of marine biodiversity in maintaining the 'gene pool'
Marine biodiversity represents a rich 'gene pool'. Ray and Grassle (1991), for example, argue that there is greater genetic variation at the molecular level within species of the marine environment than in terrestrial areas. Some have suggested that this is due to 'life existing longer in the sea' and the gene flow can be expected to be higher in seas due to the contiguous nature of oceans and higher dispersal capabilities (May 1994). It is therefore often argued that marine biodiversity is of ecological importance, as it represents a diverse 'gene pool' for evolutionary processes. That is, as May (1994) put it, 'genetic diversity is of fundamental importance, providing the natural variation which is the raw stuff of evolution'.

Economic Importance

The economic importance of marine biodiversity lies in the role it plays in providing ecosystem 'goods and services' that contribute to human welfare. This does not just include the direct economic benefit derived from exploiting marine living resources and the benefits to be gained from new pharmaceuticals and industrial compounds, but the 'indirect' benefits of ecosystem services derived from the marine environment.[2] Costanza et al. (1997) estimated marine ecosystem services to be worth $US20.9 trillion per year in 1994, compared with terrestrial ecosystem services worth $US12.3 trillion and the GDP of the global economy being $US25 trillion for the same year (refer to Table 3.1).[3]

Cultural and 'Intrinsic' Importance

For many, the importance of marine biodiversity transcends its instrumental value, whether or not this is for an economic or an ecological end-purpose. Marine biodiversity simply has 'value' in its own right, irrespective of what it can be used for. Many cultures have an intimate spiritual connection with the sea and all it embraces. Beliefs, spirituality, ethics and a 'way of life' are inextricably intertwined with the 'web of life' of the sea and its environs.

This spiritual connection with the sea and its biodiversity is evident not only in 'indigenous' cultures, but also in maritime communities in the 'western world' such as those on the east coast of Canada or fishing villages in the Mediterranean.[4] Marine biodiversity is often considered in a 'custodial, non-materialistic and communal' way in indigenous societies. It can also play a central role in storytelling, belief and creation myths. For New Zealand Māori, as with other Pacific peoples, Māori mythology abounds with reference to sea creatures and the father of the sea creature – the god, Tangaroa.

Apart from biodiversity sustaining our quality of life through the provision of ecosystem services, and apart from the ecological role it plays, biodiversity has 'intrinsic value' for many people. Deep ecologists such as Naess (1973) and Fox (1990) argue that biodiversity has value in its own right, independent of human exploitative motives or human perceptions of value. It is contended that biodiversity should be preserved not because of any immediate or potential use for humans, but because its preservation is of importance *per se*. Recognition of the intrinsic value of biodiversity is, for example, illustrated by the preamble to the Canadian Species at Risk Act of 2002, which states that 'wildlife, in all its forms, has value in and of itself'.

CHARACTERISTICS OF MARINE BIODIVERSITY

Marine Biodiversity at a Species Level

Taxonomists have to date recorded and described some 1.7 million species (May 1994; Tudge 2000). Unfortunately, the exact number of living species so far identified is not known as there is no central catalogue.[5] Estimates of the number of species on Earth vary considerably. Much of this uncertainty resides with large groups, such as nematodes and single-celled organisms, about which very little is known. Even in those groups that have been carefully analyzed the presence of potential synonymies and cryptic species[6] means that there is uncertainty as to the total number of species (Knowlton 1993; May 1994). Taking into account such uncertainties, it seems probable, however, that the total number of species on Earth greatly exceeds the number that have thus far been described, possibly by several orders of magnitude (Tudge 2000).

Table 3.1 Global value of ecosystem services derived from coastal and oceanic ecosystems, 1994

	Ecosystem Type						
Ecosystem Service	Open Ocean ($US billion/yr)	Estuaries ($US billion/yr)	Sea grass/Algal Beds ($US billion/yr)	Coral Reefs ($US billion/yr)	Continental Shelf ($US billion/yr)	Tidal Marsh/Mangroves ($US billion/yr)	Total ($US billion/yr)
Gas Regulation	1,262	0	0	0	0	0	1,262
Disturbance Regulation	0	102	0	171	0	303	273
Nutrient Cycling	3,918	3,798	3,800	0	3,806	0	15,322
Waste Treatment	0	0	0	4	0	1,105	4
Biological Control	166	14	0	0	104	0	284
Habitat	0	24	0	0	0	28	24
Flood Protection	498	94	0	14	181	77	786
Raw Materials	0	5	0	2	5	27	12
Recreation	0	69	0	186	0	109	255
Cultural	2,523	5	0	0	186	0	2,715
Total	8,366	4,110	3,801	377	4,283	1,648	22,585

Note: [1] This total does not exactly match the figure reported by Costanza (1997) of $US22,597 billion. This is due to rounding errors.

(*Source:* Costanza et al. 1997)

The proportion of Earth's species that are marine is also difficult to estimate. Of all the species currently named and recorded, fewer than 15 per cent are found in the oceans (May and Godfrey, 1994). This disparity between terrestrial and marine biodiversity is especially revealing given that the oceans cover approximately 71 per cent of the Earth's surface, and it has been estimated that the three-dimensional living space in the oceans is roughly 300 times greater than the equivalent terrestrial living space (Thorson 1971).

The extreme difficulty of estimating the number of marine species was recently highlighted by the discovery of a biodiversity 'treasure trove' at the Bird's Head Seascape, off the coast of Indonesia's Papua province (Kranz 2006). Scientists, led by Mark Erdmann of Conservation International, surveyed two locations at the seascape and uncovered more than 50 new species, including 24 fish species, 20 coral species and 8 shrimp species, of which many are considered to be endemic. These discoveries, coupled with the region's already catalogued species, make it perhaps Earth's most biologically diverse seascape. Unfortunately, only 11 per cent of the region is currently protected, with possible fishing threats looming (Kranz 2006).

Despite the lack of biologists studying some of the more common marine taxa (May 1994), and the fact that much of the marine environment is poorly explored and difficult to access, many scientists have accepted the 85:15 ratio of terrestrial to marine species as broadly representative of the actual total (May 1992, 1994). Nevertheless, some scientists predict that the number of species within the oceans may be as great as on land, with most of this diversity presumed to be located on, or within, the sea floor (Grassle and Maciolek 1992; Poore and Wilson 1993; Thorne-Miller 1999).

The extent of species diversity of the sea floor has, in particular, been debated. Of relevance is the empirical work of Grassle and Maciolek (1992), who reported on ocean floor samples taken off the coast of New Jersey and Delaware. Based on the macrofaunal diversity of the samples (mostly molluscs, crustaceans and polychaete worms) and estimates of species change along spatial gradients, they suggested that there are more than 1 million, and maybe even more than 10 million, species of macrofauna inhabiting the deep sea floor. Although Grassle and Maciolek's extrapolation methods have been questioned, with May (1992) suggesting that a more realistic estimate may be around 500 000 species, their work indicates there is potentially a large reservoir of undescribed macrofaunal species.

It is also recognized that very little is currently known about the diversity of micro-organisms (May and Godfrey 1994), despite the fact that micro-organisms, including fungi, bacteria and viruses, play vital roles in the functioning and maintenance of Earth's ecosystems. Attempts to understand micro-organism species diversity are made especially difficult by the lack of defining concepts about what constitutes a 'species'. Bacteria and viruses are particularly difficult to classify as they readily exchange genetic material and have relatively high mutation rates (May and Godfrey 1994; Torsvik et al. 1996).

With such difficulties in classification, it is no surprise that micro-organisms are often ignored in estimates and comparisons of species diversity (see, for example, May 1994). It is clear, however, that micro-organisms account for a significant proportion of diversity on Earth, including marine diversity. Breitbart et al. (2003), for example, propose that marine sediment viral communities may be one of the largest unexplored reservoirs of 'sequence space' (that is, distinct DNA sequences or genes associated with different 'species' types) on the planet.

Taxonomic Composition of Marine Biodiversity

Putting aside uncertainties about the extent of micro-organism diversity, it is generally accepted that while the oceans may be relatively species poor, they are rich in animal phyla (Briggs 1994; May 1994; Thorne-Miller 1999). While, as noted above, only 15 per cent of recorded species are found in the oceans, 80 per cent of all animal phyla are found in the oceans compared with just 20 per cent found on land. This is a remarkable reversal in land–sea patterns of biological diversity as one ascends in taxa from species to phylum, and it has been suggested that patterns at the level of genera, families and orders are appropriately intermediate (May 1994).

Several hypotheses have been put forward to explain the apparent differences between land and sea taxonomic compositions. First, it has been suggested that richness in higher taxa of ocean fauna can be attributed to the evolution of life in the sea – that is, the major groups evolved in the early oceans leaving descendants that survive in the seas today. Due to physiological or morphological constraints, however, a number of these groups never managed a successful transition to terrestrial habitats (Angel 1993; May 1994). Conversely, the relatively low diversity of marine fauna at the species level has been partly attributed to the circulating medium provided by the oceans that acts to disperse spores and larvae of many marine species over large distances. This leads to wide distributions for many marine species and the expectation of lower levels of endemism in the oceans compared with land (Thorne-Miller 1999).

Another factor that may lead to high species diversity on land is the presence of large vegetation that creates complex physical structures. This, in turn, creates greater opportunities for specialization and increased potential for biological interactions, thus promoting species diversity. Although high structural diversity is present in some marine environments (such as coral reefs and kelp beds) and the great depth of the oceans is a source of structural diversity that is not present in terrestrial environments, the oceans are generally recognized as being less structurally diverse or 'architecturally elaborate' when compared with terrestrial environments (May 1994; Thorne-Miller 1999).

Related to this idea of structural variation, the differences in the number of species recorded in the terrestrial and marine environments have been partly credited to differences in primary producers and the relative diversity of associated herbivores. On land we find that it is very common for insects to have evolved as host-plant specialists (May 1994), accounting for the largest proportion of recorded animal species (Tudge 2000). In comparison, primary producers in the sea are predominantly single-celled organisms that do not appear to offer the same opportunities for diverse producer-herbivore relations (May 1994).

Terrestrial environments are also recognized as being subject to great variations and fluctuations in climate and other physical factors, both over space and time. These factors promote species diversity by creating many opportunities for specialization to local conditions and readjustments to changing conditions (May 1999).

Large-Scale Spatial Patterns of Marine Biodiversity

Our knowledge of large-scale patterns of oceanic diversity is restricted to only a few major taxa, and is based on very limited sampling (Rex et al. 1997). The identified patterns include:

- *Latitudinal patterns of diversity.* In terrestrial systems, diversity gradients are well known, often with diversity increasing towards the tropics (Gray 1997). Although similar patterns have been demonstrated for certain taxa within some oceanic regions (for bivalves, gastropods and isopods in the North Atlantic and Norwegian Sea), oceanic latitudinal gradients in species diversity are generally less clear (Rex et al. 1993, 1997). The species diversity of sediment benthos off the coast of Australia, for example, is among the highest for samples taken anywhere (Gray 1997; Poore and Wilson 1993). In the Southern Hemisphere, in particular, pole-to-tropic gradients in diversity appear uncertain, possibly due to the relatively high diversity of many taxa in Antarctica (Clarke 1992) and pronounced interregional variations in diversity (Rex et al. 1997).
- *Pelagic diversity versus benthic diversity.* As discussed above, species

diversity of seabed biota (that is, benthos) is considered to be high, particularly for macrofaunal taxa (Gage 1996; Grassle and Maciolek 1992). Species diversity within the pelagic (open sea) environments is, by comparison, thought to be very low (Angel 1993). A number of theories have been put forward to explain the differences between ocean floor and pelagic diversity. Angel (1993), for example, suggests that pelagic speciation may have been limited by the hydrological regime of the oceans that promotes large-scale mixing of taxa and gene flow. On the other hand, it has been proposed that the high diversity in benthic species is partly attributable to the presence of biologically created 'structures' within the sea floor, such as mounds, burrows and 'mud balls', which create small-scale habitat heterogeneity, and thus enable niche specialization (Gage 1996).[7]

- *Bathymetric patterns of diversity.* Species diversity also varies within the benthic environment itself and has been shown to exhibit a strong relationship with water depth (Grassle and Maciolek 1992). In the western North Atlantic, the most extensively sampled area of the deep sea, the diversity of several groups of macrofauna, megafauna and fish has been found to vary parabolically with depth: diversity being lowest on the continental shelf, increasing to a maximum at mid-slope depths and declining in the abyssal plain (Rex et al. 1997). The causes of these species-depth patterns are not well understood, but probably relate to changes over depth in rates of nutrient input, biotic interactions and environmental heterogeneity. Further sampling is required to determine whether a similar depth-species pattern holds for other oceanic regions (ibid.).

THE LOSS OF MARINE BIODIVERSITY

Biodiversity Loss and Extinctions

There are relatively few records of modern marine extinctions and of those that have been identified the best known concern mammals and birds (Baillie et al. 2004). It is often thought that marine extinctions are rare because marine species are widely distributed – the decline or disappearance of a given species in one place therefore does not threaten the species globally. Work of recent authors (Carlton et al. 1999; Dulvy et al. 2003), however, suggests that marine extinctions are occurring but simply not being detected and documented the same way as in the terrestrial environment. There is also a growing body of evidence indicating that marine species are characterized by the same attributes that account for vulnerability in terrestrial species (Dulvy et al. 2003; Pauly et al. 1998). As an indication of this vulnerability, the IUCN 'Red List' (Baillie et al. 2004) now includes 131 threatened marine fish species, out of only 487 species that have so far been assessed by the organization. As well as global extinctions of species, it is also important to consider local extinctions and situations where a species becomes so rare that it effectively no longer plays a role in its ecosystem (so-called ecological extinction). Extinction of species that occupy pivotal roles (for example, as key predators or competitors) may have repercussions that cascade through the community. For instance, the elimination of sea otters (*Enhydra lutris*) from much of their natural range as a result of fur trade hunting, and the subsequent recovery of populations of other species, demonstrated the important role these animals play in structuring kelp forest communities in the North Pacific (Estes et al. 1989).

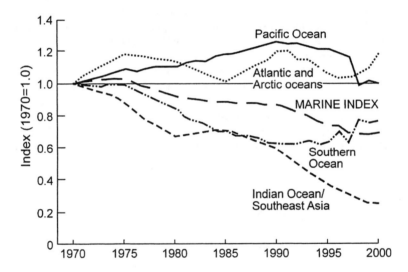

Figure 3.1 Marine species population index, 1970–2000

(*Source:* Adapted from Loh and Wackernagel 2004)

The WWF 'Marine Species Index' indicates that *populations* of species of marine mammals, birds, reptiles and fish declined by 30 per cent between 1970 and 2000 (Loh and Wackernagel 2004). Figure 3.1 indicates the trends in populations of 117 Atlantic and Arctic Ocean species, 105 Pacific Ocean species, 15 Indian Ocean species and 30 Southern Ocean species. Loh and

Wackernagel (2004) argue that these figures for the Atlantic and Arctic Oceans are misleading, as they 'hide' the effect of 'fishing down the food web'. That is, the biomass of high trophic level fishes (such as cod and tuna) have been reduced by two-thirds in the North Atlantic between 1950 and 2000, increasingly leading to species at lower levels being targeted by fishing operations (refer to Figure 3.2).

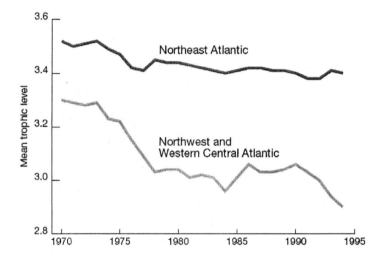

Figure 3.2 Mean trophic level of Atlantic Fisheries landings, 1970–1994

(*Source:* Loh and Wackernagel 2004)

Human Impacts on Marine Biodiversity

Fishing
Although there is much concern about the 'collapse' of fisheries due to over-exploitation (refer to Box 3.1), the long-term effects of global fisheries are perhaps best illustrated by changes in the trophic level of fish landings. A trophic level expresses the number of steps a species is removed from the primary producer in a food web (Pauly et al. 1998). Over time, the mean trophic level of global fish landings has decreased, reflecting a gradual transition in landings from large, long-lived (high trophic level) fish, towards short-lived (low trophic level) invertebrates and fish (Christensen 1998; Christensen et al. 2003; Pauly et al. 1998). This trend has been termed 'fishing down the food web' (Pauly et al. 1998).

Box 3.1 Collapse of the Newfoundland Cod Fishery: Tragedy of the Commons?

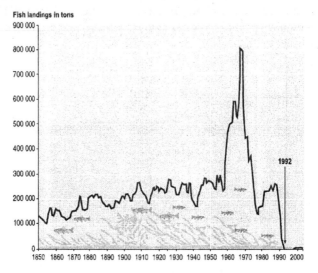

(Source: Brown et al. 2006)

The Newfoundland cod fishery dramatically collapsed in 1992. Immediately, the Canadian Minister of Fisheries and Oceans placed a moratorium on fishing for cod in Newfoundland. Until the late 1950s, the fishery was dominated by seasonal migratory fleets and inshore local fishers.

These local fishers used fixed gear and small nets, which minimized their catch. By the late 1950s, bottom trawlers made significant inroads into the fishery, not only to the cod stock, but also to non-target species. In 1977, Canada claimed a 200-nautical mile Exclusive Fishing Zone. Foreign vessels had to 'fish' outside the 200-mile zone, but the number of Canadian fishing operations increased to pick up the 'surplus' (Sinclair 1988). National quota systems were put in place, arguably based on optimistic data on the ability of cod stocks to regenerate (Palmer and Sinclair 1997). The national quota system failed to reverse the decline and the stock collapsed to extremely low levels in the late 1980s and early 1990s. A moratorium was consequently placed on the cod fishery in 1992. A small commercial inshore fishery was allowed in 1998, but catch rates declined and the fishery was again closed in 2003. Some argue this is a classic example of the 'Tragedy of the Commons'.

In terms of maximizing fish catches, it might be argued that the process of 'fishing down the food web' is advantageous because it results in an initial removal of predator fish, thus enabling populations at lower trophic levels to expand (Pauly et al. 2002). Such effects, however, have seldom been observed in marine ecosystems (Pace et al. 1999; Pinnegar et al. 2000). Plots of mean trophic levels against catches for Northwest and Northeast Atlantic, the Mediterranean (Pauly et al. 1998) and the Gulf of Thailand (Christensen 1998), for example, have shown that while an inverse relationship between catch quantity and trophic level appears to have held for some time, in all cases this relationship eventually broke down. The eventual decline in total fish landings may be attributed to a number of factors including reduced catchability of smaller and lower trophic level organisms, unreported catches and massive bycatch volumes. A further possible explanation is that fishing has induced changes in ecosystem structures that have translated into differences in the relative abundance of species (Pauly et al. 1998).

Scientists are now recognizing some of the wider ecological effects of fishing. Firstly, it has been found that fishing can affect *natural selection* processes within species (through incessant removal of certain genotypes) and within communities (through targeting of specific species), with authors noting that fishing appears to 'reverse the course of evolution' (Appollonio 1994; Parsons 1992; Pauly 1979). Secondly, it has also been noted that fishing can have profound effects on *ecosystem dynamics and stability*. For example, these effects been demonstrated in relation to the fishing of snapper (*Pagrus auratus*) in New Zealand. Snapper are one of the primary predators of sea urchin (*Evechinus chloroticus*), which in turn are heavy consumers of kelp. The decline in kelp forests off the coast of New Zealand has been attributed *inter alia* to heavy exploitation of snapper by commercial and recreational fishers resulting in an abundance of sea urchin and consequential heavy grazing of kelp. As a further feedback, heavy grazing of kelp by sea urchins has been shown to produce a habitat suitable for growth in limpet (*Cellana stellifera*) numbers (Shears and Babcock 2003).

Habitat degradation, fragmentation and loss
Habitat degradation has been identified as one of the most serious threats to marine biodiversity, particularly in coastal areas (Gray 1997). Examples include the smothering of mud flats, coral reefs and other coastal habitats by sediment as a result of changing terrestrial land use patterns (Lundin and Lindén 1993), and the removal of mangrove forests in order to make way for aquaculture (Primavera 1991). Even in those situations where habitats are ostensibly maintained, they may become fragmented as a result of human activities potentially leading to losses in diversity (Gray 1997; Huston 1994).

Marine pollution
The oceans are often the sink for much of the waste produced from human activities. Oil spills from the 1989 *Exxon Valdez* disaster in Alaska, and the more recent spill resulting from Israeli air strikes on a Lebanese power plant, are examples of major human-induced events leading to widespread losses of marine biodiversity. Many of the pollutants affecting marine biodiversity are, however, discharged in a far less dramatic fashion, tending to accumulate in the oceans over time. Eutrophication, caused by agricultural runoff, sewage discharge and the burning of fossil fuels, for example, has been recognized as a particularly serious threat to coastal marine biodiversity (GESAMP 1990).

Introduction of invasive species
Various human activities promote the transfer of organisms from one location to another. The comb jelly *Mnemiopsis leidyi,* for example, is believed to have been transported from the US East Coast to the Black Sea via ship ballast water. This has resulted in catastrophic alterations to the trophic web within the Black Sea and contributed to significant reductions in commercial fishing stocks (Gray 1997). Introduced species may also be more likely to establish and flourish if the receiving environment is already stressed.

Global atmosphere change
Coral reefs and coastal wetland habitats may be particularly affected by global warming and rising sea levels as a result of increasing greenhouse gas emissions. Other potential impacts of climate change include: the loss of species whose temperature tolerance ranges are exceeded, and changes in ocean stratification and circulation patterns. Such impacts will, in turn, result in changes to nutrient levels and phytoplankton productivity, potentially creating significant impacts on global marine biodiversity. Ozone depletion, and the resultant increase in UV-B radiation, is another human-induced atmospheric change affecting marine biodiversity. Fish eggs, which often float near the surface of the ocean, are likely to be particularly sensitive to increases in UV-B, and this has the potential to create cascading effects through entire food chains (Karentz 1992).

International Initiatives to Reduce Marine Biodiversity Loss

Biodiversity loss gained international recognition as an important environmental issue following the Earth Summit in Rio de Janeiro in 1992. As with many environmental issues, it is a complex global problem, the management of which requires at least some international cooperation. The way in which nations or states cooperate with respect to environmental and other global issues is typically through the process of negotiating and formulating instruments of international law, such as treaties and conventions, as well as various 'soft law' declarations and agreements.

United Nations Convention on the Law of the Sea

For many centuries the oceans were subject to the freedom-of-the-seas doctrine – the oceans were proclaimed to be free to all and belonging to none. By the mid 20th century, however, this doctrine was proving to be inadequate with, in particular, significant tensions developing over the rights of nations to appropriate lucrative fish and sea floor resources. These growing tensions led to the first United Nations Conference on the Law of the Sea (UNCLOS) in 1958 and the eventual adoption of UNCLOS in 1982, which was finally enforced in 1994.

Although predating the Convention on Biological Diversity, UNCLOS is particularly important to biodiversity as it enabled coastal nations to extend jurisdiction over adjacent areas of the marine environment, generally to a maximum distance of 200 nautical miles (370 km). Within these limits nations have the ability to create and enforce laws, regulate any use and set up organizations to manage issues relating to biodiversity. The convention also contains a number of other provisions that are directly relevant to biodiversity. For example, while the convention maintains the traditional right of all nations to fish the high seas (that is, waters beyond national jurisdictions), this right is qualified by an obligation to take such measures as are necessary for the conservation of living resources (Article 117). Nations are also obligated, within their areas of jurisdiction, to ensure the maintenance of living resources is not endangered by overexploitation (Article 61). An area where UNCLOS has been subject to critique is in the requirement of nations to consider 'maximum sustainable yields' when determining the appropriate measure required to conserve living resources (Articles 61 and 117). Some conservation biologists do not believe that this concept is sufficiently protective or precautionary in relation to biodiversity loss (Mace and Hudson 1999).

Convention on Biological Diversity

Signed in 1992, The Convention on Biological Diversity was the first international agreement relating specifically to biodiversity. The main objectives of the Convention are conserving biodiversity, sustainable use of its components, and equitable sharing of the benefits arising from the utilization of genetic resources (Article 1). Parties to the Convention are *inter alia* obligated to: promote the protection of ecosystems, natural habitats and the maintenance of viable species in natural surroundings; establish protected areas where special measures need to be taken to conserve biodiversity; and prevent the introduction of exotic species and eradicate or control those already introduced (Article 8).

Box 3.2 Marine Protected Areas

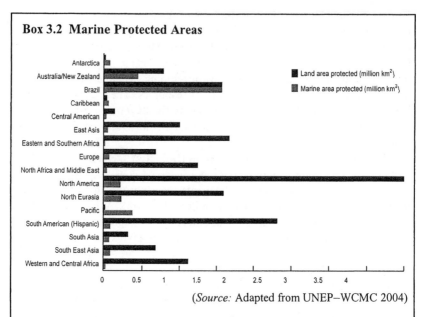

(*Source:* Adapted from UNEP–WCMC 2004)

One type of effort to conserve the world's marine biodiversity has been the establishment of Marine Protected Areas (MPAs). Despite the fact that most of Earth's fish stocks have been exploited well beyond sustainable limits, only 0.6 per cent of the earth's marine environment is protected (WWF Global Marine Programme 2006). WWF is campaigning for at least 10 per cent of marine areas to be under some form of protection by 2012.

MPAs are established to protect and conserve species, ecosystems, habitats, and/or historical/cultural sites. In fact, many of the first, although unofficial, MPAs were established by indigenous groups such as the Māori in New Zealand to conserve their sources of food and livelihoods. Restrictions in MPAs range from 'no take' zones where all forms of exploitation are prohibited; to exclusions on fishing, oil and gas mining, access for tourism, construction and development; to mere limits on technology use or catch/take. In the late 1980s, there were an estimated 1300 marine reserves worldwide (Botsford et al. 1997).

With respect to all these conservation obligations, nations are, however, only required to act 'as far as possible and appropriate' to compensate for the different capabilities, both financial and technical, of different countries. It has been commented that this phrase makes the conservation provisions weak and possibly ineffectual (Thorne-Miller 1999). (For further discussion on the role of Marine Protected Areas in conserving biodiversity, refer to Box 3.2).

Antarctica

One way in which biodiversity may be conserved is through the protection of particular geographic regions or habitats. A notable example is Antarctica. It has been subject to incremental increases in environmental protection starting with the 1959 Antarctic Treaty through to the Protocol on Environmental Protection to the Antarctic Treaty signed in 1991. This latter instrument designates Antarctica as a natural reserve (Article 2) and has been identified as one of the most stringent international agreements to date. Particularly relevant to marine biodiversity is the Convention on the Conservation of Antarctic Marine Living Resources. This came into force in 1982 and aims to protect all species of living organisms within the Southern Ocean surrounding Antarctica. It was the first international convention to take an ecosystem-based approach to the management of living resources of the of high seas and in this respect pioneered the concept of managing large areas that make sense ecologically.

Convention on migratory species

There are also various agreements that are part of the 'Convention on the Conservation of Migratory Species of Wild Animals', designed to protect particular marine species or groups of species, including: Cetaceans of the Black Sea, Mediterranean and Contiguous Atlantic Area; Small Cetaceans of the Baltic and North Seas; Seals in the Wadden Sea; Albatrosses and Petrels; and Marine turtles of the Atlantic Coast of Africa, Indian Sea and South-East Asia (Brown et al. 2006).

NOTES

1. This refers to the situation where a species is restricted to a particular geographic region, owing to factors such as response to climatic conditions or isolation.
2. In strict terms, 'ecosystem services' are broader than 'biodiversity services' as ecosystems include abiotic factors. Nonetheless, most 'ecosystem services' are a result of the interaction of biotic and abiotic factors which are difficult to analytically disentangle.
3. Matthew Wilson and Shuang Liu, in Chapter 6, provide a more detailed account of the economic valuation of 'ecosystem goods and services provided by coastal and near shore marine systems'.

4. Charlotte Šunde, in Chapter 8, explores the 'spiritual and cultural values of the oceans', and how such a perspective issues fundamental challenges for ecological economics.
5. There is, however, increasing awareness of the need to better catalogue and characterize marine biodiversity. One such initiative is the 'Census of Marine Life' – a growing global network of researchers in more than 70 nations engaged in a 10-year initiative to assess and explain the diversity, distribution and abundance of marine life.
6. The term 'cryptic species' refers to organisms that are indistinguishable from outward appearance, but qualify as separate species due to reproductive isolation.
7. Gage (1996) also suggests that high benthic diversity may be attributable to periodic disturbances in the ocean floor that enable species invasion and succession in patches of new 'open habitat'.

REFERENCES

Angel, M.V. (1993), 'Biodiversity of the pelagic ocean', *Conservation Biology*, **7**: 760–772.

Appollonio, S. (1994), 'The use of ecosystem characteristics in fisheries management', *Reviews in Fisheries Science*, **2**: 157–180.

Baillie, J.E.M., C. Hilton-Taylor and S.N. Stuard (eds) (2004), *2004 IUCN Red List of Threatened Species: A Global Species Assessment*, Cambridge: IUCN Publications Services Unit.

Botsford, L.W., J.C. Castilla and C.H. Petersen (1997), 'The management of fisheries and marine ecosystems', *Science*, **277**: 509.

Breitbart, M., B. Felts, S. Kelley, J.M. Mahaffy, J. Nulton, P. Salamon and F. Rohwer (2003), 'Diversity and population of a near-shore marine-sediment viral community', *Proceedings of the Royal Society of London B: Biological Sciences*, **271**: 565–574.

Briggs, J.C. (1994), 'Species diversity: land and sea compared', *Systematic Biology*, **43**: 130–135.

Brown, C., E. Corcoran, P. Herkenrath and J. Thonell (eds) (2006), *Marine and Coastal Ecosystems and Human Well-Being: A Synthesis Report Based on the Millennium Ecosystem Assessment*, Nairobi, Kenya: United Nations Environment Programme, 76 pp.

Capone, D.G. (2001), 'Marine nitrogen fixation: what's the fuss?', *Current Opinion in Microbiology*, **4**: 341–348.

Carlton, J.T., J.B. Geller, M.L. Reaka-Kudla and E.A. Norse (1999), 'Historical extinctions in the sea', *Annual Review of Ecology and Systematics*, **30**: 525–538.

Chisholm, S.W., R.J. Olson, E.R. Zettler, R. Goericke, J.B. Waterbury and N.A. Welschmeyer (1988), 'A novel free-living prochlorophyte abundant in the oceanic euphotic zone', *Nature*, **334**: 340–343.

Christensen, V. (1998), 'Fishery-induced changes in a marine ecosystem: insight from models of the Gulf of Thailand', *Journal of Fish Biology*, **53**: 128–142.

Christensen, V., S. Guenette, J.J. Heymans, C.J. Walters, R. Watson, D. Zeller and D. Pauly (2003), 'Hundred-year decline of North Atlantic predatory fishes', *Fish and Fisheries*, **4**: 1–14.

Clarke, A. (1992), 'Is there a latitudinal diversity cline in the sea?' *Trends in Ecology and Evolution*, **7**: 286–287.

Costanza, R., R. d'Arge, R. de Groot, S. Farber, M. Grasso, B. Hannon, K. Limburg, S. Naeem, R.V. O'Neill, J. Paruelo, R.G. Raskin, P. Sutton and M. van den Belt, (1997), 'The value of the world's ecosystem services and natural capital', *Nature*, **387**: 253–260.

Dulvy, N.K., Y. Sadovy and J.D. Reynolds (2003), 'Extinction vulnerability in marine populations', *Fish and Fisheries*, **4**: 25–64.

Elton, C.S. (1958), *Ecology of Invasion by Animals and Plants*, London: Chapman.

Estes, J.A., D.O. Duggins and G.B. Rathbun (1989), 'The ecology of extinctions in kelp forest communities', *Conservation Biology*, 3: 252–264.

Field, C.B., M.J. Behrenfeld, J. T. Randerson and P. Falkowski (1998), 'Primary production of the biosphere: integrating terrestrial and oceanic components', *Science*, **281**: 237–240.

Fox, W. (1990), *Toward a Transpersonal Ecology: Developing New Foundations for Environmentalism*, Boston: Shambhala.

Gage, J.D. (1996), 'Why are there so many species in deep-sea sediments?', *Journal of Experimental Marine Biology and Ecology*, **200**: 257–286.

GESAMP (1990), 'The state of the marine environment: UNEP regional seas', *Reports and Studies GESAMP*, **39**, 1–111.

Grassle, J.F. and N.J. Maciolek (1992), 'Deep-sea species richness: regional and local diversity estimates from quantitative bottom samples', *American Naturalist*, **139**: 313–341.

Gray, J.S. (1997) 'Marine biodiversity: patterns, threats and conservation needs', *Biodiversity and Conservation*, **6**, 153–175.

Huston, M. (1994), *Biological Diversity: The Coexistence of Species in Changing Landscapes*, Cambridge: Cambridge University Press.

Karentz, D. (1992), 'Ozone depletion and UV-B radiation in the Antarctic: limitations to ecological assessment', *Marine Pollution Bulletin*, **25**, 231–232.

Knowlton, N. (1993), 'Sibling species in the sea', *Annual Review of Ecology and Systematics*, **24**: 189–216.

Kranz, E. (2006), 'Scientists confirm Bird's Head seascape is richest on Earth', *Conservation International*, http://www.conservation.org/frontlines/2006/09180601.html 18 Sept 2007.

Lévêque, C. and J. Mounolou (2001), *Biodiversité*, Paris: Dunod.

Loh, J. and M. Wackernagel (eds) (2004), *Living Planet Report 2004*, Cambridge: Branson. © *WWF (panda.org). Some rights reserved.*

Lundin, C.G. and O. Lindén (1993), 'Coastal ecosystems: attempts to manage a threatened resource', *Ambio*, **22**: 468–473.

Mace, G.M. and E.J. Hudson (1999), 'Attitudes toward sustainability and extinction', *Conservation Biology*, **13**: 242–246.

Mackenzie, D. (1995), 'End of the line for the living fossil', *New Science*, **1978**: 14–15.

May, R.M. (1972a), 'Limit cycles in predator–prey communities, *Science*, **177**: 900–902.

May, R.M. (1972b), 'Will a large complex system be stable?', *Nature*, **238**: 413–414.

May, R.M. (1992), 'Bottoms up for the oceans', *Nature*, **357**: 278–279.

May, R.M. (1994), 'Biological diversity: differences between land and sea', *Philosophical Transactions of the Royal Society of London B: Biological Sciences*, **343**: 105–111.

May, R.M. and J. Godfrey (1994), 'Biological diversity: differences between land and sea [and discussion], generalizing across marine and terrestrial ecology', *Philosophical Transactions: Biological Sciences*, **343**(1301): 105–111.

McCann, K.S. (2000), 'The diversity–stability debate', *Nature*, **405**: 228–233.

Morel, F.M.M. and N.M. Price (2003), 'The biogeochemical cycles of trace metals in the oceans', *Science*, **300**: 944–947.

Myers, N. (1979), *The Sinking Ark: A New Look at the Problem of Disappearing Species*, Oxford, UK: Pergamon Press.

Naeem, S., L.J. Thompson, S.P. Lawler, J.H. Lawton and R.M. Woodfin (1994), 'Declining biodiversity can alter the performance of ecosystems', *Nature*, **368**: 734–737.

Naess, A. (1973), 'The shallow and the deep, long-range ecology movement: a summary', *Inquiry*, **16**: 95–100.

Odum, E.P. (1953), *Fundamentals of Ecology*, Philadelphia: W.B. Saunders.

O'Neill, R.V., D.L. DeAngelis, J.B. Waide and T.F.H. Allen (1986), *A Hierarchical Concept of Ecosystems*, Princeton: Princeton University Press.

Pace, M.L., J.J. Cole, S.R. Carpenter and J.F. Kitchell (1999), 'Trophic cascades revealed in diverse ecosystems', *Trends in Ecology and Evolution*, **14**: 483–488.

Palmer, C. and P. Sinclair (1997), *When the Fish are Gone: Ecological Disaster and Fishers in Northwest Newfoundland*, Halifax, Nova Scotia: Fernwood.

Parsons, T.R. (1992), 'The removal of marine predators by fisheries and the impact of trophic structure', *Marine Pollution Bulletin*, **25**: 51–53.

Pauly, D. (1979), 'Biological overfishing of tropical stocks', *ICLARM (International Center for Living Aquatic Resources Management) Newsletter*, **3**: 3–4.

Pauly, D., V. Christensen, J. Dalsgaard, R. Froese and F. Torres (1998), 'Fishing down marine food webs', *Science*, **279**: 860–3.

Pauly, D., V. Christensen, S. Guénette, T.J. Pitcher, U.R. Sumaila, C.J. Walters, R. Watson and D. Zeller (2002), 'Towards sustainability in world fisheries', *Nature*, **418**: 689–95.

Pinnegar, J.K., N.V.C. Polunin, P. Francour, F. Badalamenti, R. Chemello, M.-L. Harmelin-Vivien, B. Hereu, M. Milazzo, M. Zabala, G. D'Anna and C. Pipitone (2000), 'Trophic cascades in benthic marine ecosystems: lessons for fisheries and protected-area management', *Environmental Conservation*, **27**: 179–200.

Poore, G.C.B. and G.D.F. Wilson (1993), 'Marine species richness', *Nature*, **361**: 597–598.

Primavera, J.H. (1991), 'Intensive prawn farming in the Philippines: ecological, social, and economic implications', *Ambio*, **20**: 28–33.

Raven, P.H. (1980), *Research Priorities in Tropical Biology*, Washington, DC: National Academy of Sciences.

Ray, G.C. and J.F. Grassle (1991), 'Marine biological diversity', *BioScience*, **41**(7), 453–457.

Rex, M.A., R.J. Etter and C.T. Stuart (1997), 'Large-scale patterns of species diversity in the deep-sea Benthos', in R.F.G. Ormond, J.D. Gage and M.V. Angel (eds), *Marine Biodiversity: Patterns and Processes*, Cambridge: Cambridge University Press.

Rex, M.A., C.T. Stuart, R.R. Hessler, J.A. Allen, H.L. Sanders and G.D.F. Wilson (1993), 'Global-scale latitudinal patterns of species diversity in the deep-sea benthos', *Nature*, **365**: 636–639.

Shears, N.T. and R.C. Babcock (2003), 'Continuing trophic cascade effects after 25 years of no-take marine reserve protection', *Marine Ecology Progress Series*, **246**: 1–16.

Sinclair, P.R. (1988), 'The state encloses the commons: fisheries management from the 200 mile limit to factory freezer trawlers', in P.R. Sinclair (ed.), *A Question of Survival: The Fisheries and Newfoundland Society*, St John's, Newfoundland: Memorial Institute of Social and Economic Research, University of Newfoundland.

Southwood, T.R.E. (1977), 'Habitat, the template for ecological strategies?', *Journal of Animal Ecology*, **46**: 337–365.

Thorne-Miller, B. (1999), *The Living Ocean: Understanding and Protecting Marine Biodiversity*, Washington, DC: Island Press.

Thorson, G. (1971), *Life in the Sea* (Translated from the Danish by M.C. Meilgaard and A. Laurie), London: Weidenfeld and Nicolson.

Torsvik, V., R. Sorheim and J. Goksoyr (1996), 'Total bacterial diversity in soil and sediment communities: a review', *Journal of Industrial Microbiology*, **17**: 170–178.

Tortell, P.D., M.T. Maldonado, J. Granger and N.M. Price (1999), 'Marine bacteria and biogeochemical cycling of iron in the oceans', *Microbiology Ecology*, **29**: 1–11.

Tudge, C. (2000), *The Variety of Life: A Survey and a Celebration of all the Creatures that have ever Lived*, Oxford: Oxford University Press.

UNEP-WCMC (2004), *Protected Areas and Biodiversity Report: An Overview of Key Issues*, CBD 7th Conference of the Parties, 9–20 February 2004, 56 pp.

Watson, A.J. and P.S. Liss (1998), 'Marine biological controls on climate via the carbon and sulphur geochemical cycles', *Philosophical Transactions of the Royal Society of London B: Biological Sciences*, **353**: 41–51.

Whittaker, R.H. (1967), 'Gradient analysis of vegetation', *Biological Reviews*, **42**: 207–264.

Wilson, E.O. (ed.) (1988), *Biodiversity*, Washington, DC: National Academy Press.

WWF Global Marine Programme (2006), *Problems: Inadequate Protection*, http://www.panda.org/about_wwf/what_we_do/marine/problems/inadequate_prote ction/index.cfm.

4. Oceans and Coasts as Complex Adaptive Systems

Mark Gibbs and Anthony Cole

Our understanding of living systems has increased dramatically over the last four decades, and nowhere have these advances in understanding been more prominent than on sub-organism scales. This has particularly been the case in the disciplines of micro-biology and genetics, where the search for the ultimate building blocks of life has stimulated intensive scientific investigations. Interestingly, the same path was followed by physicists earlier in the 20th century, whose search for the building blocks of matter lead to investigations of particles on smaller and smaller (sub-atomic) scales. However, although our understanding of sub-organism scale processes has increased dramatically over recent decades, during the same period the ecosystem services that support life on earth have in many cases been dramatically impaired. Therefore, it can be argued that this newfound knowledge of both physical and biological processes has yet to be able to address the most pressing of issues facing humankind: the loss of resilience in both ecological and social systems, and the decline of the ability of earth to support humankind.

There are a number of reasons why societies have not been particularly successful at managing natural environments and ecosystems (natural capital), although it is convenient to classify these factors into the following two categories:

- An inability for science and stakeholders to accurately understand the complexity of ecological systems and the likely environmental consequences of development activities and management intervention on these systems. There is therefore a common inability for stakeholders to be in a position to make robust cost–benefit assessments of development and management proposals.
- Our inability or unwillingness to take appropriate action even when the weight of evidence suggests that it would be prudent to do so. This

category also includes our common unwillingness to adequately account for the future costs of present development and management decisions; or similarly, our unwillingness or inability to internalize environmental externalities.

In terms of the latter, there are many examples where, despite overwhelming evidence suggesting that drastic management intervention is required, response action is often late and insufficient. Good examples of this in the marine environment are numerous fisheries that have collapsed (for example, Atlantic cod in the Grand Banks of the north-east coast of North America – once the world's most prominent fishery). Proponents of weak sustainability approaches, however, often argue that this can be acceptable as long as the reduction in natural capital results in a corresponding increase in manufactured capital. By contrast, proponents of strong sustainability argue that harvesting fish stocks to commercial extinction is unacceptable and it is becoming clear that in many of these cases, commercial extinction was clearly not the management objective. These examples often illustrate a breakdown of the engagement between fishers and fishery managers. Fortunately, considerable work is now being done in the form of transdisciplinary research (Nicolescu 2002) and it is hoped that some of the methods that arise from these studies will facilitate better stakeholder engagement and communication processes, and allow a better understanding of complexity issues that will lead to better outcomes than in the past. Having said this, until the future costs of development activities are more closely aligned to present benefits, sustainable development and the maintenance of resilience will remain elusive (Tainter 2006). In terms of the first category, it is clear that a lack of science's ability to convince many stakeholders of the likely future outcomes of present development strategies has in many cases allowed unfettered development to proceed, even despite the widespread introduction of the Precautionary Principle in legislation.

A core aim of the natural sciences over the last century has been to understand a natural system well enough so that accurate predictions about future states of the system, or how the system will respond to human intervention, can be made. A reason for developing such an understanding is so that the full costs and benefits of natural resource management decisions can be clearly and unambiguously identified. However, despite recent dramatic advances in computing power and an explosion of scientific literature describing numerical and analytical models of natural systems, this field of science is still in its infancy and it is argued here that the very nature of oceanic and coastal ecosystems will prevent us from developing comprehensive forecasting abilities of marine ecosystems.

Robust predictive ability in marine environments has been most successful for geophysical flows dominated by Newtonian behaviour (meteorology, physical oceanography, geology), single species populations, and to a lesser extent lower trophic level marine ecological processes (nutrient-phytoplankton-zooplankton systems). The development of successful short-term predictive models for geophysical flows has raised the expectations of many stakeholders that science should be able to deliver robust predictions about a range of living marine systems. This brings into question why investigators have not been able to create more accurate predictions of the behaviour of whole ecological systems. A large part of the answer to this question is a direct result of the lack of a comprehensive theoretical basis for the behaviour of natural systems, species, population, community and ecosystem levels of organization and this is discussed in the following sections.

INVESTIGATING OCEANS – REDUCTIONIST OR WHOLE SYSTEMS APPROACHES?

Over two centuries of primarily European and American marine ecological investigations (and much longer in other cultures) have led to the development of a good understanding of specific ecological processes – for example, how species:

- alter local and global geochemical cycles,
- alter disturbance regimes,
- modify their physical environment,
- control other species through predation and parasitism,
- perform essential ecosystem services such as nutrient cycling and food production,
- are a source of essential nutrients for other consumer species.

However, a robust unified theory that is able to be translated into comprehensive mathematical models that describe the temporal and spatial variability of the relative roles of the processes listed above remains elusive. Furthermore, ecosystem properties such as resilience, and the relationship between diversity and functioning, remain hotly debated although there is growing evidence of strong linkages between resilience, diversity and sustainability (Gunderson and Holling 2002). The issue of scale and cross-scale dependence in functional processes also remains unclear, as evidenced by the debate over the Gaia Theory (Lovelock 2000). It can also be argued that the intractability of the large spatial scales, and slow timescales involved in ecosystems have reinforced reductionist approaches to ecological investigations at the expense of more holistic approaches that consider non-additive, non-linear interactions.

Ecological investigations are often classified into two broad categories: autecology (the study of individual species/processes) and synecology (the study of communities and ecosystems). Autecology leads to reductionist approaches and has been the most popular investigational approach applied to marine ecological investigations during the 20th century. Autecological approaches have also been incorporated into environmental management, and the most prominent example of this is the present reliance of the management of marine fisheries resources on single-species assessment approaches in many institutions.

Reductionist approaches have been invaluable for elucidating the details of specific processes, particularly when observational, manipulative and modelling techniques have been combined (see Wing et al. 2003). Furthermore, it is difficult to see how some reduction of scale can be avoided in many studies. However, these types of investigations generally result in some level of understanding over a synoptic period, or series of periods, when the system is behaving in a single or small number of possible behavioural modes. Invariably, this results in an understanding that is most appropriate for the particular location, spatial scale, and time period investigated. Unfortunately this does not often provide an understanding of the range of possible behaviours of the system, and hence the predictive ability is limited to the behavioural modes that have been investigated. Proponents of both deterministic and stochastic models often argue against this conclusion. However, the conspicuous lack of ecosystem-level ecological models used for active prediction suggests otherwise. While reductionist approaches are also underpinned by the assumption that if individual processes are understood on small scales, then these can be combined to provide a predictive ability over larger scales through allometric techniques, this ignores the existence of emergent properties and agents, as discussed in the following sections.

It is also human nature to attempt to simplify systems to facilitate communication to stakeholders and the wider public; as noted by Tainter (2006, p. 92): 'not only are humans not prone to complexity, we are in many situations averse to it'. As an aside, it can also be argued that our ability to predict, understand and influence the future is strongly dependent upon our ability to understand complexity. The practice of (over) simplifying complex interactions is often actively encouraged in science outreach programmes that attempt to repackage complex problems and processes so that they can be easily communicated to wider audiences. However, the fact remains that natural systems are complicated, and social-ecological systems even more complicated, and distilling such systems down to their governing dynamics (a mathematical perspective) is implicitly a reductionist type technique, and hence exposed to the limitations of autecological approaches.

The management of marine systems is presently undergoing something of a revolution that has involved the introduction of more 'ecosystem-level' approaches and a corresponding movement away from autecological approaches. For example, the management of marine systems generally focuses on two levels: managing coastal marine environments, and the management of fisheries resources. Actually what are really being managed are fishers and people that undertake activities that interact with marine environments. The management of coastal marine environments is slowly moving toward more of an Integrated Coastal Zone Management (ICZM) regime in many nations (see Chapter 14). Unfortunately this is often hindered by the multiple statutory authorities, and ill-fitting pieces of legislation governing activities in the coastal zone. However, there is at least worldwide recognition that coastal management should head towards a more holistic integrated framework; although exactly how to do this remains unclear in many cases. There has been a similar trend in the management of living marine resources recently. The collapse of a number of prominent and long-standing fisheries has led to many reviews of management frameworks of these resources that mostly relied upon single species stock assessment techniques (Walters and Martell 2004). A result of these reviews has often been increasing calls for this so-called 'ecosystem-based' management of fisheries (Pikitch et al. 2004). However, once again it is unclear exactly what this will entail, given the difficulties in acquiring data on multitudes of species, habitats and biogeochemical fluxes in the oceans. Furthermore, from a theoretical perspective, moving away from single species population techniques to even small multi-species techniques over short ecological time-scales is not straightforward. This can be illustrated by considering the simplest two-species ecological predator–prey interaction, as defined by the classical Lotka–Volterra relationships.

The predator–prey relationships described by the Lotka–Volterra set of coupled differential equations have been the subject of intense scrutiny over a number of decades:

$$\frac{dX}{dt} = rX - aXY \tag{4.1}$$

$$\frac{dY}{dt} = bXY - mY \tag{4.2}$$

The relationships have two variables (*X, Y*) and four parameters:

X = density of prey
Y = density of predators
r = intrinsic rate of prey population increase
a = predation rate coefficient
b = reproduction rate of predators per one prey eaten
m = predator mortality rate

Solutions to these equations reveal the existence of cycles of predators and prey that oscillate according to the governing predatory behaviour of the dynamics. Solutions also fall into well-defined 'attractor basins' whereby the populations effectively 'chase each other around' the solution space. However, of interest here is that, even if these relationships faithfully describe the ecological interactions among interacting species, the unstable and potentially bifurcating behaviour of even individual logistic growth population trajectories do not lend themselves to accurate deterministic modelling techniques such as Lotka–Volterra approaches (Wilson et al. 1993). This is particularly pertinent for species with high intrinsic growth rates and non-overlapping generations described by logistic difference equations that exhibit behaviour on 'the edge of chaos' that are extremely sensitive to the initial conditions of the population modelling (May 1974). Furthermore, although elegant, the Lotka–Volterra relationships do not explicitly account for the greater environment. Hence any environmental variability must be indirectly introduced through time-dependent (and spatially dependent) intrinsic growth rate or carrying capacity parameters. The intractability of the mathematical relationships for even a single Lotka–Volterra predator–prey ecological relationship, and the fact that they do not explicitly describe spatial dynamics, therefore hinders our ability to predict the detailed behaviour of any sort of real ecosystem or community. This is the case even over short timescales that are dominated by these sorts of interactions, let alone natural selection over evolutionary timescales.

WHAT IS A COMPLEX ADAPTIVE SYSTEM? A MARINE ECOLOGICAL PERSPECTIVE

If it is agreed that natural systems behave as networks (either sub-systems over the planet, or the entire planet as in the Gaia approach), then a number of interesting consequences present themselves. A key consequence of network or complex systems theory is that the relationships and fluxes between parts of the system often tend to be more revealing that the physical structure (populations, species, and so on) of the system. This is contrary to the focus of many marine ecological investigations that tend to concentrate more on the abundance of individual populations such as commercially important fishes or endangered marine mammals, rather than the fluxes or relationships between agents in the network. However, once the jump to system properties and behaviours has been made, then a number of interesting characteristics of systems present themselves. One of the most important of these is the development of emergent properties. Emergent properties or structures are those structures that can only be seen by viewing the system as a whole, and are not evident when looking at individual parts of the system. In other words, emergent properties only become evident at particular levels of complexity.

Another key property of complex systems is that of self-organization at different scales. Early work in cybernetics revealed that systems far from equilibrium could spontaneously create patterns of organization – that is, new structures and behaviour generated often through non-linear (often positive) feedback loops within the network. A good example of this, as identified by Capra (1996), is that of whirlpools above drain holes in bathtubs or basins that form when water is emptying out of the basin. Such structures emerge spontaneously through non-linear feedback mechanisms within the fluid flow and, despite the apparent stable structure, are inherently far from equilibrium and feature a continuous flux of both fluid and energy through the structure. Such spontaneous states are key properties of self-organizing complex systems. Other prominent examples of self-organizing behaviour are the architecture of termite mounds, synchronous flashing of fireflies, and the Belousov–Zhabotinski chemical reaction that generates quasi-stable patterns of spiral waves (Camazine et al. 2001). Interested readers are referred to StarLogo at the MIT Media Laboratory's website for further examples of self-organizing behaviour.

An interesting consequence of self-organization is that the system adapts to new states as required (hence complex *adaptive* systems). This system-wide adaption is not to be confused with classical Darwinian theory that describes the natural selection of individual species within an ecosystem. Self-organization implies that systems evolve together, or co-evolve (Lovelock 2000) rather than being a framework whereby species evolve on individual trajectories influenced only by externalities that change on evolutionary timescales. That is, in this framework there is no feedback between the evolution of individual species. This self-organizing attribute has significant consequences for the management of endangered species and restoration ecology as it implies that artificial ecosystems aiming to replace or enhance heavily degraded environments cannot be simply 'created'. Similarly, it also allows for populations to exhibit new behavioural patterns when transplanted into a new environment – a lesson repeatedly learned when alien species are introduced into new environments (see Shigesada and Kawasaki 1997).

Self-organizing adaptive systems do not 'evolve' in a regular fashion; rather, they often jump between different states of complexity, some of which may reveal emergent structures and behaviour. This sort of behaviour was perhaps first identified by Prigogine (from the 'Brussels School') when he investigated Bénard cells and coined the term 'dissipative structures'. Bénard cells appear on heated surfaces and appear spontaneously as regular hexagonal cells on an otherwise uniform surface that is heated beneath (Velarde and Normande 1980; see Figure 3.1). Once again these regular structures form in a system that processes energy (heat), is not in stable dynamical equilibrium, and displays adaptive and self-organizing behaviour that cannot be predicted by linear theory. Other examples of self-organizing behaviour based on Turing Instability dynamics include patterns on mammal coats and insect hives.

Modelling the multiple links within parts of networks (for example, populations within a foodweb) remained largely elusive until the widespread introduction of fast computers. Of interest is that as soon as investigators began presenting the solutions to non-linear networks (often under the guise of 'integrative biology'), the existence of these 'strange attractors', or attractor basins towards which the system converges over time became clear. These investigations have helped to explain why multiple stable states commonly occur in dynamical systems, including ecosystems. Furthermore, a key feature of non-linear networks is the sensitivity of the solutions to particular parameter values and initial conditions (measured by the Lyapunov Exponent). Small changes in these values can lead to completely different behaviour, or jumping from one state to another (bifurcation or threshold points), that is often irreversible or reverses via a different pathway (hysteresis). This sensitivity has strong implications for our ability to predict the future behaviour of ecosystems in the absence of almost perfect knowledge of key initial conditions and boundary parameter values.

It must also be highlighted that whilst economics, and some branches of marine ecology, have long embraced whole systems approaches, much of our understanding in marine ecological processes has come from reductionist investigations driven by requirements, for example, to understand individual target species. Finally, it must also be recognized that our ability to gain data from marine systems is prohibitively expensive, and this in itself acts to limit our understanding of marine systems.

CAN MARINE ECOSYSTEMS BE DESCRIBED AS COMPLEX ADAPTIVE SYSTEMS?

A key objective of this chapter is to investigate whether marine ecosystems behave as complex adaptive systems, as introduced in the previous section. Consider first the pattern of organization of marine ecosystems. Marine foodwebs generally have between four and six macro-trophic levels. The fact that there are a similar number of trophic levels across a very large range of physical environmental gradients is of interest in itself, although often taken for granted. An example of where marine ecosystems have collapsed into a smaller trophic web is during micro-algal bloom events where a dramatic expansion in a single species of micro-algae can influence the surrounding physical-chemical environment (lowering of dissolved oxygen) to a point where few higher trophic level organisms can exist. However, this is by no means always a stable equilibrium state and the system can adjust itself very rapidly. Discussions of marine trophic levels must also be tempered with the elusive details of microbial loops in the oceans – it has been argued that the larger, visible species such as finfish can be considered as a *'variable phenomenon in a sea of microbes'* (Karl 1999, p. 181). The diversity of functional groups in marine ecosystems can also be surprisingly low. For example almost all pelagic systems have a similar range of functional groups. By contrast, the diversity within functional groups of almost all marine ecosystems is large. This is an interesting question in itself – why do marine ecosystems feature high 'within trophic level diversity', but low 'between trophic level diversity'?

The widespread recognition that foodwebs are in fact 'webs', rather than as previously defined 'food chains', demonstrates acceptance of the concept of ecosystems structured as networks. It therefore follows that foodwebs, let alone the associated physical and chemical processes, must behave as non-linear systems where feedback mechanisms between system components (links in the network or foodweb) play a strong role. The mathematical construction of non-linear networks admits the existence of many of the properties of complex adaptive systems.

Marine ecosystems feature a number of key processes. Probably the most important but least often considered property of marine ecosystems, in fact ecosystems in general, is that they are able to 'recreate' themselves. Interestingly, ecosystems do not necessarily 'recreate' the exact same structure when perturbed, although the core functions (ecosystem services)are usually maintained. This reorganization–exploitation–conservation–release type adaptive cycle behaviour has been explored in the seminal book *Panarchy* (Gunderson and Holling 2002), and interestingly, in the behaviour of sandpiles under the influence of grains of sand dropped from above (self-organized criticality; Bak 1996). In other words, ecosystems are able to adapt to changing environmental conditions, and themselves influence the surrounding physical environment (Lovelock 2000). This latter point is also significant as reductionist methods often separate the functioning of the living components of an ecosystem from the non-living physical/geological/ chemical components. Yet it is known that systems, and components of systems, are able to modify their surrounding environment; for example, macro-algal/seaweed beds are able to create refugia for other species – a direct positive feedback mechanism.

It is therefore argued below that marine ecosystems display all of the following characteristics of 'complex adaptive systems': (1) emergent properties, (2) adaption, (3) self-organization, (4) non-equilibrium behaviour, and (5) path dependency.

Emergent Properties of Marine Systems

As introduced in the previous section, emergent properties are properties of a system that are not discernable among individual agents in the system. In other words, emergent properties or structures are those structures that would not be predicted to occur based on an understanding of the individual agents themselves (in this case knowledge of the behaviour of individual species does not lead to predictability). A recently investigated physical emergent process in marine systems is that of patterns of sand ripples that are commonly found on beaches and undersea sediments. These ripple structures start from a collection of individual disorganized particles that emerge into larger scale organized patterns after interactions with physical processes and bedforms over a range of spatial and temporal scales (Werner 1999). In other words, rather than the sum being greater than the combined individuals, the sum is *different* from the parts.

Another example is the fractal spatial patterns that occur during phytoplankton blooms that frequently occur in the oceans. In this case the multi-scale interactions between microscopic organisms and physical processes leads to structures and patterns developing on a range of fractal scales. These patterns would not be thought to occur based on examination of the behaviour of individual organisms themselves. A further example is so-called fish 'meatballs' in the oceans (although fish schools themselves are also an example of self-organizing behaviour; Camazine et al. 2001). These dense transient aggregations of small fish, large fish, sharks, dolphins and seabirds routinely form and disperse in seemingly featureless mid-water environments. Often these aggregations are formed by the herding behaviour of a few predatory fish that leads to rapid development of aggregations of smaller prey fish that then attracts larger predators. These rotating structures can evolve and disperse within minutes but can remain in a state of unstable-equilibrium for periods of time. This is also an ecological example of positive feedback behaviour.

Adaption in Marine Systems

The concept of biological *adaptation* of organisms (often used as a synonym for natural selection) is regarded as a key process leading to increased complexity in ecosystems. Similarly, *adaption* is a key characteristic of complex systems and this refers to the adaptive behaviour of the system to an external driver, or series of drivers. Whilst there is a plethora of work directed towards investigating the adaptation of marine organisms, there has been considerably less work carried out on how marine ecosystems adapt to external influences. However, as anthropogenic influences continue to perturb marine ecosystems, there is an increasing research focus on how marine ecosystems (not just individual organisms) respond to anthropogenic influences over a range of scales. These studies are also often decoupled from evolutionary-scale investigations, despite the concomitant existence of both processes. Early marine ecological studies often worked within a framework of a 'natural or pristine state' of ecosystems that considers ecosystems to have been in a stable equilibrium state (in a thermodynamic perspective) until intervention from humankind. In fact, much of the world's natural resource management legislation is framed this way. However, marine ecosystems have had to adapt over shorter timescales then typically associated with evolutionary scales of specific organisms to a range of (often human induced) perturbations and this occurs concurrently with the adaptation of specific organisms. Although ecosystems are regularly perturbed over a number of spatial and temporal scales, the response is not easily predicted and the same system can respond to the same perturbation in different ways (often as a result of internal self-organization processes).

As an aside, one of the key issues in the management of marine ecosystems and resources is that our rate of learning about the behaviour and adaption of ecosystems to perturbations is often slower than the rate of change that is occurring in these systems (changing baselines syndrome) and this constrains our ability to adequately manage these systems. Similarly, a key ecological science question to answer is: how much of the system response is a direct (possibly linear) response to a perturbation, and how much of the response is the associated with the triggering of internal self-organizing behaviour?

One of the most fascinating recent developments in marine science is the study of 'regime' shifts, including examples of abrupt regime shifts in ocean ecosystems (Collie et al. 2004). Evidence of 'regime shifts' associated with 'natural' drivers (large-scale, non-human-induced climate change, and so on), have been commonly observed in paeloeoceanographic records. Similar evidence of 'regime shifts' occuring in response to the fishing down of major fish stocks is now also appearing (ibid.). Such anthropogenic 'regime shifts' and threshold breaches occur over much shorter timescales than are normally associated with organism-level adaptation and can involve large-scale re-arrangement of marine foodwebs.

Self-Organization in Marine Systems

Self-organizing behaviour refers to characteristics of many open systems whereby they are able to increase their complexity without being under the influence of an external driver. Self-organizing behaviour can also lead to emergent structures, as discussed above. Oceans are inherently open systems as fluxes of energy and material are transferred between the oceans and adjoining terrestrial and atmospheric environments. The structure of ocean ecosystems is not purely a result of responses to fluxes from these external environments. In contrast, the diversity (thought to be between 10^4 and 10^5 bacteria in every millilitre of water) and structure of ocean ecosystems is also largely the result of internal processes that leads to increasing complexity through positive feedbacks enhancing external influences.

Ecosystems do not simply respond in a predictable linear way to external drivers. Rather, much of the organization and structure develops as a result of internal interactions among ecosystem components. This characteristic often gets overlooked in marine ecological studies that have for many years focused on concepts such as the relative dominance of top-down (predation or demand-side ecology) versus bottom-up (production or supply-side ecology) control at various trophic levels in marine ecosystems, often with the underpinning assumption that the relative influences will be constant in space and time. Such top-down/bottom-up response studies attempt to understand ecosystem responses to external drivers and, if nothing else, have revealed that the response of ecosystems to these external drivers can be inconsistent, non-linear and generally unpredictable (characteristics to be expected in a self-organizing system). Perhaps a more appropriate way to think about ecosystem or foodweb dynamics is in terms of the relative magnitudes of linear responses to external drivers (top-down or bottom-up), versus internal self-organizing non-linear behaviour determined by increasing and decreasing return feedback mechanisms.

Non-Equilibrium Behaviour in Marine Systems

Do marine ecosystems tend towards a Clementsian 'equlibrium' point or is their behaviour better described as being 'non-equilibrium'? In answer to this, it must be remembered that strictly speaking, equilibrium is a concept most applicable to closed or semi-closed systems and, as highlighted above, ocean ecosystems are generally not closed unless one is considering, say, deep ocean ecosystems for relatively short periods of geological time. Hence, whilst local equilibria, or basins of attraction, may exist when local processes are stationary for the scale under consideration, it is difficult to argue in a general sense that marine ecosystems remain in a single state of stable equilibria or remain within a single attractor basin. Key issues are, therefore, the timescale under consideration, the width of attractor basins and the potential for the ecosystem to flip from one state of attractor basin to another. Of interest is that this line of investigation quickly leads us to discussions of resilience or robustness in ecosystems and social-ecological systems (see Walker et al. 2005).

In addition, what is becoming clearer is that ecosystems adapt to the surrounding constraints, and adapt the constraints themselves, and this is distinct from the adaptation of individual organisms filling specific optimal niches. This concept takes key elements from Darwinian evolutionary theory, short-term type Lotka–Volterra ecological predator prey–processes, and disturbance theory. In fact, a large proportion of individual species or organisms will not be at anywhere near their scope-for-growth potential in a theoretical optimal equilibrium ecosystem state. Furthermore, the equilibrium concept implies that there should be little temporal variability in the ratio of relationships (fluxes) between agents in the network (individuals, populations, or functional groups within a foodweb). By contrast, we know that even relatively unexploited ecosystems display very large non-stationary variability on all levels that is inconsistent with single stable equilibrium states. This implies that not only are the structures of ecosystems highly variable, but also the processes (ecosystem services) performed by the ecosystems. However, more insight on the latter should be gained once the new emphasis on these ecosystems services gains momentum.

It is also worth highlighting that, because a network is not in equilibrium, this does not necessarily mean that it is in a state of chaos. For example, consider an individual population. Although some populations display extremes in variability – for example, micro-algae and insect populations – they are unlikely to be always behaving as true chaotic systems as the extinction risks associated with chaotic behaviour determine that extinction would be almost inevitable. Hence not all populations are chaotic, although some are (Hastings 1993). However, the chaotic-like behaviour of some natural systems that show evidence of highly non-linear behaviour has been coined 'near chaotic' to signify that whilst these systems may not be behaving in a truly chaotic manner, they display behaviour that is on the edge of chaos. A key outcome of this sort of behaviour is the sensitivity of the trajectory or behaviour of the system to initial conditions. This has profound implications for our ability to simulate such systems without near-perfect information on the initial state of the system. This contrasts with Newtonian viewpoints of particularly equilibrium systems where the system rapidly forgets the initial state and converges towards a stable mechanical equilibrium state. Perhaps the most obvious example of this is in the numerical simulations of low-level atmospheric conditions. Synoptic weather forecasting has been one of the more successful disciplines in terms of being able to simulate a large-scale natural system. These models essentially solve the mechanistic equations of motion (Navier–Stokes coupled partial differential equations). However, despite increasing computational capabilities coupled with real-time data from remote sensing sources, our ability to predict or forecast the weather more than a few days in the future remains limited. This lack of ability is largely a result of the inability to adequately resolve initial conditions in the models or accurately describe non-linear emergent properties leading from sub-grid scale processes.

Algal blooms, possibly resulting from coastal eutrophication, represent another example of complex behaviour in coastal ecosystems. It is clear from limnological examples that lakes and nearshore coastal systems can rapidly change from one stable state (clear water, multi-trophic state), to a eutrophied state featuring high turbidity and the collapse of higher trophic levels after nutrient inflows exceed a threshold (Carpenter and Kitchell 1996). Of interest is that the process is not always reversible simply by reducing nutrient inflows to pre-eutrophied states (that is, there is a path dependence and possibly hysteresis). Simulating these algal blooms has also proved one of the more difficult reductionist exercises, and at present only limited success in particular cases has been possible. A likely reason for this is that the trajectory of blooms is path-dependent, in other words the environment is pre-conditioned and only a very particular set of input and boundary conditions coupled with internal self-organizing behaviour can lead to bloom development.

As identified above, another classical example of complex behaviour is the regime shifts that sporadically occur in marine ecosystems. A topical example of this is the relatively recent domination of low-commercial value mackerel, dogfish (small sharks) and skate (rays) over the previously dominant populations of high commercial value cod, haddock and flounder over the Georges Bank off the north-eastern coast of North America following decades of extensive fishing (Fogarty and Murawski 1998). Interestingly, dramatic shifts in 'baseline' conditions can occur in marine ecosystems without leading to ecological disasters (Steele 1998). In the Georges Bank example, the dominant species mix has changed substantially although a major change in the trophic structure has not occurred.

Path Dependency in Marine Systems

The sensitivity of the behaviour of networks to initial conditions also implies some sort of path dependency involving the interaction of fast and slow moving variables – that is, the present state of the system is determined in part by the historical behaviour of the system. We also see examples of this characteristic in marine systems. For example, coastal marine habitat restoration projects (such as restoration of wetlands or submerged rocky reefs) almost always result in a biological community that is different in both structure and flows/fluxes from the original community. Although appearing to be qualitatively similar, it can be excruciatingly difficult to recreate the same habitat or relative species mix. A reason for this is that the original network evolved over a convoluted path involving both fast- and slow-moving variables, and attempts at restoration often attempt to reproduce the final state without the benefit of the path-dependency and time required to achieve the state that the system was in before it was modified. Similarly, wild stock fishery enhancement projects are rarely able to equivalently replace natural population recruitment processes without altering relationships among associated and dependent species within the ecosystem.

IMPLICATIONS FOR ECOLOGICAL ECONOMICS

The realization that marine systems can be described as complex adaptive systems also leads to a number of specific implications for ecological economics. Key implications for ecological economics are described below.

Theories of Organization

Marine ecology has been dominated by linear mathematical/Newtonian mechanistic views of organization and behaviour that often focus on direct cause–effect, or linear pressure-state-response paradigms. Such paradigms often feature implicit understandings about the behaviour of the system that influence which properties we focus on and these in turn tend to determine the theories of organization we embrace. However, a consequence of embracing a complex systems approach implies that we need to think more broadly about system behaviour than is typically represented in reductionist studies. For example, whilst environmental external factors undoubtedly influence biological systems, internal non-linear positive feedback mechanisms that amplify external influences and lead to the development of emergent patterns and structures can confound many standard retrospective investigational ecological approaches.

The Precautionary Principle

The use and abuse of the Precautionary Principle has been the subject of a growing body of literature. It can be argued, however, that there is a lack of general consensus on exactly when the Precautionary Principle should be invoked. For example, a disturbing trend in marine resource management fora (for example, fisheries management) is for the results of a predictive ecological model to be presented, the assumptions and results argued over – highlighting the uncertainty in predictions – and then a move is made by more conservation aligned stakeholders to invoke the Precautionary Principle in response to irreconcilable differences in opinions on the implications of the level of uncertainty in the model predictions. Such an approach, whilst sometimes leading to short-term environmental gains, often leaves other stakeholders dissatisfied, and often halts any further learning about how the social-ecological system behaves and responds to management intervention. While not degrading the value of hard-won environmental gains, it can be argued that adaptive management approaches are a more robust management framework, although this approach can also be hijacked and the process turned into an unfettered development experiment. However, remembering that resilience is based upon system attributes that are restored slowly and are difficult to predict, this lends itself to the combination of scenario modelling (rather than trying to exactly predict what will happen to all parts of the system), and learning through adaptive management.

Is Management of Marine Ecosystems an Option?

Up until now we have assumed that it was possible to manage marine ecosystems from a command-and-control basis where system properties have been attempted to be managed for an optimal yield (for example, fisheries surplus production approaches). In contrast, it is becoming increasing clear that this command-and-control approach is degrading natural capital in marine ecosystems (Gunderson and Holling 2002) and can lead to unsustainable social systems and communities that rely on marine resources. This has been partly a result of continual surprises in the way ecosystems respond, and in other cases a lack of accounting for the full future costs of marine resource management decisions. It is timely to review how marine social-ecological systems should be 'managed' in view of their 'unpredictable' behaviour. Such issues in particular are explored in Chapter 14 *Ocean and Coastal Governance for Sustainability*.

Managing for Resilience

It can be argued that maintaining or enhancing resilience or robustness should be a prime, if not the prime objective for managing marine social-ecological systems. Here resilience is defined in terms of:

- the amount of change the system can undergo and still remain within the same domain of attraction;
- the degree to which the system is capable of self-organization; and
- the degree to which the system can build capacity to learn and adapt.

Such a management approach would entail considerably different initiatives than are often currently practised. For example, as noted by Walker et al. (2005), managing for outcomes in terms of yield, stability and production may be appropriate during exploitation and conservation phases of a social-ecological system (the r and K phases of the Gunderson and Holling adaptive cycle). Management actions taken during these periods can strongly influence the overall system resilience and the capacity to reorganize following large system perturbations that lead into the breakdown (Ω) and reorganization (α) phases of the adaptive cycle. Furthermore, Walker et al. (2005, p. 182) highlight that 'It is only through the ecosystem probing the boundaries of its domain of attraction that the attributes of the system that confer resilience can be maintained'. In other words, the ecosystem, and correspondingly the social components (stakeholders) of the coupled social-ecological system must be prepared to accept, and even encourage change (that may lead to short-term costs). This once again underpins the importance of adaptive management approaches, rather than simply attempting to manage for yield sustainability in an attempt to maintain the present level of system output or yield in the face of both external perturbations, and internal self-organizing behaviour.

CONCLUSIONS

A number of conclusions emerged from this chapter that are pertinent to developing an ecological economics of the oceans and coasts. First, the history of research and theory development in marine ecology has grown from an autecological tradition based on scientific methodology, which assumes the relevance of a reductionist approach. While this approach has assisted in understanding marine ecosystems at a species and process level, fine resolution has come at the expense of whole-of-system understanding. Furthermore, it is now becoming more apparent that ecosystem component understanding is a poor predictor of the behaviour and structures of whole marine systems.

Second, we have mounted a case for recognition of marine ecosystem foodwebs as networks. A number of interesting phenomena of marine ecosystem follow from this proposition. For example, networks reveal emergent properties and constitute a basis for self-organization and movement between locally stable equilibrium states, thus reflecting collective evolutionary behaviour that is essentially different from species level natural selection.

Third, while relatively little has been written in this area, we venture to suggest that marine ecosystems can be characterized by five key attributes of complex adaptive systems: emergent properties, adaption, self-organization, non-equilibrium behaviour and path dependency. An ecological economics of the oceans and coasts must be mindful of these complex systems characteristics of marine systems.

REFERENCES

Bak, P. (1996), *How Nature Works: The Science of Self-Organised Criticality*, New York: Copernicus Press for Springer-Verlag.

Camazine, S., J.L. Deneubourg, N.R. Franks, J. Sneyd, G. Theraulaz and E. Bonabeau (2001), *Self-Organization in Biological Systems*, Princeton: Princeton University Press.

Capra, F. (1996), *The Web of Life*, New York: Anchor/Doubleday.

Carpenter, S.R. and J.F. Kitchell (1996), *The Trophic Cascade in Lakes*, Cambridge: Cambridge University Press.
Collie, J.S., K. Richardson and J.H. Steele (2004), 'Regime shifts: can ecological theory illuminate the mechanisms?', *Progress in Oceanography*, **60**(2–4): 281–302.
Fogarty, M.J. and S.A. Murawski (1998), 'Large-scale disturbance and the structure of marine systems: fisheries impacts in Georges Bank', *Ecological Applications*, **8**: S6–22.
Gunderson, L.H. and C.S. Holling (2002), *Panarchy: Understanding Transformations in Systems of Humans and Nature*, Washington, DC: Island Press.
Hastings, A. (1993), 'Complex interactions between dispersal and dynamics', *Ecology*, **74**: 1362–1372.
Karl, D.M. (1999), 'A sea of change: biogeochemical variability in the North Pacific subtropical gyre', *Ecosystems*, **2**: 181–214.
Lovelock, James (2000), *The Ages of Gaia* (2nd ed.), Oxford, UK: Oxford University Press.
May, R. (1974), *Stability and Complexity in Model Ecosystems*, Princeton: Princeton University Press.
Nicolescu, B. (2002), *Manifesto of Transdisciplinarity*, New York: State University of New York Press.
Pikitch, E.K., C. Santora, E.A. Babcock, A. Bakun, R. Bonfil, D.O. Conover, P. Dayton, P. Doukakis, D. Fluharty, B. Heneman, E.D. Houde, J. Link, P.A. Livingston, M. Mangel, M.K. McAllister, J. Pope and K.J. Sainsbury (2004), 'Ecosystem-based fishery management', *Science*, **305**: 346–347.
Shigesada, N. and K. Kawasaki (1997), *Biological Invasions: Theory and Practice*, Oxford, UK: Oxford University Press.
Steele, J.H. (1998), 'Regime shifts in marine ecosystems', *Ecological Applications*, **8**(1): 33–36.
Tainter, J.A. (2006), 'Social complexity and sustainability', *Ecological Complexity*, **3**: 91–103.
Velarde, M.G. and C. Normande (1980), 'Convection', *Scientific American*, **243**(1): 92–108.
Walker, B., G. Peterson, J.M. Anderies, A. Kinzig and S. Carpenter (2005), 'Robustness in ecosystems' in Erica Jan (ed.), *Robust Design: A Repertoire of Biological, Ecological and Engineering Case Studies*, Oxford, UK: Oxford University Press, pp. 173–190.
Walters, C.J. and S.J.D. Martell (2004), *Fisheries Ecology and Management*, Princeton, NJ, USA: Princeton University Press, 448 pp.
Werner, B.T. (1999), 'Complexity in natural landform patterns', *Science*, **284**: 102–104.
Wilson, W.G., A.M. de Roos and E. McCauley (1993), 'Spatial instabilities within the diffuse Lotka–Volterra system: an individual-based simulation result', *Theoretical Population Biology*, **43**: 91–127.
Wing, S.R., M.T. Gibbs and M. Lamare (2003), 'Spatial structure of the sea urchin (*Evechinus chloroticus*) population in a New Zealand fjord', *Marine Ecology Progress Series*, **248**: 109–123.

PART II

Economic and Other Values of the Marine Environment

These chapters focus on the critical issue of how we value the marine environment. 'Value' is arguably the most important and fundamental concept in economics, not only from a theoretical point of view but also because it guides our thinking on how to deal with questions of practical action. Ecological economists have adopted a broader approach to 'value' that emphasizes the multidimensional characteristics of values, particularly those relating to ecology. Ecological economists have also attempted to move beyond the utilitarian and anthropocentric concepts used in neoclassical economics.

Chapter 5 is an important chapter as it outlines the standard neoclassical economic approach to analyzing the question of optimal use of marine resources. The particular approach described in this chapter is based on capital theory, but more broadly it is framed in terms of neoclassical analytics – that is, a theory of value that integrates 'cost' and 'utility' ideas through the mechanism of demand and supply curve analysis.

Chapter 6 is also fundamentally based on the neoclassical economics theory of value, focusing on questions of how to value marine ecosystems services that normally don't have a market price.

Chapter 7 also addresses the question of how to value marine ecosystem processes, but uses the contributory value concept derived from ecology. This chapter attempts to provide a more biophysical perspective on value by focusing on the interdependencies that occur in marine ecosystems.

Chapter 8 presents a fundamentally different view to all the other chapters about how we 'value' the oceans. Drawing on cross-cultural understandings of nature, it shows that many of the concepts of value are not reducible to the type of metrics we commonly use in economics, and therefore we need to be cautious before we universally apply either neoclassical or ecological economics ideas to the context of the oceans and coasts.

5. Neoclassical Frameworks for Optimizing the Value of Marine Resources

Basil Sharp and Chris Batstone

INTRODUCTION

The notion of capital generally means anything which yields a flow of services over time and is subject to control – in this particular case public policy. Thus sustainable development focuses *inter alia* on the substitution of manufactured for natural capital. Capital theory can be used to provide a broad framework for developing ocean resource policy and to derive rules for optimizing the value of ocean resources. Capital theory structures the optimization problem as one in which the objective is to maximize the present value of a flow of future net benefits subject to a set of constraints, namely, the asset. Models presented in this chapter share the same generic objective function and the notion that labour and capital are used to recover the resource, but they differ in the way the asset is represented. Hotelling's (1931) model, which provides the foundations for a wide range of neoclassical models dealing with the optimal depletion of a non-renewable resource, is first presented. The structure of this model considers a stock as a non-renewable asset that generates a flow of returns over time. An important opportunity cost is revealed because current extraction and consumption means that there is less to extract and consume in later periods. The pioneering work of Clark (1976), Clark et al. (1979) and Clark and Munro (1975, 1978) provide the foundations for optimal renewable resource use and management, which is presented in the latter part of the chapter. Although the stock-flow concept carries over, a natural production function is used to represent the rate at which the resource is replenished conditional on use. The ideas of an asset providing a flow of services and the existence of an inter-temporal opportunity cost also apply. However, in contrast to a non-renewable resource, the flow of services can be sustained indefinitely provided the asset is not reduced to a critical level where it becomes impossible to reverse the prospect of extinction. The models presented in this chapter are elementary and not particularly sophisticated because the aim is to provide the rudimentary elements of the neoclassical approach and to derive insights for oceans policy. Furthermore, we assume that there are no externalities associated with resource use. Those 'externalities' are, however, covered in the following chapter.

TOTAL ECONOMIC VALUE

Ocean resources can be broken down into two broad categories: non-renewable resources and renewable resources. *Non-renewable resources* are defined as resources whose quantity *in situ* does not significantly change within the time frame being considered. If the quality of a non-renewable ocean resource is affected by natural deterioration, then this should be explicitly recognized in the optimization model. We assume that quality does not change with time. Offshore natural gas is an obvious example of a non-renewable resource – use of the resource now reduces the size of the resource available in the future. In contrast, a natural replenishment process is an integral part of a *renewable resource* and it is possible to sustain a given flow of services over many years provided the use rate does not exceed the rate of replenishment. Fish stocks and other biotic resources are obvious examples. Ciriacy-Wantrup (1968) further divides renewable resources into those that are not significantly affected by human action and those that are. For example, tidal activity is not significantly affected by human action, whereas the flow of services from fish stocks can be affected by harvesting decisions. This latter class of renewable resources is particularly important in ocean resource policy because current use rates can influence future use rates. Furthermore, the resource stock could be depleted to a level where the decrease in flow of services cannot be reversed with current technology.

Clearly there will be resources that span this dichotomy. For example, sand in some situations might be classified as a non-renewable resource, while in other locations it is a renewable resource. From an economics perspective both non-renewable and renewable ocean resources provide society with opportunities to derive benefit. In some situations the benefits associated with use will be valued in the market. For example, manganese recovered from the ocean floor will have a market price as will the fish harvested by commercial fishing vessels. However, the flow of other services associated with the ocean may not be priced in the market. For example, some members of society will value recreational fishing, boating, swimming and marine habitat, which are not priced by the market mechanism. Methods for valuing the flow of non-market services are reviewed in Chapter 6.

Figure 5.1 illustrates how the total economic value (TEV) framework can be used to describe the flow of services associated with ocean resources. *Use values* arise from the fact that factors of production are applied to the resource *in situ*. For example, mining technology is used to recover manganese. Similarly, vessels and labour are used to harvest seafood. In both cases the inputs used to recover the resource and the outputs have market prices. However, not all use values are market valued. For example, although the inputs necessary for recreational use of the ocean – boat, fishing gear, fuel, and so on – are market priced, the flow of services associated with the ocean are not. A revealed preference approach – such as the travel cost method – could be used to estimate the value of recreational services (Vaughan and Russell 1982). *Non-use values* arise in situations where a value is attached to a resource even though it is not used. For example, it is not used in an extractive sense but nevertheless makes a valuable contribution to the functioning of marine ecosystems. The value of services associated with marine habitat would have to be estimated using a stated preference approach such as the choice modelling approach (Lew and Larson 2005).

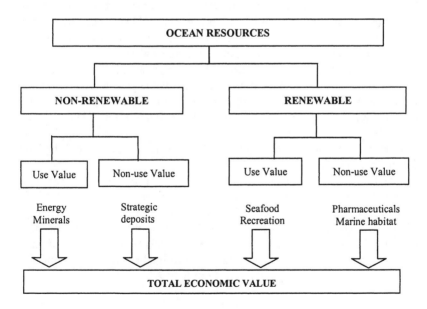

Figure 5.1 Total economic value of ocean resources

In principle, therefore, the concept of TEV provides an overarching framework for policy aimed at maximizing the value of the flow of services from ocean assets. Interdependencies can be easily woven into the framework. For example, if ocean mining were to proceed then the net benefits associated with mineral recovery could be weighed against the damage to marine habitat and flow-on impacts to commercial fishing. The allocation of fish stocks between commercial fishing and recreational fishing can also be assessed within the TEV framework. In the sections that follow we do not attempt to cover external impacts associated with resource use, nor do we provide an overview of non-market values as they relate to ocean resources.

NON-RENEWABLE RESOURCES

When dealing with non-renewable assets, the most obvious economic problem has to do with the optimal rate of depletion over time. Consider the situation where a resource owner has the exclusive rights to a stock of natural gas (S). The price of recovered gas is p and the cost of recovery is $C(q,S)$. Assume that the owner can, in any year t, make a profit π_t. Before deciding whether to recover the gas, the profit-seeking owner should first consider the opportunity cost of recovery now with profit that could be earned by recovery at some later date, say π_{t+1}. To make decisions over time we need an additional variable – one that enables resource owners to decide upon an inter-temporal sequence of depletion. The interest rate plays this role. If the present value of waiting and earning π_{t+1} exceeds the present value of π_t then the owner will push depletion out into the future. Optimal policy therefore requires information on prices, cost and the interest rate. This example illustrates the arbitrage process. Unless bound by contracts to supply, firms can delay depletion and get higher returns by reallocating their depletion decisions into the future.

The bogey of the interest rate also applies when the resource owner has multiple deposits of identical quality but different extraction costs. For example, other things being equal, the marginal cost (MC_1) of extracting gas from a near-shore deposit is likely to be lower than the marginal cost (MC_2) of extracting gas from a field located further offshore. If the price of gas is expected to increase by δ per cent then the marginal return of depleting field 1 will be less than the marginal return from field 2:

$$\frac{[p(1+\delta)-MC_1]}{(p-MC_1)} < \frac{[p(1+\delta)-MC_2]}{(p-MC_2)} \qquad (5.1)$$

The left-hand side of equation (5.1) is compared with the interest rate r. Value is enhanced if the marginal net profit of extracting the gas is less than r. If the return associated with leaving it in the ground is greater than r then value is enhanced by leaving the gas in the ground. If the resource owner has rights to a number of deposits then fields with the lowest marginal extraction costs should be developed first. The test is simple – if the net value of the resource is expected to grow at a rate faster than the interest rate *in situ* then the owner should leave the resource in the ground and only deplete the resource when the net return is less than the interest rate. Therefore, it is the net value of marginal reserves that should appreciate at the interest rate for value maximization. Inferior reserves will appreciate at a rate faster than the interest rate.

In order to generalize on the above discussion let us assume that the firm's problem is to decide on a depletion profile that maximizes the value (V) of a resource S.

$$\max V(q(t), S(t)) = \int_0^T [pq(t) - c(q(t), S(t))] e^{-rt} dt \qquad (5.2)$$

s.t.

$$\int_0^T q(t) \leq S$$

The current value Hamiltonian is

$$H = pq(t) - c(q(t), S(t)) - \rho(t)q(t) \qquad (5.3)$$

where ρ is the co-state variable. The necessary conditions for value maximization are

$$\frac{\partial H}{\partial q(t)} = 0 \Rightarrow p = \frac{\partial c}{\partial q(t)} + \rho(t)$$

$$\frac{\partial H}{\partial S} = 0 \Rightarrow \dot{\rho}(t) = r\rho(t) + \frac{\partial c}{\partial S(t)} = 0 \qquad (5.4)$$

Along the optimal depletion path, equation (5.4) states that the price of the resource should equal the marginal cost of extraction plus the undiscounted royalty ρ. The depletion literature uses resource rent and user cost interchangeably with the notion of a royalty. User cost is the opportunity cost of depleting a unit today. Hotelling's (1931) model is the classic in the field of optimal depletion of a stock resource. In the Hotelling formulation the unit cost of extracting the resource does not vary with the amount of stock remaining which means that there is no stock effect in the cost function ($c_S =$ 0). According to equation (5.4) the necessary condition for value maximization is:

$$\frac{\rho(t)}{\rho(t)} = r \qquad\qquad (5.5)$$

which has the solution:

$$\rho(t) = \rho(0)e^{rt}$$

Equation (5.5) states that, under the assumption of constant marginal extraction cost, the undiscounted user cost $\rho(t)$ will rise over time at the rate of interest r. At each point in time user cost is equivalent to net price ($p\text{-}c_q$). Combining these conditions gives the Hotelling rule: in a competitive equilibrium net price will rise over time at the rate of interest (or equivalently discounted net price is constant over time) if marginal extraction costs are constant until the date at which the reserves are exhausted.

Arbitrage Argument

Hotelling's rule requiring the price of the resource to rise over time at the interest rate is generated by the interaction of supply and demand. Any deviation from this rule presents an opportunity for arbitrage – that is, resource owners can profit by advancing or deferring their extraction plans. Under the assumptions listed above, particularly the assumption that the entire path of future prices is known by everyone with certainty, the opportunity for arbitrage would rapidly remove any deviation from the Hotelling path. For example, suppose some of the resource owners were aware that price was actually rising over time at a rate exceeding the rate of interest. Such a situation would provide an incentive for them to defer their current extraction plans in anticipation of greater future returns, even if they found it necessary to borrow at rate r to finance current consumption. Delaying extraction in this way would result in a reduction in current supply and increase in the current price, and a corresponding increase in supply in the future and a price fall. These adjustments will reduce the rate at which the price rises over time, so the arbitrage action moves the market towards equilibrium.

Extensions to the Model

Numerous extensions aimed at increasing the range of applications of the above-value maximizing model to real world situations have been developed. Non-homogeneous resource deposits are represented by variations in the cost function. In this case the cost of extraction is constant within a given deposit but may differ across deposits. As noted earlier, if the cost of extraction from the low quality deposit exceeds that from the high quality deposit then it is not in the low quality owner's interest to supply because the resource is earning a higher rate of return *in situ*. The situation where marginal extraction costs rise with cumulative extraction is referred to as the 'stock' or 'depletion' effect, which is cumulative and drives a wedge between price and marginal extraction costs. If extraction costs are an increasing function of cumulative part extraction, then the total physical stock need not be completely depleted.

Comparative dynamics can be used to examine the sensitivity of the equilibrium conditions to changes in key parameters, including changes in cost, demand and interest rate. Higher extraction costs will affect the equilibrium path by involving a higher initial price, and a longer period of time before the resource is exhausted. A higher interest rate results in a lower user cost and a shorter period of extraction until the resource is exhausted. The impact of an increase in the stock, say from S to $S+\Delta S$, results in the royalty and the sequence of prices falling. If demand falls because the price of a substitute falls, then the royalty will fall and the period to exhaustion increases.

An examination of the extraction path of a non-renewable resource under monopolistic conditions and its relationship to the competitive path were first indicated by Hotelling (1931). Under monopolistic conditions the resource owner is the sole supplier and therefore has control over the total amount of the resource supplied to the market at any point in time. The profit maximizing problem for the monopolist is identical to that of the competitive firm, except that the monopolist can influence the price of the resource by varying the quantity supplied. By selecting an extraction rate the monopolist also determines price via the demand curve.

In general, with monopoly, the price and extraction paths will vary from those arising in the competitive case. The extent of the deviation depends on the relationship between price and marginal revenue. Hotelling concluded that the rate of resource extraction would be slowed following the result from static analysis, that there is a 'general tendency for production to be retarded under monopoly' (1931, p. 152). Later examinations of this issue have provided counter-examples in which the rate of extraction is either identical to or faster than that under a competitive equilibrium. These have been generalized to show that whether the resource is depleted more or less rapidly by the monopolist depends on the nature of the demand curve. Hotelling's intuitive conclusion that the monopolist structure will encourage a more conservationist extraction path has been shown to rest on the assumption that the elasticity of demand is decreasing over output levels or time (Dasgupta and Heal 1979). If the elasticity of demand decreases as extraction rises, the monopolist will deplete the resource more slowly than under a competitive market outcome.

Demand elasticity that decreases as output expands might arise where price increases for the resource stock generate incentives for the research, development and use of substitutes. Dasgupta and Heal (1979) suggest the example of higher oil prices providing encouragement for the development of shale oil, which would increase the elasticity of demand faced by oil suppliers. When demand becomes less elastic over time the monopolist would do best by speeding up extraction in the early part of the time horizon, since net marginal revenue when demand is elastic can be expected to exceed that on later sales when demand is less elastic. That is, the monopolist will increase early sales to restrict the quantities sold in later periods enabling it to take advantage of less elastic demand. The situation of elasticity falling over time does not seem very likely. A more realistic approach would be to expect demand to become increasingly elastic as substitutes become available. If this is the case, the depletion path under monopolistic extraction will be slower than under the competitive structure. Intuitively, the reasoning is that the monopolist will restrict extraction early in order to take advantage of the relatively inelastic demand. Most authors accept the result that, in general, monopolistic control of resources will generate more conservationist extraction paths than those arising in a competitive market structure. This conclusion is reinforced if cumulative depletion dependent costs are included.

Sustainability

Many definitions of the popularized term 'sustainable development' have been proposed but the basic concern is whether or not future generations will be at least as well off as the present generation (Krautkraemer 1998). The prospect for sustainable development is indeed bleak if population growth continues unabated, technology does not change and there is no opportunity to substitute other forms of capital for non-renewable resources (Stiglitz 1974). However, sustained growth depends *inter alia* on whether or not the economy is patient enough to allow technological progress or capital-resource substitution to overcome the drag arising from non-renewable resource depletion. The ability to substitute renewable capital for non-renewable capital is an important factor in determining whether non-decreasing consumption is feasible (Dasgupta and Heal 1979).

In order to sustain a constant level of consumption, Hartwick (1977) proposed that rents from non-renewable resources should be invested in renewable capital. The basic idea is to treat a non-renewable resource as natural capital and the depreciation of this natural capital is balanced by investment in another capital asset thus preserving the total stock of capital (Solow 1974, 1986). The logic behind the Hartwick rule is seen by considering the present value of the resource depleting firm at a particular point in time with $S(t)$ reserves remaining

$$V(S(t)) = \int_t^T (pq^*(u) - c(q^*(u))) e^{-r(u-t)} \, du \qquad (5.6)$$

differentiating with respect to time yields the following asset equation

$$\dot{V}(S(t)) = rV(S(t)) - (pq^*(t) - c(q^*(t))) \qquad (5.7)$$

Equation (5.7) shows that the change in the value of the firm equals the market value of the firm less the Hotelling rent. The Hartwick rule seeks to maintain capital in the economy by investing the Hotelling rent associated with depleting natural capital in manufactured capital. If price is a function of time, then the Hartwick rule changes to include the investment of rent including any capital gains or losses associated with future price changes. One implication of the Hartwick rule is that national accounts should be adjusted to account for the economic depreciation of stock resources (Hartwick 1990).

Stock Resource Policy

Government policy can be designed to influence the rate at which marine non-renewable resources are being used. Pricing instruments are used to encourage different patterns of resource use. For example, the government might think that current rates of gas use are excessive and prices too low, and therefore tax gas depletion. Government legislation could be reframed in a way that provided for competitive access to offshore exploration and mining sites. In this section we look at access rights and taxation as two major policy instruments.

Access rights

A simple, and quite common, approach to controlling access is to award rights on the basis of first-in–first-served. The approach has shortcomings. Entry is decided by a 'race' that involves little, if any, consideration of opportunity cost. From the economy's point of view, access rights may not fall into the hands of firms that can maximize value. From the firm's point of view there is an incentive to substitute away from high cost inputs in favour of the relatively lower priced non-renewable asset. This undesirable outcome is compounded if the access right is not transferable, because other more profitable enterprises would be denied access simply because the incumbent right holder got in first. More recently, the auctioning of rights to extract ocean resources has been used to establish initial entitlements. If there is sufficient competition for rights and firms have sufficient information on the deposit, then the firm's willingness to pay for a right to mine in an offshore area would be bounded by the net present value of the expected rents from the site. All expected rents would be captured in a single payment. Mining rights would therefore gravitate to those firms deriving the greatest value from mining and selling the output. If the mining industry is not competitive, the full value of the deposit might not be realized.

Taxation

A severance tax is a tax on raw material as it is recovered. The tax can take the form of specific tax levied at a rate per unit of output; or as an ad valorem tax levied on the dollar value of output. A constant rate of tax will result in a postponement of production (Dasgupta and Heal 1979). The tax introduces a distortion, resulting in higher initial consumer prices, greater conservation, and a reduction of the value of the stock *in situ*. The initial royalty price is higher with the tax, the depletion rate is lower, the depletion date is extended, and the present value of deposits is lower because the royalty is reduced.

A profit's tax is very common in resource-based industries. In the context of the simple model it may also be called a rent or royalty tax. Providing the tax is a flat rate and not expected to change in the future, depletion rates will be unaffected. The net price of the resource rising at the interest rate also means that the tax liability will rise at the rate of interest. Altering the date of production will not change the present value of the tax paid. Therefore a constant profits tax is identical to a specific severance tax growing at the rate of interest. However, it is conceivable that lower profits in the industry will also influence the willingness, and indeed the ability, of firms to allocate funds to exploration and to the development of new sites.

In conclusion, without a tax, the profit per unit sold rises over time at the interest rate. If a constant profits tax is introduced, then the tax liability per unit sold will also rise at the interest rate. Therefore the present value of tax liability incurred by the sale of a unit is constant and independent of the date of sale and there is no reason to suspect that the firm would change its sale profile. But if the tax rate were to rise over time, then so would the present value of the tax liability per unit sold, thereby inducing the firm to bring sales forward to minimize tax liability. If the tax rate were to fall through time, then the reverse would hold.

Empirical evidence
The above overview of the basic Hotelling model and extensions provides some insights into the huge literature on the optimal depletion of non-renewable resources. Each extension attempts to capture real-world phenomena such as uncertainty over stock quantity, variable quality, price expectations and capital investment. Empirical evidence of non-renewable resource prices and *in situ* values do not, in general, support the results of the basic Hotelling model. Time series analyses do not reveal a persistent upward trend in resource prices; rather prices fluctuate and the direction of change depends on the period being considered (Berck and Roberts 1996; Slade 1982). As Krautkraemer (1998) correctly points out, it is the *in situ* value of the resource that should be increasing over time; but again, empirical studies find no support for this hypothesis.

Significant capital investment is necessary to explore and recover a non-renewable resource and beneficiate it for supply. Capital intensity is, of course, common to other forms of manufacture but the size of resource stock and the nature of the upstream resource using industry can have an important bearing on scale, capital specificity and time horizon. For example, the *in situ* value of a large capital stock might be relatively small and the impact of high interest rates on the cost of capital could dominate depletion decisions. Similarly, high interest rates could delay the development of alternative supply. If capital used in resource recovery and beneficiation is not malleable, then plant capacity can constrain output and the firm's output could remain constant as opposed to declining over time. The time horizon for investment decisions in capital-intensive industries can easily span a period of 20 years. Price expectations *ex ante* may deviate markedly from those that play out over the duration of the project. One need only reflect on the changes that have occurred over the past 20 years in terms of leading economic indicators, technological change and government policy. At this stage, the impact of these and other factors make it very difficult to make predictions on the inter-temporal price of non-renewable resources and extraction paths. The development of substitutes and technological change, while uncertain, will continue. Perhaps the most relevant concern for oceans policy is the protection of the life-supporting services associated with oceanic resources for which there are few substitutes.

Case study

The following case study of an ocean stock resource illustrates an application of the neoclassical model. The case study involves New Zealand's Maui gas field. In 1969 a private sector consortium discovered the Maui gas field with an estimated 75 million barrels of condensate and 5446 PJ of natural gas. The find was reasonably large by world standards. The New Zealand Government played a significant role in development of the field: it owned the gas, the gas-using industry and the gas reticulation system, and controlled the planning and development of electricity generation. Thus the Government was considered the only viable long-term, large-scale purchaser of the gas (Sharp and Simon 1992).

In 1973, after an extended period of negotiations over price, a 30-year contract was executed whereby the government purchased a 50 per cent interest in the field and accepted a base price of 37 cents per million British therma units for contractual take-or-pay quantities. The contract encouraged use of the gas beyond the take-or-pay quantities by charging 85 per cent of the take-or-pay price. The take-or-pay clause put pressure on the Government to find uses for the gas, particularly when projected growth in electricity demand did not materialise. The Government decided to allocate 28 per cent of the reserves to a synthetic fuel plant, 8 per cent to a methanol plant and 3 per cent to an ammonia urea plant; and to contribute to equity capital to these projects. The capital cost of these projects was about $NZ2.5 billion. In 1984 the net present value of the three projects was about –$NZ390 million.

The impact of stock uncertainty, market power and asset specificity are clearly evident from development of the Maui gas field. Would a better outcome have resulted if policy had been based on the Hotelling model and, possibly, the Hartwick rule? With asset specific investments there was an incentive on both sides of the contract to obtain a degree of certainty over price and quantity. However, locking parties into a 30-year take-or-pay agreement with little room for adjustment runs counter to the resource rent trajectory proposed by the capital-theoretic model. Furthermore, the Hartwick rule would not be satisfied by government-subsidized capital-intensive energy projects because the combined present value of these projects was negative. In the case of Maui gas, depletion and development policies agreed to and implemented by the New Zealand Government in the mid-1970s were not value enhancing.

RENEWABLE RESOURCES

Neoclassical models of renewable resources are distinguished by the inclusion of a function used to describe the natural rate of replenishment. Although we provide an overview of the model used in fisheries economics, the model can be used to derive optimality conditions for the use of other renewable ocean resources. Stock production models are particularly appropriate for use where large, single species, resources exhibit low year-to-year fluctuations. For more dynamic fisheries, with yield variation and high risk of irreversibility, these models may be inappropriate. The fisheries natural production function is defined as:

$$\dot{X}_t = g(X) = \beta X - \gamma X^2 \text{ with } \beta \text{ and } \gamma > 0 \qquad (5.8)$$

where

X = an aggregate measure of the stock, such as tonnes.

There are two roots to equation (5.8)

X_e = minimum biologically viable population
X_m = maximum stock size possible

Integrating both sides yields the logistic curve:

$$X_t = \frac{\beta X_0}{[\gamma X_0 + (\beta - \gamma X_0)e^{-\beta t}]} \qquad (5.9)$$

A production function is incorporated into the model where Y_t is the harvest and E the level of effort.

$$Y_t = f(E, X) \qquad (5.10)$$

The sustainable yield in the fishery occurs when the harvest rate equals the natural rate of replenishment.

$$\dot{X} = g(X_t) - Y_t = 0 \qquad (5.11)$$

Gordon (1954) provided the conceptual basis for much of the literature on the economics of fisheries management. Under conditions of open access, the natural resource is exploited by users competing with one another for a greater share of the harvest. Assuming the price of landed fish is constant at p and the cost of applying effort to harvest fish is given by w, then the profit that firm i gains is given by

$$\pi_{it} = pY_{it} - wE_{it} = 0 \qquad (5.12)$$

Equation (5.12) shows that economic rent associated with the resource is dissipated; aggregate value is zero. This result is important because labour and manufactured capital will be over-allocated and the stock of natural capital depleted. In this situation labour and capital could be more productively employed elsewhere in the economy.

Fisheries economics has long been framed in capital-theoretic terms. The fish population is viewed as a capital stock capable of providing a sustainable flow of harvest through time. When cast in this way it becomes possible to explicitly examine the inter-temporal implications of resource use. In particular, we can determine the optimal harvest over time which, in turn, implies selecting an optimal stock level as a function of time (Peterson and Fisher 1977). The present value Hamiltonian for society's maximization problem is

$$MaxV(E,X,\mu)=(pf(E,X)-wE)e^{-rt}+\mu(g(X)-f(E,X)) \quad (5.13)$$

The conditions describing optimality are:

$$\frac{\partial H}{\partial E} = (p\frac{\partial f}{\partial E}-w)e^{-rt}-\mu\frac{\partial f}{\partial E}=0$$
$$\Rightarrow p=\frac{w}{f_E}+\mu e^{rt} \qquad (5.14)$$

$$g(X)-f(E,X)=0 \qquad (5.15)$$

$$\frac{\partial H}{\partial X} = (p\frac{\partial f}{\partial X})e^{-rt}+\mu(\frac{\partial g}{\partial X}-\frac{\partial f}{\partial X})=0 \qquad (5.16)$$
$$\Rightarrow pf_X e^{-rt}+\mu(g_X-f_X)=-\dot{\mu}$$
$$\Rightarrow f_X(p-\lambda)+\lambda(g_X-r)=-\dot{\lambda}$$

The discounted shadow price associated with the renewable resource is:

$$\mu = \lambda e^{-rt}$$
$$\Rightarrow \dot{\mu} = e^{-rt}(\dot{\lambda} - r\lambda)$$

The marginal user cost of fish *in situ* is μ. This is the amount by which the present value of the fishery at t is reduced (or increased) when an additional unit of the stock is harvested (or added). We now provide an interpretation of the first order conditions for value maximization. First, equation (5.14) tells us that in the steady state solution, price equals marginal cost plus the current value of the marginal user cost. Second, equation (5.15) requires catch to equal natural replacement. Finally, equation (5.16) can be broken down into two parts. The first part of the left-hand side represents the net marginal benefits generated by an additional unit of the stock. The second part represents the opportunity cost of holding an additional unit of the stock. If the sum of these two components is positive, then additional harvesting should be delayed because of capital gain. If the sum is negative then the opportunity cost of holding fish *in situ* is higher than future gains and it would be better to harvest marginal units now.

Using a linear model, Clark and Munro (1975) provide an illuminating alternative to equation (5.16):

$$g_X(X^*) - \frac{c_X(x^*)g(X^*)}{p - c(X^*)} = r \qquad (5.17)$$

Equation (5.17) is a modified golden rule equilibrium equation which requires the marginal physical productivity of capital less the marginal stock effect to equal the discount rate. If the biomass is managed at Maximum Sustainable Yield (MSY) and if:

$$Z \equiv - \frac{c_X(X_{MSY})g(X_{MSY})}{p - c(X_{MSY})}$$

then:

$$X^* = \begin{cases} < X_{MSY} & \text{if } r > Z \\ = X_{MSY} & \text{if } r = Z \\ > X_{MSY} & \text{if } r < Z \end{cases}$$

Following Clark and Munro (1975), results obtained using the static model can be replicated by setting the discount rate equal to zero. Figure 5.2 shows the fishery managed under two property right arrangements: (1) under open access, effort expands out to E_O and economic rent in the fishery is dissipated; (2) under optimal management, effort is controlled at E^* where rent is maximized.

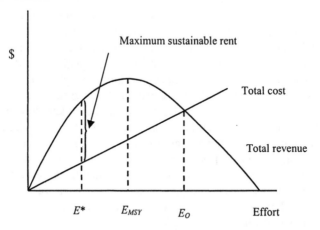

Figure 5.2 Fishing effort under open access and optimal management

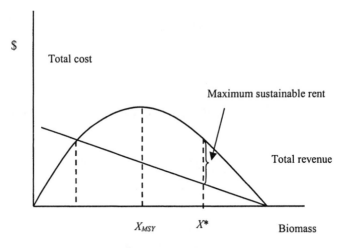

Figure 5.3 Biomass under open access and optimal management

The consequence of open access in terms of biomass is illustrated in Figure 5.3. Moving from the right, positive economic rent is shown to reduce the biomass until X_O where rent is dissipated. The static model shows the optimal management policy resulting in higher biomass levels (X^*) than, either, open access (X_O) or maximum sustained yield (X_{MSY}). Figures 5.2 and 5.3 serve to show that open access results in both an over allocation of labour and capital and in the depletion of the resource. Hartwick (1990) also proposes that national accounts be adjusted to account for the economic depreciation of the stock.

Renewable Resource Policy

In the absence of any limitations on harvest, economic theory predicts that rent will be dissipated. This prediction has been observed in many fisheries throughout the world. There are at least two reasons why policy makers should be concerned about a fishery operating at zero rent. First, the economy is foregoing rent by over-allocating resources in fishing. Second, stock levels will be lower and the stock itself can experience recruitment fluctuations that eventually work their way through to lower replenishment levels. Therefore the problem of fisheries management is to enhance value in the fishery and to ensure sustainable utilization. In general terms, two policy instruments are required: (a) regulated outputs and inputs, (b) property rights.

Maximum sustainable yield is often promoted as an objective for fisheries management (Larkin 1977). Indeed this objective is legislated in New Zealand's Fisheries Act 1996. Economists were quick to attack the idea of MSY saying that the objective neglects the fact that labour and capital must be allocated in order to catch fish in the first place. These inputs have an opportunity cost in the economist's framework. In contrast, the economic objective is to maximize the present value of the difference between benefits and costs subject to a sustainability constraint. This is the essence of the optimization model described above. If fisheries policy is directed at maximizing rent in the fishery, then the challenge is to find an instrument or set of instruments that can deliver, in theory at least, maximum economic value. Economists typically focus on the relative merits of input controls such as regulated access, limits on the number of vessels, limits on the size of vessels and so on; output controls such as competitive catch limits; taxes; and tradable quota rights.

Regulated output and inputs
The essential feature of regulations is that they are aimed at controlling the quantity of fish caught and/or the effort applied in the fishery. Let us assume that the management agency sets a harvest limit Y_m. The problem now is how to allocate the limit. Should it be carved up with each fisher getting an equal share? Should open entry to the fishery be allowed up to the point at which

the limit on harvest Y_m is reached? If the agency sets Y_m and allows competition up to Y_m, then even though the regulation might produce positive economic rent in the short run, the policy creates an incentive to race and capture rent that will lead to increased costs and eventual dissipation of the rent. Regulations could be applied to vessel numbers, engine size, length of boat, and so on. Technology regulations are inherently inefficient. They embed harvesting technology which once adopted often proves difficult to change during the economic life of the technology. The incentive to innovate is effectively removed by input regulations.

Property rights
Important dimensions of property rights are described in Chapter 13. As already noted, open access describes a situation where there is no residual claimant on rent in the fishery and, as a result, rent is dissipated by unfettered competition. There are many alternatives available to craft property right arrangements. For example, a system of non-transferable licences could be used to limit effort, based perhaps on the number of vessels that currently harvest fish in a particular fishery. Once introduced and the number decided upon, effort will be reallocated from less productive to more productive areas. If there is rent to be captured then there will be an incentive for licence holders to invest in technologies that will enhance their ability to catch a greater share of the allowable harvest.

Faced with the twin problems of achieving positive economic rent and some notion of sustainable harvest, fisheries management agencies in a growing number of countries are implementing tradable quota rights. New Zealand and Iceland are two countries to implement so-called rights-based systems of governance. The idea is relatively simple. The fisheries management agency sets a total allowable catch (TAC) that conforms to some notion of sustainability, and individual fishers own tradable rights to harvest. The total holdings of individual tradable quota (ITQ) is constrained by the TAC. Operation of the system can be illustrated using a simple model.

Let us assume that fishing firm i's profit function is given by $\pi[p,w,\alpha(TAC)]$ where p is the landed price of fish, w is a vector representing input prices and $\alpha(TAC)$ is the firm's share of the allowable catch. If w_q represents the price of ITQ then we can represent the firm's demand function for quota rights as

$$x_q = -\frac{\partial \pi[p,w,\alpha(TAC)]}{\partial w_q} \qquad (5.19)$$

Market demand for quota is a function of *inter alia* the price of landed fish, harvesting costs, and the TAC which in turn is a function of the stock level. Two exogenous forces come into play here. First, we assume that firms are price takers, thus if profit increases then *ceterus paribus* the demand for quota rights will increase. Second, the quota market is output constrained, therefore the TAC can directly influence market demand for quota rights. The sign associated with the impact of changes to the TAC will depend on the level of the stock.

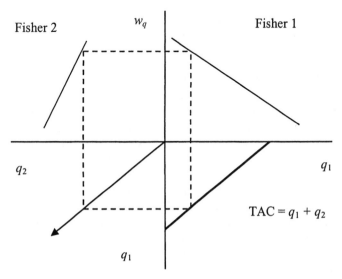

Figure 5.4 Simple model of rights-based fishing

The idea behind rights-based fishing is illustrated in Figure 5.4. Typically a fisheries management agency announces a TAC for the fishing season, which is allocated to commercial fishers on the basis of their quota holdings. Figure 5.4 shows how market demand maps the TAC into quota holdings for two fishing firms. Comparative static analysis follows quite easily. If, for example, firm 1 is able to lower its harvesting costs then its demand for quota rights will increase and rights would flow from firm 2 to firm 1. If the TAC is adjusted then this can be expected to impact the quota market. The structure of rights-based governance is discussed in more detail in Chapter 13.

In a shared fishery, interdependencies between commercial fishers and recreational fishers will need to be considered. Returning to the TEV model, the allocation of scarce fish stocks between competing interests should, in principle, reflect relative value. However, it is usual, from the fisheries manager's perspective, that there is an asymmetric supply of value information. In Chapter 14 we show how quota market information can be used when setting the commercial catch but there is no value revealing mechanism in place for the recreational catch. Allocating a harvestable yield to cover the recreational catch remains one of the major challenges facing rights-based governance in shared fisheries. Obviously this is not an issue in many deep water fisheries.

Case Study

Setting aside the complications of dynamic optimization, application of the static fisheries model to real-world fisheries management problems has served to highlight the biological and economic shortcomings of contemporary policy. Many fisheries throughout the world have, at one time or another, been characterized by the twin problems of low economic performance and stock depletion (Henderson and Tugwell 1979). Low rents and depleted stocks are sure signs that the institutional structure needs re-organization. The case study of New Zealand's rock lobster fishery traces the evolution of policy from regulated access through to rights-based management.

In terms of economic value, the rock lobster fishery has been one of New Zealand's most important fisheries since the mid-1950s. For many years the fishery was controlled by regulations aimed at input controls and addressing minimum biological requirements such as minimum legal size, a requirement that all pots be fitted with escape gaps, and closed seasons and spatial controls. During the late 1940s, profitable export markets for rock lobster developed, which fuelled entry into the fishery. The number of vessels increased through 1955, tapering off slightly in the early 1960s and then increasing again in the 1970s. Average harvest per vessel peaked at around 15 tonnes in the mid-1950s and generally fell off through 1980 to around 4 tonnes. This pattern of development is characteristic of newly exploited fisheries where the rapid increase in landings is sustained by harvesting larger sized age classes. During the early stages of development entry was limited by restrictive licensing which was removed in 1963. In the absence of entry controls fishers only needed a permit to catch rock lobster. With unlimited entry production will progressively decrease as smaller animals are harvested. In 1963, 950 vessels harvested an average of 4.8 tonnes. When a moratorium on the issue of new licenses was introduced in the early 1980s, 1125 vessels landed 4534 tonnes, an average of 4.0 tonnes per vessel.

Prior to the 1980 moratorium on entry, a survey of registered fishers in 1979 provided the following insights into the economic conditions of commercial rock lobster fishing: (i) 38 per cent of the respondents reported a harvest of less than one tonne, and 42 per cent between one and six tonnes;

(ii) most vessels were fished single handed, the average crew size was 1.6; (iii) the break-even income and quantity increased significantly between 1976 and 1978 for most vessel classes (Annala 1983). Against this backdrop of declining average harvest and lower profit, 78 per cent of the respondents indicated they would not support a competitive TAC and 64 per cent were against a catch quota per vessel. It is of interest to note that the survey was undertaken over ten years before rock lobster were introduced in the quota management system (QMS). Not only had profitability in the sector declined, the trajectory of biomass estimates also declined from 1945 through the mid-1970s. These outcomes are consistent with the predictions of the bioeconomic static model.

Rock lobster was introduced into the QMS in 1990. The aim was to rebuild fish stocks and improve profitability through the creation of tradable property rights to catch fish within an administered TAC. The basic structure of the QMS and its performance is covered in more detail in Chapter 14. However, to complete the case study we can point to a number of outcomes since 1990: (1) a general improvement in biomass; (2) an increase in catch per unit effort, measured in terms of kilograms per pot lift; and (3) a drop in the number of registered rock lobster vessels and increased average landings per vessel. The fact that the rock lobster quota is traded at a positive price indicates the existence of economic rent. On both counts – biology and economics – the QMS outscores the system of governance that it replaced.

CONCLUSIONS

The neoclassical approach to ocean resources begins by classifying ocean resources into renewable and non-renewable resources. The distinction is important because renewable resources, if managed well, can provide an indefinite supply of services. Non-renewable resources, once used, are not available for use in the future – unless of course some 'waste' materials can be economically 'recycled'.

Starting with the assumption of maximizing 'total economic value', or more specifically the present value of net benefits, we identified services that are priced in the market and those that are not. The market pricing mechanism is obviously contingent on governance and the structure of property rights in particular. For example, rights-based access to recreational fishing stocks is feasible but not common. If implemented, the value attached to recreational harvest would be revealed in the market. However, in the absence of price-revealing mechanisms, the neoclassical economist must turn to selecting a method from the large toolkit of non-market valuation methods to assign values to flows of non-market services (see Chapter 6). The objective of maximizing net present value is common to both models of renewable and non-renewable resources.

In both cases the resource is treated as a capital asset. However, in the case of modelling renewable resources, a natural production function is included to capture the essence of replenishment. The broad structure of the capital theoretic model is thus one of maximizing net present value subject to a set of constraints that describe characteristics of the resource. Equilibrium conditions yield important insights for policy makers. In both cases the interest rate provides the inter-temporal price necessary for maximizing economic value over time. The notion of a user cost or rent is common to both non-renewable and renewable resources. In the simple case of a non-renewable resource, rent should grow at the discount rate. With renewable resources, a slightly different rule applies because the natural production function of the resource enters into the equilibrium conditions for value maximisation. The basic capital theoretic model has been extended to address specific issues. For example, a large literature has evolved about issues such as market structure, asset specificity, problems of excess capital in fisheries, stock uncertainty, and so on. Empirical evidence of the outcomes expected is quite mixed. It would appear that the explanatory power of the Hotelling type model is quite low and cannot adequately capture forces that co-determine resource prices and resource values *in situ*. In contrast, the Clark–Munro class of bioeconomic models has proved to be quite accurate in predicting the outcomes associated with alternative systems of renewable resource management.

Two case studies were used to illustrate the application of economic theory to resource policy. In the case of natural gas, the New Zealand Government committed itself to a fixed price take-or-pay contract and artificially created demand for gas by investing in energy intensive projects. Only one of these projects yielded a positive net present value. At the time, energy markets could hardly be described as competitive and the decisions of the Government were certainly not consistent with that expected of a single large buyer. Even with the idiosyncratic nature of energy investment, the present value of Maui gas could have been enhanced by applying basic capital theoretic principles to contract design and the depletion of the gas field. The rock lobster case study clearly demonstrates the outcomes predicted by the bioeconomic model. Policy based on regulated open access led to low economic performance and depleted fish stocks. The rights-based system of governance has clearly outperformed its predecessor. Biomass levels have steadily improved and the industry is producing positive rents.

REFERENCES

Annala, J.H. (1983), *New Zealand Rock Lobsters: Biology and Fishery, Fisheries Research Division*, Occasional Publication No. 42, Wellington: Ministry of Agriculture and Fisheries.

Berck, P. and M. Roberts (1996), 'Natural resource prices: will they ever turn up?' *Journal of Environmental Economics and Management*, **31**(1): 65–78.

Ciriacy-Wantrup, S.V. (1968), *Resource Conservation, Economics and Policies* (3rd edn), Berkeley: University of California Press.

Clark, C.W. (1976), *Mathematical Bioeconomics*, New York: John Wiley.

Clark, C.W. and G.R. Munro (1975), 'The economics of fishing and modern capital theory: a simplified approach', *Journal of Environmental Economics and Management*, **2**: 92–106.

Clark, C.W. and G.R. Munro (1978), 'Renewable resource management and extinction', *Journal of Environmental Economics and Management*, **5**(2): 198–206.

Clark, C.W., F.H. Clark and G.R. Munro (1979), 'The optimal exploitation of renewable resource stocks: problems of irreversible investment', *Econometrica*, **47**(1): 25–47.

Dasgupta, P. and G. Heal (1979), *Economic Theory and Exhaustible Resources*, Welwyn, UK: James Nisbet and Co. and Cambridge University Press.

Gordon, H.S. (1954), 'The economic theory of a common property resource: the fishery', *Journal of Political Economy*, **62**(April): 124–42.

Hartwick, J.M. (1977), 'Intergenerational equity and the investing of rents from exhaustible resources', *American Economic Review*, **57**(5): 972–74.

Hartwick, J.M. (1990), 'Natural resources, national accounting and economic depreciation', *Journal of Public Economics*, **43**: 291–304.

Henderson, J.V. and M. Tugwell (1979), 'Exploitation of the lobster fishery: some empirical results', *Journal of Environmental Economics and Management*, **6**: 287–96.

Hotelling, H. (1931), 'The economics of exhaustible resources', *Journal of Political Economy*, **39**(2): 137–75.

Krautkraemer, J.A. (1998), 'Nonrenewable resource scarcity', *Journal of Economic Literature*, **36**: 2065–107.

Larkin, P.A. (1977), 'An epitaph for the concept of maximum sustained yield', *Transactions of the American Fisheries Society*, **106**(1): 1–11.

Lew, D.K. and D.M. Larson (2005), 'Valuing recreation and amenities at San Diego County beaches', *Coastal Management*, **33**: 71–86.

Peterson, F.M. and A.C. Fisher (1977), 'The exploitation of extractive resources: a survey', *Economic Journal*, **87**(4): 681–721.

Sharp, B.M.H. and B. Simon (1992), 'Long-term natural resource contracts', *New Zealand Economic Papers*, **26**(1): 27–46.

Slade, M.E. (1982), 'Trends in natural resource commodity prices: an analysis of the frequency domain', *Journal of Environmental Economics and Management*, **9**(2): 122–37.

Solow, R.M. (1974), 'Intergenerational equity and exhaustible resources', *Review of Economic Studies, Symposium on the Economics of Exhaustible Resources*, **40**: 29–45.
Solow, R.M. (1986), 'On the intergenerational allocation of natural resources', *Scandinavian Journal of Economics*, **88**(1): 141–49.
Stiglitz, J.E. (1974), 'Growth with exhaustible natural resources: efficient and optimal growth paths', *Review of Economic Studies, Symposium on the Economics of Exhaustible Resources*, **40**: 123–37.
Vaughan, W.J. and C.S. Russell (1982), 'Valuing a fishing day: an application of a systematic varying parameter model', *Land Economics*, **58**(4): 450–63.

6. Non-Market Value of Ecosystem Services Provided by Coastal and Nearshore Marine Systems

Matthew Wilson and Shuang Liu

INTRODUCTION

The population and development pressures that coastal and nearshore marine areas are now experiencing raise significant challenges for coastal planners and decision makers. Communities must often choose between competing uses of the coastal environment and the myriad goods and services provided by healthy, functioning ecosystems. Should this shoreline be cleared and stabilized to provide new land for development, or should it be maintained in its current state to serve as wildlife habitat? Should that coastal wetland be drained and converted to agriculture, or should more wetland area be created to provide freshwater filtration services? Should this coral reef be mined for the production of lime, mortar and cement, or should it be sustained to provide renewable seafood products and recreational opportunities?

To choose from among these competing options, it is important to know not only what ecosystem goods and services will be affected but also what they are actually worth to different members of society (Farber et al. 2006). When confronting decisions that pit different ecosystem services against one another, decision makers cannot escape making a *social choice* based on values – whenever one alternative is chosen over another, that choice indicates which alternative is deemed to be worth more than other alternatives. In short, 'we cannot avoid the valuation issue, because as long as we are forced to make choices, we are doing valuation' (Costanza and Folke 1997, p. 50). In this chapter, we show that efforts to assess and quantify *all* the benefits associated with coastal and nearshore marine ecosystem services will be necessary for policy and managerial decisions that seek to maximize the social benefit derived from such complex systems.

CONCEPTUAL FRAMEWORK

Coastal and nearshore marine systems, including fish nurseries, coral reef systems, estuaries, wetlands and sandy beaches, provide many different ecosystem goods and services to human society. An ecosystem service, by definition, contains 'the conditions and processes through which natural ecosystems, and the species that make them up, sustain and fulfill human life' (Daily 1997). Ecosystem goods, on the other hand, represent the material products that are obtained from natural systems for human use (DeGroot et al. 2002). Ecosystem goods and services occur at multiple scales, from climate regulation and carbon sequestration at the global scale, to flood protection, water supply, soil formation, nutrient cycling, waste treatment and pollination at the local and regional scales (DeGroot et al. 2002; Heal et al. 2005). They also vary in terms of how directly they contribute to human welfare, with those listed above contributing less directly; while food, raw materials, genetic resources, recreational opportunities, and aesthetic and cultural values contributing more directly.

Figure 6.1 represents an integrated framework that the authors have developed for the assessment of ecosystem goods and services within the coastal and nearshore marine environment. This includes a consideration of ecological structures and processes, their biophysical drivers, coastal and marine management and policy, ecosystem services and human welfare goals, as well as the feedbacks between them. As Figure 6.1 shows, ecosystem goods and services form a pivotal conceptual link between human and ecological systems – namely, ecosystem structures and processes are influenced by long-term, large-scale biophysical drivers, which in turn create the necessary conditions for providing the ecosystem goods and services people value.

The concept of ecosystem goods and services used in this chapter is inherently *anthropocentric* – it is the presence of human beings as welfare-maximizing agents that enables the translation of basic ecological structures and processes into value-laden entities. Through laws and rules, land use management and policy decisions, individuals and social groups make tradeoffs between these values. In turn, these land-use decisions directly modify the structures and processes of the coastal zone by engineering and construction and/or indirectly by modifying the physical, biological and chemical processes of the natural system (Boumans et al. 2002).

In this chapter, we use the concept of ecosystem goods and services to describe a diversity of human values associated with coastal and nearshore systems (Farber et al. 2002). We focus on peer-reviewed estimates of non-market economic values and discuss how these values can be used to inform decisions about the future of the coastal and marine environments.

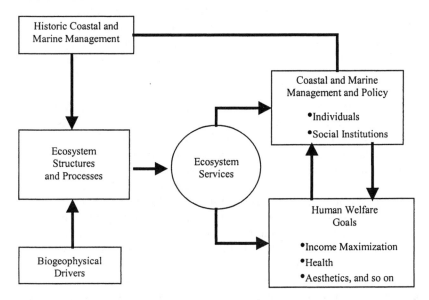

Figure 6.1 Framework for integrated assessment and valuation of ecosystem functions, goods and services in the coastal and marine environment

(*Source:* Adapted from Wilson et al. 2005)

CLASSIFYING ECOSYSTEM GOODS AND SERVICES IN COASTAL AND NEARSHORE SYSTEMS

Coastlines and marine systems around the world exhibit a variety of physical types and characteristics, the result of differences in geophysical and biophysical processes. There are also a number of distinct habitat and ecosystem types within the coastal and nearshore zone, each suggesting unique management and planning needs. Coastal and marine regions are dynamic interface zones where land, water and atmosphere interact in a fragile balance that is constantly being altered by natural and human influences. When establishing classification schemes for the coastal and nearshore zone, it is important to remember that critical biological and physical drivers and interconnections extend beyond these areas and that coastal zones can be significantly affected by events that happen great distances (temporal and spatial) from the coast itself.

Accurate ecosystem definition and classification are essential preliminary steps in the valuation and management of coastal and nearshore systems. In this chapter, we adopt an ecosystem classification system with a high level of standardization that builds on previous work by the authors (Wilson et al. 2004, 2005). In Table 6.1, we have identified specific coastal and nearshore features using this typology.

For example, nearshore ocean is distinguished here from open ocean by those ocean areas that are either 50 m in depth or 100 km offshore. Nearshore islands and nearshore open space analogously fall within the 100 km zone offshore or inshore from the physical coastline, respectively. Estuaries and lagoons are classified as those highly productive areas in the nearshore environment where mixing between salt and freshwater take place. Saltwater wetlands, marshes or salt ponds are distinguished from the former by the fact that they occur inland of the physical coastline. Beaches or dunes may occur on nearshore islands or within nearshore open space, but are given a distinct class of their own due to the significant value attached to them by humans. Analogously, coral reefs or coral atolls are distinguished from nearshore islands (Moberg and Folke 1999). Finally, both mangrove systems and seagrass beds or kelp forests are recognized as a separate ecosystem classes due to their unique ecological features and high levels of productivity (Barbier 2000).

Accurate definition and classification of ecosystem goods and services are also essential preliminary steps in the valuation of coastal and nearshore systems. In this chapter, we adopt a modified version of the newly standardized system developed in the UN-sponsored Millennium Ecosystem Assessment (2005) and adapt that system to a typology of ecosystem goods and services developed in collaboration with colleagues (DeGroot et al. 2002; Farber et al. 2006). The Millennium Assessment (2005) provides a useful way of grouping ecosystem goods and services into four basic categories based on their functional characteristics:

- *Regulating Services*: ecosystems regulate essential ecological processes and life support systems through biogeochemical cycles and other biospheric processes. These include things like disturbance prevention and flood control.
- *Cultural Services*: ecosystems contribute to the maintenance of human health and wellbeing by providing spiritual fulfillment, historic integrity, recreation and aesthetics.

Table 6.1 Number of peer reviewed non-market valuation studies of coastal-marine ecosystems (1970–2006), 70 studies in total

Ecosystem Type	Supporting Services					Regulating Services								Cultural Services				Total Observations
	Nutrient cycling	Net primary production	Pollination and seed dispersal	Habitat	Hydrological cycle	Gas and climate regulation	Disturbance regulation	Biological regulation	Water regulation	Soil retention	Waste regulation	Nutrient regulation	Water supply	Recreation	Aesthetic	Science and education	Spiritual and historic	
Estuaries and Lagoons				2									9	6	5			22
Beaches and Dunes		1		1			2						7	11	3			25
Saltwater Wetlands				3			2						4	9	1		3	23
Nearshore Freshwater Wetlands							1		3				1	5	1		1	11
Seagrass or Kelp beds				1				1						1				3
Nearshore Islands				2			1											4
Coral Reefs and Atolls													1	8				9
Mangrove				1														1
Semi-enclosed Seas				2											1			3
Open Ocean																		0
Nearshore Ocean				4									5	24	1			34
Nearshore Open Space				1									4	13	2			20
Total Observations	0	1	0	17	0	0	6	1	3	0	0	0	31	77	15	0	4	155

123

- *Supporting Services*: ecosystems also provide a range of services that are necessary for the production of the other three service categories. These include nutrient cycling, soil formation and habitat functions.
- *Provisioning Services*: the provisioning function of ecosystems supply a large variety of marketed ecosystem goods and other services for human consumption, ranging from food and raw materials to energy resources.

As this list shows, not all ecosystem goods and services are the same – there is no single category that captures the diversity of what functioning coastal and nearshore systems provide humans. In Table 6.1, we identify studies in the valuation literature, and match them with relevant landscape features and ecosystem goods and services to create a matrix of the best available data. Since this chapter is focused on the non-market values, *provisioning* services are left out of this analysis.

The information depicted in Table 6.1 shows that ecosystem service values can be associated with a variety of coastal and nearshore ecosystems. Numbers in the table represent ecosystem goods and services that have been empirically measured in the non-market valuation literature and the number of observations associated with each 'ecosystem type–ecosystem service' pairing.

VALUATION OF COASTAL AND NEARSHORE MARINE ECOSYSTEM SERVICES

In economic terms, the ecosystem goods and services depicted in Table 6.1 yield a number of important values to humans. When discussing these values, however, we first need to clarify what the underlying concept actually means (Farber et al. 2002). The term 'value' as it is employed in this chapter has its conceptual foundation in economic theory (Freeman 1993). In this limited sense, value can be reflected in two theoretically commensurate empirical measures. First, there is the amount of money people are willing to pay for specific improvements in a good or service – *willingness to pay* (WTP). Second, there is the minimum amount an individual would need to be compensated to accept a specific degradation in a good or service – *willingness to accept compensation* (WAC). Simply put, economic value is the amount of money a person is willing to give up in order to get a thing, or the amount of money required to give up that thing. To date, in the literature WTP has been the dominant measure of economic value. However, WTP is not restricted to what we actually observe from people's transactions in a market. Instead, 'it expresses how much people would be willing to pay for a given good or service, whether or not they actually do so' (Goulder and Kennedy 1997).

A central concern in coastal management is one of making social tradeoffs – allocating scarce resources among society's members. For example, if society wished to make the most of its endowment of coastal resources, it should be possible to compare the value of what society's members receive from any improvement in a given coastal ecosystem with the value of what its members give up to degrade the same system. The prevailing approach to this type of assessment in the literature is cost–benefit analysis (Ableson 1979; Kneese 1984; Turner 2000). Cost–benefit analysis is characterized by a fairly strict decision-making structure: 'defining the project, identifying impacts which are economically relevant, physically quantifying impacts as benefits or costs', and then 'calculating a summary monetary valuation' (Hanley and Spash 1993). Given this approach, a key question comes down to: what gets counted?

In addition to the production of marketable goods, coastal ecosystems provide natural functions such as nutrient recycling as well as conferring aesthetic benefits to humans (Costanza et al. 1997). Coastal goods and services may therefore be divided into two general categories: (1) the provision of direct *market* goods or services such as drinking water, transportation, electricity generation, pollution disposal and irrigation; and (2) the provision of *non-market* goods or services which include things like biodiversity, support for terrestrial and estuarine ecosystems, habitat for plant and animal life and the satisfaction people derive from simply knowing that a beach or coral reef exists.

The market value of ecosystem goods and services are the observed trading ratios for services that are directly traded in the marketplace – that is: price = exchange value. The exchange-based, welfare value of a natural good or service is its market price net of the cost of bringing that service to market. For example, the exchange-based value of fresh fish to society is based on its catch rate and 'value at landing', which is the market price of fish, minus harvest and time management costs. Estimating exchange-based values in this case is relatively simple, as observable trades exist from which to measure value.

Since individuals can be observed making choices between objects in the marketplace while operating within the limits of income and time, economists have developed several market-based measures of value as imputations from these observed choices. While monetary measures of value are not the only possible yardstick, they are convenient since many choices involve the use of money. Hence, if you are observed to pay $9 for a pound of shrimp, the imputation is that you value a pound of shrimp to be at least $9, and are willing to make a tradeoff of $9 worth of other things to obtain that shrimp. The money itself has no intrinsic value, but represents other things you could have purchased. Time is often considered another yardstick of value: if someone spends two hours fishing, the imputation is that the person values the fishing experience to be worth more than two hours spent on other activities. Value is thus a result of the expressed tastes and preferences of persons, and the limited means with which objects can be pursued. As a result, the scarcer the object is, the greater its value will be on the margin.

Box 6.1 – Economic Valuation Techniques to Establish WTP or WTA

Avoided Cost (AC): services allow society to avoid costs that would have been incurred in the absence of those services. For example, flood control provided by barrier islands avoids property damages along the coast.

Replacement Cost (RC): services could be replaced with man-made systems. For example, nutrient cycling waste treatment can be replaced with costly treatment systems.

Factor Income (FI): services provide for the enhancement of incomes. For example, water quality improvements increase commercial fisheries catch and incomes of fishermen.

Travel Cost (TC): service demand may require travel, the costs of which can reflect the implied value of the service. For example, recreation areas attract distant visitors whose value placed on that area must be at least what they were willing to pay to travel to it.

Hedonic Pricing (HP): service demand may be reflected in the prices people will pay for associated goods: For example, housing prices along the coastline tend to exceed the prices of inland homes.

Marginal Product Estimation (MP): service demand is generated in a dynamic modelling environment using production function (that is, Cobb–Douglas) to estimate value of output in response to corresponding material input.

Contingent Valuation (CV): service demand may be elicited by posing hypothetical scenarios that involve some valuation of alternatives. For example, people would be willing to pay for increased preservation of beaches and shoreline.

Group Valuation (GV): This approach is based on principles of deliberative democracy and the assumption that public decision making should not result from the aggregation of separately measured individual preferences, but from *open public debate.*

By estimating the economic value of ecosystem goods and services not traded in the marketplace, the otherwise 'hidden' social costs or benefits are revealed. While measuring exchange values requires monitoring market data for observable trades, non-market values of goods and services are much broader and more difficult to measure. Indeed, it is these non-market values that have captured the attention of environmental and resource economists who have developed a number of techniques for valuing ecosystem goods and services (Bingham et al. 1995; Freeman 1993). When there are no explicit markets for services, more indirect means of assessing economic values must be used. A spectrum of economic valuation techniques commonly used to establish the WTP or WTA when market values do not exist is identified in Box 6.1.

As these brief descriptions suggest, each economic valuation methodology has its own strengths and limitations, thereby restricting its use to a select range of goods and services associated with coastal systems. For example, Travel Cost is useful for estimating recreation values, and Hedonic Pricing (HP) for estimating coastal property values. Rather, a full suite of valuation techniques is required to quantify the economic value of goods and services provided by a naturally functioning coastal-marine ecosystem. By using a range of methods for the same site, the so-called 'total economic value' of a given coastal ecosystem can thus be estimated (Freeman 1993).

Figure 6.2 depicts a model based on the idea of functional diversity, linking different ecosystem structures and processes with the output of specific goods and services, which can then be assigned monetary values using the range of valuation techniques described above. Here, key linkages are made between the diverse structures and processes associated with the coastal zone, the landscape and habitat features that created them, and the goods and services that result. Once delineated, economic values for these goods and services can then be rationally assessed by measuring the diverse set of human preferences for them. In economic terms, the natural assets of the coastal zone can thus yield direct (for example, fishing) and indirect (for example, nutrient cycling) use values as well as non-use (for example, preservation of rare species) values of the coastal system. Once accounted for, these values can then be aggregated to estimate the total value of the entire system (Anderson and Bishop 1986).

In principle, a global picture of the potential economic value associated with the coastal zone can be built up via the aggregation of a number of existing valuation studies. For example, in a preliminary estimate of the total economic value of ecosystem services provided by global systems, Costanza et al. (1997) showed that while the coastal zone, including mangroves, covers only 6.3 per cent of the world's surface, the goods and services provided by it are responsible for approximately 43 per cent of the estimated total value of global ecosystem services: US$14.2 trillion (1997 dollars). While controversial (Pearce 1998; Pimm 1997), this preliminary study made it abundantly clear that coastal ecosystem services do provide an important portion of the total contribution to human welfare on this planet. Furthermore, it demonstrated the need for additional research and indicated the fact that coastal areas are among the most in need of additional study (Costanza 2000).

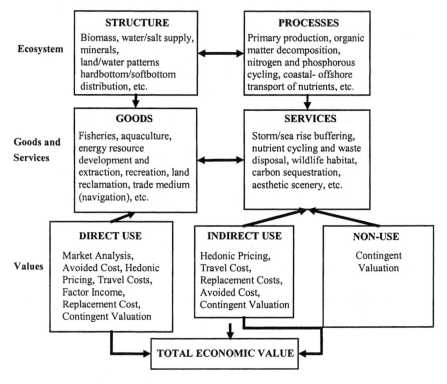

Figure 6.2   Total economic value of coastal-marine ecosystem goods and services

(*Source:* Adapted from Turner 2000, and Wilson et al. 2005)

'Environmental benefit transfer' studies,[1] such as that by Costanza et al. (1997), often form the bedrock of practical policy analysis because only rarely can policy analysts or managers afford the luxury of designing and implementing an original study for every given ecosystem (Wilson and Hoehn 2006). Instead, decision makers must often rely on the limited information that can be gleaned from past empirical studies that are often quite limited or even contradictory (Desvouges et al. 1998; Smith 1992). Primary valuation research, while being a 'first best' strategy, is also very expensive and time consuming. Thus, secondary analysis of the valuation literature is a 'second best' strategy that can nevertheless yield very important information in many scientific and management contexts (Rosenberger and Loomis 2000). When analyzed carefully, information from past studies published in the literature can form a meaningful basis for coastal zone policy and management (Beatley et al. 2002; French 1997). In the final section of this chapter, we demonstrate this integrative approach for coastal and nearshore marine ecosystem service valuation by providing a brief review of case studies drawn from the literature.

LITERATURE REVIEW RESULTS

Empirical valuation data for coastal and nearshore ecosystems often appear scattered throughout the scientific literature and is uneven in quality. To elucidate this unevenness, we present here a review of existing non-market valuation literature in order to provide useful insights for further research in the area. Such an exercise provides scientists, coastal managers and policy makers with a sense of where the science of coastal and nearshore ecosystem valuation has come from, and where it might go in the future. Below we synthesize peer-reviewed economic data on coastal and nearshore ecosystems depicted in Table 6.1.

All information presented below was obtained from studies that were published in peer-reviewed journal or book chapters. They deal *explicitly* with non-market coastal and nearshore ecosystem services measured throughout the world. The literature search involved an intensive review of databases on the World Wide Web available at the University of Vermont. Several keywords such as economic value, economics, valuation, management, coastal, marine, wetland, estuary, mangrove, contingent valuation and ecosystem service and so on, were combined in various patterns to elicit studies that might be relevant to coastal and nearshore ecosystem valuation. This search yielded more than 300 citations. Each citation was then located and reviewed by the authors. About 230 citations (77 per cent) were rejected because they were not peer-reviewed or did not explicitly address the economic valuation of coastal and nearshore ecosystem goods and services. The literature review yielded a total of 70 studies with 155 data observations studies for further analysis and discussion.

Results from these studies were sorted by ecosystem type, ecosystem good and service, valuation methodology and region of study. On this basis, each study was classified as measuring an ecosystem good, service or any combination thereof (several studies report data for more than one good or service). Selected valuation studies for coastal goods or services are discussed in greater detail below.

Our review of the peer-reviewed literature reveals that many different landscape features and ecological processes within the coastal and nearshore marine zone provide essential natural services to humans, but that the reporting of their economic values remains unevenly distributed. For example, as the pattern of data in Figure 6.3 confirms, opportunities for recreation and natural amenities (for example, nearshore fisheries, white sandy beaches) get inordinate attention in the economic literature while other services such as spiritual and historic or biological control do not get much attention at all.

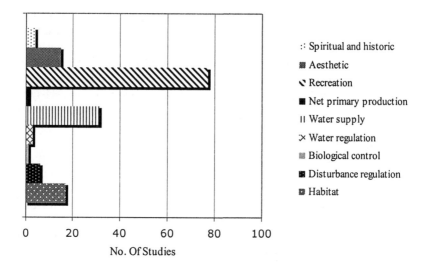

Figure 6.3   Peer-reviewed non-market valuation studies of coastal ecosystems by type of ecosystem service, 1970–2006

Similarly, in Figure 6.4, nearshore ocean, open space, freshwater wetlands and saltwater wetlands, marshes or salt ponds have tended to receive the most attention in the peer-reviewed literature, while areas such as mangroves and coral reefs have received far more limited attention by economists.

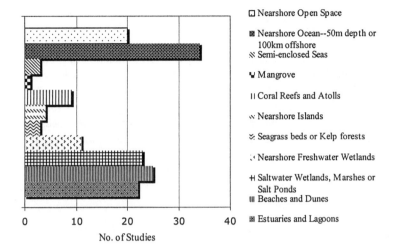

☐ Nearshore Open Space

▓ Nearshore Ocean--50m depth or 100km offshore

⋉ Semi-enclosed Seas

⅃ Mangrove

‖ Coral Reefs and Atolls

⋎ Nearshore Islands

⋩ Seagrass beds or Kelp forests

⦂⋅ Nearshore Freshwater Wetlands

+⊢ Saltwater Wetlands, Marshes or Salt Ponds

⊪ Beaches and Dunes

▨ Estuaries and Lagoons

No. of Studies

Figure 6.4   Peer-reviewed non-market valuation studies of coastal ecosystems by type of ecosystem, 1970–2006

Finally, as Figure 6.5 shows, the vast majority of economic valuation studies in the peer-review literature have been conducted in the US, with other regions such as Europe, Australia and New Zealand lagging behind. While perhaps not surprising, given the early development of environmental and ecological economics as a field of study, the uneven distribution of empirical analyses raises critical issues for decision makers that will need to be addressed in the not-too-distant future (Wilson and Hoehn 2006).

To provide a more in-depth account of the specific types of non-market valuation literature available today, below we briefly review a select group of published valuation studies reported in Table 6.1 and group them according to the type of ecosystem services discussed. As this chapter does not focus specifically on market goods, provisioning services (for example, food, fuel and fibre) are left out of the analysis. The results from each empirical study are reported in their original monetary metric.

Supporting Services

As mentioned previously, the coastal and nearshore marine environment is one of the most productive habitats in the world. Mangroves, eelgrass, salt marsh and intertidal mud flats all provide a variety of services to the public associated with their nursery and habitat functions. Improvements in the ecological integrity of these habitats may ultimately lead to measurable increases in the production of market goods such as fish, birds and wood products. In other cases, ecological productivity itself can represent a unique class of values not captured by traditional market-based valuation methods. Instead, these values represent an increase in the production of higher trophic levels brought about by the increased availability of habitat (Gosselink et al. 1974; Turner et al. 1996). Here, it is critical to realize that one may not, in general, add productivity value estimates to use values estimated using other market-related methodologies (that is, hedonic and travel cost) because to do so would risk double counting some aspects of value, or measuring the same benefits twice (Desvouges et al. 1992, 1998).

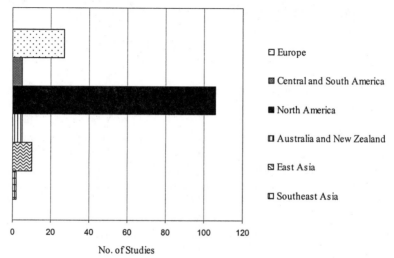

Figure 6.5   Peer-reviewed non-market valuation studies of coastal ecosystems by region, 1970–2006

Valuation studies of the supporting functions provided by coastal and nearshore marine habitat have predominantly focused on the economic value of fishery related services (Barbier 2000; Kaoru et al. 1995; Lynne et al. 1981). Most often, the market price of seafood products is used as a proxy when calculating the non-market value of ecosystem goods provided by coastal and nearshore systems. For example, Farber and Costanza (1987) estimated the productivity of coastal habitat in Terrebonne Parrish, Louisiana, US by attributing commercial values for several species to the net biomass, habitat, and waste treatment of the wetland ecosystem. Arguing that the annual harvest from an ecosystem is a function of the level of environmental quality, the authors chose to focus on the commercial harvest data for five different native species – shrimp, blue crab, oyster, menhaden, and muskrat – to estimate the marginal productivity of wetlands. The annual economic value (marginal product) of each species was estimated in 1983 dollars: shrimp $10.86/acre; blue crab $67/acre; oyster $8.04/acre; menhaden $5.80/acre; and muskrat pelts $12.09/acre. Taken together, the total value marginal productivity of wetlands in Terrebonne Parrish, Louisiana was estimated at $37.46 per acre.

In an earlier study, Lynne et al. (1981) suggested that the value of the coastal marsh in southern Florida could be modelled by assuming that seafood harvest is a direct function of salt-marsh area. The authors then derived the economic value of a specified change in marsh area through the marginal productivity of fishery harvest. For the blue crab fishery in western Florida salt marshes, a marginal productivity of 2.3 lb per year for each acre of marshland was obtained. By linking the market price of harvested blue crab to this estimate, the authors were able to estimate the total present value of a marsh acre in human food (blue crab) production at $3.00 for each acre (with a 10 per cent capitalization rate).

Regulating Services

A critically important service provided by coastal landscapes such as barrier islands, inland wetlands areas, beaches and tidal plains is disturbance prevention. Significant property damages have been attributed to flooding from tidal surges and rainfall as well as wind damage associated with major storm events. For example, Farber (1987) has described an 'Avoided Cost' method for measuring the hurricane protection value of wetlands against wind damage to property in coastal Louisiana, US. Using historical probabilities for storms and wind damage estimates in Louisiana, an expected wind damage function was derived, and from this the author estimated reductions in wind damage from the loss of one mile of wetlands. Based on 1983 US dollars, the expected incremental annual damage from a loss of one mile of wetlands along the Louisiana coastline was $69 857 which, when extrapolated to a per-acre estimate, amounts to $0.44 per acre (Farber 1987).

In another study, Lindsay et al. (1992) measured 985 coastal beach visitors' willingness to pay (WTP) for a dedicated fund for a beach erosion programme in Maine and New Hampshire. Beach erosion had been a substantial problem for many coastal communities, forcing them to choose between active management techniques and the possible loss of valuable waterfront acreage. Using a tobit regression technique, the authors estimated average WTP for beach protection of $30.80 per person in 1992 US dollars.

Cultural Services

Stretches of beach, rocky cliffs, estuarine and coastal marine waterways, and coral reefs provide numerous recreational and scenic opportunities for humans. Boating, fishing, swimming, walking, beachcombing, scuba diving, and sunbathing are among the numerous leisure activities that people enjoy worldwide and thus represent significant economic value. Both travel cost (TC) and Contingent Valuation (CV) methods are commonly used to estimate this value. For example, the Chesapeake Bay estuary on the eastern seaboard of the United States has been the focus of an impressive amount of research on non-market recreational values associated with coastal systems. When attempting to estimate the monetary worth of water quality improvements in Chesapeake Bay, Bocksteal et al. (1989) focused on recreational benefits because it was assumed that most of the increase in wellbeing associated with such improvements would accrue to recreationists. The authors estimated the average increases in economic value for beach use, boating, swimming, and fishing due to a 20 per cent reduction in total nitrogen and phosphorus introduced into the estuary. Using a combination of CV and TC methods, the annual aggregate WTP for a moderate improvement in the Chesapeake Bay's water quality was estimated to be in the range of $10 to $100 million in 1984 US dollars (Bocksteal et al. 1989). In a similar study, Kawabe and Oka (1996) used TC to estimate the aggregate recreational benefit (viewing the bay, clam digging, bathing, sailing, snorkelling and surfing) from improving nitrogen contamination of Tokyo Bay at 53.2 billion yen. Using the CV method, the authors also estimated the aggregate value of improving chemical oxygen demand to reduce the reddish-brown colour of the bay at 458.3 billion yen (Kawabe and Oka 1996).

Open space, proximity to clean water, and scenic vistas are often cited as a primary attractor of residents who own property and live within the coastal fringe (Beach 2002). Hedonic pricing (HP) techniques have thus been used to show that the price of coastal housing units vary with respect to characteristics such as ambient environmental quality (that is, proximity to shoreline, water quality) because buyers will bid up the price of units with more of a desirable attribute (Johnston et al. 2001). For example, Leggett and Bockstael (2000) use hedonic techniques to show that water quality has a significant effect on property values along the Chesapeake Bay. The authors use a measure of water quality – faecal coliform bacteria counts – that has serious human health implications and for which detailed, spatially explicit information from monitoring is available. The data used in this hedonic analysis consist of sales of waterfront property on the western shore of the Chesapeake Bay that occurred between 1993 and 1997 (Leggett and Bockstael 2000). The authors consider the effect of a hypothetical localized improvement in observed faecal coliform counts – 100 counts per 100ml – on a set of 41 residential parcels. The projected increase in property values due to the hypothetical reduction totals approximately $230,000. Extending the analysis to calculate an upper bound benefit for 494 properties, the authors estimate the benefits of improving water quality at all sites at $12.145 million (Leggett and Bockstael 2000).

DISCUSSION

Ecosystem goods and services form a fundamental connective link between people and ecological systems. In this chapter, we have shown how coastal and nearshore marine ecosystem goods and services not commonly traded in the marketplace contribute significantly to human welfare. Using an integrated framework developed for the assessment of ecosystem goods and services, we have considered how ecological structures and processes, land-use decisions, and human values interact in the coastal and nearshore marine environment. The concept of ecosystem goods and services has thus allowed us to analyze how human beings as welfare-maximizing agents actively translate complex ecological structures and processes into value-laden entities.

The literature reviewed here demonstrates both the opportunities and the challenges inherent in estimating the total economic value of coastal ecosystem goods and services. As the pattern of data in Table 6.1 suggests, one of the major insights from our analysis is the discrepancy between the ecosystem goods and services that have been documented in the published valuation literature and those that could potentially contribute significantly to human welfare, both directly and indirectly. Accounting for these missing economic values represents a significant challenge for scientists, planners and decision makers involved in coastal zone and nearshore marine management.

Through laws and rules, land-use management and policy decisions, individuals and social groups ultimately will make tradeoffs between these values as they continue to live, work and play in the coastal zone. In turn, these land-use decisions will directly modify the structures and processes of the coastal zone through engineering and construction and/or indirectly by modifying the physical, biological and chemical processes of the natural system. Resource managers and ecologists should therefore be aware that non-use values have been shown to comprise a sizeable portion of total economic value associated with coastal and nearshore ecosystems.

As we have shown, assigning economic values to landscape features and habitat functions of coastal and nearshore ecosystems requires a fuller understanding of the nature of the natural systems upon which they rest. Ecosystem structures and processes are influenced by long-term, large-scale biophysical drivers (that is, tectonic pressures, global weather patterns) which in turn create the necessary conditions for providing the ecosystem goods and services people value. Ecological information must be thoroughly integrated before a meaningful assessment of economic value can be made. This is a formidable challenge, but we believe that the classification system presented in section 3 of this chapter provides a critical first step.

We conclude with the observation that the most non-market valuation studies to date have been performed for a relatively small subset of coastal and nearshore marine ecosystem goods and services at a limited number of sites in the world. Hence, our ability to generalize from studies presented in this review remains limited but promises to grow as more environmental valuation studies are done (Wilson and Hoehn 2006). The observations and results presented here provide valuable insights into the challenges and limitations of ecosystem service valuation as it is currently being practised. The experiences summarized should be useful to ecologists, managers, and social scientists as they collaborate to estimate the future direction for development in the coastal and nearshore marine environment.

NOTE

1. The 'benefit transfer method' enables valuation data, which is collected in other surveys, to be used in a new location/context without the need to re-survey. This is done so analysts don't need to repeat (expensive) evaluation surveys. For example, values for 'recreational use of coral reef' in country 'x' could be transferred to country 'y' with appropriate adjustments and caveats. Wilson and Hoehn (2006) review benefit transfer methods that can be used in a special edition of the journal *Ecological Economics*, which they edited.

REFERENCES

Ableson, P. (1979), *Cost Benefit Analysis and Environmental Problems*, London: Saxon House.
Anderson, G.D. and R.C. Bishop (1986), 'The valuation problem', in D.W. Bromley (ed.), *Natural Resource Economics: Policy Problems and Contemporary Analysis*, Boston, MA: Liuwer Nijoff Publishing, pp. 89–137.

Argady, T., J. Alder, P. Dayton, S. Curran, A. Kitchingman, M.A.Wilson, A. Catenazzi, J. Restrepo, C. Birkeland, S. Blaber, S. Saifullah, G. Branch, D. Boersma, S. Nixon, P. Dugan and N. Davidson, C. Vorosmarty (2005), 'Coastal systems: an assessment of ecosystem services, in millennium ecosystem assessment', in R. Hassan, R. Scholes and N. Ash (eds), *Ecosystems and Human Well-Being: Current States and Trends Vol. 1*, Washington, DC: Island Press, pp. 515–49.

Barbier, E.B. (2000), 'Valuing the environment as input: review of applications to mangrove-fishery linkages', *Ecological Economics*, **35**: 47–61.

Beach, D. (2002), *Coastal Sprawl: The Effects of Urban Design on Aquatic Ecosystems in the United States*, Arlington, VA: Pew Oceans Commission.

Beatley, T., D.J. Brower and A.J. Schwab (2002), *An Introduction to Coastal Zone Management*, Washington, DC: Island Press.

Bingham, G., R. Bishop, M. Brody, D. Bromley, E. Clark, W. Cooper, R. Costanza, T. Hale, G. Hayden, S. Kellert, R. Norgaard, B. Norton, J. Payne, C. Russell, G. Suter (1995), 'Issues in ecosystem valuation: improving information for decision making', *Ecological Economics*, **14**: 73–90.

Bockstael, N.E., K.E. McConnell and I.E. Strand (1989), 'Measuring the benefits of improvements in water quality: the Chesapeake Bay', *Marine Resource Economics*, **6**: 1–18.

Boumans, R.M.J., R. Costanza, J. Farley, M.A. Wilson, J. Rotmans, F. Villa, R. Portela and M. Grasso, (2002), 'Modelling the dynamics of the integrated earth system and the value of global ecosystem services using the GUMBO model', *Ecological Economics*, **41**: 529–60.

Costanza, R. (2000), 'The ecological, economic and social importance of the oceans', in C.R.C. Sheppard (ed.), *Seas at the Millennium: An Environmental Evaluation*, New York: Pergamon, pp. 393–403.

Costanza, R., R. d'Arge, R. deGroot, S. Farber, M. Grasso, B. Hannon, K. Limburg, S. Naeem, R.V. O'Neill, J. Paruelo, R.G. Raskin, P. Sutton and M. van den Belt, (1997), 'The value of the world's ecosystem services and natural capital', *Nature*, **387**: 253–60.

Costanza, R. and C. Folke (1997), 'Valuing ecosystem services with efficiency, fairness, and sustainability as goals', in Gretchen D. Daily (ed.), *Nature's Services*, Washington, DC: Island Press, pp. 49–68.

Daily, G.C. (1997), *Nature's Services: Societal Dependence on Natural Ecosystems*, Washington, DC: Island Press.

DeGroot, R., M.A. Wilson and R.M. Boumans (2002), 'A typology for the classification, description, and valuation of ecosystem functions, goods and services', *Ecological Economics*, **41**: 393–408.

Desvouges, W.H., F.R. Johnson, H.S. Banzhaf (1998), *Environmental Policy Analysis with Limited Information: Principles and Applications of the Transfer Method*, Cheltenham, UK and Lyme, US: Edward Elgar.

Desvousges, W.H., M.C. Naughton and G.R. Parsons (1992), 'Benefit transfer: conceptual problems in estimating water-quality benefits using existing studies', *Water Resources Research*, **28**: 675–83.

Farber, S. (1987), 'The value of coastal wetlands for the protection of property against hurricane wind damage', *Journal of Environmental Economics and Management*, **14**: 143–51.

Farber, S. and R. Costanza (1987), 'The economic value of wetlands systems', *Journal of Environmental Management*, **24**: 41–51.

Farber, S., R. Costanza, D. Childers, J. Erickson, K. Gross, M. Grove, C. Hopkinson, J.R. Kahn, S. Pincetl, A. Troy, P. Warren and M.A. Wilson (2006), 'Linking ecology and economics for ecosystem management', *Bioscience*, **56**: 117–29.

Farber, S., R. Costanza and M.A. Wilson (2002), 'Economic and ecological concepts for valuing ecosystem services', *Ecological Economics*, **41**: 375–92.

Freeman, M. (1993), *The Measurement of Environmental and Resource Values: Theory and Methods.* Washington DC: Resources for the Future.

French, P.W. (1997), *Coastal and Estuarine Management*, New York: Routledge.

Gosselink, J.G., E.G. Odum and R.M. Pope (1974), *The Value of the Tidal Marsh*, Center for Wetland Resources: Louisiana State University.

Goulder, L.H. and D. Kennedy (1997), 'Valuing ecosystem services: philosophical bases and empirical methods', in Gretchen C. Daily (ed.), *Nature's Services: Societal Dependence on Natural Ecosystems*, Washington, DC: Island Press, pp. 23–48.

Hanley, N. and C. Spash (1993), *Cost–Benefit Analysis and the Environment*, Aldershot, UK and Brookfield, US: Edward Elgar.

Heal, G.M., E.B. Barbier, K.J. Boyle, A.P. Covich, S.P. Gloss, C.H. Hershner, J.P. Hoehn, C.M. Pringle, S. Polasky, K. Segerson and K. Schrader-Frechette (2005), *Valuing Ecosystem Services: Toward Better Environmental Decision-Making*, Washington, DC: The National Academies Press.

Johnston, R.J., J.J. Opaluch, T.A. Grigalunas and M.J. Mazzotta (2001), 'Estimating amenity benefits of coastal farmland', *Growth and Change*, **32**: 305–25.

Kaoru, Y., V.K. Smith and J.L. Liu (1995), 'Using random utility-models to estimate the recreational value of estuarine resources', *American Journal of Agricultural Economics*, **77**: 141–51.

Kawabe, M. and T. Oka (1996), 'Benefit from improvement of organic contamination of Tokyo Bay', *Marine Pollution Bulletin*, **32**: 788–93.

Kneese, A. (1984), *Measuring the Benefits of Clean Air and Water*, Washington, DC: Resources for the Future.

Leggett, C.G. and N.E. Bockstael (2000), 'Evidence on the effects of water quality on residential land prices', *Journal of Environmental Economics and Management*, **39**: 121–44.

Lindsay, B.E., J.M. Halstead, H.C. Tupper and J.J. Vaske (1992), 'Factors influencing the willingness to pay for coastal beach protection', *Coastal Management*, **20**: 291–302.

Lynne, G.D., P. Conroy and F.J. Prochaska (1981), 'Economic valuation of marsh areas for marine production processes', *Journal of Environmental Economics and Management*, **8**: 175–86.

Millennium Ecosystem Assessment (2005), *Ecosystems and Human Well-Being: A Framework for Assessment*, Washington, DC: Island Press.

Moberg, F. and C. Folke (1999), 'Ecological goods and services of coral reef ecosystems', *Ecological Economics*, **29**: 215–33.

Pearce, D. (1998), 'Auditing the earth', *Environment*, **40**: 23–8.

Pimm, S.L. (1997), 'The value of everything', *Nature*, **387**: 231–2.

Rosenberger, R.S. and J.B. Loomis (2000), 'Using meta-analysis for benefit transfer: in-sample convergent validity tests of an outdoor recreation database', *Water Resources Research*, **36**: 1097–107.

Smith, V.K. (1992), 'On separating defensible benefit transfers from "smoke and mirrors"', *Water Resources Research*, **28**: 685–94.

Turner, R.K. (2000), 'Integrating natural and socio-economic science in coastal management', *Journal of Marine Systems*, **25**: 447–60.

Turner, R.K., S. Subak and W.N. Adger (1996), 'Pressures, trends and impacts in coastal zones: interactions between socioeconomic and natural systems', *Environmental Management*, **20**: 159–73.

Wilson, M.A. and J.P. Hoehn (eds) (2006), 'Special issue. Environmental benefits transfer: methods, applications and new directions', *Ecological Economics*, **60**(2): 335–342.

Wilson, M.A., A. Troy and R. Costanza (2004), 'The economic geography of ecosystem goods and services: revealing the monetary value of landscapes through transfer methods and Geographic Information System", in M. Dietrich and Van der Straaten (eds), *Cultural Landscapes and Land Use*, Boston, MA: Kluwer Academic.

Wilson, M.A., R. Costanza, R.M.J. Boumans and S.L. Liu (2005), 'Integrated assessment and valuation of ecosystem goods and services provided by coastal systems', in James G. Wilson (ed.), *The Intertidal Ecosystem*, Dublin, Ireland: Royal Irish Academy Press, pp. 1–24.

7. Ecological Shadow Prices and Contributory Value: A Biophysical Approach to Valuing Marine Ecosystems

Murray Patterson

A recurrent theme in ecological economics literature is the call for valuation methods that are more biophysical/biocentric, to provide a counterbalance to the anthropocentric valuation methods used in neoclassical economics and which were reviewed in the last chapter (Cleveland et al. 1984, Proops 2003). Ecological shadow pricing, as developed in this chapter, is seen as a constructive move in this direction, being based on measuring 'biophysical interdependencies' (or contributory values) implicit in ecological systems. Although some of these biophysical interdependencies are clearly a result of human interventions, and hence indirectly reflect human preferences, ecological pricing does, however, tend to highlight species and ecological functions that may not usually be detected by other valuation methods such as WTP (Costanza et al. 1991). For example, it is unlikely that the value of phytoplankton in the ecosystem would be measured in a WTP survey, whereas in ecological pricing the value of phytoplankton would be taken account of by the forward and backward linkages they have with other components of the ecosystem. In this sense, ecological pricing is more biocentric than neoclassical valuation methods that tend to have a more anthropocentric emphasis (Hannon 1998).

Ecological prices are 'shadow prices' inferred from data (energy and mass flows) that describe the ecological processes that support human and non-human activity. Inferred prices or 'shadow prices' are frequently used tool in economics where real markets don't exist for a good. For example, 'hedonic pricing', as used in resource/environmental economics, *statistically infers the price of an environmental good* based on observing differences in property values, wages and other phenomena. Ecological prices are *relative prices,* which means any commodity can be used as the numeraire-commodity resulting in the same relativities between prices. In this chapter monetary units are used as numeraire as these units are readily understood but in addition solar units are also used in one example.

COMPONENTS OF CONTRIBUTORY VALUE IN ECOSYSTEMS

The idea of 'contributory value', as advocated by Ulanowicz (1991), is important in the ecological pricing approach to valuation. Contributory value refers to the 'contribution' that one ecological entity or compartment makes to the existence of another – for example, plankton provides contributory value to a fish species, as it is a source of food for fish. The 'ecological entities' being referred aren't necessarily human or even known to humans. Therefore, the idea of contributory value *can be* defined in terms of the 'needs' of non-human species and in this way it can be considered to be a more biocentric valuation concept.

The concept of contributory value can be illustrated and appreciated by referring to Figure 7.1. This figure depicts some simplified structural relationships in the Schlei Fjord ecosystem (Germany), an example that is analyzed later in this chapter. Essentially, this figure shows that the contributory value has two aspects in any ecosystem – 'donor value' where an ecological compartment donates value to another ecological compartment, and 'receiver value' where an ecological compartment receives value to another ecological compartment.

Donor Value Only – Ecological Compartments that only have Forward Linkages

Some ecological compartments only have *forward linkages* (or forward interdependencies) in the ecosystem. That is, *they only donate value* to other compartments further up the food web. Solar energy is a good example of such an ecological compartment in the Schlei Fjord ecosystem (see Figure 7.1). In the Schlei ecosystem, solar energy directly 'donates value' to phytoplankton; and indirectly 'donates' value to other compartments in the food web that depend on phytoplankton, via so-called forward linkages. These ecological compartments that only have forward linkages are said to be *primary inputs* into the ecosystem, as they are not produced by the ecosystem. They are important as they are the source of all value that flows through ecological systems.

At the global scale, primary inputs include not only solar energy, which is often assumed to be the case, but also inputs of gravitational energy, geothermal energy, nuclear energy and lunar energy. There are also inputs of mass into the biosphere (for example, meteorites), although these are very small and normally trivial. At the ecosystem level, however, the system is typically more much more *open* in character with a wider array of primary inputs of mass and energy.

Receiver Value Only – Ecological Compartments that only have Backward Linkages

Some ecological compartments only have *backward linkages* (or backward interdependencies). In the Schlei Fjord ecosystem, 'harvested fish' is an example of such an ecological compartment (see Figure 7.1). Such ecological compartments, by definition, directly and indirectly only 'receive' value from other ecological compartments. They do not donate value (via mass and energy flows) to any other compartments in the ecosystem. The value of such compartments is therefore solely defined by their backwards linkages – that is, the embodied (direct and indirect) inputs required to produce one unit of the compartments' output.

To some extent, the existence of these types of ecological compartments that only have 'receiver' value is just *an artifact of where the system's boundary is drawn*. For instance, in Figure 7.1, the system's boundary is drawn at 'harvested fish' which by definition does not permit any forward linkages from harvested fish. In actuality, however, 'harvested fish' does have forward linkages, namely 'harvested fish' → consumed by humans → human wastes → sewerage system effluent → aquatic biomass → etc. These forward linkages are analytically ignored in Figure 7.1 and overlooked in the calculation of the ecological prices, because they are outside the system boundary for the Schlei Fjord ecosystem.

Both Donor and Receiver Value – Ecological Compartments with both Backward and Forward Linkages

Most ecological compartments and species that are encountered in real-world ecosystems have *both backward and forward linkages*. That is, they both receive and donate value and therefore their ecological function is to 'transfer value' through the system.

In the Schlei Fjord ecosystem, for example, zooplankton has backward linkages directly to phytoplankton, and then indirectly back to the system's primary input of solar energy (see Figure 7.2).

Zooplankton also has a direct backward linkage to detritus and therefore has a whole set of indirect backward linkages to all the ecosystem compartments that produce detritus. As well as these backward linkages, zooplankton also has forward linkages to planktivores and small fish and eventually further up the food chain to medium and apex predators. Zooplankton is, therefore, an example of an ecological compartment that is a receiver and donator of value, and hence a compartment that transfers value in the Schlei Fjord ecosystem.

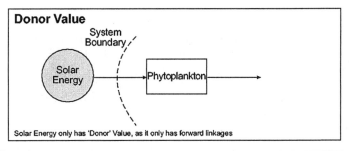

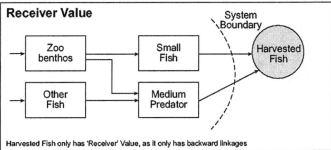

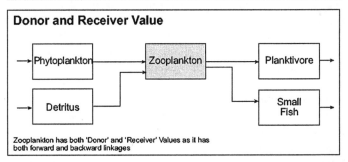

Figure 7.1 Components of contributory value using simplified diagrams for the Schlei ecosystem

ECOLOGICAL PRICING APPROACH TO CONTRIBUTORY VALUE

As argued elsewhere by Patterson (1998b, 2002), the ecological pricing approach provides an operational measure of the contributory value concept, as it explicitly measures forward and backward linkages in the ecosystem, and summarizes these data in one indicator. Ecological compartments are evaluated in terms of how efficiently they 'donate' or 'receive' value from other compartments. The ecological pricing approach, which measures these interdependencies between ecological and economic compartments, has been advocated by a number of ecological economists including Costanza and Neill (1984), England (1986), Judson (1989), Patterson (1998a), Hannon (1998) and Klauer (2000). The idea, however, actually has a long history in economics and somewhat more recent antecedents in ecological thinking, which are reviewed by Patterson (2002).

What are Ecological Prices?

Price, whether a market or ecological price, measures 'the *value* of a commodity, per physical unit of that commodity'[1] – for example, so many dollars per tonne of apples. 'Value' is usually measured in terms of monetary units but can with equal theoretical justification be measured in terms of any 'numeraire-commodity'. In ecological pricing, usually 'value' is measured in terms of an 'ecological numeraire' – for example, in solar energy equivalents. However, as shown elsewhere by Patterson (2002), ecological prices can actually be measured using any the system quantities including money, and *the same relative prices result*. Indeed, it is often sensible to use money as the numeraire-commodity as this enhances the communication of the analytical results to audiences more accustomed monetary measures of value.[2]

Market prices are *real* in the sense that they measure the real exchange value of a commodity as observed in markets. Ecological prices are *implied or shadow prices*, based on the biophysical interdependencies between ecological commodities that exist in ecosystems. Incidentally, shadow prices are often used in resource and environmental economics when a real market doesn't exist for a commodity.

Probably the most important difference between 'market prices' and 'ecological prices' is that 'ecological prices' are based on the *biophysical interdependencies in the system (forward and backward linkages)*, while 'market prices' are measurements based on consumer preferences and 'willingness to pay', and other factors that determine the exchange value in markets. 'Ecological prices' implicitly exist in nature. They do not require a human valuer or even a human presence in ecosystems.

This issue of how to 'commensurate' different quantities (in different units) to take account of qualitative differences is central to the idea of 'ecological pricing', and is further discussed by Patterson (1998b). For example, a joule of incident solar energy is not equivalent to a joule of metabolic energy in harvested fish, because it takes many joules of solar energy to produce this metabolic energy as it is concentrated along the food chain. It would, therefore, be incorrect simply to add a joule of solar energy and a joule of metabolic energy without some sort of commensuration, as they are of differing qualities. This issue becomes even more evident when there is a need to compare or add-up quantities that are measured in different units – for example, how to compare a gram of marine detritus with a joule of solar energy. This 'mixed units' or 'commensuration' problem was first raised in the marine ecology context by Costanza and Hannon (1989), who outlined an ecological pricing approach to resolve this problem. Odum (1996) developed a similar concept called EMERGY analysis, which is also based on commensurating energy types in terms of equivalence factors called transformities.

The calculation of ecological prices, as discussed by Patterson (2002), also has linkages to economic theory. Ecological pricing is based on classical economics ideas of 'cost of production', where the value of a commodity was seen to be a result of the labour inputs (cost). In the 1960s, this cost-of-production approach was resurrected and formalized in terms of matrix algebra by Sraffa (1960) in his landmark publication *Production of Commodities by Means of Commodities*.

Simple Numerical Example of the Determination of Ecological Prices

For illustrative purposes, consider the following marine ecosystem, which consists of the following processes described in incommensurable units:[3]

  100 GJ solar energy $\rightarrow$ 50 kg phytoplankton

  46 kg phytoplankton + 6 kg detritus $\rightarrow$ 36 kg zooplankton

  4 kg phytoplankton + 26 kg zooplankton $\rightarrow$ 30 kg detritus

These flows can be described in terms of a system of simultaneous linear equations:

$$100\beta_1 = 50\beta_2 \qquad (7.1)$$
$$46\beta_2 + 6\beta_4 = 36\beta_3$$
$$4\beta_2 + 26\beta_3 = 30\beta_4$$

Any one of the quantities (GJ solar energy, kg phytoplankton, kg zooplankton, kg detritus) can be used as the numeraire in order to solve these equations. If solar energy is used as numeraire (as is conventionally the case), then the unique solution to these equations is:

$\beta_1 = 1$ (by definition)
$\beta_2 = 2.00$
$\beta_3 = 3.04$
$\beta_4 = 2.90$

These beta (β) values are the 'ecological prices' or shadow prices of the respective ecological commodities considered in this example. They are expressed in terms of multiples of the selected numeraire (solar energy, GJ), but the same 'relative prices' result irrespective of which quantity is arbitrarily used as the numeraire – that is, the relativities between $\beta_1, \beta_2, \beta_3,$ and β_4 do not vary according to the selection of the numeraire.

Implicit in these ecological prices are the following set of equivalencies:

1 GJ or solar energy ⟺ 1 GJ of solar energy equivalents (by definition)
1 kg of phytoplankton ⟺ 2.00 GJ of solar energy equivalents
1 kg of zooplankton ⟺ 3.04 GJ of solar energy equivalents
1 kg of detritus ⟺ 2.90 GJ of solar energy equivalents.

Like any properly mathematically defined 'equivalence', these relationships are reflexive, symmetrical and most importantly transitive.

Mathematical Determination of Ecological Prices in 'Square Matrix Systems'

Conventional matrix algebra can be used for these systems of equations, so-called 'square matrix systems'.[4] In this chapter, the 'simple numerical example' (equation 7.3) and the 'Schlei Fjord ecosystem example' (equation 7.7) both represent 'square matrix systems'. Such systems, by definition, are overdetermined by one degree of freedom (that is, they have one more quantity than the number of processes). The determination of ecological prices for this type of systems can be compactly described in matrix notation. That is, the *inputs and outputs of processes* can be described by:

$$\mathbf{W}\beta = \mathbf{V}\beta \qquad (7.2)$$

where:

W = matrix $(m \times n)$ representing n inputs into m processes in the ecological-economic system, measured in physical units, known.

V = matrix $(m \times n)$ representing n outputs into m processes in the ecological-economic system, measured in physical units, known.

β = vector $(n \times 1)$ of n prices for each quantity, to be solved for.

For such a system, the price vector **β** can readily be determined by using straightforward matrix algebra. That is, by rearrangement we have:

$$(\mathbf{V} - \mathbf{W})\boldsymbol{\beta} = 0 \qquad (7.3)$$

More compactly, let $\mathbf{V} - \mathbf{W} = \mathbf{X}$:

$$\mathbf{X}\boldsymbol{\beta} = 0 \qquad (7.4)$$

One of the columns in **X** is used as the numeraire, and is defined as the column vector **y** after it has been multiplied by the scalar -1.[5] With the removal of this column from **X**, the resultant matrix becomes **Z**. Therefore, we have:

$$\mathbf{Z}\boldsymbol{\beta} = \mathbf{y} \qquad (7.5)$$

To solve for the ecological shadow prices **β** we have:

$$\boldsymbol{\beta} = \mathbf{Z}^{-1}\mathbf{y} \qquad (7.6)$$

The matrix **Z** is square (rows = columns) and therefore can readily be inverted using standard methods. As it turns out, the choice of the numeraire **y** is purely arbitrary, as the relativities between the elements in the solution vector **β** remain constant.

ECOLOGICAL PRICES IN THE SCHLEI FJORD ECOSYSTEM

This example focuses on the determination of ecological shadow prices for the Schlei Fjord ecosystem in 1984. It primarily draws on data originally collected by Nauen (1984), and then manipulated by Christensen and Pauly (1992), using the Ecopath II software, in order to obtain a steady-state model of the ecosystem.

Characteristics of the Schlei Fjord System

The Schlei Fjord is a narrow inlet of the Baltic Sea in North Germany, being a remnant of the last glaciation. It is a 43 km long, 3.4 km wide tidal fjord with 135 km of coastline (Kesting et al. 1996). It is a brackish and eutrophified ecosystem. Salinity gradually decreases from the western Baltic surface level of the fjord to the inner parts. Except for very narrow parts where high current velocities prevail, there are extensive areas at the bottom that are mud-covered (Nauen 1984).

There is a long history of fishing in the Schlei Fjord which Nauen (1984) traces traced back to King Christian I of Denmark in 1480. Nauen's analysis shows that only a very small component of the net primary production of the fjord ecosystem is passed onto the fish components – most is diverted into the detritus drain, bacterial growth and the expansion of H_2S mud. Data presented by Nauen showed that 'degradation of the environment' had in fact resulted in steadily decreasing freshwater fish yield in the decades leading up to 1984. The main types of fish caught in the Schlei Fjord were: Apex Predators (Pike, Pike Perch), Medium Predators (Perch, Eel, Flounder), White Fishes (Roach, Bream) and Pelagic Filter Feeders (Smelt, Herring).

Input–Output Model of the Schlei Fjord Ecosystem

A model of the Schlei Fjord ecosystem can be constructed from data on mass flows obtained from Christensen and Pauly (1992), supplemented by data on fish prices from Eurostat (2006) and solar insolation for ecosystems at latitude (54° 36′ N) and longitude (9° 51′ E). This model is diagrammatically depicted in Figure 7.2, which enumerates the flows of mass between 11 ecological compartments (phytoplankton, detritus, zooplankton, zoobenthos, planktivore, temporary planktivore, white fish, small fish, apex predator, fishing). In addition, solar energy input into the system is enumerated in energy terms. This model demonstrates that only 446 tonnes/yr (0.4 per cent) of the net primary production of 117 100 tonnes/yr is caught fish. A very of the net primary production of 117 100 tonnes/yr is caught fish. A very significant amount of this net primary production (72.4 per cent) is lost from the system due to respiration, with a further 27.2 per cent being exported from the fjord to the Baltic Sea as detritus.

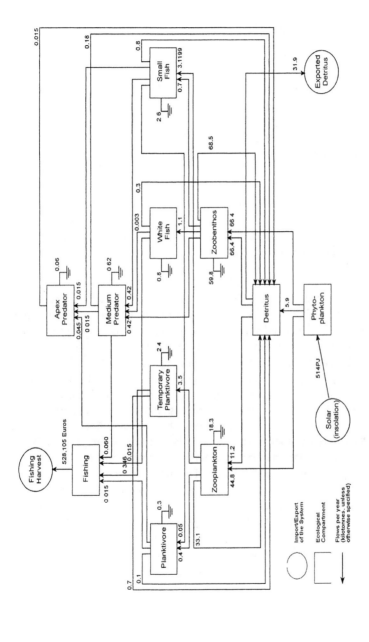

Figure 7.2 Input–output model of the Schlei Fjord ecosystem; in kilotonnes/yr, except 'fishing harvest' in Euros/yr and 'solar insolation' in PJ/yr

Determination of the Ecological Shadow Prices for the Schlei Fjord

The following system of simultaneous linear equations that describe the mass/energy flows in the Schlei Fjord ecosystem (as described by Figure 7.2)[6] were solved in order to determine the ecological prices for each quantity (compartment) in the system:

$$5.85\beta_3 + 33.13\beta_4 + 68.48\beta_5 + 0.09\beta_6 + 0.71\beta_7 + 0.23\beta_8 + 0.80\beta_9 \qquad (7.7)$$
$$+ \ 0.18\beta_{10} + 0.02\beta_{11} = 109.47\beta_2$$
$$514.17\beta_1 = 117.07\beta_3$$
$$11.21\beta_2 + 44.82\beta_3 = 37.76\beta_4$$
$$66.40\beta_2 + 66.40\beta_3 = 73.04\beta_5$$
$$0.42\beta_4 + 0.05\beta_9 = 0.15\beta_6$$
$$3.45\beta_4 = 1.05\beta_7$$
$$1.07\beta_5 = 0.27\beta_8$$
$$0.77\beta_4 + 3.07\beta_5 = 1.28\beta_9$$
$$0.42\beta_5 + 0.05\beta_8 + 0.42\beta_9 = 0.26\beta_{10}$$
$$0.05\beta_6 + 0.02\beta_9 + 0.02\beta_{10} = 0.02\beta_{11}$$
$$0.02\beta_6 + 0.35\beta_7 + 0.02\beta_8 + 0.06\beta_{10} = 528.10\beta_{12}$$

Each of these equations describes the production of each compartment (quantity) in the Schlei Fjord ecosystem – namely, the flow of inputs into each compartment (left-hand side of equation) required to produce the output of the compartment (on right-hand side of the equation). These compartments include: (1) Detritus, (2) Phytoplankton, (3) Zooplankton, (4) Zoobenthos, (5) Planktivore, (6) Temporary Planktivore, (7) White Fish, (8) Small Fish, (9) Medium Predator, (10) Apex Predator, (11) Harvested Fish. The first simultaneous equation describes the production of the first compartment 'Detritus'; the second equation describes the production of the second compartment 'Phytoplankton; and so on. One of the compartments, 'solar energy', has no equation that describes its production because solar energy is a primary input into the ecosystem, and therefore is not produced by the ecosystem. In these equations (7.2), the ecological prices are denoted by β_2 ....β_{12} of the respective quantities (compartments), with β_1 being the ecological price of solar energy. The flows of solar energy are measured in petajoules of solar insolation, the flows of harvested fish are measured in 10^3 Euro (2001 prices), and all other flows are measured in kilotonnes.

By setting the coefficient for solar energy to unity ($\beta_1=1$), the following ecological shadow prices for the Schlei Fjord ecosystem are determined:

4.39 solar energy equivalents (PJ) per 1 ktonne of phytoplankton
9.82 solar energy equivalents (PJ) per 1 ktonne of zooplankton
18.09 solar energy equivalents (PJ) per 1 ktonne of zoobenthos
42.49 solar energy equivalents (PJ) per 1 ktonne of planktivore
32.12 solar energy equivalents (PJ) per 1 ktonne of temporary planktivore
71.37 solar energy equivalents (PJ) per 1 ktonne of white fish
49.31 solar energy equivalents (PJ) per 1 ktonne of small fish
119.42 solar energy equivalents (PJ) per 1 ktonne of medium predator
295.59 solar energy equivalents (PJ) per 1 ktonne of apex predator
0.04 solar energy equivalents (PJ) per Euros (10^3) caught fish
15.51 solar energy equivalents (PJ) per 1 ktonne of detritus
1.00 solar energy equivalents (PJ) per 1 PJ of solar energy

By setting the coefficient of any other quantity to unity, the same 'relative prices' will result. For example, by setting β_{12} to unity, the following ecological shadow prices for the Schlei Fjord ecosystem are determined:

115.90 Euros (10^3) per 1 ktonne of phytoplankton
259.00 Euros (10^3) per 1 ktonne of zooplankton
477.30 Euros (10^3) per 1 ktonne of zoobenthos
1115.60 Euros (10^3) per 1 ktonne of planktivore
847.40 Euros (10^3) per 1 ktonne of temporary planktivore
1882.80 Euros (10^3) per 1 ktonne of white fish
1301.00 Euros (10^3) per 1 ktonne of small fish
3150.50 Euros (10^3) per 1 ktonne of medium predator
7798.20 Euros (10^3) per 1 ktonne of apex predator
1.00 Euros (10^3) per Euros (10^3) of caught fish
6109.20 Euros (10^3) per 1 ktonne of detritus
26.40 Euros (10^3) per 1 PJ of solar energy

These price data illustrate that the choice of numeraire in the solution process is arbitrary – that is, the 'relative prices' are the same. For example, ratio between zooplankton and phytoplankton prices is always 2.23, irrespective of the choice of numeraire.

'Ecological' Interpretation of the Results

For ecologists, the ecological prices reported in solar energy equivalents would seem to be 'very familiar'. Indeed, if the denominator in these ratios was expressed in 'available energy' terms, these ecological prices would be exactly the same units as Odum's (1996) 'transformity' measures – that is, solar energy equivalents per unit of available energy.

As matter (or energy) flows up the trophic levels in the ecosystem, there are losses due to respiration at each step. Ecologists measure these losses in terms of 'trophic chain efficiency', which is the energy output divided by the energy input for each trophic (food) chain step. The losses become very much more magnified the further you move up the trophic levels due to the multiplicative effect of combining the efficiencies of each individual step. In other words, very little matter (or energy) ends up getting to the highest trophic levels due to the cumulative effects of these 'inefficiencies'. This cumulative effect is reflected in the ecological prices for the Schlei Fjord ecosystem when the data are expressed in 'solar energy equivalents' – that is, the further you move up the trophic levels the higher the ecological price, due mainly to more and more solar energy (PJ) being required to produce 1 kilotonne of biomass: 4.39 PJ/kt for phytoplankton, 9.82 PJ/kt for zooplankton, 18.09 PJ/kt for zoobenthos, 44.29 PJ/kt for planktivores, 32.12 PJ/kt for temporary planktivores, 71.37 PJ/kt for white fish, 49.31 PJ/kt for small fish, 119.42 PJ/kt for medium predators, 295.59 PJ/kt for apex predators and, interestingly, 13.51 PJ/kt for detritus.

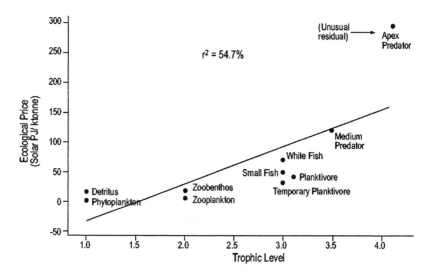

Figure 7.3   Correlation between ecological price and trophic level in the Schlei Fjord ecosystem

Figure 7.3 demonstrates that this relationship between 'ecological price' and 'trophic level' is relatively significant (r^2 = 0.55) for the Schlei Fjord ecosystem. That is, as the trophic level index of each compartment increases, so does its ecological price. The relationship is even more significant (r^2 = 0.61) when the apex predator is removed from the analysis.[7] It would, however, be false to claim on *a priori* grounds that the trophic level index is the only determinant of ecological price. This is because: (1) although in effect the 'trophic level' index is a good proxy for 'cumulative inefficiencies' in the trophic chain, it does not exactly measure 'cumulative inefficiencies; (2) the effects of forward linkages are taken account of in the calculation of ecological prices, in addition to the backward linkages that are measured by the trophic chain perspective.[8]

'Economic' Interpretation of the Results

Most economists would probably consider the 'ecological prices' generated in this analysis as 'shadow prices'. That is, they are an imputed price in the absence of an actual market. For example, if it took two trees to produce a tonne of apples and a tonne of apples has a market price of $1000, then implicitly one tree has a shadow price of $500 if there was no market price for the tree. Shadow prices are routinely estimated in the 'non-market valuation' of ecosystem services, by using indirect methods of valuation such as hedonic pricing (refer to Chapter 6). Shadow prices can also be found in linear programming applications where the solution to the problem results in hypothetical prices for scarce inputs.

The input–output model of the Schlei Fjord ecosystem can be evaluated in terms of the shadow prices. That is, the *flow of quantities* (in Figure 7.2) is *multiplied by the prices*, in order to obtain measurement of the *value flows* (Figure 7.4) between compartments in the ecosystem. The value flows are measured in Euros (€) although as the evaluation is based on relative prices, any other numeraire such as solar energy, could have been used. This evaluation means that the equivalent market value (€) of all compartments in the Schlei Fjord ecosystem is measured, even though only a very small portion of this ecosystem (caught fish) has an actual market value.

Table 7.1 provides another way of summarizing these 'Price × Quantity = Value' calculations. Overall, the most valuable compartment is detritus (€44,797,000), followed by zoobenthos (€34,861,000), phytoplankton (€13,569,000), zooplankton (€9,780,000), small fish (€1,664,000), temporary planktivore (€893,000), medium predator (€117,000), caught fish (€528,000), white fish (€510,000), planktivore (€168,000) and apex predator (€117,000).

Table 7.1 Calculation of value (price × quantity) of compartment outputs in the Schlei Fjord, in Euro (000s)

Compartment	Price of Output[1] (Euros x 10^3 per kilotonne)	Quantity of Output (kilotonnes)	Value of Output[2] (Euros × 10^3)
Detritus	409	109.47	44 797
Phytoplankton	116	117.07	13 569
Zooplankton	259	37.76	9 780
Zoobenthos	477	73.04	34 861
Planktivore	1116	0.15	168
Temporary Planktivore	847	1.05	893
White Fish	1883	0.27	510
Small Fish	1301	1.28	1664
Medium Predator	3151	0.26	806
Apex Predator	7798	0.02	117
Caught Fish	1210	0.44	528

Notes:
1. All prices are shadow prices, except caught fish, which is the actual market price.
2. Value = Price × Quantity.

These gross output values (€) reported in Table 7.1 are of interest because they show the relative value of each compartment in the Schlei Fjord ecosystem. They highlight the 'importance' of detritus and zoobenthos in the ecosystem functioning, and the relative 'unimportance' of high-trophic level species including apex predators. However, the net output value is probably of more 'economic' importance. Figure 7.4 shows that the net input into the Schlei Fjord ecosystem is €13,574 000 of solar energy with net output of €13,037 000 of detritus and €526,000 of caught fish. The net output of the Schlei Fjord ecosystem is €$_{2001}$ 928 per hectare, or US_{2001}$ 1083 per hectare, which is significantly below the figures reported by Costanza et al. (1997) for marine and coastal ecosystems.

Contributory Value to Non-Human Species and Humans

It is apparent from Figure 7.2 (in physical units) how different organisms and species contribute to others. For example, an apex predator in the Schlei Fjord depends on medium predators, planktivores and small fish. In turn these depend on inputs from zooplankton and zoobenthos, and eventually on solar energy captured by phytoplankton. Similar 'food chain sequences' can be drawn for all the ecosystem organisms (as represented by 'ecological compartments'), either in a backwards sequence as above, or in a forwards direction. That is, all organisms in the Schlei Fjord system both 'receive' and 'donate' 'value'. Only rarely do compartments in an ecosystem have only backward linkages (receivers only) or only forward linkages (donors only).

So what more do the Figure 7.4 data (in ecological pricing values) tell us about contributory value of ecosystem compartments, compared with the data in Figure 7.2 (in physical terms)? Quite simply, the data allow us to compare values in the same 'commensurated' units – you cannot, for example, validly add PJ (solar energy) and kilotonnes (white fish). As pointed out some time ago by Odum (1971), and more recently by Costanza and Hannon (1989), efficiency and other ecosystem indicators often require the so-called 'mixed unit problem' to be resolved, which is the explicit purpose of the ecological pricing approach (Patterson 1998b).

By using the ecological pricing data (for example, solar equivalents), the contributory value of all species in the Schlei Fjord ecosystem can be readily appreciated and validly compared. First, it is demonstrated that only a very small percentage (1 per cent) of the net output of the Schlei Fjord system is appropriated by humans and hence directly contributes to human welfare. By far the largest net output in solar equivalent terms is detritus, which mainly provides contributory value to species apart from humans. The idea that ecosystems exist only to provide 'services' solely for humans is not only anthropocentric, but manifestly false, as shown in the Schlei Fjord ecosystem. Second, the contributory value of detritus (1698 PJ solar equivalents), zoobenthos (1321 PJ solar equivalents), phytoplankton (514 PJ solar equivalents) and zooplankton (371 PJ solar equivalents) demonstrates the ecological 'importance' of these species in the lower trophic levels. Their contributory value far outweighs the species in the higher trophic levels, which collectively adds up to only 117 PJ solar equivalents in the Schlei Fjord ecosystem.

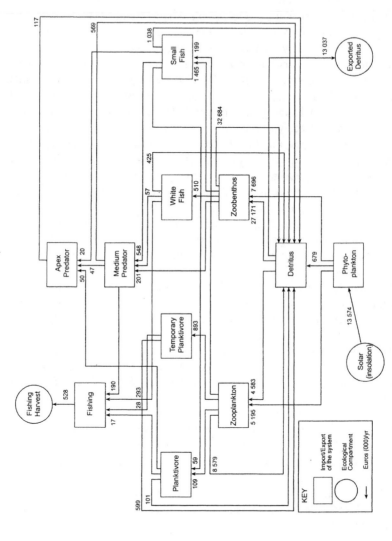

Figure 7.4 The contributory value between compartments of the Schlei Fjord ecosystem, evaluated in Euros (000s)

ECOLOGICAL PRICES IN THE GLOBAL MARINE SYSTEM

A brief illustrative coverage of the determination of ecological prices for the global marine system is specifically included here to provide an example of: (1) the determination of ecological prices in a larger scale and more complicated system than the Schlei Fjord; (2) a model that requires the solution of a 'rectangular' system of equations – that is, a system where in the final solution matrix there are more processes than quantities. More processes (equations) are added to the model in order to more aptly describe the functioning of the global marine ecological system than would be possible in 'square matrix' format; (3) the inclusion of abiotic processes that were assumed only to be 'background' processes in the Schlei Fjord example.

Input–Output Model of the Global Marine System

The global marine system model is described by Figure 7.5. This is a model of 24 processes and 15 quantities. The *quantities* include: marine plants, marine consumers, soil humus, marine humus, marine skeletons, HCO_3^- in surface water, HCO_3^- in deep sea, oil shale, sedimentary rocks, petroleum, natural gas, solar energy, CO_2, CO, and economic output. These quantities are measured in energy, mass and monetary units, which present an immediate commensuration problem that is, of course, is the central focus of the ecological pricing approach.

The *processes* in the global marine input–output model include:[9] gross marine production, marine plant respiration, production of marine skeletons, marine humus formation (from plants), marine consumption, marine humus formation (from consumers), transfer of soil humus to sea, oxidation of marine humus in the surface sea, oxidation of marine humus in the deep sea, oil shale (kerogen) formation, formation of limestone, dissolution of CO_3^{2-} in deep sea, transfer of HCO_3^- to the surface sea, transfer of HCO_3^- to the deep sea, weathering of limestone, release of CO_2 from the surface sea, absorption of CO_2 by the surface sea, petroleum formation, natural gas formation, fishing, petroleum exploitation and use, natural gas exploitation and use, and use of sedimentary rocks.

Data for the energy and mass flows quantified by this model of the global marine system were obtained from Bolin et al. (1979), Bowen (1979), Charlson et al. (1987), Schlesinger (1991), Butcher et al. (1992), Holmen (1992), Jahnke (1992), Mackenzie et al. (1993), Wollast et al. (1993), den Elzen et al. (1995), Mackenzie and Mackenzie (1995), Ayres (1996), and

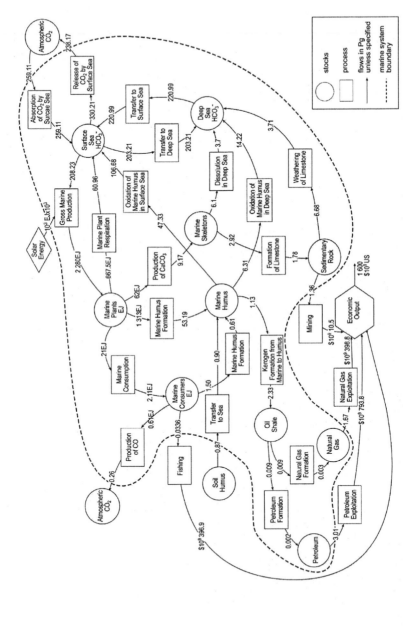

Figure 7.5 Input–output model of the global marine system for 1994, in Pg except where stated

Smil (1997, 2000, 2002). Price and quantity data for the economic processes quantified by this model were obtained from the United Nations (1999, 2000) for the year 1994.

Derived Ecological Shadow Prices for the Global Marine System

As for the Schlei Fjord ecosystem, ecological prices are determined from the input–output model of the global marine system. This input–output of the global marine system is hence described by a system of simultaneous linear equations, which on solution yield a vector of ecological shadow prices. The solution method, however, is different in the case of global marine system, as the system of simultaneous linear equations is over-determined (more equations than unknowns). The over-determined system of equations is solved using 'regression-like' methods developed by Patterson et al. (2006) and yields valuable information concerning the 'relative efficiency' of each process in the system.[10]

The ecological shadow prices of products from the global marine system are:

$US42.00 billion per Pg of CO_2
$US69.30 billion per Pg of CO
$US2.77 billion per Ejoules of marine plants
$US29.50 billion per Ejoules of marine consumers
$US70.70 billion per Pg of soil humus
$US68.30 billion per Pg of marine humus
$US18.41 billion per Pg of marine skeletons
$US30.30 billion per Pg of surface sea HCO_3^-
$US30.30 billion per Pg of deep sea HCO_3^-
$US33.10 billion per Pg of oil shale
$US17.40 billion per Pg of sedimentary rock
$US263.72 billion per Pg of petroleum
$US238.80 billion per Pg of natural gas
$US60.90 billion per EJ $\times 10^3$ of solar energy
$US1.00 billion per $US billion of economic output (by definition).

Generally speaking, the global marine system is more complex than the Schlei Fjord System, as it includes abiotic processes. Also, human use processes deplete 'natural capital' (use of fossil fuels and minerals), which adds a temporal dimension to the interpretation of results. Nevertheless, the contributory value of biotic and abiotic processes to each other is apparent and is reflected in the ecological prices. For example, as in the Schlei Fjord

Table 7.2 *Calculation of the value (price × quantity) of process outputs in the global marine system, in solar equivalents*

Process	Price of Output (Solar Equivalents per Exajoule) [2]	Price of Output (Solar Equivalents per Petagram) [1]	Quantity of Output (Petagram)	Quantity of Output (Exajolues)	Value of Output [3,4] (Solar Equivalents) [1]
Release of CO$_2$ from Surface Sea		0.69	238.17		164.26
Absorption of CO$_2$ by Surface Sea		0.50	359.24		178.74
CO Production by Marine Biota		1.14	0.26		0.29
Gross Marine Production	0.05			2,280.01	103.70
Marine Plant Respiration	0.50			60.96	30.33
Production of Marine Skeletons		0.30	9.17		2.77
Marine Humus formation (by Plants)		1.12	53.19		59.65
Marine Consumption		0.48	2.11		1.02
Marine Humus Formation (by Consumers)		1.12	0.61		0.68
Transfer of Land Humus to Sea		1.12	0.90		1.01
Oxidation of Marine Humus in Surface Sea		0.50	106.68		53.08
Oxidation of Marine Humus in Deep Sea		0.50	14.22		7.08
Oil Shale Formation from Marine Humus		0.54	2.33		1.26
Formation of Limestone		0.29	2.92		0.83
Dissolution of CO$_3$ in Deep Sea		0.50	3.71		1.85
Transfer of HCO$_3$ to Surface Sea		0.50	220.99		109.95
Transfer of HCO$_3$ to Deep Sea		0.50	203.21		101.10
Weathering of Limestone		0.50	1.78		0.88
Petroleum Formation		4.33	0.00		0.00
Natural Gas Formation		3.92	0.00		0.00
Fishing		57.47	0.11		6.52
Petroleum Use		4.33	3.01		13.03
Natural Gas Use		3.92	1.67		6.55
Use of Carbon Sedimentary Rocks		0.13	1.36		0.17

Notes: 1. Solar Equivalents are measured in EJ $\times$ 10^3. 2. Odum (1996) would consider 'solar equivalents per exajoule', to be the same as his 'transformity' measure. 3. Odum (1996) would consider these embodied 'solar equivalents' to be the same as his 'emergy' measure. However, there is the issue of Odum's treatment of forward linkages, as discussed by Patterson (1998b), which makes this equivalence only approximate. 4. Value = Price $\times$ Quantity.

system, 'humus' (detritus) again plays a critical role in the contributory value of the system – it is not only important to the biotic and abiotic processes that sustain life, but has also been important over geological time in the processes of forming shale oil and eventually fossil fuels (gas and petroleum), which significantly contribute to human welfare.

The relative importance of each process in the global marine system can be evaluated (Price × Quantity = Value) to determine the value (in solar equivalents) of the output (see Table 7.2).[11] The coupled processes of the release and absorption of CO_2 from the surface ocean is found to have the highest contributory value, with fluxes of 164 EJ × 10^3 solar equivalents/year and 178 EJ × 10^3 solar equivalents/year, respectively. Similarly, the coupled processes of transfer of HCO_3^- between the surface and deep ocean are also significant. Of the biotic processes, gross marine production, at 103 EJ × 10^3 solar equivalents/year, is highest followed by marine humus formation, at 53 solar equivalents/year. The 'human appropriation processes' of fossil fuel use, mineral exploitation and fishing amount collectively to 27 EJ × 10^3 solar equivalents, which are 17.7 per cent of the direct solar energy input into the global marine system.

Global marine system resources directly contributed $US1600 billion to human welfare in 1994. This is equal to 6.4 per cent of the global GDP of $US25 trillion as reported by the World Bank (1996). Most of this contribution is via the use of natural gas and petroleum usage, but also includes minerals extraction and fishing. The global marine system also provides a 'sink' for atmospheric CO_2 valued at $US879 billion, as well as a 'sink' for soil humus valued at $US61 billion, according to the shadow pricing approach used here. *By including these 'sink functions' in addition to the before-mentioned 'resource inputs', the total contribution of the global marine system to human welfare is valued at 10.1 per cent of the global GDP.*

CONCLUDING REMARKS

The 'ecological pricing' method is a useful emerging tool for operationalizing a more biophysical/biocentric concept in a way that can communicate to both ecologists and economists. Its practical application has shown it can highlight not only those species that are 'visible', but also species that are ignored or undervalued in neoclassical valuations. It is well known, for example, that the so-called 'charismatic megafauna' such as dolphins and whales receive high value in contingent valuation studies, while the inconspicuous phytoplankton, although critical in the food chain and in terms of ecosystem functioning, may not be recognized in these studies. The ecological pricing approach attempts to address this issue by adopting a valuation approach that is firmly grounded in understanding the underlying biophysical processes in the ecological-economic system that is being evaluated.

ACKNOWLEDGEMENT

I wish to acknowledge Tanja Mildner's contribution in providing me with information about the Schlei Fjord and fish prices in Germany.

NOTES

1. The term 'commodity' is used here to refer to a physical quantity of anything observed in the physical world, ranging from a litre of water to a kilogram of zooplankton. The use of the term 'commodity' does not necessarily imply that it is traded or exchanged on markets. Perhaps we could use the more neutral (and less emotionally loaded) term of 'quantity' instead of 'commodity'.
2. Odum (1996) similarly sometimes uses 'emdollars' to measure the 'value' of a quantity, instead of his usual 'solar energy equivalents'. Odum uses these money units ('emdollars') for the same reason that I do in this chapter – that is, to improve the communication of the analytical results.
3. This marine ecosystem example is exactly analogous to the example used by Sraffa (1960) in *Production of Commodities by Means of Commodities*. The example Sraffa used was:
240 qr wheat +12 tons iron + 18 pigs → 450 qr wheat
90 qr wheat + 6 tons iron + 12 pigs → 21 tons iron
120 qr wheat + 3 tons iron + 30 pigs → 60 pigs
4. 'Square matrix' systems are overdetermined by exactly 1 degree of freedom (that is, they have one more quantity than the number of processes). Once one of these quantities is set to unity, there remains an equal number of processes and quantities, giving a 'square matrix', which is then used in the solution of ecological prices.
5. This multiplication by −1 is necessary, as the vector is taken to the 'other side of equation' (7.5).
6. The numbers in these equations are rounded to two decimal places, whereas in Figure 7.2, in some cases, the flows are reported to greater than two decimal places.
7. The apex predator is an 'outlier' in the regression/correlation analysis because it has a significantly lower than 'average' trophic efficiency of only 20 per cent. This compares with the trophic efficiency of other compartments in the Schlei Fjord ecosystem such as zooplankton (67 per cent), zoobenthos (55 per cent), planktivores (32 per cent), white fish (25 per cent), small fish (33 per cent) and medium predators (29 per cent).
8. The idea of food (trophic) chain analysis is predicated on the assumption that there is a chain with 'a beginning' and 'an end' to the food chain (Christensen 1994). The analysis by Odum (1996) therefore 'looks backwards' from the end point in the food chain – for example, looking backwards from the apex predator to the primary input of solar energy. This type of analysis only takes account of backward linkages. It does not take account of the 'forward linkages' of the apex predator as it dies and creates detritus, which then in turn is an input

into the production of phytoplankton – in this forward linkages sense, 'phytoplankton' could be considered be the next step level in the food chain.

9. Not all the known biogeochemical processes are included is this global marine input–output model – for example, the formation of other sedimentary rocks (in addition to limestone formation which is covered), as well as aspects of the hydrological cycle that impinge on the marine environment. The exclusion of these processes from the input–output model of the global marine system, however, is not expected to significantly affect the numerical magnitude of the ecological shadow prices estimated from the input–output model.

10. A further problem that needs to be taken account of in solving the equations for the global marine system is that the base matrix used in solving the equation may be singular and therefore cannot be inverted. This is due to circularity of the flows between 'Marine Plants' and 'Surface Sea HCO_3^-'. This problem was 'resolved' by 'breaking the cycle', by removing from the base matrix, the return flow of 'Surface HCO_3^- to 'Marine Plants'. This issue of 'cycling' is often encountered in matrix algebra manipulation of ecosystem data (for example, Patten 1992; Ulanowicz 1991) and is often dealt with by 'removing such cycles from the analysis'. Costanza and Neill (1984) specifically encountered this problem in determining the ecological prices of the biosphere processes and dealt with it by reallocating water flows to other ecological compartments.

11. Although the measurement units of the 'transformity' unit and the 'ecological prices' are the same, caution needs to be displayed here. That is, Odum (1996) claims that transformity only measures 'backward linkages' or what he refers to as 'looking back upstream'. As Patterson et al. (2006), however, point out: (1) Odum (1996) actually uses 'forward linkages' when calculating the transformity of geothermal heat for the obvious reason that there are no backward linkages to 'solar energy' from 'geothermal heat'; (2) 'Ecological Prices', as pointed out elsewhere in the text, measure both forward and backward linkages.

REFERENCES

Ayres, R.U. (1966), *Industrial Metabolism and the Grand Nutrient Cycles*, Fontainebleau, France: INSEAD Centre for the Management of Environmental Resources.

Bolin, B., E.T. Degens, S. Kempe and P. Kettner (eds) (1979), *The Global Carbon Cycle*, SCOPE Report No. 13, Chichester: Wiley.

Bowen, H.J.M. (1979), *Environmental Chemistry of the Elements*, London: Academic Press.

Butcher, S.S., R.J. Charlson, G.H. Orians and G.V. Wolfe (1992), *Global Biogeochemical Cycles*, New York: Academic Press.

Charlson, R.J., J.E. Lovelock, M.O. Andreae and S.G. Warren (1987), 'Oceanic phytoplankton, atmospheric sulphur, cloud albedo, and climate', *Nature*, **326**: 655–661.

Christensen, V. (1994), 'Emergy-based ascendancy', *Ecological Modelling*, **72**: 129–144.

Christensen, V. and D. Pauly (1992), 'ECOPATH II: a software for balancing steady-state ecosystem models and calculating network characteristics', *Ecological Modelling*, **61**: 169–185.

Cleveland, C.J., R. Costanza, C.A.S. Hall and R. Kaufmann (1984), 'Energy in the United States economy: a biophysical perspective', *Science*, **225**: 890–897.

164   *Economic and other values of the marine environment*

Costanza, R. and C. Neill (1984), 'Energy intensities, interdependence and value in ecological systems: a linear programming approach', *Journal of Theoretical Biology*, **106**: 41–57.

Costanza, R., H.E. Daly and J.A. Bartholomew (1991), 'Goals, agenda and policy recommendations for ecological economics', in R. Costanza (ed.), *Ecological Economics: The Science and Management of Sustainability*, New York: Columbia University Press, pp. 1–20.

Costanza, R., R. d'Arge, R. De Groot, S. Farber, M. Grasso, B. Hannon, K. Limburg, S. Naeem, R.V. O'Neil, J. Paruelo, R.G. Raskin, P. Sutton and M. van den Belt (1997), 'The value of the world's ecosystem services and natural capital', *Nature*, **387**: 253–260.

Costanza, R. and B. Hannon (1989), 'Dealing with the mixed units problem in ecosystem network analysis', in F. Wulff, J.G. Field and K.H. Mann (eds), *Network Analysis in Marine Ecology: Methods and Applications*, Berlin: Springer, pp. 90–115.

den Elzen, M., A. Beusen and J. Rotmans (1995), *Modelling Global Biogeochemical Cycles: an Integrated Assessment Approach*, Global Dynamics and Sustainable Development Programme, GLOBO Report Series No. 7, Bilthoven: National Institute of Public Health and the Environment (RIVM).

England, R.W. (1986), 'Production, distribution and environmental quality: Mr Sraffa reinterpreted as an ecologist', *Kyklos*, **39**: 230–244.

Eurostat (2006), *Facts and Figures on the CFP: Basic Data on Common Fisheries Policy*, Luxemburg: Office for Official Publications of the European Communities.

Hannon, B. (1998), 'How might nature value man?', *Ecological Economics*, **25**(3): 265–279.

Holmen, K. (1992), 'The global carbon cycle', in S.S. Butcher, R.J. Charlson, G.H. Orians and G.V. Wolfe (eds), *Global Biogeochemical Cycles*, London: Academic Press, pp. 239–262.

Jahnke, R.A. (1992), 'The sulfur cycle', in S.S. Butcher, R.J. Charlson, G.H. Orians and G.V. Wolfe (eds), *Global Biogeochemical Cycles*, London: Academic Press, pp. 301–314.

Judson, D.H. (1989), 'The convergence of neo-Ricardian and embodied energy theories of value and price', *Ecological Economics*, **1**: 261–281.

Kesting, V., S. Gollosch and C.D. Zander (1996), 'Parasite communities of the Schlei Fjord (Baltic coast of northern Germany)', *Heloglander Meeresunters*, **50**: 477–496.

Klauer, B. (2000), 'Ecosystem prices: activity analysis applied to ecosystems', *Ecological Economics*, **33**(3): 473-486.

Mackenzie, F.T. and J.A. Mackenzie (1995), *Our Changing Planet: An Introduction to Earth System Science and Global Environmental Change*, New Jersey: Prentice-Hall.

Mackenzie, F.T., L.M. Ver, C. Sabine, M. Lane and A. Lerman (1993), 'C, N, P, S global biogeochemical cycles and modelling of global change', in R. Wollast, F.T. Mackenzie and L. Chou (eds), *Interactions of C, N, P and S Biogeochemical Cycles and Global Change*, Berlin: Springer-Verlag, pp.1–62.

Nauen, C. (1984), 'The artisanal fishery in Schlei Fjord, eastern Schleswig-Holstein, Federal Republic of Germany', in J.M. Kapetsky and G. Lasserne (eds), *Management of Coastal Lagoon Fisheries*, Stud. Rev. Gen. Fish. Council, Medit., 1(61): 403–428.

Odum, E.P. (1971), *Fundamentals of Ecology*, Philadelphia: W.B. Saunders.

Odum, H.T. (1996). *Environmental Accounting: EMERGY and Environmental Decision Making*, New York: Wiley.

Patten, B.C. (1992), 'Energy, emergy and environs', *Ecological Modelling*, **62**: 29–69.

Patterson, M.G. (1998a), 'Commensuration and theories of value in ecological economics', *Ecological Economics*, **25**(1): 105–123.

Patterson, M.G. (1998b), 'Understanding energy quality in ecological and economic systems', in *Advances in Energy Studies: Energy Flows in Ecology and Economy*, Rome: Museum of Science and Scientific Information, pp. 257–274.

Patterson, M.G. (2002), 'Ecological production based pricing of biosphere processes', *Ecological Economics*, **41**: 457–478.

Patterson, M.G., G.C. Wake, R. McKibbon and R.O Cole (2006), 'Ecological pricing and transformity: a solution method for systems rarely at equilibrium', *Ecological Economics*, **56**: 412–423.

Proops, J. (2003), 'Research challenges for ecological economics in the 21st century', in S. Dovers, D.I. Stern and M.D. Young (eds), *New Dimensions in Ecological Economics: Integrated Approaches to People and Nature*, Cheltenham, UK and Northampton, MA, USA: Edward Elgar, pp.13–22.

Schlesinger, W.H. (1991), *Biogeochemistry: An Analysis of Global Change*, San Diego: Academic Press.

Smil, V. (1997), *Cycles of Life: Civilization and the Biosphere*, New York: Scientific American Library.

Smil, V. (2000), 'Phosphorous in the environment', *Annual Review of Energy and the Environment*, **25**: 53–88.

Smil, V. (2002), 'Global biogeochemical cycles', in R.U. Ayres and L.W. Ayres (eds), *A Handbook of Industrial Ecology*, Cheltenham, UK and Northampton, MA, USA: Edward Elgar, pp. 249–259.

Sraffa, P. (1960), *Production of Commodities by Means of Commodities: Prelude to a Critique of Economic Theory*, Cambridge: Cambridge University Press.

Ulanowicz, R.E. (1991), 'Contributory values of ecosystem resources', in R. Costanza (ed.), *Ecological Economics: The Science and Management of Sustainability*, New York: Columbia University Press, pp. 253–268.

United Nations (1999), *Industrial Commodity Statistics Yearbook*, New York: United Nations.

United Nations (2000), *World Commodity Survey 1999–2000. Markets, Trends and the World Economic Environment*, New York: United Nations.

Wollast, R., F.T. Mackenzie and L. Chou (eds) (1993), *Interactions of C, N, P and S Biogeochemical Cycles and Global Change*, Berlin: Springer-Verlag.

World Bank (1996), *The World Bank Atlas*, Washington DC: World Bank.

8.   The Open Horizon: Exploring Spiritual and Cultural Values of the Oceans and Coasts

Charlotte Šunde

When our leaders and planners say that our future lies in the sea, they are thinking only in economic terms, about marine and seabed resources and their development. When people talk of the importance of the oceans for the continuity of life on Earth, they are making scientific statements. But for us in Oceania, the sea defines us, what we are and have always been. (Hau'ofa 1998, p. 405)

INTRODUCTION: APPROACHING THE OCEAN

The focus of this chapter necessitates a navigational shift in one's position to allow a different perspective – an opening of the horizon – on the nature of value. Although many economists, among others, accept the existence of social and cultural values that they may or may not consider commensurable, relatively few seem comfortable in acknowledging spiritual values in their economic, scientific and political decision-making methodologies. In presenting a case for weak comparability of values as a foundation for ecological economics, Joan Martinez-Alier et al. (1998, p. 278) define weak comparability in terms such that 'irreducible value conflict is unavoidable but compatible with rational choice employing practical judgement'. This presupposes that value is always informed by rational ways of approaching reality. However, I submit that non-rational ways of relating to the ocean (for example, spiritual values) are often neglected because they are incommensurable and incomparable with other values that are subject to rational choice and practical judgement. Love and reverence for the ocean are not irrational or emotional sentiments, but may be understood as expressions of an immediate contact with the Real that emerges from a fundamentally different way of approaching reality.

I do not wish to be misunderstood as making an unreasonable case for the outright rejection of rationality. However, I do wish to assert that by reducing reason to that which is rational, the modern mind excludes other ways of approaching reality such as the nondual intuition or the mystical experience – and that secular rejection of the sacred is unreasonable. As the etymology of the words 'reason' and 'rationality' suggest, what is rational is that which is held in *ratio* to another thing. This implies a duality whereby the seer and the seen are separated, creating a subject–object dichotomy that divorces the subjective mind from the so-called objective world. This line of thought has dominated in Western philosophy following the influence of René Descartes' famous proclamation 'cogito ergo sum' and his ideas on scientific thinking in his *Discourse on Method.* However, the Cartesian division between matter and mind or between soul and body was fundamentally challenged in quantum physics. Werner Heisenberg's (1958, p. 75) wave-particle experiments led him to conclude that there can be no 'objective observer' in our relation to nature as the very act of observation changes the outcome of the study or experiment: thus, '...the sharp separation between the world and the I [is] impossible.'

In the opening quotation of this chapter, Epeli Hau'ofa (1998) draws attention to another way of valuing the ocean than the rational methodology employed in economic valuations or scientific studies. Whereas Hau'ofa does not reject the validity of those perspectives, he raises a challenge for political leaders and economic planners to become aware of different relationships to, and ways of relating with, the ocean. Like many others who were raised in thalasso-centric cultures, Hau'ofa draws his identity from a radical interrelatedness with the ocean. Thus, when he appeals for an awareness of 'the ocean in us', Hau'ofa touches on a deep insight. This insight might be interpreted as an expression of the nondual intuition or supreme experience as when the seer and seen merge as one in an inseparable whole or unity.

The Indian poet, Rabindranath Tagore (2006, p. 79), offers these words: 'I dive down into the depth of the ocean of forms, hoping to gain the perfect pearl of the formless'. One reaction to this way of approaching the ocean may ridicule or reject all non-rational values as irrational. Another response may assert that the unsustainable plundering of the oceans without regard to the holistic interconnectedness of the 'web of life' is irrational, unreasonable and foolhardy.

THE IRRATIONAL PLUNDER OF THE OCEAN

The geographical world-picture that prevailed in Europe from the 4th to 15th centuries mapped the possibility of an Antipodes or southern land as the 'torrid zone' whereupon ships might '...melt in a kind of boiling soup' (Collis 1976, p. 12). Even though Ptolemy postulated the earth as a sphere, it was only in the 15th and 16th centuries that geographical explorations and circumnavigations confirmed it as a fact that became widely known and accepted beyond educated circles. Since then the earth's vast oceans have been sailed numerous times over, charted and, more recently, digitized by satellite imagery. Science and technology have explored the surface of the oceans and, to a lesser extent, probed its depths. Much is known about the importance of the oceans in the thermoregulation of the planet, and the fact that without the oceans, life on land would not be possible (see Chapter 2). However, despite an overwhelming abundance of information shared globally, we still treat the oceans irrationally as if they are an endlessly replenishing food basket – depleting entire populations of fish for commercial profit and hunting whales for the 'scientific' delicacy of their flesh. As Barbara Ward and René Dubos (1972, pp. 271–272) deplore, we also treat the ocean as a receptacle into which our city and farm pollutants are poured and then quickly forgotten:

> We all tend to feel that once a polluted river empties into the open sea, once we conduct city sewer systems far enough away from land, all industrial and urban discharge will disappear somehow into blue space beyond the horizon, as if we piped it away from our own planet. We seem in this conception of the ocean to forget for a moment that the world is round and without edges.

In 1969, when a man took his first step on the moon, one of the most powerful images was projected back to those who remained firmly rooted to *terra firma*. The image of Planet Earth spinning in space reaffirmed the ancient wisdom of Gaia, Mother Earth, and strengthened the calls of the then burgeoning environmental movement to protect 'spaceship earth' as both unique and fragile in its entirety. Kenneth Boulding (1966) used this phrase in his essay, *The Economics of the Coming Spaceship Earth*, to distinguish between the different economic principles required in the 'closed earth of the future' (that is, the 'spaceman economy') from the 'open earth of the past'. He associated the open economy of apparently limitless resources with the reckless, exploitative, and violent behaviour of the 'cowboy economy'. Boulding (1966, p. 218) was critical of the economic orthodoxy of the 1960s, in particular for their lack of appreciation of the biophysical limitations of 'spaceship earth':

> Even now we are very far from having made the moral, political, and psychological adjustments which are implied in this transition from the illimitable

plane to the closed sphere. Economists in particular, for the most part, have failed to come to grips with the ultimate consequences of the transition from the open to the closed earth.

As Boulding (1966) and many others point out, the reality of our biophysically limited biosphere is not generally shared by those who direct the dominant political systems and global economy – this was particularly so in the mid-1960s when Boulding's seminal article was first published. Original attempts to establish a Law of the Sea to protect the oceans as commons have been undermined by the legal division of the oceans into 'exclusive economic zones'. When driven by motives of 'individual utility maximization', short-term capital gain and greed, corporate and government leaders display the characteristics of *Homo economicus*, gambling with the oceans as an economic lottery game. In the global super-market trade of goods, the life cycle of a fish is destroyed when it is netted, tinned, stacked on a shelf and priced for purchase by an anonymous consumer. The intrinsic value of the fish does not enter this rational version of reality. At our inevitable peril, the world's economic leaders denigrate the intrinsic qualities of oceanic ecosystems and ignore the rich and complex interconnections on which we all depend and of which we are part (see Chapter 2).

The rationale for the global market economy is underpinned by neoclassical economic theory and valuation models that reduce complex marine ecosystems and the mysterious deep oceans to a single category known as 'natural capital'. As it is used today, the neoclassical model assumes that money is the universal standard of valuation, and that everything is potentially commensurable – an assumption that many people (including some economists) vehemently disagree with.[1] Yet, this attitude towards nature has not always been the dominant one in economics. The classical economists (for example, Adam Smith, Thomas Malthus, David Ricardo) and pre-classical economists (for example, François Quesnay) wrote about 'natural values' and 'natural law' and regarded value as intertwined in nature and divinity and the natural balance of things. Only when economics became mathematical, with the *marginalist revolution* led by Alfred Marshall, was value abstracted away from nature and moral philosophy. Therefore, an urgent challenge for ecological economics is to address this dualistic division and to restore moral values and ethical guidelines in models and valuations of the ocean and marine resources. If such a critical task is taken up, then economists will be required to think beyond the safe grounds of their discipline and to accept the fluidity of cross-boundary thinking that is open to other ways of approaching the ocean and, ultimately, to new horizons.

POLAR EXTREMES: LAND AND SEA IN DIALECTICAL CONTENTION

On land, humans have for centuries built fortified structures to keep out the enemy. These are often located strategically on promontories overlooking the sea: the defensive stance renders the gaze insular – toward defending one's castle, village or nation from outsiders. On the sea, however, the gaze is forever pulled toward the open horizon and up to the sky to read the climatic conditions, and into the ocean to trace the currents. On land, survey lines are carved across landscapes, dissecting and fragmenting ecosystems with linear roads and property boundaries. At sea, a different tack is required. Aboard the sailing ship, the course is always a cybernetic zigzag of give-and-take; tacking into the wind and responding to its changes so that the ship's sails are filled. At sea, the sailor's mind must think differently and his or her senses must be acutely attuned to the rhythms of the natural elements.[2] The human footprint does not carry the same weight of authority at sea as it seems to with the imprint of human impact on land.

I do not wish to generalize, nor to set up an oversimplified dichotomy. However, I do wish to explore the apparent differences between those whose worldview emanates from the north polar perspective, where the ratio of land-to-sea favours a stronger influence by the land, in contrast to the southern oceanic peoples whose cosmology embraces the expansiveness of the sea. Oceania writer Hau'ofa (1994) suggested this cultural difference when he challenged the northern Eurocentric description of the Pacific as 'islands in a far sea' with a Polynesian view of the Pacific as 'a sea of islands'. He explains that there is a 'world of difference' between these two views: 'The first emphasizes dry surface in a vast ocean far from the centers of power. Focusing in this way stresses the smallness and remoteness of the islands. The second is a more holistic perspective in which things are seen in the totality of their relationships' (Hau'ofa 1994, pp. 152–153).

The Eurocentric view of the Pacific as 'islands in a far sea' is, according to Hau'ofa and other critics, economically and geographically deterministic. That view is promoted by World Bank economists and developers whose interests are well served in defining the Pacific in terms of what it *lacks* (that is, Western development and economic growth) and stressing the inevitability of its dependency on the larger centres of power due to the isolation and smallness of the islands and their populations.[3] However, the peoples of Oceania *do not* live in 'tiny confined spaces' simply because they have never limited their view of the world to the land surfaces they occupy. As the rich and varying myths, legends, oral traditions and cosmologies of the peoples of

Oceania attest, and as Hau'ofa (1994, p. 152) goes on to explain:

> Their universe comprised not only land surfaces, but the surrounding ocean as far as they could traverse and exploit it, the underworld with its fire-controlling and earth-shaking denizens, and the heavens above with their hierarchies of powerful gods and named stars and constellations that people could count on to guide their ways across the seas. Their world was anything but tiny.

When considering this apparent tension between land and sea as a dialectic, it is easy to be lured into a fixation on one or other polar opposite and therefore to exaggerate this tension. Yet, many people who dwell near the water's edge are not drawn into such a dialectical framework. They might prefer to distinguish their reality as existing at the margins or coastal 'soft boundary' between land and sea. To them, the beach may be considered a transition zone. Although, as Solomon Islanders put it, there are two kinds of peoples: 'man belong bush' and 'man belong saltwater', there are also 'ecosystem people', who have one foot in the sea and the other firmly on land.[4] Those people embrace the opportunities and challenges presented by both land and sea as complementary and equally important. Pacific Islanders, for example, far from being stuck on 'islands in a far sea', have both *roots* in the land and *routes* on the sea (Jolly 2001, p. 419).

FRESHWATER AND SALTWATER IN DYNAMIC BALANCE

Traditionally, indigenous peoples have been comfortable living with the tension between the natural and supernatural realms – the rational and non-rational ways of knowing. Many indigenous peoples do not accept the type of duality that has elevated rational reasoning to near-exclusive dominance in moderns' fixation with having to know and define reality and place economic values on nature. Rather than perceiving polar differences as competing or opposing extremes to be either overcome or united, an alternative embraces polarity as a complementary interrelationship.

In fact, such polar tensions are more likely to be cherished and therefore nurtured for their ability to give rise to conditions that enhance expressions of diversity within unity. The acceptance of things as they are is fundamental to indigenous cultures that seek harmony and a dynamic balance in the cosmos, in contrast to other cultures that attempt to assimilate plurality within a universal version of reality.

For the Yolngu Australian Aboriginal people of northeast Arnhem Land, one such place that holds this significance for them is known as *ganma* – an area (such as a still lagoon or mangrove swamp) where freshwater streams flowing down from the land and springs bubbling up from the earth meet and mix with saltwater coming in from the sea. In ecological terms, *ganma* is an extremely productive food source because it exists at the interface between land and sea and is fed by a rich tidal exchange of nutrients and organisms. Yet, the significance of *ganma* goes far beyond its ecological functions and critical role in sustaining the physical survival of the Yolngu over hundreds of generations. *Ganma* also has a symbolic role as a metaphor for environmental philosophy and praxis where the ways of relating to the environment are infused with moral, social and spiritual elements, as illustrated in the following passage:

> On Elcho Island, six kilometres off the northeast Arnhem Land coast of Australia's Northern Territory, a senior Yolngu woman sat by a riverbank in the shade, keening a crying-song for her recently deceased uncle. She was singing his spirit and essence out to sea, to his ancestral waters. The words of her song spoke of the river's rushing floodwaters – of the bubbling, frothing foam that builds as the river rushes toward the sea, eventually mixing with the salt water of the incoming tide in a swirling whirlpool known as *ganma* (or *garma*). The freshwater embraces the salt and is enveloped by it to be carried inside and underneath to the deep sea and on to Indonesia. In her mournful singing, as in all Yolgnu songs, there was no clear separation between the environment and the person; waters have moral, social, and spiritual consequences. In the concept of *ganma*, ancestral waters come together as a foaming, frothy substance – the embodiment of new life and ideas. (Magowan 2002, p. 18)

The metaphorical significance of *ganma* to the Yolgnu also extends to moral guidance on appropriate forms of social conduct among kin and also between the Yolgnu and those not known to the country. An allegory for cross-cultural interaction emerges from within the swirling patterns and undercurrents of *ganma*. As the incoming tide rises to its full capacity and then recedes with the ebb-tide, a dynamic interaction of energies takes place.

This, according to the Yolgnu, is akin to the dynamic interaction of knowledge traditions. Raymattja Marika-Munungguritj explains: 'In this way, the Dhuwa and Yirritja sides of Yolngu life work together. And in this way, *balanda* (non-Yolngu) and Yolngu traditions can work together. There must be balance; if not, either one will be stronger and will harm the other' (Magowan 2002, pp. 19–20). What can be drawn from this insight is a simple yet eloquent expression of the need for pluralism – an acknowledgement of the other and acceptance, with genuine openness, of the possibilities for working together across the boundaries of very different ways of knowing.

CROSSING BOUNDARIES: TRANSDISCIPLINARY OPENNESS

Proponents of ecological economics, such as Richard Norgaard (1985, 1989), also plead for pluralism, but they do so in the context of 'methodological openness' to encourage the growth of knowledge across the boundaries of various disciplines and their models. In contrast to the mechanistic-reductionist approach that underpins neoclassical economics, ecological economists assert a transdisciplinary approach that works across – and goes beyond – traditional disciplinary boundaries. According to Basarab Nicolescu (2002 [1996], p. 44), transdisciplinarity '...concerns that which is at once between the disciplines, across the different disciplines, and beyond all discipline.' As Manfred Max-Neef (2005, p. 15) clarifies: 'Transdisciplinarity, more than a new discipline or super-discipline is, actually, a different manner of seeing the world, more systemic and more holistic.' However, Max-Neef cautions against simply replacing the neoclassical economic paradigm with a new universal model of economics – albeit a more holistic one, such as ecological economics. Indeed, proponents of transdisciplinarity will need to be careful to ensure that in seeking the 'unity of knowledge' a more humble horizon of openness is retained so as to avoid the pitfalls of universalism.

Universalism is the fundamentalist imposition of one cultural set of values, beliefs or knowledge over all others. Universalism is at the root of many critical problems of social and environmental injustice in the world today – problems that cannot now be solved by any one group, be they political, economic, social or religious. Instead, the critical and urgent task facing humankind today is to address our present situation through open and dialogical communication across worldviews and other ways of approaching reality. This is the challenge of pluralism, which should not be misunderstood as a simple recognition of differences (that is, quantitative *plurality*) – as with the multidisciplinary approach, or as a sensitivity to variety (that is, qualitative *pluriformity*) – as with relativism. Rather, pluralism has to do with 'radical *diversity*' – it is grounded in the belief that truth itself is pluralistic (Pannikar 1995). Thus, if ecological economics is to truly embrace the uncertainty, complexity and pluralistic nature of truth, its practitioners must willingly accept and explore that 'region of reality' not limited to empirical rationality or pure reason. As Max-Neef (2005, pp. 11–12) asserts:

> Werner Heisenberg introduced in his *Manuscripts of 1942*, the idea of what he called *Regions of Reality*. The first region is that of classical physics, the second is that of quantum physics, of biology and of psychic phenomena; and the third is

that of religious, philosophical and artistic experiences. ... what appears to be increasingly evident is that we can no longer assume that there is just one reality, fully describable and understandable in terms of pure reason.

The pluralism of truth and the pluralistic nature of approaching reality can also be illustrated by analogy to skilled ocean-goers and the differences in method that distinguish the 'way-finder' from the 'navigator'. Greg Dening (2004) highlights this distinction and explains: '*Way-finding* is the word that modern islanders use to describe their craft and the craft of their ancestors in piloting their voyaging canoes around the Great Ocean, the Pacific'. In their sea journeys, navigators and way-finders pay close attention to the signs of nature: the sea currents and wind patterns; the trajectory of the sun and stars to guide them. However, the navigator has the security of taking recourse in 'a more universal science of instruments', whereas way-finding is an 'interpretive craft' whereby for a way-finder: '...no knowledge, no image is stilled either in time or in space. ... [Furthermore,] no voyage is ever the same. His way is always different, but always ruled by his confidence that he will find it' (Dening 2004).[5]

The difference between a navigator and a way-finder is akin, I argue, to the difference between 'methodology' and 'method'. A formally accepted methodology produces replicable results by methodically following a systematic procedure, technique, experiment or predetermined mode of enquiry. Hence, compass and chart already prescribe a rational reality that the navigator accepts almost without questioning in his vocation. Method, however, denotes the *way* of approaching reality – and indeed the *transformation of the way* of approaching and experiencing reality in the pursuit of knowledge – as indicated by the etymology of the Greek root *meta-hódos* (*meta-* transformation; *hódos* way, manner). Method includes, but is not restricted to, rational ways of knowing. Most importantly, method also includes non-rational ways of knowing and therefore overcomes the dualistic separation of subject and object, allowing the nondual (neither one nor many) approach to emerge.

A way-finder achieves far more than traversing great oceans – his is a truly sacred journey in which his entire being merges with the Way. This undertaking reveals and, indeed, reveres those sacred bonds that unite human beings with the cosmos – the Earth and the Divine. In the nondual perception, the seer and the seen are one in an inseparable whole or unity – the supreme experience of immediate contact with the Real. The shamans and *tohunga* (holy men, spiritual healers) who see beyond the horizon, that is, further than the limited vision of normal eyesight, were regarded as valuable *taonga* (treasures) on early ocean-going voyages of discovery. Their cultures also respect them for their ability to see beyond the visible horizon to what theologian and philosopher Raimon Panikkar (1995) calls the invisible 'horizon of intelligibility' or *mythos*, recognizing that reality can never be fully captured by the *logos*. Reality is always more than what the Enlightenment philosophers, with their sharp focus on reason and the intellect, could ever illuminate.

Transdisciplinarity has been described as a 'more holistic and more systemic' way of seeing the world than the approach taken in neoclassical economics. However, as long as ecological economists stay firmly entrenched within a theoretical framework – or a rational mode of methodology – the holistic nature of their enquiry remains severely limited. Whether reality is approached through a reductionist lens or a complex systems methodology, both enforce a dualistic standpoint whereby human subjects distance themselves from their so-called objects of study. Although ecosystem theories assert that humans are part of ecosystems, that 'part' is typically reduced to a functional or organizational role defined in secular terms. Ecological economists may be more willing to accept the possibility of spiritual values in addition to economic and other values, but unless they are genuinely open to exploring wider horizons that include non-rational relationships, such a stance will remain a philosophical platitude or a post-modern diversion.[6]

The challenges presented by transdisciplinarity and holism may require going beyond the constraints of academic theory to find authentic expression in living relationships within communities and their environments. The following example of a traditional Fijian village highlights a range of values (including spiritual) that villagers hold in their relationships with the ocean and each other. Such values are not exclusive to indigenous peoples or to the Oceania region. Many European maritime communities hold a similar depth of values with respect to the ocean, which they express through their own rich cultural traditions and folklore. My intention here is to allow a space for voices to be shared with terra-centric moderns who may be less familiar with the lifestyles and values that bind citizens of Oceania to their sea environment.

EXPLORING NONDUAL RELATIONSHIPS: THE OLD WOMEN WHO SING THE SEA

As the day draws to an end in a small coastal village on Fiji's main land, Vitu Levu, an air of anticipation and great excitement rises amongst the children:

the grandchildren of the old women of the village. At night the children go together down to the beach, armed with torches or simple sticks alight at one end. Their beacons illuminate a beach full of small, scuttling hermit crabs inhabiting their protective shells. With an occasional scream of delight, the children eagerly gather handfuls of the small crabs into buckets which they give to their grandmothers for the following day's fishing. The grandmothers, well into their sixties and seventies, know and love the sea intimately: the sea keeps them alive and they respect, nurture and value those abiding patterns and reciprocal relationships. In the morning they take their pouch of small crabs and wade into the lagoon. They may be immersed in the sea for six or seven hours, long enough for the tide to rise to mid-chest height and recede again.

With intricate and intimate skill and knowledge, the women coax the small crabs from the shells where they have retreated. They do this by singing to the crab the sounds of the sea: the sound of waves washing through the crab's home. The crab, lulled into believing it is back amongst the ocean, pops out of its shell, only to meet its fate, for the old woman expertly and deftly hooks the crab and lowers it as bait for the fish in the lagoon. The shell, the crab's former home, is returned to the ocean for the cycle of renewal: another crab will make the shell its home. All day the women enjoy and value each other's lifelong friendship and the companionship they share with the sea. They live for the sea, and the sea lives in them. Their day's activity is rewarded with a pouch of fish, which they take home to feed and sustain their grandchildren and other loved ones. Late into the night, the children sit at the feet of their grandfathers as the elders pass on their stories of the sea – the journeys, fishing exploits, and myths that abound from the special relationship between their people and the ocean.

For generations, traditional fishers have depended on the sea for their sustenance and livelihood. They have long-term, vested interests in monitoring the abundance of marine life, and the relative health and balance of the aquatic ecosystem. Yet, their role is not limited to that of ecological monitoring or guardianship. They have deeper responsibilities to the rituals that maintain correct relationships within the very kosmos of which their culture is an interconnected and integral part – see Šunde (2004) for further exploration of ritual and indigenous kosmology. Thus, they must strictly observe those rituals, myths and cultural mores that sustain the interrelationships between their people, the sea, their totem species, and the ancestral deities. In keeping with these obligations, customary fishing rights are tightly guarded and defended. But the offerings of the sea are always shared communally in a generosity of spirit that affirms the generosity of the spirits who guide them. Walter Nona, an elder of the Torres Strait Islander people – a people who are 'of the Land and Sea' – describes a ritual of reciprocity that he performs in preparation for hunting:

> When I go hunting, I give something that is with me to the sea – drinking water I give to the sea, some food I give, that's in our culture. That's how you get everything easy for you – because you ask the sea for permission again. If you don't ask, you won't get. You have got to treat the sea with respect. (Nona 2003, p. 81)

Kalaveti Batibasaga (personal communication 1999)[7] recalls the negotiated harmony between families in the Fijian village who share with each other the gifts of food in a similar spirit of generosity. The adults of each household would spend the day gathering from their gardens, or hunting in the forests, or fishing in the lagoon. By the end of the day, some might have a net of fish or shellfish, another a basket of taro, and another perhaps a wild boar. Most likely, each would have more than sufficient to feed their own household. In the tropical heat of Fiji, fish must be eaten fresh, preferably on the same day as it is caught. Therefore, surplus fish were collected into a basket and a child would be sent to distribute the fish to the other families in the village. However, that child would not return with an empty basket; rather, the basket would be filled with other food items or gifts offered in exchange. Each family would have, more-or-less, a balanced diet of fish, taro, coconuts, green vegetables, and whichever crop or fruit was in season. In this example, food is valued beyond its instrumental use (for example, as a source of nutrition) to include social and cultural values that often hold greater significance for the people. Thus, benefits to any one individual are considered less important than the honouring of reciprocal relationships that ensure the health and wellbeing of the entire community.

However, when the first refrigerator was brought into the village, the intricate relationships that bound the villagers to each other began to change. Because the net of fish caught in one day could now be stored in the refrigerator, the fishers did not have to return to the sea as often. Furthermore, it was no longer necessary to share surplus fish with the other villagers. In fact, a catch of fish could be accumulated until market day and then sold for monetary gain rather than simply given away, free, to the other villagers. In this process, fish became a commodity. Soon after, as Kalaveti laments, the first locked door sealed the fate of the traditional Fijian village. Mistrust and resentment began to unsettle village relations, as did the perceived need to protect the stash of fish and the cash received from sales at the market. The bonds of reciprocity that for generations wove villagers together are now under considerable strain from the intrusion of modern technology and a growing tendency to define the value of oceanic and coastal resources in terms of economic profit and private wealth, rather than in terms of traditional communal values.

Not only are the slow rhythms of village life disrupted, but natural rhythms are also being artificially accelerated. In some cases, entire ecological cycles of renewal and the livelihoods that depend directly on the natural environment are in jeopardy because of the very development projects that were promoted as improving quality of life. Even the old women who 'sing the sea' now protest that the lagoons are filling with sediment and that fish populations have noticeably diminished. With the rains comes a brown slurry of mud visible around river mouths as a dark stain seeping out to sea. Logs washed down rivers signify deforestation in the mountainous interior by multi-national forestry corporations. Not only does this deforestation devastate ecosystems, but some of the mountain villages who sold their forest rights are left in abject poverty once their initial profits were carelessly spent by people unfamiliar with the ways of manipulating currency. Here, we witness a story that has equivalents all over the world wherever *Man of Nature* meets *Man of Money* (see Panikkar 1993, pp. 20–53).

RESTORING WISE VALUES: FROM *CHREMATISTICS* TO *OIKONOMIA*

These stories from Fiji provide simple illustrations of the distinction that Aristotle made in his *Politics* between *oikonomia* and *chrematistics*. The word 'economics' derives from the Greek root *oikos-nomos*, meaning 'management or administration of the household'. Where members of a household (or village) shared things, there was no purpose for ownership. As or when need arose for the exchange of useful goods, such as food, a barter or gift-giving transaction served to satisfy the needs of sufficiency. According to Aristotle, this art of exchange is 'natural', whereas the 'unnatural' art of acquisition developed as exchange extended to distant transactions and the import and export of goods from and to foreign sources. It was perhaps inevitable, therefore, that money-currency became the common, standardized measure of value. Aristotle referred to wealth produced from the 'lower form of the art of acquisition' as *chrematistics*, in which the unlimited pursuit of money-making and increasing profits became the purpose for retail trade – as it is today in the global economic market.

Ecological economist Herman Daly and theologian John Cobb state the case for an 'economics of community' based on the principles that characterize *oikonomia* (Daly and Cobb, 1994). While there is little doubt that Aristotle's definition of household was not limited literally to one household but to a much larger political unit, Daly and Cobb suggest the term household should be further extrapolated to include wider resources of land and community and the tangible and intangible values they entail. While the neoclassical economic paradigm is preoccupied with *chrematistics*, the reunion of economics and ecology – that is, ecological economics – could potentially restore the responsibilities of *oikonomia* or wise management of the 'household' defined in terms of all its myriad facets, as Daly and Cobb (1994, p. 138) suggest:

> Chrematistics ... can be defined as the branch of political economy relating to the manipulation of property and wealth so as to maximize short-term monetary exchange value to the owner. Oikonomia, by contrast, is the management of the household so as to increase its use value to all members of the household over the long run. If we expand the scope of household to include the larger community of the land, of shared values, resources, biomes, institutions, language, and history, then we have a good definition of 'economics for community'.

VALUING LOVE FOR THE OCEAN: FROM ECOLOGY TO ECOSOPHY

I suggest, however, that the 'study of the house' (ecology) and the 'management of the house' (economics) do not go far enough in thinking about *how* human beings ought to relate to and perceive the *oikos*, the earth. As long as ecologists and economists refer to the earth in terms of a house rather than a *home*, then moderns will continue to encounter nature as a stranger and therefore suffer the associated feelings of loss and estrangement from nature. Perceiving the *oikos*, Gaia, or 'Mother Earth' as many indigenous peoples refer to our planet, as our home embodies a sense of familiarity and belonging that comes with the acceptance of our relatedness to nature as part of a wider family of beings. This difference between house and home has radical implications that are worth exploring further.

Consider a house: it is property; it has a price based on market valuation; it is a piece of real estate that can be sold to the highest bidder. A house can be abandoned by someone and reoccupied by someone else. Furthermore, it can be owned and the owner has a legal right to alter the structure of the house (for example, to add or remove rooms) to suit his or her preferences. In contrast, a home can never truly be abandoned: we carry our sense of home within us even as we venture away from its physical location (New Zealand

Māori call this *turangawaewae*; their ancestral birthplace). A home implies a much richer connection and layers or depths of belonging to place. Far beyond the 'rights' of a house owner, those who feel at home also accept responsibilities to share and care for their home. Home is – or should be – a sanctuary, a safe haven where caring and love embrace family members and visitors alike, for 'home is where the heart is'. Hau'ofa (2000, p. 468) affirms this relationship as spiritual:

> There is a vast difference here that shows diametrically opposed perceptions of our relationship with our world: world as property, and world as lasting home. Home as a heritage, a shrine for those who have cared for it, and passed it on to us, their descendants. For those of us who hold this view, our relationship with our Earth is indeed spiritual.

What this calls for is a profoundly different way of relating to the earth – one that entails entering a personal relationship with her. As Panikkar (1993, p. 142) states, 'Obviously, a relationship with the Earth, like any personal relation, cannot be measured in scientific parameters.' Nor can such a personal relationship be 'studied' or 'managed' as the methodologies and etymologies of ecology and economics suggest. Indeed, the acceptance of 'relationship' requires acceptance that two or more things are *related*, and therefore the consideration that not only do human beings relate to the earth, but also that the earth relates to and responds to humans. This would require going far beyond the disciplinary boundaries of contemporary ecology to the sort of deep understanding and relationship with the ocean that moved marine biologist Sylvia Earle to exhort: 'You have to love it before you are moved to save it' (cited by Rosenblatt, 1998).

An enlarged respect for the earth is hinted at in the term *ecosophy*, which means: '...the wisdom of the biosphere, of the ecosphere, of nature, of the universe, rather than that of human thought concerning nature. ... Nature is the great educator, the great economy' (Vachon 1997, p. 2). It is with this recognition of the vast intelligence and, indeed, the ancient wisdom of the earth that indigenous peoples (and many other peoples) approach their relationships with nature; that is, with reverence, humility, and love – much as they would a parent or grandparent who they adore. That love is boundless, for it not only crosses cultural boundaries it also offers hope as a basis for pluralism, as Panikkar (1999, p. 11) affirms: 'We are more, not less, than "rational". And perhaps the more realistic basis on which to ground human conviviality is not rational knowledge but loving awareness'. Again, Hau'ofa (2000, pp. 155–156) summarizes this nondual relationship in a way that is as open and affectionate as the ocean herself:

we all know that only those who make the ocean their home and love it, can claim it as their own. Conquerors come, conquerors go, the ocean remains, mother only to her children. This mother has a big heart though; she adopts anyone who loves her.

CONCLUSION: THE OPEN HORIZON

The ocean is so much more than an 'economic externality' or a 'provider of ecosystem services', as some economists and ecologists assume (see Chapters 5 and 6). Rather, for many, the ocean is a living reality and a reality that gives us life precisely because '...the ocean is in us' (Hau'ofa 2000). This explanation cannot be restricted to a physical definition or reduced to a commensurable value. That is because the relationships that Epeli Hau'ofa and many others refer to are non-rational – that is, non-rational in the sense that their expressions in lived experience go beyond the dualistic limitation of rational values. Expressions of love and reverence for the ocean may indeed push up against the rational boundaries that define the privileged comfort zone in neoclassical economic theory – but it is precisely those insulating theoretical limits that need revising and, indeed, pushing through. Like the navigator sailing the vast oceans, economics should encourage an open and extensive search of its horizon for openings to other ways of approaching and valuing reality.

NOTES

1. Silvio Funtowicz and Jerry Ravetz (1994, p. 199) are alert to the irreducible complexity of the issues at stake in considering the value of an irreplaceable songbird. They explain: 'The issue is not whether it is only the marketplace that can determine value, for economists have long debated other means of valuation; our concern is with the assumption that in any dialogue, all valuations or 'numeraires' should be reducible to a single one-dimensional standard.'
2. Joseph Conrad's (1906, p. 38) personal reflections of his time at sea reveal his great passion for the sea and respect for the sailing ship of yesteryear: 'Such is the intimacy with which a seaman had to live with his ship of yesterday that his senses were like her senses, that the stress upon his body made him judge of the strain upon the ship's masts.'
3. This perspective is reinforced in maps of the world that place North America at the centre and therefore enlarge its hold on the world. Buckminster Fuller (1981, p. 3) challenged this cartographic distortion when he produced his own world map, explaining that: 'The Dymaxion World Map shows one world island in one world ocean with no breaks in the continental contours and with no visible distortion of the relative size or shape of any of the cartographic patterning'.
4. Raymond Dasmann (1976, p. 3) originally coined the term 'ecosystem people' to distinguish those people who are adapted to their local ecosystem from the 'biosphere people'

who he describes as those who can draw from the resources of the entire world. Whilst ecosystem people (for example, indigenous traditional cultures) have to live simply within the carrying capacity of their own ecosystem, biosphere people (for example, the global technological civilization) can exploit the resources of one ecosystem to the point of causing great devastation – something that would be impossible or unthinkable for people who were dependent upon that particular ecosystem.

5. A way-finder has rare and unusual talent and impressive skills that are displayed in his (he was usually male) acute attention to the environment in which he guides his vessel, always searching for signs in the paths of stars, in cloud formations, in bird zones, and in wave patterns as they break around islands and radiate outward to intersect his sphere of influence. His knowledge also embraces the experiences of his ancestors and the ancient masters whose teachings have been passed down through the generations. A way-finder may draw upon these ancient lessons through their expression and celebration in rich cultural narratives, myths, songs and chants. However, the application of those timeless lessons is always unique and always renewed or challenged by his own experiences.

6. Daly and Farley (2004, p. 50) claim that ecological economics adopts a kind of 'practical dualism', which they define as entailing: '...the mysterious problem of how the material and the spiritual interact.' They qualify this 'radically empirical' position with the following note: 'Although we suspect that mystery is an enduring part of the human condition and not just another word for "future knowledge not yet discovered," we nevertheless respect the scientific and philosophical quest to solve mysteries, including the mystery inherent in the dualism we advocate as a practical working philosophy'.

7. Kalaveti Batibasaga is an indigenous Fijian who lives in the village of Navola on the southern coast of Fiji's main island, Viti Levu. One of his many personal narratives on the traditional Fijian way of life is related here.

REFERENCES

Boulding, K.E. (1966), 'The economics of the coming spaceship earth', in N. Nelissen, J.V.D. Straaten and L. Klinkers (eds), *Classics in Environmental Studies: An Overview of Classic Texts in Environmental Studies*, Utrecht: International Books, pp. 218–228.

Collis, J.S. (1976), *Christopher Columbus*, London: Macdonald and Jane's.

Conrad, J. (1906), *The Mirror of the Sea: Memories and Impressions*, London: JM Dent and Sons Ltd.

Daly, H.E. and J.B. Cobb, Jr (1994), *For the Common Good: Redirecting the Economy toward Community, the Environment, and a Sustainable Future* (updated and expanded edition), Boston: Beacon Press.

Daly, H.E. and J. Farley (2004), *Ecological Economics: Principles and Applications*, Washington, DC: Island Press.

Dasmann, R. (1976), 'Toward a dynamic balance of man and nature', *The Ecologist*, **6**(1): 3.

Dening, G. (2004), *Beach Crossings: Voyaging Across Times, Cultures and Self*, Victoria, Australia: Melbourne University Publishing, www.common-place.org.

Fuller, R.B. (1981), *Critical Path*, New York: St. Martin's Press.

Funtowicz, S.O. and J.R. Ravetz (1994), 'The worth of a songbird: ecological economics as a post-normal science', *Ecological Economics*, **10**: 197–207.

Hau'ofa, E. (1994), 'Our sea of islands', *The Contemporary Pacific*, 6(Spring): 148–161.

Hau'ofa, E. (1998), 'The ocean in us', *The Contemporary Pacific*, 10(Fall): 391–410.

Hau'ofa, E. (2000), 'Epilogue: pasts to remember', in R. Borofsky (ed.), *Remembrance of Pacific Pasts: An Invitation to Remake History*, Honolulu: University of Hawai'i Press, pp. 452–471.

Heisenberg, W. (1958), *Physics and Philosophy: The Revolution in Modern Science*, London: George Allen & Unwin.

Jolly, M. (2001), 'On the edge? Deserts, oceans, islands', *The Contemporary Pacific*, 13(2): 417–466.

Magowan, F. (2002), 'Ganma: negotiating indigenous water knowledge in a global water crisis', *Cultural Survival Quarterly*, 26(2): 18–20.

Martinez-Alier, J., G. Munda and J. O'Neill (1998), 'Weak comparability of values as a foundation for ecological economics', *Ecological Economics*, 26: 277–286.

Max-Neef, M.A. (2005), 'Foundations of transdisciplinarity', *Ecological Economics*, 53(1): 5–16.

Nicolescu, B. (2002[1996]), *Manifesto of Transdisciplinarity* [Translated from the French by K.C. Voss (2002)], New York: SUNY Press.

Nona, W. (2003), 'The sea', in *Elders: Wisdom From Australia's Indigenous Leaders*, Cambridge: Cambridge University Press, pp. 79–97.

Norgaard, R.B. (1985), 'Environmental economics: an evolutionary critique and a plea for pluralism', *Journal of Environmental Economics and Management*, 12: 382–394.

Norgaard, R.B. (1989), 'The case for methodological pluralism', *Ecological Economics*, 1: 37–57.

Panikkar, R. (1993), *The Cosmotheandric Experience: Emerging Religious Consciousness*, S.T. Eastham (ed.), Maryknoll, New York: Orbis Books.

Panikkar, R. (1995), *Invisible Harmony: Essays on Contemplation and Responsibility*, H.J. Cargas (ed.), Minneapolis: Fortress Press.

Panikkar, R. (1999), *The Intra-Religious Dialogue*, Rev. Ed., New York: Paulist Press.

Rosenblatt, R. (1998), 'Call of the sea: SYLVIA EARLE Her Deepness welcomes us into her world of wonders', *Time Magazine*, 4 October.

Šunde, C. (2004), *The Water or the Wave? Toward a Cross-Cultural Ecology of Understanding for Environmental Practice*, Unpublished PhD, Palmerston North, New Zealand: Massey University.

Tagore, R. (2006), 'Ocean of forms', *Gitanjali*, New Delhi: Rupa & Co., retrieved 13 October from http://www.schoolofwisdom.com/gitanjali.html.

Vachon, R. (1997), 'Preface: ecosophy and silvilization', *INTERculture*, 132: 2.

Ward, B. and R. Dubos (1972), *Only One Earth: The Care and Maintenance of a Small Planet*, Middlesex, England: Pelican Books.

PART III

Marine Sustainability: Integrating Ecology, Economics and Social Dimensions

If the oceans and coasts are to be sustainably managed, it is imperative that ecological economists have tools, methods, processes and examples of how ecological, economic and social factors can be simultaneously considered in a 'connected-up' way. Unfortunately, this is often not achieved because of the fragmented (disciplinary-based) way economists, social scientists and ecologists tend to investigate the issues.

Chapter 9 is about connecting the economic and ecological dimensions. It shows how the ecology of oceans and coasts are inextricably linked to economic activity. This chapter provides an understanding of the 'economic drivers' that directly and indirectly affect marine ecosystems: growth in the coastal economy, increasing demand for marine products (fish, energy, minerals, tourism), and the indirect effects of inland agriculture and industry.

Chapter 10 provides a practical example of a tool (dynamic simulation modelling) that can facilitate better understanding of the complex relationships that exist between economic and ecological systems. It shows how dynamic simulation models can help us test policy alternatives for solving problems that occur in the marine environment. Two case studies are used in this chapter to demonstrate the power of such tools, which are increasingly being used by ecological economists.

Chapter 11 is about connecting the social dimension to the question of the ecological economics of the oceans and oceans, by examining the particular issues of poverty and inequity. All too often ecological economists ignore this 'social dimension', despite persistent calls to include it. As such, poverty and inequity are issues that remain largely ignored in the ecological economics discourse. This chapter is about making sure that, in developing an ecological economics of the oceans and coasts, these 'social' issues don't continue to be neglected.

9. Economic Drivers of Change and their Oceanic–Coastal Ecological Impacts

Murray Patterson and Derrylea Hardy

The focus of this inquiry is on how economic drivers of change impact on oceanic and coastal ecosystems. This chapter is approached from a narrative perspective, rather than relying on the insights of formal 'growth theory' models,[1] which tend to be highly abstracted accounts of economic growth trajectories relying on single-sector models and a highly reduced set of explanatory variables. Instead, we attempt to think of the connections between the economy and the oceanic-coastal system in terms of a 'messy mosaic' of spatial, economic, ecological and other factors, rather than relying on the 'stylized facts' that underpin growth neoclassical theory models, such as those advanced by Solow (1956) and more recently by Romer (1990). We believe our approach is more sympathetic to the endeavor of ecological economics, which attempts to view economy–environment relationships in a more holistic rather than reductionist fashion.

Understanding the nexus between the economy and the environment is, of course, the central question to which ecological economists seek answers. The discussions of this question can be wide-ranging and touch on many areas of common interest to conventional (neoclassical) economists, such as: the 'de/coupling' of economic growth and environmental impacts; the role of technology in progressing (and working against) sustainability and economic goals; the substitutability of natural and manufactured capital; and the pertinence of biophysical/thermodynamic limits. Most of the areas have been thoroughly debated, albeit in many cases without clear resolution, and almost entirely in the context of the land-based economy and industrial processes. For example, there has been much analysis of the relationship between land-based industrial pollution and economic growth via Environmental Kuznet Curve analysis (Harbaugh et al. 2002). However, there have been very few studies, if any, specifically addressing these issues that have an oceanic–

coastal focus. The purpose of this chapter, therefore, is to draw some initial conclusions about the connections between 'the economy' and the 'oceanic–coastal' ecological system that may suggest future in-depth analysis.

ECONOMIC DRIVERS OF CHANGE THAT AFFECT THE OCEANIC–COASTAL SYSTEM

Growth of Coastal Economies and Population Centers

A significant proportion of the world's population (about 44 per cent)[2] and associated economic activity is located in a 150-km-wide zone extending inland from the coast. Furthermore, this 'coast-based economy' is growing faster than the 'non-coastal economy'. For example, GDP growth in coastal Chinese provinces has consistently outpaced that of inland regions for many years, with per capita GDP in coastal China being 79 per cent above the national average (Early Warning 2004).

All of this increased economic activity in the coastal zone puts increasing pressures on coastal ecosystems including estuaries, coastal wetlands, coastal waters and offshore ecosystems such as seagrass beds (refer to the next section for details of these ecological impacts). Most (16 out of 20) of the world's megacities are in coastal locations, which further exacerbates and intensifies the impacts on coastal ecosystems in specific growth corridors and nodes along our planet's coasts. With the exception of Tokyo, New York, Los Angeles and Osaka, all of these coastal megacities are in the developing world where both population and economic growth are occurring more rapidly and having ever-accelerating impacts on the coastal environment.

The majority of these coastal megacities are on navigable rivers with access to the sea. Cities usually develop around areas of industry, and ports have historically been the life blood that feed many megacity industries (UN 2005). In particular, the sea-orientated megacity is a frequent phenomenon in South Asia, the Atlantic coast of Africa and Mediterranean countries. The role of colonization in the choice of these cities in Asia and West Africa has been stressed by many scholars such as Dogan (2003). For example, most of the 20 Chinese maritime cities with populations of more than 1 million inhabitants are former treaty ports.

A pertinent and meaningful explanation was formulated by Charles Horton in the late 1800s as to why so many of today's megacities were built on waterfronts. He elaborated a theory of the 'break' in transportation – that is, an interruption or 'break' in the movement of goods and their temporary storage, meant that cities grew up around the location of these 'breaks'. Thus, port cities grew at these locations and became the junctions between maritime and rail and, later, air transportation. For less developed countries, portal cities represented gateways to the rest of the global marketplace (Dogan 2003). The map of contemporary air traffic coincides largely with the map of maritime traffic and the map of highways. The explanation is obvious – the aeroplane comes to the mega-city and not the opposite.

Accelerated coastal growth through 'circular and cumulative causation'
During the 20th century, coastal populations have been growing rapidly around the globe because of the many economic opportunities and environmental amenities that coastal zones provide. According to Martin and Ottaviano (2001), growth and geographic agglomeration of economic activities are mutually self-reinforcing processes. Growth fosters agglomeration because, as sectors at the origin of innovation expand, new firms tend to locate close to these sectors, which are often located in coastal locations.

Likewise, the theory of *circular and cumulative causation* originated by Gunnar Myrdal shows that large-scale migration has increasingly occurred from developing (periphery) to developed (core) regions that are often on the coast. This is due to both the employer-led demand for low-wage workers, and the worker-led demand for employment. Social networks also play a significant role in migration, whereby networks build a self-perpetuating momentum into the migration process that leads to its growth over time, in spite of fluctuating wage differentials, recessions, and increasingly restrictive immigration policies in developed nations. Additionally, tourists have been increasingly attracted to these large, coastal agglomerations that were more easily accessed because of their coastal locations, and because of the many and varied activities that were available in larger cities, over and above that developed specifically for the tourist market (Heer 2002).

Further reinforcing the momentum of coastal agglomeration growth is the fact that, as population increases, a process of circular and cumulative causation occurs as greater amenities and infrastructure are created. The growing concentration of industry, manufacturing and commercial activities, investment and trade, in turn attracts increased migration due to the prospect of greater job availability and/or higher wages. There is also a further 'knock-on' effect of people migrating to these 'core' growth regions in order to be where their families reside. International 'hubs', and associated ports and transportation infrastructure, are further developed, and the growth continues. However, this theory applies only to a certain point, after which the increases in migration become 'gluts' and cease to be causative of further migratory population increases – unless, of course, economic opportunities to sustain population growth are created, which has often occurred by way of targeted investments and/or growth in new industries such as tourism.

Uneven development of coastal economies
Sub-national sociological data suggest that people living in coastal areas experience higher wellbeing than those living in inland areas, but the acute vulnerability of coastal ecosystems to degradation puts coastal inhabitants at greater relative risk (Agardy 2004). The world's wealthiest populations occur primarily in coastal areas (per capita income being four times higher in coastal areas than inland), and life expectancy is thought to be higher while infant mortality is thought to be lower in coastal regions (ibid.). In 1994, 18 of the top 20 US counties ranked by per capita income were coastal counties (Culliton 1998). One end result of coastal communities getting wealthier is a more resource-intensive lifestyle with larger ecological footprints that inevitably put an even greater strain on coastal ecosystems.

However, in spite of this wealth accumulation in coastal populations in the West, other coastal communities are politically and economically marginalized, particularly in the developing world (see Chapter 11). Wealth disparity and poverty has led to denied access to resources for many coastal communities. Fisheries decline has also reduced a readily accessible source of protein for many coastal communities in developing countries. Communities reliant on 'common pool coastal resources', such as fisheries, may also have their access to these resources further eroded by privatization and other economic reforms.

Growth in the World Economy and the Increasing Demand for Products

The world economy expanded a remarkable 6.3 times from 1950 to 1998, increasing from US_{1990}$5.3 to 33.7 billion (Maddison 2001). This was mainly due to the consumption by each person of more goods and services (2.7 times on average) and, to a lesser extent, the increase in the global population (2.3 times) (Maddison 2001).

Oceanic and coastal ecosystems are being affected significantly by this dramatic expansion of the global economy, both directly and indirectly. *Direct* impacts emanate from the ever-increasing demand for oceanic–coastal goods and services including fish, oil, gas, minerals, tourism products and international travel. As is explained elsewhere in this chapter, the increased demand for these goods and services is putting severe strain on many oceanic and coastal ecosystems. In many cases, such as fisheries, this demand can no longer be met on a sustainable basis. Cases such as oceanic energy and mineral stocks represent a finite resource (natural capital) that cannot be exploited indefinitely without being depleted.

Oceanic and coastal ecosystems are also being affected *indirectly* as the demand for goods and services increases in the global economy. Probably the most important indirect effect is the link between growth in the global economy and global warming. As the global economy grows, fuelled primarily by the burning of fossil fuels, so do CO_2 emissions – resulting in enhanced global warming and climate change. The link between global economic growth and increasing CO_2 emissions is strong, as indicated by Tucker's (1995) analysis. Indeed, as the global economy increased 6.3 times from 1950 to 1998, CO_2 emissions increased 3.4 times, being more closely correlated with economic growth than population increase (Marland et al. 2003). The effect of climate change (global warming) on oceanic and coastal ecosystems has been well documented. The effects include: inundation of coastal wetlands, contributing to the bleaching of coral reefs, changing oceanographic processes including upwelling and surface currents that affect marine productivity, and the loss of both marine habitat and biodiversity. Such climate change impacts are further discussed in the next section.

It can be argued that *all* sectors of the expanding global economy have at least some ecological impact on the oceanic–coastal environment, either directly or indirectly. However, as discussed in the following sections, some sectors have a disproportionate impact on the oceanic–coastal environment, including: coastal tourism, fishing, energy, minerals and agricultural sectors.

Growth of coastal tourism

Further exacerbating the concentration of human populations in coastal cities around the world is the rise of coastal tourism. Seasonal tourist numbers are often not reflected in national population figures, indicating that the pressures on coastal communities are much greater than would be suggested by coastal population figures alone. According to the WWF Global Marine Programme (2006), on top of the increasing movement of people taking up residence along the world's coastlines, 80 per cent of all tourism takes place in coastal areas. The coastal environment is a magnet for tourists, with ocean and coastal tourism widely regarded as one of the fastest growing areas of contemporary tourism.

Tourism is the world's biggest and fastest growing industry (Phillips and Jones 2006) and the major source of foreign exchange earning and employment for many developing countries (CBD/UNEP 2005). International tourism has grown exponentially in the last 50 years, with tourist numbers expanding a massive 65 times from about 10 billion in 1950 to 650 billion in 2000 (Rekacewicz, UNEP/GRID-Arendal 2001). This is a

much faster rate of growth than the global economy, which only expanded
six-fold over the same period (Maddison 2001). Furthermore, World Travel
and Tourism Council (2006) projections are that the industry is expected to
grow 4.6 per cent (real terms) to total $US6.5 trillion in 2006, and an average
4.2 per cent per annum growth for 2007 to 2016 is then forecast.

The drivers of tourism growth are diverse and complex, and motivations to
travel vary greatly. However, key drivers of increased tourism, generally
speaking, relate to greater affordability (in terms of cheaper travel and
increased societal and personal wealth, primarily in the developed world),
greater knowledge of and exposure to tourism opportunities, greater ease of
travel and accessibility of tourist locations such as coastal resorts, and
increasing globalization or 'local internationalization' (Hall and Page 2006;
Theobald 2005).

Europe accounts for 60 per cent of international tourists and is the world's
largest holiday destination, with business growing by 3.8 per cent a year
(EEA 2005). Much of this tourism is concentrated in the Mediterranean
region, with over 100 million of the 220 million tourists to this region every
year flocking to the beaches (WWF Global Marine Programme 2006). In less
than 20 years, the annual number of tourists visiting the area is expected to
increase to 350 million (WWF 2005). As the big resorts of the western
Mediterranean fill up, areas to the east are becoming increasingly popular,
including the Greek islands and Cyprus, as well as Malta to the west. Malta
receives more than 1 million tourists a year, three times its permanent
population (EEA 2005). The tourism infrastructure developments and
associated urban populations that have arisen to cater for the tourism industry
in Europe have significantly affected the natural dynamics of many
Mediterranean coastal ecosystems. This infrastructure alone is a major cause
of habitat loss in the region (WWF Global Marine Programme 2006).
Ironically, in Europe as elsewhere in the world, the very resources that attract
tourists to a region are increasingly becoming so degraded that they may
become the reason for declines in tourism, thereby creating substantial
declines in regional economic activity and foreign exchange earnings and
associated employment and household income.

A further trend of importance to the impact on oceanic and coastal
ecosystems is cruise ship tourism, one of the major growth areas of the
international tourism market. Cruise tourism has increased at almost twice the
rate of tourism overall, with an annual increase of 8 per cent for the last few
decades (Wood 2000), and up to 15 per cent more recently (Dowling 2006).
Charlier and McCalla (2006) estimate a cruise supply of 109.2 million bed-
supply days, of which 57.1 per cent was in North and Central American
waters, 24.1 per cent in Europe and 16.2 per cent in the rest of the world

(with 2.7 per cent of vessels being 'idle' at any one time).

Increasing demand for fish products and subsidization of fishing

A critical driver of change in coastal and oceanic ecosystems is the increasing human demand for fish and fish products to meet the needs of the ever growing global population. Consequent overfishing not only results in the collapse of a significant number of commercial fisheries, but also in habitat loss through bottom trawling, thus negatively affecting non-target species both directly and indirectly (Worm et al. 2002).

Worldwide annual per capita consumption of fish and shellfish is approximately 34 pounds (15 kg), but this varies considerably among regions and individual countries. Europeans and Asians tend to have the highest per capita consumption (Lackey 2005). Fish proteins provide at least 20 per cent of the average intake of animal protein for more than 2.6 billion people – more than 50 per cent in parts of Asia and Africa (FAO 2004; Greenfacts 2005), and up to 100 per cent in Southeast Asia and the South Pacific (Hinrichsen 2004).

Fish is the most heavily traded food commodity and the fastest growing 'agricultural' commodity on international markets. In 2002, half the $US58.2 billion world fish trade was from developing countries, exceeding the value of the combined net exports of rice, coffee, sugar and tea (World Bank 2004, 2005). Demand for seafood products has doubled over the last 30 years and is projected to continue growing at 1.5 per cent per year to 2020 as global population grows and per capita fish consumption rises. To meet this demand, the number of fishers and fish farmers also grew markedly, having doubled in the last 20 years, with much of this increase occurring in developing countries as people have turned to fishing for an alternative or supplemental income source (Kura et al. 2002). The total demand for fish products is expected to increase to 127.8 million metric tons by 2020 (World Bank 2005). Given the issues of overexploitation of fisheries stocks and oceanic and coastal habitat degradation and loss occurring worldwide, the capacity to increase food sources from the oceans seems at the least problematic.

It can be argued that heavy government subsidization of the fishing industry has artificially increased the demand for fish products by making them available at cheaper prices to the consumer. Subsidy levels supporting the fisheries sector – mostly in industrialized countries – are estimated to be $US20–50 billion per year (Pauly and Alder 2006). Industrial countries have increasingly 'subsidy-supported' fishing fleets to operate in developing countries, often in direct competition with local fishers. According to the World Bank (2004, pp. x–xi) 'during 1993–97, the European Union fishing fleet caught over 600 000 tons per year, or 11 per cent of their catch, in distant waters; and in 1998, Japan, Korea, Taiwan and the US caught about 1.8 million tons of tuna in the 200-mile Exclusive Economic Zones of the Pacific Island countries'.

Government subsidization not only results in encouraging overfishing with negative ecological outcomes, but can also disadvantage local fishers in poorer countries. Furthermore, many economists would see this level of government subsidization as being economically 'inefficient'.

The practice of farm raising fish and shellfish, known as *aquaculture or mariculture*, emerged in response to dwindling ocean fish catches. This industry has burgeoned and diversified to take up the slack and meet food and income needs. Over the past three decades, aquaculture has become the fastest growing food production sector in the world, with 37.9 million metric tons of fishery products in 2001 – nearly 40 percent of the world's total fish supply (Kura et al. 2002). Pauly et al. (2002), however, warn that aquaculture cannot be expected to compensate for the shortfall in global fish catches, and in fact may well exacerbate it. It is argued that aquaculture operations are also largely 'unsustainable' because of their heavy dependence on inputs such as water, energy and chemicals. Aquaculture also poses a threat to native biodiversity due to habitat modification, the spread of diseases into wild populations, and because escapees may out-compete native species (in the case of exotic species) or modify existing gene pools (in the case of indigenous species).

Increasing demand for mineral and energy products

Arguably, fossil fuels are the most commercially valuable resources extracted from the seas and oceans, totally $US438 billion per annum in 1994, compared with the fish catch at $US397 billion for the same year (refer to Chapter 7). Offshore fossil fuel sources account for about 30 per cent of the world's oil production and about 50 per cent of the world's natural gas production (UNDOA/ISA 2002). The most significant known source of offshore oil and gas is in the Persian Gulf, which holds about 57 per cent of the world's crude oil reserves and 45 per cent of total proven world gas reserves (Persian Gulf Committee 2005). However, such marine sources of fossil fuels are coming under increasing pressure in every continent around the world, as terrestrial sources of oil and gas are being rapidly exhausted.

The total value of offshore mineral exploitation is valued by the International Seabed Authority (2003) at $2 billion per annum, being only a very small proportion of the value of offshore fossil fuel exploitation. According to Corbett (2004, cited in UNDOA/ISA 2002, p. 2), offshore production of tin in South East Asia is 'considerable', gold has been intermittently mainly offshore-led in Alaska, and diamonds are currently mined from the seabed offshore from Namibia and South Africa.

The future potential of offshore minerals is, however, difficult to assess, particularly as much of the seabed has not been surveyed in detail. For example, the International Seabed Authority (2003) reports that only about 5 per cent of the 60 000 kilometres of oceanic ridges worldwide have been surveyed 'in any detail'. Nonetheless, considerable reserves of minerals are known to exist on the ocean floor including: reserves of 'polymetallic modules' (golf-ball to tennis-ball size modules of nickel, cobalt, iron and manganese in varying proportion), cobalt rich ferromanganese crusts, and 'polymetallic massive sulphides'. To what extent these are 'realizable resources' is an unanswered question at this stage, given the significant technological, thermodynamic and economic constraints they have in their development. For many people, however, the oceans and seas, including the pristine environment of Antarctica, remain the 'final frontier' for exploiting energy and mineral resources.

Increasing demand for agricultural and food products
The ever-increasing demand for food to nourish the world's expanding population is an important economic driver of change in oceanic and coastal ecosystems – not just for the obvious pressure it exerts on fish resources, but also for the 'knock-on' effects that terrestrial food production has on oceanic–coastal ecosystems. Runoff of nutrients (phosphorus and more particularly nitrogen) into the world's oceans and seas have dramatically increased over the last 50 years, as agriculture has expanded and become more intensive and reliant on fertilizers. The consequential 'over-enrichment' of oceanic and coastal environments that is occurring on a worldwide scale has a number of significant ecological effects. These effects include a greater occurrence of hypoxic or 'dead zones', loss of habitat and biodiversity, particularly in near-shore situations, and even impacts on climate change as marine rates of carbon sequestration are affected.

Over the last 50 years, global food production has tripled; the average food intake per person has also increased (International Food Policy Research Institute 1995). This dramatic increase in food production was mainly due to the so-called 'Green Revolution', whereby yields increased by using improved crop varieties, expansion of irrigation schemes, and the heavier application of fertilizers and pesticides (Duda and El-Ashry 2000).

The amount of nitrogenous fertilizers has increased from about 12 million tons in 1961 to about 83 million tons in 2002 (Brown et al. 2006). The increase in phosphorus fertilizers was not quite so dramatic, increasing from about 11 million tons in 1961 and peaking at 29 million tons in 1989, but

declining slightly in the 1990s (Brown et al. 2006). Data collated by UNEP
(2005) show that, at least for nitrogen, the flows from various watersheds to
the ocean increased proportionately according to the level of nitrogen
fertilizer application to land. Nitrogen flow rates into the marine environment
are arguably the most relevant as scientific evidence shows that nitrogen is
usually the 'limiting factor' (to biomass production) in most marine
ecosystems – refer to Valiela (2006) and Howarth (1988).

Consequently, the 'over-enrichment' of oceanic and coastal ecosystems is
highly correlated with increased food production, which requires ever
increasing amounts of nitrogen and phosphorus fertilizers. As well as 'over-
enrichment' of the marine environment mainly attributable to more intensive
use of fertilizers, agricultural expansion and intensification have also had
other negative impacts on oceanic and coastal ecosystems: (1) increased
pesticide residues have been recorded in many marine ecosystems; (2) soil
loss and sedimentation from agricultural sources have had an adverse effect
on coastal and oceanic habitat; and (3) fossil fuel use by agriculture is
significant, materially contributing to greenhouse gas emissions worldwide
which have a series of negative consequences for coastal and oceanic
ecosystems.

IMPACTS ON COASTAL ECOSYTEMS

Even though coastal ecosystems cover only a very small percentage (1.2 per
cent) of the earth's surface, they are remarkably productive, dynamic and
ecologically important ecosystems. Given the close proximity of these
ecosystems to centers of population and the pressures exerted by adjoining
agricultural catchments, coastal ecosystems are, however, the most affected
by human economic development and the most under threat.

Loss of Habitat in Coastal Ecosystems

Economic growth and development over the last 50 years has had a severe
impact on all coastal ecosystems, leading to significant habitat loss.

Loss of mangroves

Many areas of mangroves are being degraded or eliminated by human
activity and associated development pressures. The global rate of mangrove
deforestation and habitat loss is estimated to be 1–2 per cent per annum,
resulting in them being one of the world's most threatened tropical

ecosystems (Dulvy et al. 2003; Valiela et al. 2001; Walters 2003). Local losses, however, are often much larger than this – for example, 90 per cent loss in the Philippines: from one million hectares in 1960 to around 100 000 hectares in 1998 (Hinrichsen 2004; Walters 2003). Globally, for countries for which there are available data, it is estimated that 35 per cent of mangroves have disappeared in the last two decades (Brown et al. 2006). The main economic activities that have caused mangrove habitat loss are conversion for use for agriculture and aquaculture; urban industrial and port development; and the use of mangroves for fuelwood.

Loss of estuaries

The loss of estuaries is more difficult to estimate on a global scale. However, data show significant loss of estuaries, particularly those in close proximity to urban centers and ports. Dayton (2003) indicates that half the original estuaries and wetlands areas of US coasts have now been 'substantially' altered. Estuaries are not only lost or modified due to port development, infilling and civil engineering works, but are also significantly affected by their urban and agricultural watersheds. Agricultural runoff, for example, often causes estuarine areas to become eutrophied and/or hypoxic (oxygen depleted). The hydrology of estuaries is also often affected by upstream dams which may, for example, reduce the fresh water supply to estuaries thus causing hypersalinization.

Loss of coral reefs

Coral reefs are arguably the most 'finely-tuned' and fragile of ecosystems, and thereby the most vulnerable to human-induced impacts. Human activities that impact on coral reefs include construction works, destructive and over-fishing, removal of coral for ornamental purposes, runoff from adjoining land, and human-induced climate change causing bleaching.

More than half the world's coral reefs are potentially threatened by human activities, with up to 80 per cent at risk in the most populated areas (UNEP 2005). Of the world's 600 000 km^2 of reefs found in tropical and semi-tropical seas, scientists estimate that 70 per cent of them – some 400 000 km^2 – could be lost within 40 years (Hinrichsen 2004). A global effort to assess the status of coral reefs by The World Conservation Union found that 20 per cent of the world's coral reefs have been effectively destroyed and show no immediate prospect of recovery; that 24 per cent of the world's reefs are under imminent risk of collapse through human pressures, with a further 26 per cent being under a longer term threat of collapse; while 40 per cent of the 16 per cent of the world's reefs that were seriously damaged by El Nino in 1998 are either recovering well or have recovered (Wilkinson 2004). In the

Caribbean, the rate of living coral is only 20 per cent; Southeast Asia has the second lowest rate of coral reefs in good condition (30 per cent), with more than 80 per cent of corals in this Asian region at risk (Hinrichsen 2004).

Loss of seagrass beds

In the Millennium Ecosystem Assessment, Brown et al. (2006) report 'major losses' of seagrass habitat in the Mediterranean, Florida and Australia. These losses are mainly attributable to human activities including coastal development, runoff from agricultural land which causes eutrophication, habitat conversion for things such as algae farming, and human-induced climate change effects. Indeed, Hemminga and Duarte (2000) report large-scale seagrass decline at over 40 locations, 70 per cent of which were 'unambiguously attributable' to human-induced disturbance. Present losses are expected to accelerate, particularly in developing tropical regions such as South-East Asia, East Africa and the Caribbean, as human pressure on the coastal zone grows and capacity to implement conservation policies is limited (Duarte 2002). Given that the bulk of extant seagrass meadows are found on the coastline of developing nations, which are experiencing the greatest rate of environmental degradation at present and will continue to do so in the future, this problem can only be exacerbated.

Loss of kelp forests

Brown et al. (2006) concluded that it is likely that no kelp systems exist in their 'natural condition'. Fishing, in particular, has had an impact on kelp forests. With the removal of predators through fishing, populations of other species such as sea urchins have exploded, greatly simplifying the ecosystem structure.

Impacts of Nutrient-Bearing Pollutants on Coastal Ecosystems

Coastal ecosystems have been greatly affected by nutrient-bearing non-point source runoff from agricultural land, as well as by point source discharges from industrial and sewage sources. This nutrient over-enrichment of the coastal zone has led to the eutrophication of coastal ecosystems with consequential loss of habitat, alteration of ecosystem structure and, sometimes, biodiversity loss.

The increase in nutrients flows from the terrestrial to the marine environment is reasonably well documented. UNEP (2005) reports that nitrogen flows since the Industrial Revolution have increased markedly from the following watersheds: North Sea Watersheds (15×), North Eastern US (11×), Yellow River (10×), Mississippi River (5.7×), Baltic Sea (5×), Great

Lakes/St Laurence River Basin (4×), and South Western Europe (3.7×). Bouman et al. (2005) report that by 2030, global river nitrogen exports from the terrestrial to the marine environment are projected to be 49.7 Tg/yr, with natural sources contributing 57 per cent, agricultural 34 per cent, and sewage 9 per cent. A similar picture also emerges for phosphorus enrichment of the coastal zone, although nitrogen is the chief culprit in eutrophication and other impacts of nutrient over-enrichment in temperate coastal waters.

The ecological impacts of this nutrient over-enrichment vary across ecosystem type and geographical location in the coastal zone. Typically, however, the range of ecological impacts includes:

- blooms of algae become more frequent and extensive, resulting in increased mortality of fish and other species;
- submerged plant communities, such as seagrass beds and kelp forests, can be harmed by loss of light due to other nutrient induced growth, which can lead to consequential loss of spawning and nursing grounds for fish;
- high nutrient levels in coral reefs are usually detrimental, as they stimulate movement away from coralline algae that helps build up coral structure towards dominance by algae turfs or sea weeds that cover reefs (Howarth et al. 2000);
- moderate nutrient enrichment of the coast can be seen as 'beneficial' as it can lead to increased catches of commercial fish, but this may also be a 'cost' in terms of loss of biodiversity of other species and the simplification of community structure;
- estuarine environments are particularly susceptible to nutrient enrichment as they are often the 'confluence point' for nutrients flowing from the terrestrial to the marine environment. Bricker et al. (1999), for example, found that 65 per cent (in surface area terms) of estuaries in the US had moderate to high eutrophic conditions. More eutrophic estuaries are characterized by macroalgal abundance problems, epiphyte abundance, low dissolved oxygen, nuisance and toxic algal blooms and loss of submerged aquatic vegetation.

Impacts of Non-Nutrient Pollutants on Coastal Ecosystems

Economic activities in urban and rural areas also produce an array of non-nutrient pollutants that find their way into the coastal environment, primarily through runoff and hydrological processes. These 'non-nutrient' pollutants (persistent organic substances, heavy metals, oil and oil by-products, litter, pathogens) directly impact on coastal ecosystems and the quality of the coastal environment.

Pesticides and other persistent organic chemicals from industry are toxic and can accumulate in organisms for decades. Although the use of persistent organic pesticides (POP) such as DDT, chloridene and heptachlor stopped in most countries 20–30 years ago, they can still be found in oceanic and coastal environments. Through the process of bioaccumulation, they concentrate further up the food chain in fish, predatory birds, mammals and humans. Even in the most remote coastal environments, such as in the Arctic and Canada, high levels of POPs have been detected in wildlife.

Urban runoff and industrial activity are also significant sources of 'non-nutrient' pollutants into coastal regions. Valiela (2006), for example, provides a comprehensive analysis of the effect of polychlorinated biphenyls (PCBs) on organisms in the New Bedford Harbour, including bacteria, dinoflagellates, shellfish, eels and fish species. The water quality inevitably deteriorates and intensifies around all the world's most urbanized coastal areas as a result of urban runoff, stormwater runoff, leachate from landfills, sewage disposal and point-source industrial discharges. Urban runoff, for example, typically contains a cocktail of oil, grease, pesticides from turf management, road salts, metals, bacteria and viruses. Often such urban runoff will accumulate in shellfish and other species.

Impacts of Alien Species on Coastal Ecosystems

Economic activity often results in invasive or alien species being introduced into coastal environments, albeit mostly by accident rather than by intention nowadays. Many (accidental) invaders into the coastal environment have been introduced by either being attached to ship's hulls or, more commonly, in ballast water. Many species of diatoms, protozoans and copepods may last up to 10 months, dinoflagellates 5 months, and flagellates, ciliates, nematodes, larvae of worms and bivalves 1–2 months (Cohen 1998). Other species have been deliberately imported for biological control – for example, for stabilizing eroding shores. Yet other species have been introduced by canal construction between two water bodies – for example, Lessepsian aliens have spread throughout the Mediterranean coastline from the Red Sea to the Suez Canal. Such 'alien species' can sometimes significantly change the compositional make up of coastal ecosystems (see examples of estuary invasions in Valiela 2006). In other cases the impact is either temporary, or more minor or 'accepted' by local residents. However, irrespective of the 'acceptability' to local residents of the invasion of alien species, there is compelling evidence of an increasing rate of the growth of new invasive species with the globalization of world trade and commerce – for example, Brown et al. (2006) reported at increase of around 52 non-native marine plant species on the European coast over the period 1970–1999.

Brown et al. (2006) also report that infectious diseases are a serious problem associated with aquaculture developments. Any infected fish that escape from aquaculture operations can infect natural populations of fish. As an example, Norwegian studies have shown migrating salmon to be more infected with sea lice in salmon-farming areas.

Impacts of Climate Change on Coastal Ecosystems

It is increasingly accepted that climate change is the most profound ecological impact of economic activity. Many of these ecological impacts are important to the coastal environment.

Sea level rises due to global warming, however, will have the greatest impact on coastlines and coastal ecosystems. Of all the coastal ecosystems, coastal wetlands including salt marshes and mangroves are most vulnerable to the rise in sea level. The key factor is the rate of accretion of the wetland surface relative to sea level rise (Valiela 2006). If the accretion rate (accumulation of organic and sediments) of the surface does not exceed or equal the rate of sea level rise, it is likely coastal wetlands habitat will be lost. One adaptation to sea level rise is the inland migration of coastal wetlands, but this largely depends on the topography of inland areas. Nicholls et al. (1999) conclude that accelerated sea level rises (due to global warming) could lead to world coastline losses of up to 2 per cent by the 2020s.

In human terms, however, the most critical effect on the coastal environment is likely to be the potential inundation of the foreshore of low-lying areas in countries such as Bangladesh, Egypt, Senegal, Nigeria, Pacific Island states, and low-lying island groups such as the Maldives. Many major cities, as previously pointed out, are situated on low-lying lands on the coast. Although is has proven difficult to estimate the economic cost and number of people affected by projected accelerated sea level rise in the coastal zone, it is likely to be tens of millions of people and billions of dollars on a global scale over the next century (Darwin and Tol 2001).

As discussed earlier, coral reefs, for example, are particularly vulnerable to the effects of global warming, and the risk of the loss of vast areas of coral reefs is high. Climate change will have a disproportionate impact on coral reef ecosystems due to their delicate physio-chemical balance. Coral bleaching is known to occur when the ocean warms beyond a critical threshold – usually when waters become 2°C warmer than average (see Chapter 2).

Impacts of Coastal Sedimentation and Erosion

The supply of sediments to the coastal zone is important, for example, to sustain habitat in deltas and to maintain the sedimentation–erosion equilibrium. Human economic activity has played an important role in both decreasing (in some geographic locations) and increasing (in other geographic locations) the sediment supply to the coastal zone. Walling and Fang's (2003) analysis of 145 major river systems throughout the world found that 50 per cent of rivers over the last 36–66 years showed no statistically significant change in sediment loads. However, 30 per cent showed increasing loads and 20 per cent decreasing loads, resulting in a net reduction of sediment loads to the coast of about 10 per cent (Agardy and Alder 2006).

Dams, levees (stop banks), dikes, irrigation canals and other engineering structures can intercept sediments that otherwise would be transported to the coast by rivers. Perhaps the most dramatic example of sediment interception is the building of the Aswan High Dam on the Nile in 1964. After the High Dam was built, water input into the Nile delta decreased by 80 per cent and sediment input by 98 per cent (Stanley and Warne 1993). As a result, there has been erosion along parts of the Mediterranean coastline, salinization of cultivated land, and declines in sardine yields. Geographically, the coastlines of Asia and more particularly China (currently 22 000 dams) are most affected by dams that halt sediment flow to the coast.

Land-use changes, such as clearance of forests for agriculture and settlement, as well as poor farming and soil conservation practices, can have significant effects on increasing sediment yields in some geographical localities. Increased sedimentation change has a significant affect on mangroves, coral reefs and other coastal ecosystems. Excessive sedimentation can smother and kill coral tissue and reduce the light supply to symbiotic algae associated with corals.

On balance, however, *most coastal areas are ecologically affected by the net reduction of sediment loads*, which can significantly increase the rate of coastal erosion along with other factors such as sea level rise and wave/current action. Without sufficient replenishment by sediments, many coasts have eroded. For example, Valiela's (2006) forecasted developments on the Ebro River in Spain predict a continuing recession of the present delta.

This type of reduction of sediment loads reaching the coasts can markedly affect the area of coastal wetlands. The consensus view (Phillips 1986; Salinas et al. 1986), is that the salt marshes of the Mississippi delta have been subsiding principally as a result of the reduction of sediment loads, with the extraction of groundwater and sea land rise being contributing factors.

IMPACTS ON OCEANIC ECOSYSTEMS

For many people, the seas and oceans are the 'last frontier' for economic development. Ecosystems of the continental shelf and the open oceans cover a vast area of 35.9 million hectares (69 per cent) of the earth's surface. Ecologically, these ecosystems are important as they account for 44.5 per cent of the world's primary productivity (photosynthesis), although they have a relatively low productivity per hectare (Costanza et al. 1998; Field et al. 1998). Economically, in terms of contribution to human welfare, these ecosystems are also important, providing ecosystem services worth $US12.4 trillion, which is similar to the contribution of terrestrial ecosystem services of $US12.23 trillion (Costanza et al. 1997).

Impacts of Fishing on Oceanic Ecosystems

The most profound and widespread impact from economic activity on oceanic ecosystems is that of commercial fishing. The *Millennium Ecosystem Assessment* (Brown et al. 2006) concluded that 'it [fishing] is the major direct anthropocentric force affecting the structure, function and biodiversity of the oceans'.

Watson and Pauly's (2001) data show that global marine catches peaked in the late 1980s, after a period of sustained growth following World War II (refer to Box 9.1). Before then, depth and distance from coast meant that fisheries away from the continental shelf were essentially out of reach to most commercial fishing operations, thereby providing a refuge for the spawning of many species. Technological advancements (such as refrigeration freezer technology, electronic fish detection devices, GPS technology), as well as the heavy investment and subsidization of fisheries, have led to fishing fleets now covering most of the world's oceans.

The ecological impact of this 'industrial scale' fishing is highlighted by a number of indicators:

- The Food and Agricultural Organization's (2004) assessment of World Fish Stocks indicates that most of the world's fish stocks are being exploited beyond accepted 'sustainable limits': 47 per cent are 'fully exploited'; 21 per cent 'moderately exploited'; 9 per cent depleted; and 1 per cent 'recovering'. FAO (2004b) considers that only 4 per cent of world fish stocks are 'underexploited'. Figure 9.1, however, shows there is considerable regional variation in the 'state' of world fishery stocks.
- Pauly et al.'s (1998) comprehensive measurement of Average Trophic

Level of Fish Landings shows consistent decline since 1950 in four areas: the North Pacific, the North West and Central Atlantic, the North East Atlantic and the Mediterranean (see Figure 9.1). Pauly et al. (1998) refer to this phenomenon as 'fishing down the food web'. As top level predators are becoming scarcer, fishers are forced down the food chain, often catching species previously considered 'bait'. According to Pauly et al. (1998), the principal ecological impacts of fishing down the food chain are: (1) increases in the numbers of previously suppressed species, which are often invertebrates; and (2) simplification of food webs (reduction in number and length of food web pathways) leading to increased variability and lack of predictability in population sizes.

- FAO's (2004) database of world fisheries catch indicates that 366, or 24.1 per cent of the world's fisheries, collapsed between 1950 and 2000 (Mullon et al. 2005). Not all these collapses were due solely to overexploitation – climate change, for example, may also be a factor. However, Mullon et al. identified effective fishing effort as the principal cause of past fisheries collapses.

Bottom trawling has now been extended well beyond the 'traditional' fishing grounds of the continental shelf and is increasingly being recognized as having a significant impact on the ocean floor (benthos ecology). Bottom trawling is estimated to cover half the global continental shelf and now accounts for more of the world's catch than any other method (Dayton et al. 1995; Watling and Norse 1998). It is often likened to the clear-felling of forests in the terrestrial environment (Watling and Norse 1998). In this vein, the area bottom-trawled each year is equivalent to 150 times the total forest area clear-felled yearly, and corresponds to an area about twice the size of the contiguous US (Norse 1998). Until the 1950s, some areas were naturally protected from trawling, being too rocky, too deep or too remote to allow access. However, new technologies have permitted bottom trawling to occur almost anywhere. In intensively fished areas such as the North Sea, areas are bottom trawled from one to seven times yearly, providing little opportunity for populations to recover (UNEP/DEWA/Earthwatch 2005). Jones (1992) catalogues the main ecological impacts of bottom trawling: (1) zero relative increase in 'k strategist' (fast growing) compared with 'r strategist' (longer living) species because of frequent disruptions due to trawling; (2) permanent removal of macro-benthos where there is insufficient time for recovery; and (3) the adverse affect on plant and animal life of sediment re-suspension that can last for decades in areas of little water movement such as the deep ocean.

Another significant ecological impact of commercial fishing activity is the effect on non-target species. Leong (1998) estimates one quarter of the

Box 9.1 Future of World Fisheries: Malthusian Collapse or Ricardian Stationary State

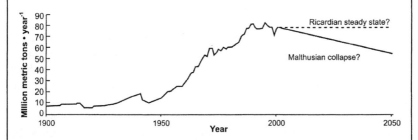

Malthus, in *An Essay on the Principles of Population* published in 1798, argued that the human population increased according to a geometric ratio, while land reserves (for food production) increased only in an arithmetic fashion. In this way, Malthus envisaged that population growth would eventually outstrip increases in food production. This, according to Malthus, would result in an 'overshoot' of carrying capacity and hence catastrophic decline in population. In modern parlance, Malthus considered population growth unsustainable as it outstripped the natural resource base.

Ricardo, another classical economist, also analyzed the land sustainability problem. Ricardo concluded that food resources would gradually diminish over time, as progressively poorer quality land (less fertile) would have to be farmed as the population increased. He envisaged 'diminishing marginal returns' of food production from land as the best land (resources) were exploited first. Ricardo's analysis did not predict the catastrophic decline of the human population; rather, he foresaw a slow and gradual decline in economic activity and population growth as the economy eventually moved to 'a stationary state'.

Pauly et al. (2003) identify two 'scenarios' for the future of world fisheries – one a 'best case' that corresponds to the Ricardian Stationary State, and the other a 'worst case' that corresponds to the Malthusian Collapse. Pauly et al. claim that the best case scenario would result from implementing proactive components of (their) 'Market First' and 'Policy First' scenarios. Both these scenarios involve a very significant reduction in current fishing effort ranging from 'half present' levels for the Market. First scenario to 'massive reductions' for the Policy First scenario. Without these reductions, Pauly et al. predict a dramatic collapse in World Fish Landings, akin to the Malthusian collapse.

world's annual fish catch (about 20 million tonnes) is discarded or not used each year. MacAllister (1998) similarly puts the bycatch at 17–39 million tonnes per annum. Besides fish, other non-target animals, notably including dolphins, sea turtles and sea birds are (unintentionally) caught in drift nets and long lines.

A final ecological consideration relating to commercial fisheries that is often canvassed is the issue of the 'fossil fuel subsidy' of fishing operations. Considerable oil-based products are required to power the world's fishing fleet and this is increasingly due to the need for vessels to search longer and in more remote locations to catch fish. Tydemers et al. (2005) estimate that 50 billion litres of oil is consumed to catch fish – equivalent to 1.2 per cent of the world's total per year oil consumption, or the amount of oil consumed by the Netherlands, which is the eighteenth ranked oil-consuming country globally.

Tydemers et al. (2005) found that worldwide, 12.5 times more fuel energy is used to catch the fish, compared with the edible protein energy yielded from the fish. That is, harvesting fish for food has a very low energy efficiency of only 8 per cent. Although this is a low energy efficiency, it is better than many other systems such as grain-feed animal protein systems; but unfortunately it is worse than crop protein systems and pasture-fed animal protein systems, which are both more energy efficient (Leach 1978).

Impacts of Pollutants and Wastes on Oceanic Ecosystems

The oceans and seas are not only a 'source' of biophysical resources such as biomass (fish), fossil fuels and mineral resources. They are also a 'sink' of wastes/pollutants from the global economy including carbon dioxide, nutrients sediments, nuclear wastes[3] and so forth. The ability of the oceans and seas to continue to absorb and process these wastes/pollutants is often mistakenly considered to be virtually limitless due to their vastness and size. The attitude is very much 'out of sight out of mind'. There is increasing evidence, however, of significant ecological impacts resulting from wastes and pollutants unsustainably flowing into the marine environment.

Impacts of nutrient-bearing pollutants on oceanic ecosystems

Nutrient loading of the ocean, principally from agricultural runoff, human sewage and burning of fossil fuels, is increasingly impacting on the oceans and seas, as well as on estuaries and wetlands, as previously discussed. The main ecological effect of this nutrient loading is hypoxic or 'dead zones' in the oceans and seas. Increased nutrients lead to excess growth of phytoplankton – as the phytoplankton and zooplankton die and sink below the photic zone, bacterial degradation causes a lack of dissolved oxygen in the water. These low dissolved oxygen levels make it difficult for fish and other species to survive – hence the label 'dead zones'.

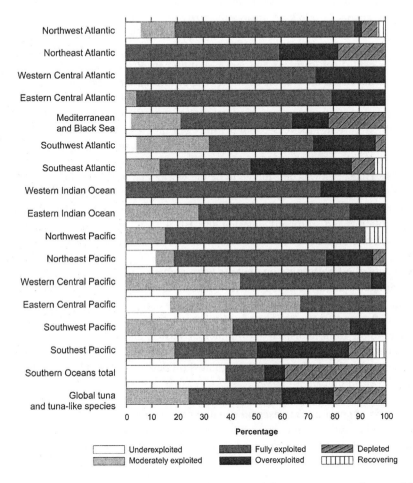

Figure 9.1 State of exploitation of marine fishery resources by world geographic regions

(*Source:* Adapted from FAO 2004b)

The world's largest dead zone is in the Baltic Sea, covering some 70 000 km^2 of seabed (Hinrichsen 2004). The largest zone of oxygen depleted coastal waters in the US and the entire western Atlantic Ocean, is found in the northern Gulf of Mexico on the Louisiana/Texas continental shelf, influenced by freshwater discharge from nutrient loads of the Mississippi River system. The dead zone in the Gulf of Mexico, now the world's second largest, covers 21 000 km^2, an area the size of Israel (Hinrichsen 2004). In the last half of the 20th century, the average annual nitrate concentration in the Gulf of Mexico doubled, and the mean silicate concentration was reduced by 50 per cent. Each summer, nutrient pollution causes a dead zone the size of Massachusetts in the Gulf of Mexico, with such problems occurring in almost every coastal state in the US (Panetta 2003). More than 60 per cent of US coastal rivers and bays are moderately to severely degraded by nutrient runoff. If current practices continue, nitrogen inputs to US coastal waters in 2030 may be as much as 30 per cent higher than at present and more than twice what they were in 1960 (ibid.).

The Black Sea was considered to be the world's largest dead zone until the early 2000s. UNEP (2005) reports that changes such as rising prices of fertilizers have resulted in significantly decreased levels of nutrients (phosphorus and nitrogen) entering the Black Sea, which has caused the Black Sea's dead zone to largely disappear and the fisheries to rebound.

Impacts of oil pollutants on oceanic ecosystems
Significant quantities of oil wastes associated with economic activity find their way into the seas and oceans. According to UNEP (2005), in 2003, 306 000 tonnes were deliberately discharged from vessels, 140 000 tonnes were runoff from industrial and municipal wastes, and 100 000 tonnes were from accidental tanker spills. Oil slicks kill birds, marine mammals and fish, particularly near the coasts, and coagulated oil destroys coastal habitats. Even low levels of oil can kill larvae.

Impacts of greenhouse gases on oceanic ecosystems
Climate change, brought about principally by the combustion of fossil fuels (in the economy), is becoming a major driver of environmental change in the marine environment (see Chapter 2). Many of the ecological impacts are only now being understood. These impacts include:

- Acidification of the oceans brought about by increasing amounts of CO_2 being absorbed. As pH levels of the ocean drop, the shells and hard skeletons of plankton and corals dissolve. These losses that have consequences for the entire marine food chain.
- Changing wind patterns and sea temperatures will impact on a number of oceanic processes. The *Millennium Ecosystems Assessment*, for example,

reports that recent studies of the North Atlantic suggest the Gulf Stream may be slowing down (Brown et al. 2006). More generally, sea temperature changes will affect the viability of species ecosystems in all oceans and seas.

• With the predicted reduction of 10–30 per cent nutrient supply to the upper ocean (due to less mixing because of warmer waters), there are expected to be significant decreases in biological productivity in the ocean and seas (Matear and Hirst 1999).

CONCLUDING REMARKS

It is clear that the rapid post-WWII growth of the world economy is now having a profound impact on oceanic and coastal ecosystems. Many of these impacts are *indirect* and related to economic activity occurring in regional economies far away from the coast. For example, agricultural activity in inland catchments in the US is a major contributor to the occurrence of hypoxic (dead) zones in the Gulf of Mexico. In this respect, there is not only a fundamental need for scientists to better understand these land–oceans–coasts interactions,[4] but for ecological economists to take this information to work towards a more holistic understanding of exactly how the global economy is impacting on oceanic and coastal ecosystems. This involves understanding and quantifying complex relationships between economic and ecological processes, which often traverse the terrestrial and marine environments (see Chapter 10). The resulting research agenda for ecological economics is a challenging one, not only because of its complexity and difficulty, but also because it is an area virtually untouched by ecological economics. Previous ecological economics research on 'economy–environment interactions' has almost exclusively had a terrestrial focus or at the very least has not teased-out the implications of global economic growth for the oceanic–coastal environment in any depth at all.

NOTES

1. In addition to 'growth theory models', 'growth accounting' explanations of economic growth are also used in neoclassical economics. They, like growth theory models, are also characteristically reductionist, although they are more grounded, insofar as they use empirical facts to explain economic growth trends in the macro-economy (for example, Denison 1974).
2. Cohen et al. (1997) state that 44 per cent of the 1994 world population lived within 150 km of the coast. According to Hinrichsen (1998), nearly half the world's population lives within 200 km of the seashore and this number could increase up to 75 per cent by 2025. Small and

Nicholls (2003) apply stricter criteria and therefore they arrive at a more conservative estimate of the world's coastal population. They estimate that the coastal population living within both 100 km of the shoreline and 100 m of sea level is estimated to be 1.2 billion people. This represents 23 per cent of the world's 1990 population of 5.25 billion, as reported by Maddison (2001).
3. It is difficult to ascertain the exact extent of nuclear waste disposals in the oceans and their possible ecological impacts. UNEP (2005), however, reports that 85 petaquerrels (PBq) of radioactive waste has been deliberately dumped into the oceans at over 80 locations worldwide, and all contemporary practices involving amounts of radionuclides are authorized in conformity with the International Safety Standards for Protecting against Ionizing Reduction and the Safety of Radiation Sources. UNEP (2005) concludes that most contamination comes from natural sources rather than human activities, and public concern on the subject is not generally supported by objective risk assessments.
4. A number of scientific research programs are investigating the interactions between terrestrial, oceanic and coastal systems. One example includes the 'Land–Ocean Interaction in the Coastal Zone' (LOICZ) international project, started in 1992 and scheduled to finish in 2012 (Hartwig et al. 2005). Another example includes 'Land Ocean Interaction Study' (LOIS) a £30 million project funded by the Natural Environment Research Council (UK).

REFERENCES

Agardy, T. (2004), 'Coastal ecosystems, industrialization, and impacts on human well-being', in Proceedings of the World Ocean Forum, 15–16 November, New York City.

Agardy, T. and J. Alder (2006), 'Chapter 19: Coastal systems' in C. Brown, E. Corcoran, P. Hekerenrath and J. Thonell (eds), *Marine and Coastal Ecosystems and Human Wellbeing: A Synthesis Report Based on the Findings of the Millennium Ecosystem Assessment*, New York: United Nations Environment Programme.

Bouman, A.F., G. van Drecht, J.M. Knoop, A.H.W. Beusen and C. Meiardi (2005), 'Exploring changes in river nitrogen export to world's oceans', *Global Biogeochemical Cycles*, **19**: 1002.

Bricker, S.B., C.G. Clement, D.E. Pirhalla, S.P. Orlando and D.R.G. Farrow (1999), *National Estuarine Eutrophication Assessment: Effects of Nutrient Enrichment in the Nation's Estuaries*, Silvery Spring, Maryland: National Ocean Service.

Brown, C., E. Corcoran, P. Hekerenrath and J. Thonell (eds) (2006), *Marine and Coastal Ecosystems and Human Wellbeing: A Synthesis Report Based on the Findings of the Millennium Ecosystem Assessment*, New York: United Nations Environment Programme.

CBD/UNEP (2005), *Biological Diversity and Tourism: Introduction*, Secretariat of the Convention on Biological Diversity, United Nations Environmental Programme.

Charlier, J.C. and R.J. McCalla (2006), 'A geographical overview of the world cruise market and its seasonal complementarities', in R.K. Dowling (ed.), *Cruise Ship Tourism*, Oxon, UK: CAB International, 441 pp.

Cohen, A.N. (1998), *Ship's Ballast Water and the Introduction of Exotic Organisms into San Francisco Estuary: Current Status of the Problem and Options for Management*, CALFED Category III Steering Committee, California Water Agencies.

Cohen, J.F., C. Small, A. Mellinger, J. Gallup, J. Sachs (1997), 'Estimates of coastal populations', *Science*, **278**: 1211–2.

Costanza, R., R. d'Arge, R. De Groot, S. Farber, M. Grasso, B. Hannon, K. Limburg, S. Naeem, R.V. O'Neil, J. Paruelo, R.G. Raskin, P. Sutton and M. van den Belt (1997), 'The value of the world's ecosystem services and natural capital', *Nature*, **387**: 253–260.

Costanza, R., R. d'Arge, R. De Groot, S. Farber, M. Grasso, B. Hannon, K. Limburg, S. Naeem, R.V. O'Neil, J. Paruelo, R.G. Raskin, P. Sutton and M. van den Belt (1998), 'The value of ecosystem services: putting the issues in perspective', *Ecological Economics*, **25**: 67–72.

Culliton, T.J. (1998), *Population, Distribution, Density and Growth: NOAA's State of the Coast Report*, Silver Spring, MD: National Oceanic and Atmospheric Administration (NOAA).

Darwin, R.F. and S.J. Tol (2001), 'Estimates of the economic effects of sea level rise', *Environmental and Resource Economics*, **19**: 113–129.

Dayton, P.K. (2003), 'The importance of the natural sciences to conservation', *American Naturalist*, **162**: 1–13.

Dayton, P.K., S.F. Thrush, M.T. Agardy and Hofman (1995), 'Environmental effects of marine fishing', *Aquatic Conservation – Marine and Freshwater Ecosystems*, **5**: 205–232.

Denison, E.F. (1974), 'Accounting for United States economic growth', Washington, DC: The Brookings Institution.

Dogan, M. (2003), 'Four hundred giant cities atop the world', *International Social Science Journal*, **56**(181): 347–360.

Dowling, R.K. (2006), 'The cruising industry', in R.K. Dowling (ed.), *Cruise Ship Tourism*, Oxon, UK: CAB International, 441 pp.

Duarte, C.M. (2002), 'The future of seagrass meadows', *Environmental Conservation*, **29**(2): 192–206.

Duda, A.M. and M.T. El-Ashry (2000), 'Addressing the global water and environmental crises through integrated approaches to the management of land, water, and ecological resources', *Water International*, **25**: 115–126.

Dulvy, N.K., Y. Sadovy and J.D. Reynolds (2003), 'Extinction vulnerability in marine populations', *Fish and Fisheries*, **4**: 25–64.

Early Warning (2004), *China's Regional Gap: Coasts to stay in the Lead*, 6 December, retrieved 20 November 2006 from http://www.earlywarning.com/articles/2004_12_06_china_regional_gap.

EEA (European Environment Agency) (2005), *The European environment – State and outlook 2005*, State of Environment Report No 1/2005, Denmark: EEA/OPOCE.

FAO (2004), *The State of Food Insecurity 2004*, http://www.fao.org/newsroom/en/focus/2004/51786/article_51791en.html.

FAO (2004b), *The State of the World Fisheries and Aquaculture 2004*, Rome: FAO.

Field, C.B., M.J. Behrenfeld, J.T. Randerson and P. Falkowski (1998), 'Primary production of the biosphere: integrating terrestrial and oceanic components', *Science*, **281**: 237–240.

Greenfacts (2005), *Scientific Facts on Fisheries: FAO 2004 Data.*

Hall, C.M. and C.M. Page (2006), *The Geography of Tourism and Recreation: Environment, Place, and Space*, Abingdon, Oxon; New York, NY: Routledge.

Harbaugh, W.T., A. Levinson and D.M. Wilson (2002), 'Re-examining the empirical evidence for an environmental Kuznet's curve', *Review of Economics and Statistics*, **84**(3): 541–551.

Hartwig, H.K., M.D.A Tisser, P.R. Burbridge, L. Talaue-McManus, N.N. Rabalais, J. Parslow, C.J. Crossland and B. Young (2005), *Land–Ocean Interactions in the Coastal Zone: Science Plan and Implementation Strategy*, Stockholm: Royal Institute for Sea Research.

Heer D.M. (2002), 'When cumulative causation conflicts with relative economic opportunity: recent change in the Hispanic population of the United States', *Migraciones Internacionales*, **1**(3): 32–53.

Hemminga, M. and C.M. Duarte (2000), *Seagrass Ecology*, Cambridge, UK: Cambridge University Press.

Hinrichsen, D. (1998), *Coastal Waters of the World: Trends, Threats, and Strategies*, Washington, DC: Island Press.

Hinrichsen D. (2004), 'People and coasts: an overview. Ocean planet in decline', in *Coastal Waters of the World, People & Planet*, Washington, DC: Island Press.

Howarth, R. (1988), 'Nutrient limitation of primary productivity in marine ecosystems', *Annual Review of Ecological Systems*, **19**: 89–110.

Howarth, R., D. Anderson, J. Cloern, C. Elfring, C. Hopkinson, B. Lapointe, T. Malone, N. Marous, K. McGlathery, A. Sharpley and D. Walker (2000), 'Nutrient pollution of coastal rivers, bays and seas', *Issues in Ecology*, **7**: 1–15.

International Food Policy Research Institute (IFPRI) (1995), *A 2020 Vision for Food, Agriculture and the Environment*, Washington, DC: IFPRI.

International Seabed Authority (2003), *Seabed Authority Brochures: Marine Mineral Resources; Contractors for Seabed Exploration; Polymetallic Sulphides; & Cobalt-Rich Crusts*, retrieved 4 May 2006 from http://www.isa.org.jm/en/default.htm.

Jones, J.B. (1992), 'Environmental impact of trawling on the seabed: a review', *New Zealand Journal of Marine and Freshwater Research*, **26**: 59–67.

Kura, Y., C. Revenga, E. Hoshino and G. Mock (2002), *Fishing for Answers: Making Sense of the Global Fish Crisis*, Washington, DC: World Resources Institute.

Lackey, R.T. (2005), 'Fisheries: History, science, and management', in J.H. Lehr and J. Keeley (eds), *Water Encyclopedia: Surface and Agriculture Water*, New York: John Wiley & Sons, pp. 121–129.

Leach, G. (1978), *Energy and Food Production*, Guildford, Surrey: IPC Science and Technology Press.

Leong, C.C. (1998), 'Oceans of the world: in troubled waters', *Straits Times*, 21 January.

MacAllister, D. (1998), Quoted in Oceanspace issue 100, 22 December.

Maddison, A. (2001), *The World Economy: A Millennial Perspective*, Paris: Organization for Economic Development and Cooperation.

Marland, G., T.A. Boden and R.J. Andres (2003), 'Global, Regional and National CO_2 Emissions', in *Trends: A Compendium of Data on Global Change*, Oak Ridge, Tennessee, US: Carbon Dioxide Information Analysis Center, Oak Ridge National Laboratory, US Department of Energy.

Martin, P. and G.I.P. Ottaviano (2001), 'Growth and agglomeration', *International Economic Review*, **42**(4): 947–968.

Matear, R.J. and A.C. Hirst (1999), 'Climate change feedback on the future oceanic CO_2 uptake', *Tellus Series B-Chemical and Physical Meteorology*, **51**: 722–733.

Mullon, C., P. Freon and P. Cury (2005), 'The dynamics of collapse in world fisheries', *Fish and Fisheries*, **6**(2): 111–120.

Nicholls, R.J., F.M.J. Hoozemanns and M. Marchand (1999), 'Increased flood risk and wetland losses due to global sea level rise: regional and global analysis', *Global Environment Change*, **9**: 569–587.

Norse, E. (1998), Quoted in Oceanspace, Issue 100, 22 December.

Panetta, L.E. (2003), *America's Living Oceans: Charting a Course for Sea Change*, A Report to the Nation – Recommendations for a New Ocean Policy, May, South Carolina, US: Pew Oceans Commission.

Pauly, D. and Alder, E.F. (2006), 'Marine Fisheries Systems'. in R. Watson, A.H. Zakari, A. Cropper, H. Mooney and W. Reid (eds.), *Ecosystems and Well-Being*, Washington, DC: Island Press.

Pauly, D., J. Alder, E. Bennett, V. Christensen, P. Tyedmers and R. Watson (2003), 'The future for fisheries', *Science*, **302**: 1359–1361.

Pauly, D., V. Christensen, J. Dalsgaard, R. Froese and F. Torres (1998), 'Fishing down marine food webs', *Science*, **279**: 860–863.

Pauly, D., V. Christensen, S. Guenette, T.J. Pitcher, R. Sumaila, C.J. Walter, R. Watson and D. Zeller (2002), 'Towards sustainability in world fisheries', *Nature*, **418**: 689–692.

Persian Gulf Committee (2005), 2005 Inquiry Simulation, *Conference on the World's Oceans: Security, Economics and the Environment*, International Ocean's Forum 7–10 April, Tufts University.

Phillips, J.D. (1986), 'Coastal submergence and marsh fringe erosion', *Journal of Coastal Research*, **2**: 247–436.

Phillips, M.R. and A.L. Jones (2006), 'Erosion and tourism infrastructure in the coastal zone: problems, consequences and management', *Tourism Management*, **27**: 517–524.

Rekacewicz, P. and UNEP/GRID-Arendal (2001), *Tourism Growth: Vital Signs 2000*, Washington, DC: Worldwatch Institute, and World Tourism Organization (WTO).

Romer, P.M. (1990), 'Endogenous technological change', *Journal of Political Economy*, **98**: S71–S102.

Salinas, L.M., R.D. DeLaune and W.H. Patrick (1986), 'Changes occurring along a rapidly submerging coastal area: Louisiana, U.S.A.', *Journal of Coastal Research*, **2**: 269–284.

Small, C. and R.J. Nicholls (2003), 'A global analysis of human settlements in coastal zones', *Journal of Coastal Research*, **19**(3): 584–599.

Solow, R.M. (1956), 'A contribution to the theory of economic growth', *Quarterly Journal of Economics*, **70**: 65–94.

Stanley, D.J. and A.G. Warne (1993), 'Nile delta: recent geological evolution and human impact', *Science*, **260**: 628–634.

Theobald, W.F. (ed.) (2005), *Global Tourism Vol. 3*, New York: Butterworth-Heinemann/Elsevier.

Tucker, M. (1995), 'Carbon dioxide emission and global GDP', *Ecological Economics*, **15**: 215–223.

Tydemers, D.H., R. Watson and D. Pauly (2005), 'Fuelling global fishing fleets', *Ambio*, **34**(8): 635-638.

United Nations (UN) (2005), *UN Atlas of the Oceans: Megacities*, New York: United Nations.

United Nations Environment Programme (UNEP) (2005), *Major Global Trends: The State of the Environment*, New York: UNEP.

United Nations Division for Ocean Affairs and the Law of the Sea, Office of Legal Affairs, and the International Seabed Authority (UNDOA/ISA) (2002), Official Records of the General Assembly, 57th session, 70th plenary meeting [verbatim record], 9 December 2002. *Proceedings of the Twentieth Anniversary Commemoration of the opening for signature of the United Nations Convention on the Law of the Sea,* New York, 9–10 December, New York: ISA, UN.

UNEP/DEWA/Earthwatch (2005), *United Nations System-Wide Earth Watch: Oceans and Coastal Areas*, retrieved 29 Sept from http://earthwatch.unep.net/oceans/oceanfisheries.php.

Valiela, I. (2006), *Global Coastal Change*, Malden, US: Blackwell Publishing.

Valiela, I., J.L. Bowen and J.K. York (2001), 'Mangrove forests: one of the world's threatened major tropical environments', *Bioscience*, **51**: 807–815.

Walling, D.E. and D. Fang (2003), 'Recent trends in the suspended sediment loads of the world's rivers', *Global Planetary Change*, **39**(1–2): 111–126.

Walters, B.B. (2003), 'People and mangroves in the Philippines: fifty years of coastal environmental change', *Environmental Conservation*, **30**(3): 293–303.

Watling, L. and E.A. Norse (1998), 'Disturbance of the seabed by mobile fishing gear: a comparison to forest clearcutting', *Conservation Biology*, **12**(6): 1180–1197.

Watson, R. and D. Pauly (2001), 'Systematic distortion in world fisheries catch trends', *Nature*, **414**(6863): 534–536.

Wood, R.E. (2000), 'Caribbean cruise tourism: globalization at sea', *Annals of Tourism Research*, **27**(2): 345–370.

Wilkinson, C. (ed.) (2004), *Status of the Coral Reefs of the World: 2004 – Executive Summary*, Switzerland: International Union for Conservation of Nature and Natural Resources (The World Conservation Union).

World Bank (2004), *Saving Fish and Fishers: Toward Sustainable and Equitable Governance of the Global Fishing Sector*, Report No. 29090-GLB, The International Bank for Reconstruction and Development/The World Bank, Agriculture and Rural Development Department, Washington DC.

World Bank (2005), World Bank and Partners Launch Initiative to 'Turn the Tide' of Fisheries Depletion, 29 September, from: http://web.worldbank.org/WBSITE/EXTERNAL/NEWS/0,,contentMDK:20624610~pagePK:34370~piPK:34424~theSitePK:4607,00.html.

Worm, B., H.K. Lotze, H. Hillebrand and U. Sommer (2002), 'Consumer versus resource control of species diversity and ecosystem functioning', *Nature*, **417**: 848–851.

World Travel and Tourism Council (WTTC) (2006), *Introduction: Global Travel and Tourism Summit*, 10–12 April, Washington, DC: WTTC.

WWF (2005), *Oil or Gas Extraction in Marine Protected Areas*, retrieved 19 September from http://www.panda.org/about_wwf/what_we_do/marine/ what_we_do/ protected_areas/extractive_industries.cfm.

WWF Global Marine Programme (2006), *Problems: Tourism and Coastal Development*, retrieved 4 May from http://www.panda.org/about_wwf/ what_we_do/marine/problems/.

10. Integrative Economy–Ecology Models for Marine Management

Matthias Ruth

The primary difference between marine and terrestrial environments has been described as one of medium – air versus water. The buoyancy of organisms in the respective medium, the rate of medium flow and the thermal stratification within each medium all contribute to the development of very different functional morphologies of organisms. Conducting research in the marine environment presents many challenges not encountered on land. Individual researchers are often limited in their ability to observe organisms in their environment, either by maximum bottom times for scuba or by the expense of deploying manned submersibles and remotely operated vehicles (ROVs). In many instances, marine science – literally – only skims the surface and often provides fragmentary insights into a vast system. Computer-based, dynamic modelling can help put the pieces of the marine puzzle together and can provide researchers with the opportunity to explore the implications of their knowledge and refine research questions prior to field experiments. Simple, yet powerful, models of a given system or sub-system can provide important information to scientists and managers alike on future trajectories of a system's development under a variety of conditions. The following sections briefly describe key concepts and tools of dynamic modelling and show-case two applications.

USING ECONOMY–ECOLOGY MODELS FOR MARINE MANAGEMENT

The problems of generating consensus about the behaviour of dynamic systems are particularly pronounced when decisions need to be made about complex environmental issues and when the stakes are high. The problems are exacerbated when there are little data and undisputed facts on which assessments of the behaviour of a dynamic system can be based. Marine conservation is a case in point. Although much is known about many aspects of the marine system, in many cases sizeable gaps exist in our knowledge, making the assimilation of what we do know all the more difficult.

There is a need to capture our knowledge, and that of others, in a consistent and transparent way so that we can identify pertinent gaps in data and better understand the behaviour of complex systems. New graphical programming languages, such as the STELLA language (ISEE Systems 2005) used in the models below, can empower people to assemble knowledge in a structured and transparent way, and to then use the resulting computer model to play out the likely implications of alternative assumptions or actions. Such knowledge-capturing is essential to the learning process. Just as we use microscopes and telescopes to extend the reach of the eye, we can use dynamic modelling to extend the reach of our mind. In this process, the computer becomes a facilitator – it is not the 'truth-generating machine' it has often been portrayed to be.

Computer modelling becomes 'dynamic' not just by capturing the time-varying behaviours of systems, but when model development is based on the dynamic exchange of data and information among a group of model developers and users. It is the pluralism in perspectives that helps identify key features and behaviours of complex systems, and the starting point for the generation of consensus on which recommendations for actions must ultimately be based. Pluralism is also an important ingredient for the usefulness of models in creating new knowledge and in providing decision support.

The modelling tools presented here have been used extensively to explore, for example, spatial dynamics of sea level rise (Ruth and Pieper 1994), atmosphere–ocean interactions (Grzymski et al. 2002), nutrient dynamics in coastal oceans (Moline et al. 2002), dynamics of marine invertebrate populations (Lohrer and Whitlatch 2002), fisheries impacts on benthic habitat (Lindholm et al. 2001), world shrimp markets (Johnston et al. 2002), and more (see, for example, Ruth and Lindholm 2002). This chapter concentrates on the management of biological systems, not on biochemical or physical processes.

BASIC TOOLS FOR DEVELOPMENT OF DYNAMIC ECONOMY–ECOLOGY MODELS

Some of the elements that make up the system for which a model is being developed are referred to as state variables. State variables may represent an

accumulation or stock of materials or information. System elements that
represent the action or change in a state variable are called flows or control
variables. As a model is run over time, control variables update the state
variables at the end of each time step. Examples of control variables are: the
number of births per month, a variable that changes the state variable
'population'; or investments per year, which changes the state variable
'number of boats'. In the modelling language STELLA represents stocks,
flows and parameters, respectively, with the following three symbols:

Small visual variations of these symbols can be used graphically to
indicate the specific functionalities of the modelling elements in a model. For
example, stocks, flows and parameters can be named and modified to indicate
arrays of stocks, flows and parameters, as done here, where some of them
may even be connected with each other:

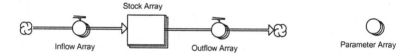

Several other variations exist; for example, a parameter that can be
interactively changed by a user as the model runs. The new symbol is a
variation of the old one, as shown here:

Parameter

Similarly, parameters that are the sum of other elements in the model are
indicated by a summation sign inside the circle, such as follows:

Summation

Icons can be selected and placed on the computer screen to define the
main building blocks of the computer model. The structure of the model is
established by connecting these symbols through 'information arrows':

Once the structure of the model is laid out on the screen, simply clicking on the respective icons can specify initial conditions, parameter values and functional relationships. Dialogue boxes appear that ask for the input of data or the specification of graphically or mathematically defined functions.

Typically, components of the system that is being modelled interact with each other. Such interactions of system components are present in the form of feedback processes. Feedback processes are said to occur if changes in a system component initiate changes in other components that, in turn, affect the component that originally stimulated the change. Negative feedback exists if the change in a component leads to a response in other components that counteracts the original stimulus. For example, the increase in the density of a prey species leads to an increase in predator density that, in turn, reduces prey density. Analogously, positive feedback is present if the change in a system component leads to changes in other components that then strengthen the original process. For example, if there are unlimited resources, an increase in the number of births leads to an increase in population size, which in turn, causes the number of births to increase. Positive feedback can result in 'explosive dynamics' – dynamics that lead a system away from its original state. In the case of population dynamics, we sometimes speak of population explosions.

Negative feedback processes tend to counteract a disturbance and lead systems towards steady-state. One possible steady-state for interacting predator and prey populations would be that the size of each population stabilizes in the long run. Such stabilizing dynamics contrast with the positive feedback processes, which tend to amplify any disturbance, leading systems away from equilibriums.

Typically, systems exhibit both positive and negative feedback processes that have different and varying strengths. Predator–prey relationships are a case in point. The increase in prey population will mean a tendency to produce even more prey. This is a positive feedback. Similarly, an increase in the number of predators means more predators can be born. The negative feedback is present in the interaction between the two populations, and the strength of this feedback depends on what happens with each of the two populations. One possible outcome is a continuous fluctuation in both populations, in which neither settle down to a long-term steady state nor result in explosive dynamics.

Variation in the strength of feedback processes is often reflected in non-linear relationships among system components. Such nonlinear relationships are present if a control variable does not depend on other variables in a linear fashion but changes, for example, with the square of some other variable. As a result of nonlinear feedback processes, systems may exhibit complex behaviour.

Another source for changes in the strength of a feedback through time is delays whereby one component changes in response to changes in another component. In some cases, the length of the time lag is known. For example, an increase in horseshoe crab populations means an increased number of eggs being laid in a bay, and thus higher food supply for sea birds. An increase in food supply translates fairly quickly into higher body mass of the birds but also has time-delayed effects on the population dynamics of birds. Well-fed birds are more likely to survive migration and are more likely to breed successfully. The effects of higher horseshoe crab populations on the size of sea bird populations is delayed by the time it takes sea birds to reach nesting grounds, lay eggs, raise offspring, and return to feed on horseshoe crab eggs. The feedback from changes in sea bird populations to horseshoe crab populations (triggered by an initially higher horseshoe crab population) is felt a year later in the crab population when the now larger number of sea birds prey on the eggs of the horseshoe crabs.

The following section presents examples of linked economy–ecology models. The first of these concentrates on the interactions of horseshoe crabs and shorebirds, and points at implications of crab harvest for crab and bird populations, and thus for the local economy. The second example explores how a marine sanctuary may affect a regional economy that relies both on fishing and tourism.

EXAMPLES OF ECONOMY–ECOLOGY MODELS

Interactions of Horseshoe Crab and Shorebird Population Dynamics

Horseshoe crabs are among the oldest creatures on the planet – their fossil evidence dates back as many as 250 million years. Within this span, thousands of species of animals have become extinct, while horseshoe crab populations have continued. However, currently horseshoe crab populations are threatened by anthropogenic activities. Adult crabs are caught to serve the American eel and conch fisheries. The eel fishery exploits primarily female adult horseshoe crabs with eggs; the conch fishery harvests both male and female crabs (ASMFC 1998).

Since horseshoe crab eggs provide nutrition for seabirds and shorebirds, a decline in the crab population may influence bird population dynamics. Declining bird populations, in turn, can affect local ecosystems through the disturbance of predator–prey regimes, and affect local economies as a consequence of disrupted ecosystems and reduced abundance of birds for bird watching. These secondary and tertiary effects of declining horseshoe crab populations are difficult to quantify, yet they may be relevant if we wish to understand better the full extent of anthropogenic effects on horseshoe crab populations.

Population surveys have shown a general decline in horseshoe crab populations since the late 1980s, most notably on the North American Atlantic coastline. While the issue has received much attention in recent media, census counts and population studies of horseshoe crabs are few in number.

Horseshoe crab ecology

The model presented here focuses on horseshoe crab and seabird populations in the Delaware Bay, a part of the US Mid-Atlantic Coast, during the peak spawning and migration period, and documents the impacts on both populations due to commercial exploitation. The region consists of approximately 160 kilometres of beaches along both the New Jersey and Delaware shoreline. With its protected beaches and suitable temperatures, the Bay is home to one of the world's largest spawning areas for horseshoe crabs. In the Delaware Bay, peak spawning activity usually occurs during May and June during peak high tides (ASFMC 1998). About 90 per cent of the total population of the crab species *Limulus polyphemus* lives along the mid-Atlantic coastline, with the largest concentration in Delaware Bay (Virtual-birder 2000). The Delaware Division of Fish and Wildlife reports an increase in horseshoe crab landings of 1 500 000 lb, approximately 43 000 crabs, from 1990 to 1997 (ASMFC 1998). Management programmes exist to protect horseshoe crab populations from overexploitation, though recent evidence shows their success to be questionable.

Limulus polyphemus is the most common species of horseshoe crab in North America. Each year for a period spanning a number of weeks, adult crabs emerge from their ocean habitat along the continental shelf and approach the beach to spawn. Males attach themselves to females, fertilizing the eggs as the female lays them in a burrow in the dry sand. Studies have shown that female horseshoe crabs can lay up to 88 000 eggs per season (Virtualbirder 2006). The larvae hatch and enter the open ocean. Juvenile crabs move further away from the shore with increasing age until they are sexually mature (Shuster 1982). Although there are notably more males than females on the beach, surveys conducted in deeper water show an opposite trend (ibid.). While accounts vary, the model below assumes a 1:1 sex ratio. After spawning, adult crabs return to their yearly habitat on the bay floor. In general, high fecundity, 'high egg and larval mortality, and low adult mortality' characterize crab populations (Botton and Loveland 1989).

Horseshoe crabs live to be 17–19 years old, but do not reach sexual maturity for 9–11 years. Juvenile and adult horseshoe crabs experience mortality due to predators and the harshness of the aquatic environment. Juvenile crabs are most susceptible to predation from other marine organisms. Adult crabs are susceptible to predation, but also to stranding, which occurs when spawning crabs become 'lost' and fail to return back to the open sea after spawning. Reported stranding rates range from 0.84 per cent of male crabs (Brockmann and Penn 1994) to 10 per cent of all spawning crabs, and result in death (Botton and Loveland 1989). Commercial exploitation, as discussed below, is increasingly becoming the major threat to adult crab populations.

Shorebird ecology
Botton et al. (1994) estimate 425 000–1 000 000 shorebirds use Delaware Bay as a staging area each May and June, though other reports estimate as many as 1 000 000 birds or more. Due to its ecological importance, the Bay has been the centre for horseshoe crab and shorebird population studies in recent years.

Travelling as much as 30 000 km each year, shorebirds require stop-over sites to build up fat reserves (Clark et al. 1993). During stop-over periods shorebirds in the Delaware Bay reportedly double their mass with crab eggs – their primary food resource. Each bird consumes as many as 135 000 eggs per season (Virtualbirder 2006). Castro and Myers (1993) suggest approximately 3 640 000 adult horseshoe crabs are required to sustain all shorebirds stopping-over in the Delaware Bay. Many different species of shorebirds utilize the Bay as a staging area. Clark et al. (1993) report the four most abundant species to be the Semipalmated Sandpiper (*Calidris pusilla*), Ruddy Turnstone (*Arenaria interpres*), Red Knot (*Calidris canutus*) and Sanderling (*Calidris alba*). In the model below (Figures 10.1–10.4), these species are lumped together into one category of shorebirds, effectively assuming that their impact on horseshoe crabs and the effects of crab egg availability are uniform across the different species. Specifically, for simplicity we assume here that the birds have similar body masses, and similar birth and death rates.

Model structure and assumptions
The STELLA model is divided into four main modules describing the inter-relationships between the following components: horseshoe crab eggs, juvenile horseshoe crabs, adult horseshoe crabs and bird populations. Horseshoe crab spawning, bird predation/migration and harvesting are

assumed to each take place during two months out of the year. Harvesting in the Delaware Bay is assumed to occur solely within these two months out of the year. Each time step of the model run therefore refers to a single season within a year. The model is run for 100 seasons.

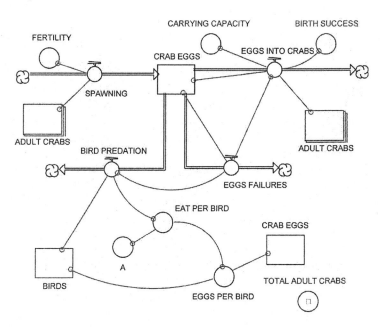

Figure 10.1 Module for horseshoe crab population dynamics

Due to the lack of consistent data, a two-step modelling procedure is applied to specify initial conditions and parameter values. In the first step, published data are used as much as possible to specify the model under the assumption that no exploitation takes place (ASMFC 1998; Botton et al. 1994; Virtualbirder 2006). Given a set of initial conditions, the model is run until a steady state is reached. Then, in a second step, the steady state conditions are used to re-initialize the model. The 'new' initial conditions and parameter values yield a consistent set of conditions that describe the system under investigation. Although the model-generated data are close to information published in the literature, it is difficult to tell how good the actual match is, because all too often confidence intervals for empirical and census information are not properly documented. Furthermore, the actual horseshoe crab–shorebird system has for a long time been affected by exploitation and other anthropogenic disturbances, none of which are perfectly known or quantifiable. Yet, by establishing consistent conditions for steady-state population dynamics, the model allows us to explore the impacts of exploitation. In essence, we are using the model here to recreate a past that we do not know, on the basis of mechanisms that guide the system and that we know still exist today.

The first component of the model is the horseshoe crab egg module is described by Figure 10.1. Each year the supply of eggs is determined by the number of female adult crabs multiplied by the fertility rate. The success rate of eggs is captured in the variable BIRTH SUCCESS, which, together with the carrying capacity, influences the number of eggs that turn into crabs. The corresponding flow EGGS INTO CRABS functions such that if the carrying capacity for adult crabs is surpassed, the birth success or egg-hatching rate is decreased. This illustrates the overcrowding effect when new nesting sites replace existing egg nests, and overall hatching success diminishes. The remaining eggs are eaten by birds, and subtracted from the stock. Eggs that are not eaten or do not develop into juvenile crabs, are considered to be failures and therefore are removed from the stock.

The BIRD PREDATION outflow is a function of the stock of birds and the number of eggs eaten per bird. It is assumed that birds eat only horseshoe crab eggs as part of their stop-over diet, and that a doubling of their body mass provides sufficient energy to complete their migration and successfully breed (Harrington and Flowers 1996; Virtualbirder 2006). The Parameter A in the model captures this assumption about the 'optimal' number of eggs for body mass doubling. The mating 'fitness' of birds is affected if they do not double their body mass.

The complete life cycle of adult shorebirds is not specifically accounted for in the model. Only their stop-over activity and its direct implications on an individual's health and mortality are modelled here. Shorebird mating and birth activities occur well beyond the extent of the Delaware Bay.

A second module captures juvenile crabs (Figure 10.2). Growth of the juvenile crab stock is determined by the birth success rate. Juveniles are promoted to adults after 10 years. The only outflow from the juvenile stock is a natural death rate. It is presumed that juveniles are not harvested, since they do not approach the beach with the adult crabs during the spawning season and are not capable of bearing the eggs needed for these harvesting industries.

Once crabs are promoted to the adult stage, male and female crabs need to be distinguished so we are able later to explore effects of different types of crab harvest on the crab and bird populations. This distinction is achieved by using arrays of the state and control variables (Figure 10.3).

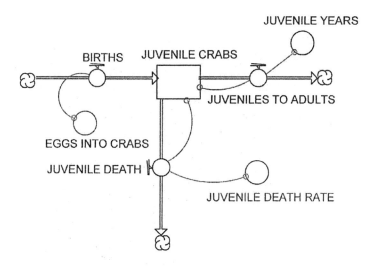

Figure 10.2 Module for juvenile horseshoe crab population dynamics

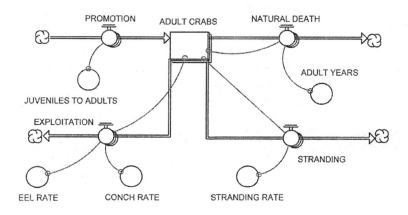

Figure 10.3 Module for adult horseshoe crab population dynamics

We assume that only eel and conch fisheries exploit horseshoe crabs, with the eel fishery removing only adult female crabs, and the conch fishery exploiting adult crabs of both sexes. For either fishery, exploitation is represented as constant, exogenously defined rates. Consequently, the model does not account, for example, for adjustments in exploitation rates based on previous exploitation.

The bird population module (Figure 10.4) is based on estimates of the total amount of birds using the Delaware Bay as a stop-over site, for a period of two months. The population of birds returns to the Bay each year, fluctuating as a function of the number of eggs each bird receives and their overall fitness level. Since one bird hatches from every clutch of eggs a female lays when she is completely 'fit', the existing stock gets fully replenished the next season.

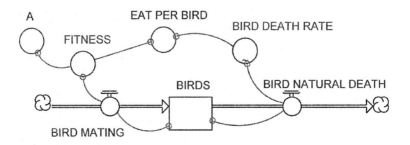

Figure 10.4 Module for shorebird population dynamics

Model results and findings

The model has been run over 100 years. Figures 10.5 and 10.6 show the effects of incremental changes in exploitation for the eel industry on horseshoe crab and shorebird populations, respectively. As the exploitation rate increases, horseshoe crab and shorebird populations decline. Since the eel industry harvests only female crabs, their numbers are naturally lower than the males and decline more sharply from the outset.

A host of model conditions yield horseshoe crab and migratory shorebird populations in the Delaware Bay that are stable in the long run. Since shorebird populations depend on horseshoe crab spawning for energy to complete their migrations and successfully reproduce, any decrease in horseshoe crab spawning noticeably affects bird populations. The opposite, however, is not true. Fluctuations in the amount of bird predation activity do not noticeably affect horseshoe crab populations. Commercial exploitation of adult horseshoe crabs, however, has a profound impact on crab and shorebird populations. Total exploitation levels of 0 to 0.11 crabs per season for both the eel and conch fisheries impact on crab population levels, but do not take the system out of steady state. Rates above 0.12 send crab and bird populations into permanent decline.

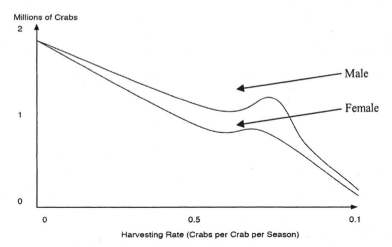

Figure 10.5 Horseshoe crab population changes with variation in harvesting rates

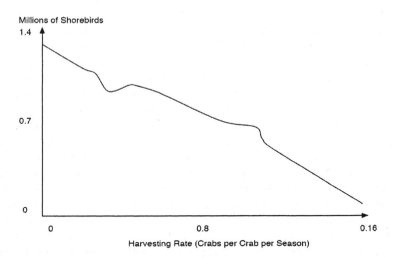

Figure 10.6 Shorebird population changes with variation in harvesting rates of horseshoe crabs

Commercial exploitation of horseshoe crabs is on the rise throughout much of the Atlantic coast. In 1996, an estimated 2 000 000 lb of horseshoe crabs were reported caught in the Bay (Virtualbirder 2006). Assuming each crab weighs an average of 3.5 lb and a high count of 3 700 000 crabs spawned that year, fishermen took 15 per cent of the total population. Given the results of our model, it is argued that current trends are not sustainable.

Effectiveness and Economic Benefits of Marine Sanctuaries

Marine protected areas (MPAs) are frequently seen as mechanisms to 'manage' the complexity of marine ecosystems effectively (refer to Box 3.2). Rather than concentrating management on individual species or groups of species (as illustrated in the example above), ideally the totality of an ecosystem is preserved by limiting human access or use. However, few areas totally limit access, and where such limits exist they are often not effectively enforced. The economic debate about marine sanctuaries is frequently dominated by estimates of job losses associated with the closure of marine areas to fishing and other economic activities. Yet, not closing some key areas such as spawning and nursery grounds while increasing fishing effort may result in the ultimate collapse of a fishery and a total loss of jobs.

The following example of a dynamic model explores some of the combined ecological and economic benefits associated with a marine sanctuary off the east coast of the northern US Stellwagen Bank National Marine Sanctuary. This Sanctuary comprises the waters and underlying lands of an area covering approximately 638 nautical square miles.

Stellwagen Bank, as does the Gulf of Maine region as a whole, supports four dominant taxonomic groups of macrobenthic invertebrates: annelids, crustaceans, molluscs and echinoderms. Many of these benthic organisms provide the main sustenance for groundfish species. Because of its particular topography, a thermal inversion effect is generated that brings cold, nutrient rich waters from the basin to the top where nutrients are exposed to sunlight and made available to the complex web of organisms. In addition, Stellwagen Bank acts as part of the geographic and thermal transition zone, which separates the Gulf of Maine, generally populated by boreal, non-migratory species, from the mid-Atlantic, generally populated by warm-water migrating species. These conditions result in a community of organisms that includes a wide variety of pelagic and demersal fish and shellfish species. Pelagic species include herring, mackerel, sharks, swordfish, bluefish, bluefin tuna, capelin and menhaden. Demersal species include cod, haddock, hake, pollack, whiting, cusk and several species of flatfish such as flounder and halibut. The products of this rich ecosystem are harvested both commercially and recreationally.

Pertinent conservation and management issues

Management of the sanctuary is directed towards balancing the dual objectives of resource conservation and public use. More specifically, management must ensure the sanctuary is utilized for the purposes of: resource protection, research, interpretation/education and visitor use (commercial and recreational). Activities subject to regulation are those that have the potential to degrade resources despite the existing regulatory structure (Barr 1990).

Fishing. Perhaps the most economically important resource within SBNMS is its fish populations. NOAA determined early in the planning process that the existing regulatory structure is adequate in managing this resource. Thus, fishing is not listed as an activity subject to sanctuary management. Management of commercial and recreational fisheries within the boundaries of Stellwagen Sanctuary remains the sole responsibility of The National Marine Fisheries Service and the New England Fishery Management Council (NEFMC). The corresponding management plan established minimum size regulations for several major commercial and recreational species, closure of spawning areas over George's Bank and southern New England, and major increases in the mesh size of mobile trawl gear. Despite these measures, stocks continued to decline for much of the 1990s.

Commercial bluefin tuna is the area's most lucrative species, representing almost 50 per cent of the economic value of all fisheries in the Stellwagen Bank Area. This species is regulated under the International Commission for the Conservation of Atlantic Tuna (ICCAT), as implemented under the Atlantic Tunas Convention Act of 1975. Though ICCAT sets quotas for the US for this species, NMFS provides additional management of the Atlantic bluefin tuna fishery.

Whale-watching. Whale-watching is one of New England's most important recreational industries, with annual revenues of over $21 million (Hoagland and Meeks 2000). Whale-watching is valued by its customers for both its recreational and educational attributes, and offers opportunities for scientific study and data collection. The number of whales to be seen limits the growth of the industry and, perhaps more importantly, the amount of dock space available (Rumage 1990). Increasing demand, however, results in more trips per vessel, and increased activity has led to concerns about the impact of the whale-watching industry on the whales themselves.

Vessel activity may have several detrimental effects on populations of rare and endangered whales. Disturbance of the marine environment, most notably by noise pollution, may cause marine mammals to disrupt feeding, displace cow/calf pairs, or induce avoidance (Tyack 1990). As a result, marine mammals require increased energy expenditure when vessels interfere in migratory paths or feeding activities. Increased vessel traffic also increases the chances of collision and injury to marine mammals (Pett and McKay 1990).

All marine mammals are protected under the Marine Mammal Protection Act of 1972. Species that are listed as 'endangered' or 'threatened' are also protected under the Endangered Species Act of 1973. Under these acts, marine mammals are protected from harassment, injury, killing, capturing or attempts to do any of these. NMFS Northeast Region also issued whale-watch guidelines in 1985 that detail the manner in which commercial and private vessels should approach mammals. It is unclear whether populations of threatened and endangered species of whales are adversely affected by the activity of these vessels, even when vessel operators follow these guidelines.

Shipping. A main thoroughfare of commercial shipping cuts through the south-central portion of the Sanctuary from Boston Harbour and the Cape Cod Canal. A 1990 review suggests annual traffic to be in the order of 2700 vessels crossing the bank per year. This high traffic zone has many direct implications for Sanctuary management. Vessel traffic entails many problems, such as collisions with whales, noise disturbance to whales, vessel collision resulting in cargo spillage and pollution and disposal of debris into the Bank's waters.

Disturbance to whale populations remains a continuous problem. Guidelines exist when navigating in the presence of marine mammals, but, unlike whale-watching cruises, commercial ships' captains are often not aware they are approaching the animals. As a result, at least five Right Whales were killed in the North Atlantic by ship collisions from 1970 to 1990 (Pett and McKay 1990). Since the viable population of Right Whales is the most threatened of all the marine mammals, a consortium of organizations implemented the northeast Right Whale Early Warning System in 1997. Through the Early Warning System, mariners are advised of the general vicinity of Right Whales, which allows ships' captains to plan an appropriate course around the whales, or slow their vessels where Right Whales have been located.

Sand and gravel mining. Within the past decade, an increase in demand and on-land transportation costs has made extensive sand and gravel deposits within Sanctuary borders economically viable. Mining and removal of sand and gravel deposits would have several potentially adverse effects on the ecosystem within the Sanctuary, including alteration of the bottom sediment and topography, sediment suspension, exposure of new sediments, and alteration of fish and benthic habitats (Pett and McKay 1990). To prevent the occurrence of these disruptions, Sanctuary regulations preclude the possibility of sand and gravel mining with the prohibition on the dredging, excavating or any other alteration of the seabed within the Sanctuary (alterations resulting from traditional fishing operations are excluded from this prohibition).

Other sources of pollution. One of the most widely disputed issues surrounding the creation of the sanctuary and the designation of its borders was the area's proximity to the Massachusetts Bay Disposal Site (MBDS). The MBDS is located approximately 5.5 km west of the northern tip of Stellwagen Bank and 40 km east of Boston. The MBDS and associated sites in Stellwagen Basin have been used since the 1940s as a repository for anthropogenic wastes including low-level radioactive wastes, explosives, toxic and other industrial wastes, ships, dredged material (including from contaminated harbours) and construction debris (Pett and McKay 1990).

There are both long-term and short-term effects associated with the disposal of dredged materials in a marine environment. Short-term effects include violations of the US Environmental Protection Agency water quality criteria, entrainment within the disposal plume, increased turbidity and entrapment of benthic organisms under the deposited sediments (Pett and McKay 1990). Long-term impacts are associated with the effects of contaminated sediment on biota. Sediments at the MBDS display elevated levels of both organic chemicals and metals, and in the range found to cause adverse effects to organisms. In response to consumer concerns related to contamination of seafood originating from the area of the disposal sites, the US Food and Drug Administration conducted extensive tests over the area in 1994. The results of this study indicated that of 55 finfish, lobster and shellfish, none had levels of contaminants considered hazardous to consumers (Raulinaitis 1994).

Hydrocarbon activities. Based on initial exploratory studies, the oil and gas industry has expressed little interest in the area of Stellwagen Bank. At the time of its designation, Stellwagen Bank was protected from hydrocarbon activities by a presidential moratorium that extended to the year 2000. To protect the Sanctuary from the disturbance of hydrocarbon activity after the moratorium expired, the Sanctuary lists hydrocarbon activities as being subject to regulation. NOAA thought that by listing the activity as subject to regulation, it could maintain authority to review, condition, or prohibit any application to lease for development areas that are within the Sanctuary. In addition, the prohibition of alteration of, or construction on, the seabed, and discharges into the sanctuary would preclude most of the activities involved in the development of hydrocarbon resources. Many felt, however, that hydrocarbon activity should be explicitly prohibited within the boundaries of the Sanctuary, and that the development of hydrocarbon resources within Sanctuary borders is incompatible with the protection of its ecosystem.

Modelling sanctuary dynamics and value

On the basis of publicly available data, interviews with Sanctuary personnel, fishers, whale-watching businesses, and researchers at government agencies, non-profit organizations and universities (see, for example, Doeringer and Terkla 1995; ICCAT 2000a, b; Hoagland and Meeks 2000; Jarvis 1990; Nickler 1999; NMFS 2001; Rumage 1990; Scida 2002), we developed a dynamic model to represent: the movement of whales into and out of the Stellwagen Banks National Marine Sanctuary (SBNMS), the whale-watching and bluefin tuna fishing industries that depend on the Sanctuary's resources, and the total economy-wide contributions these two industries provide to the Commonwealth of Massachusetts. Key elements of the STELLA model of SBNMS are shown in Figures 10.7–10.9.

The purpose of the model is to: (1) organize and synthesize existing data on the abundance and distribution of whales and tuna, as well as the impact of the whale-watching and tuna fishing industries in the Sanctuary; (2) identify data gaps and needs for future research; (3) explore potential relationships between whale-watching and tuna fishing activities on the whales in the Sanctuary; (4) determine the implications of alternative assumptions about the data, functional relationships, and policy interventions; and (5) explore the effectiveness and some of the economic benefits associated with Stellwagen Banks.

The dynamic model is based on a model designed by Lindholm et al. (2001) that disaggregated SBNMS into 11 × 16 grid cells (176 cells). In the present study, two grid systems were employed to trace whales and whale-watching boats on the one hand, and tuna boats on the other hand. Both systems were modelled simultaneously, and interactions between the two were captured in the form of interference from tuna fishing vessels with whales. Monthly and annual revenue from both the whale-watching and tuna fishing industries was also modelled, as well as the total economy-wide impact.

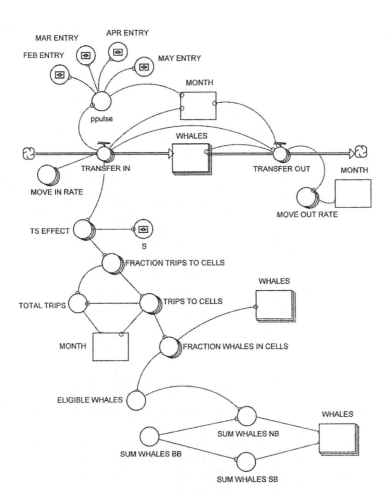

Figure 10.7 Module for whale movement on SBNMS

Notes:
TS = Total Shipping Effects.
SB = Number of Whales on South Bank.
NB = Number of Whales on North Bank.
ppulse = Monthly Onward Movement of Whales.

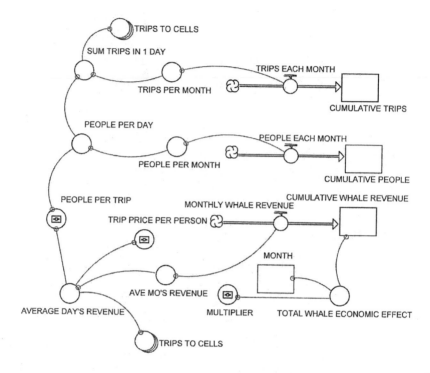

Figure 10.8 Module of whale-watching and associated economic impacts

Impact of sanctuary closure on whale movement and whale-watching industry

Overall, because Stellwagen Bank represented only 28 cells out of the 176 model cells, the impact of whale-watching trips and closures on whale movements was not that large. A Base Case Scenario was run to represent the situation when whales are insensitive to the movement of vessels. Thus, 200 whales were assumed to enter the model system, proceed along their prescribed pathway and all 200 exited the system, as expected (Table 10.1).

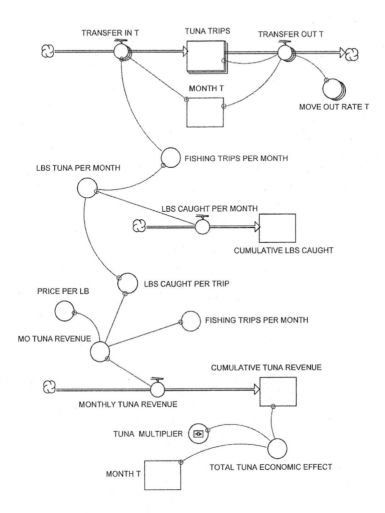

Figure 10.9 Tuna fisheries module

Notes:
Transfer In T = Biomass of Tuna moving into Region.
Transfer Out T = Biomass of Tuna Moving out of Region.
MO Tuna Revenue = Monthly Revenue from Tuna Catch.
Month T = Indicator for Month of Year in Tuna Module.

Table 10.1 Number of whales that remained on idealized pathway in SBNMS under four scenarios and ten levels of sensitivity

Scenario	Sensitivity Factor										
	0	0.1	0.2	0.3	0.4	0.5	0.6	0.7	0.8	0.9	1
Base Case Scenario	200										
North Bank Closure	200	195	191	186	182	178	175	171	167	164	159
South Bank Closure	200	195	188	182	176	171	165	159	153	147	142
Whole Bank Closure	200										

Similarly, under a Whole Bank Closure Scenario, when no whale-watching or tuna fishing vessels are allowed to enter the Bank's 28 cells, all 200 whales are not 'annoyed' by any vessels and thus entered and exited the system as expected. Figures 10.10 and 10.11 show a linear relationship between the percentage differences in the Base Case Scenario and the two closure scenarios for increasing sensitivity of whales to boating (with zero implying no effects of boats on whale, and one implying maximum diversion of whales from a chosen migratory pattern).

For the North Bank Closure Scenario, a 1 per cent change in the Sensitivity Factor around the midpoint of the line (x = 0.5) led to slightly less than a 1 per cent change in the number of 'annoyed' whales. For the South Bank Closure Scenario, a 1 per cent change in the sensitivity factor led to slightly more than a 1 per cent change in the number of 'annoyed' whales. Using a regional input–output model of the Massachusetts economy (Perez and Ruth 2002), we calculated the direct and indirect revenues generated by the whale-watching industry. Under each scenario, 4500 whale-watching trips were conducted each season carrying nearly 600 000 visitors, which generated $10.5 million in direct revenue for the whale-watching industry, spurring an economy-wide effect of nearly $18 million (see Table 10.2).

Impacts of sanctuary closure on tuna fishery
Under the Base Case Scenario, wherein no closures occur, there were 18 300 bluefin tuna fishing trips made in a season that yielded 200 000 lb of tuna. Cumulative direct revenue from tuna fishing was $2.4 million and the economy-wide total effect was nearly $3.5 million.

The number of trips falls to 17 000 under the North Bank Closure Scenario while cumulative catch falls to 189 000 lb – a difference of 6 per cent from the base case. The direct revenue from the bluefin tuna fishing industry under this scenario is $2.2 million and the economy-wide effect is $3.3 million. Thus, the economic loss associated with the North Bank Closure Scenario is a $150,000 reduction (in direct revenue and a $220,000 loss in the total economic effect as compared to the base case.

The number of trips is reduced to 16 000 under the South Bank Closure Scenario and the cumulative lbs caught falls to 180 000 for a difference of 19 000 lbs or nearly 10 per cent from the base case. The direct revenue from the tuna fishing industry under the South Bank Closure Scenario is $2.2 million and the economy-wide effect is $3.2 million. The loss in direct revenue from the South Bank Closure scenario is $230,000) and the loss in the total economic effect is $340,000 from the base case.

North Bank Closure

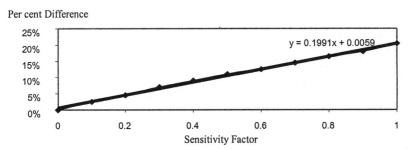

Figure 10.10 Per cent difference in number of whales from the Base Case scenario according to sensitivity factor under North Bank Closure

South Bank Closure

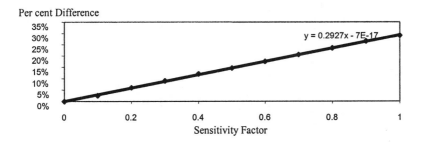

Figure 10.11 Per cent difference in number of whales from the Base Case scenario according to sensitivity factor under South Bank Closure scenarios

Table 10.2 Trips, people, revenue and total economic effect from whale-watching on SBNMS

Trips Per Day	Trips Per Month	Cumulative Trips	People Per Day	People Per Month	Cumulative People	Daily Revenue $	Monthly Revenue $	Cumulative Revenue $	Total Whale Economic Effect $
0	0	0	0	0	0	-	-	-	-
0	0	0	0	0	0	-	-	-	-
0	0	0	0	0	0	-	-	-	-
3	90	0	390	11 700	0	9,784	234,821	-	-
13	390	90	1 690	50 700	11 700	36,638	879,313	234,821	-
19	570	480	2 470	74 100	62 400	54,340	1,304,160	1,114,134	-
25	750	1 050	3 250	97 500	136 500	71,500	1,716,000	2,418,294	-
50	1 500	1 800	6 500	195 000	234 000	143,000	3,432,000	4,134,294	-
35	1 050	3 300	4 550	136 500	429 000	100,100	2,402,400	7,566,294	-
7	210	4 350	910	27 300	565 500	20,020	480,480	9,968,694	-
0	0	4 560	0	0	592 800	-	-	10,449,174	-
0	0	4 560	0	0	592 800	-	-	10,449,174	17,645,520

238

Under the Whole Bank Closure Scenario, the number of tuna fishing trips is 15 000 and the cumulative pounds caught are 169 000, which is a difference of 32 000 (16 per cent). The direct revenue from the fishing industry when the entire bank is closed to operations is $2 million and the economy-wide effect is $3 million. The loss in direct revenue from the Whole Bank Closure is $384,000 while the loss in total economic effect is $560,000.

Discussion

The results, which are summarized in Table 10.3, indicate that a 6–16 per cent reduction in direct and indirect revenues from the bluefin tuna fishing industry could be expected in association with a closure of the northern or southern bank or the entire bank area. The reduction in revenue from tuna catch under the whole bank closure could be viewed as a $1 million investment by the Massachusetts economy in the Atlantic bluefin tuna stock using SBNMS. However, to the extent that other regions do not make similar investments and to the extent that others cash in on the investments made by limiting bluefin tuna catch in SBNMS, the benefits to this investment are not reaped by the local economy.

Similarly, limiting impacts on whales within SBNMS may prove in some cases insufficient to limit anthropogenic disturbances of whales. Rather, it seems obvious that the effectiveness of SBNMS critically depends on activities outside the Sanctuary. Consequently efforts to increase the effectiveness of the Sanctuary and its economic benefits to the region must occur in coordination with other regions.

Table 10.3 Difference in the cumulative revenue and total economic effect between three scenarios and the base case

Closure Scenario	Difference from Base Case – Cumulative Revenue $	% Change	Difference from Base Case – Total Economic Effect $	% Change
North Bank	151,008	6.3	222,199	6.3
South Bank	233,376	9.7	343,280	9.7
Whole Bank	384,384	15.9	565,063	15.9

The lack of up-to-date and detailed information about the abundance and distribution of whale and tuna – let alone less charismatic or less economically important species – makes it difficult for policy makers to assess the effectiveness and economic benefits of SBNMS and other marine protected areas, in general. Although various research activities are currently underway or at various stages of planning, the model presented here has begun to identify essential data gaps and pointed at the need for systematic organization of what is known about SBNMS.

CONCLUSIONS

This chapter presents concepts and tools that make the complexity of marine systems amenable to systematic investigation. Easy-to-use software can help organize data and information, relate individual system components to each other, and explore the possible contributions of those components to the overall system's dynamics. An understanding of the sensitivity of (modelled) dynamics to alternative assumptions can help guide data collection and further analysis, as well as management intervention.

While the illustrations above have only highlighted the application of dynamic modelling within two well-described settings in the US – horseshoe crab–shorebird dynamics in the Delaware Bay, and whale population dynamics on Stellwagen Bank National Marine Sanctuary – the concepts and tools demonstrated here can, and have been, used widely to advance knowledge of combined ecological–economic marine systems. As the library of ecological–economic models of marine systems increases, new scientific insights into their dynamics are generated and new opportunities and constraints are discovered that may guide the management of marine systems towards sustainable practices.

ACKNOWLEDGMENTS

My special thanks go to Mark Maguire for his contributions to research presented in the section 'Interactions of Horseshoe Crab and Shorebird Population Dynamics', and to Michelle Perez who helped develop the model in section 'Effectiveness and Economic Benefits of Marine Sanctuaries'. The latter model was made possible, in part, with the financial support by Environmental Defense, Washington, DC, USA. The usual disclaimers apply.

REFERENCES

ASMFC (1998), *Interstate Management Plan for Horseshoe Crab*, Atlantic States Marine Fisheries Commission, Retrieved 25 October 2006 http://www.mbl.edu/animals/Limulus/issues/management.htm.

Barr, B. (1990), 'Management of the proposed Stellwagen Bank National Maine Sanctuary: opportunities and obstacles', in *The Resources and Uses of Stellwagen Bank, Part II: Conference Proceedings*, Boston, MA: Urban Harbors Institute, University of Massachusetts at Boston.

Botton, M.L. and R.E. Loveland (1989), 'Reproductive risk: high mortality associated with spawning by horseshoe crabs (Limulus polyphemus) in Delaware Bay, USA', *Marine Biologist*, **101**: 143–151.

Botton, M.L., R.E. Loveland and T.R. Jacobsen (1994), 'Site selection by migratory shorebirds in Delaware Bay, and its relationship to beach characteristics and abundance of horseshoe crab (Limulus polyphemus) eggs', *The Auk*, **111**(3): 605–616.

Brockmann, J. and D. Penn (1994), 'Age-biased stranding and righting in male horseshoe crabs, Limulus polyphemus', *Animal*, **49**: 1531–1539.

Castro, G. and J.P. Myers (1993), 'Shorebird predation on eggs of horseshoe crabs during spring stopover on Delaware Bay', *The Auk*, **110**(4): 927–930.

Clark, K.E., L.J. Niles and J. Burger (1993), 'Abundance and distribution of migrant shorebirds in Delaware Bay', *The Condor*, **95**: 694–705.

Doeringer, P.B. and D.G. Terkla (1995), *Troubled Waters: Economic Structure, Regulatory Reform, and Fisheries Trade*, Toronto: University of Toronto Press.

Grzymski, J., M.A. Moline and J.T. Cullen (2002), 'Modelling atmosphere-ocean interactions and primary productivity', in M. Ruth and J. Lindholm (eds), *Dynamic Modelling for Marine Conservation*, New York: Springer-Verlag, pp. 125–143.

Harrington, B. and C. Flowers (1996), *Flight of the Red Knot*, New York: W.W. Norton & Co.

Hoagland, P. and A.E. Meeks (2000), *The Demand for Whale-watching at Stellwagen Bank National Marine Sanctuary. The Economic Contribution of Whale-watching to Regional Economies: Perspectives from Two National Marine Sanctuaries*, Department of Commerce, Washington, DC: NOAA Marine Sanctuaries Conservation Series MSD-00-2.

ICCAT (2000a), *Report of the ICCAT SCRS West Atlantic Bluefin Tuna Stock Assessment Session*, Madrid, Spain, 18–22 September 2002.

ICCAT Advisory Committee Meeting (2000b), *Atlantic Bluefin Tuna (BFT) Commercial Landings and Permit Data: 1999 and 2000 Fishing Season Summary Review, Highly Migratory Species Management Division*, 29–31 October 2000, International Commission for the Conservation of Atlantic Tuna, http://www.iccat.es/ (last accessed October 25, 2006).

ISEE Systems (2005), *STELLA Software*, Lyme, New Hampshire.

Jarvis, R. (1990). 'Recreational fisheries of Stellwagen Bank', in *The Resources and Uses of Stellwagen Bank, Part II: Conference Proceedings,* Boston, MA: Urban Harbors Institute, University of Massachusetts, 26–27 April.

Johnston, D., C. Soderquist and D. Meadows (2002), 'The global shrimp market', in M. Ruth and J. Lindholm (eds), *Dynamic Modelling for Marine Conservation*, New York: Springer-Verlag, pp. 395–417.

Lindholm, J., P. Auster, M. Ruth and L. Kaufman (2001), 'Modelling the effects of fishing and implications for the design of Marine Protected Areas: juvenile fish responses to variations in seafloor habitat', *Conservation Biology*, **15**(2): 424–437.

Lohrer, A.M. and R.B. Whitlatch (2002), 'Life-stage-based recovery dynamics of marine invertebrates in soft-sediment habitats', in M. Ruth and J. Lindholm (eds), *Dynamic Modelling for Marine Conservation*, New York: Springer-Verlag, pp. 191–213.

Moline, M.A., O. Schofield and J. Grzymski (2002), 'Impact of dynamic light and nutrient environments on plankton communities in the coastal oceans', in M. Ruth and J. Lindholm (eds), *Dynamic Modelling for Marine Conservation*, New York: Springer-Verlag, pp. 144–164.

Nickler, P.A. (1999), 'A tragedy of the commons in coastal fisheries: contending prescriptions for conservation, and the case of the Atlantic Bluefin Tuna', *Boston College Environmental Affairs Law Review*, **26**(3): 123–134.

NMFS (2001), 'National Marine Fisheries Service, Office of Protected Resources. Northern Right Whale', www.nmfs.noaa.gov/prot_res/species/Cetaceans/rightwhales.html#Thenorthern right whale.

Perez, M. and M. Ruth (2002), *Effectiveness and Economic Benefits of Stellwagen Bank National Marine Sanctuary*, Report Prepared for Environmental Defense, Maryland School of Public Affairs, College Park, Maryland, February 2002.

Pett, S. and C. McKay (1990), *The Resources and Uses of Stellwagen Bank. Part I: Technical Report on the Resources and Uses of Stellwagen Bank*, Boston, MA: University of Massachusetts.

Raulinaitis, J. (1994), 'FDA goes fishing for toxic waste', www.fda.gov/bbs/topics/CONSUMER/CON00274.html.

Rumage, W. (1990), 'The economic value of whale-watching at Stellwagen Bank', in *The Resources and Uses of Stellwagen Bank. Part II: Conference Proceedings'*, Urban Harbors Institute, University of Massachusetts, 26–27 April.

Ruth, M. and F. Pieper (1994), 'Modelling spatial dynamics of sea level rise in a coastal area', *System Dynamics Review*, **10**: 375–389.

Ruth, M. and J. Lindholm III (eds) (2002), *Dynamic Modelling for Marine Conservation*, New York: Springer-Verlag.

Scida, P. (2002), Personal Interview, National Marine Fisheries Service, Highly Migratory Species Management Division, Washington, DC.

Shuster, Carl N. Jr (1982), 'A pictorial review of the natural history and ecology of the horseshoe crab Limulus polyphemus, with reference to other Limulidae', in J. Bonaventure, C. Bonaventure and S. Tesh (eds), *Physiology and Biology of Horseshoe Crabs: Studies on Normal and Environmentally Stressed Animals*, New York: Alan R. Liss, Inc.

Tyack, P. (1990), 'Potential effects of vessel noise on whales in Stellwagen Bank', in *The Resources and Uses of Stellwagen Bank. Part II: Conference Proceedings*, Urban Harbors Institute, University of Massachusetts, 26–27 April.

Virtualbirder (2006), 'Shorebird crisis: the horseshoe crabs of Delaware Bay', http://www.virtualbirder.com/vbirder/realbirds/dbhsc/index.html (last accessed October 25, 2006).

11. Poverty and Inequity at Sea: Challenges for Ecological Economics

Bruce Glavovic

Poverty and inequity pose fundamental challenges to the emerging field of ecological economics, and to ocean and coastal governance more generally. The central message of this chapter is that prevailing discourse and practice is 'lost at sea' when it comes to meaningfully confronting the dismal reality of ocean and coastal poverty and inequity. Poverty and inequity are issues that remain largely ignored in the ecological economics discourse. This chapter therefore aims to redress this imbalance in our attempt, in this text, to develop an 'ecological economics of the oceans and coasts'. Insights from a South African case study, and reflections on environment–poverty–inequity interactions, highlight challenges for extending the field of ecological economics to more effectively address poverty and inequity in the coasts and oceans context.

UNDERSTANDING ENVIRONMENT–POVERTY–INEQUITY INTERACTIONS

Human Development: The Social Dimension of Ecological Economics

Human development encompasses the full spectrum of concerns pertinent to realizing 'our potential', including economic, cultural, social, political and even spiritual dimensions relevant to people as individual and social beings (Alkire 2002; Sen 1999). Realizing and sustaining human potential – the pursuit of 'sustainable human development' or 'intra- and inter-generational equity with ecological integrity' – is central to ecological economics. From the genesis of this field, the 'social dimension', and in particular inter-generational equity, has been recognized as a cornerstone of sustainable development. But relative to the analysis of the ecological and economic dimensions that define this field, social sustainability remains relatively poorly developed (Lehtonen 2004). Consequently, there is an urgent and compelling need to focus sharper attention on this issue, particularly on poverty and inequity.

Meanings of Poverty and Equity

As a point of departure, what do the terms 'poverty' and 'equity' mean? *Poverty* is a complex suite of factors and constraints that prevents people from living healthy, meaningful and long lives: it is essentially *deprivation* that can be expressed in terms of, among other things, income, basic needs, human capabilities and social exclusion (World Bank 2000). *Equity* is a normative concept that has been defined in a wide variety of ways, but it has remained a marginal issue in development economics (Cling et al. 2006). In sum, equity refers to a fair and just distribution of resources within society; it connotes *equal opportunity* (economic, social and political aspects of a person's life should be independent of their background, such as gender, race, social group and so on), and avoidance of *absolute deprivation* (all people should have a decent livelihood – that is, above a specified absolute poverty line) (UNDP 2005; World Bank 2005). The two concepts are therefore distinct but interconnected. Equity is a more encompassing concept within which the challenge of poverty can often be located.

The nature of poverty can be explored further by distinguishing the key themes of poverty analysis and measurement that have evolved in recent decades (Baluch 1996; Lipton 1997; Maxwell 2001; Wagel 2002). First, poverty discourse has been dominated by a preoccupation with *economic deprivation*; that is, does a person have enough income to secure adequate food and so on? This perspective can be viewed in an absolute (that is, levels of income, consumption and welfare) or relative sense (comparing sectors of populations), or from an objective or subjective (for example, from the perspective of poor people themselves) point of view. Absolute poverty refers to levels of subsistence that are below minimum, socially acceptable living standards. It is typically defined in terms of nutritional requirements and other essential indicators of human health and physical wellbeing. Relative poverty reflects 'degrees of deprivation' between different segments of populations, and is usually measured in income quintiles or deciles. There is a moral imperative to confront absolute poverty, but relative poverty also demands attention because it sets the context for formulating and implementing initiatives, policies, and so on, to reduce absolute poverty.

Second, because human wellbeing is more than 'economic', it is constructive to focus on human *capabilities* – that is, does a person have the necessary capabilities to achieve a basic level of human wellbeing or, conversely, what factors prevent a person from achieving wellbeing? Capabilities include education, health, and so forth. According to Sen (1985, 1992, 1999), the key is the capability to make informed decisions and to live a long and healthy life. Capability is thus directly related to the freedom to make meaningful choices that improve human wellbeing (Sen 1999). This perspective demands consideration of both individual agency and the social processes that foster or constrain freedoms. 'Development consists of the removal of various types of unfreedoms that leave people with little choice and little opportunity of exercising their reasoned agency. The removal of substantial unfreedoms, it is argued here, is *constitutive* of development' (Sen 1999, p. xii).

Critics nonetheless argue that the approach taken by Sen (1999) does not pay sufficient attention to the social structures, institutions and relationships that create and perpetuate poverty – hence, the third poverty theme: *social exclusion*. People who have sufficient incomes and means of survival, and who have adequate capabilities to produce basic wellbeing, may nonetheless be poor if they are excluded from mainstream processes and activities encapsulated in political, social, cultural and civic activities. More powerful interests marginalize the poor through 'social exclusion': preventing or limiting access to resources, economic opportunities, social networks, political processes, and so forth. In other words, social exclusion reflects partial or complete exclusion from full participation in society. Poverty and social exclusion are inextricably linked and reinforce each other, though which comes first may depend on the context. Thus, notwithstanding the traditional preoccupation with economic or physiological deprivation, poverty transcends low incomes and consumption to encompass all dimensions of deprivation, including the denial of basic human rights, and the psycho-social reality of impoverishment, including poor people's perceptions and life-experiences of insecurity, marginalization, powerlessness and humiliation (Chambers 1997; Narayan et al. 2001).

Each of the three foregoing perspectives, therefore, adds valuable and progressively deeper insights about the complex and multi-dimensional nature of poverty: the deprivation of opportunities and choices essential for human development, including living long, healthy and creative lives, enjoying a decent standard of living, freedom, dignity, self-respect and the respect of other people (UNDP 1997).

The Intersection of Poverty and Inequity with Environmental Concerns

How, then, do poverty and inequity intersect with environmental concerns? Human development and environmental imperatives have traditionally been compartmentalized as separate fields of inquiry, and addressed as distinct and separate challenges. But the necessity to understand the interconnections between and, where possible, to reconcile these imperatives has come to the fore in recent years (Adams et al. 2004; Lele 1991; WCED 1987).

Until recently, it was posited that poor people are locked in an inexorable environmentally destructive 'downward spiral' or 'vicious circle'. In a nutshell, poor people focus on meeting their immediate needs and, given their impoverishment, they have no alternative but to use and, if necessary, deplete their natural resources in order to survive. As the supply of natural resources dwindles and environmental degradation spreads, the poor are compelled to exploit more marginal and fragile resources, thus intensifying environmental degradation, deepening their impoverishment and making their future prospects even more dismal. This view of the poverty–environment nexus suggests an inevitable but simplistic two-way process in which poor people are compelled by immediate necessity to overexploit their natural resources, degrading their environment, and thereby ensuring their long-term deprivation.

But poverty–environment relationships are far from simple or deterministic; they are diverse, complex and multi-dimensional – reflecting, among other things, the diverse circumstances in which these relationships unfold (Duraiappah 1998; Gray and Moseley 2005; Lonergan 1993; Martinez-Alier 2002; Reardon and Vosti 1995; Scherr 2000). In sharp contrast to the 'vicious circle' rationale, there is mounting evidence from diverse contexts that many poor households will undertake extreme short-term measures (for example, depriving the family of food) to preserve productive capital (for example, retaining stock) and conserve natural resources to meet their longer term needs. Examples of such behaviour have been documented in poor households in Africa (Cavendish 2000; Moseley 2001), the Philippines (Broad 1994) and Latin America (Swinton et al. 2003).

Poor people are often only proximate drivers of environmental degradation. It is structural inequality at various levels that is typically the ultimate driver of environmental degradation. Such degradation is driven primarily by wealthier and more powerful role-players who benefit from economic and political institutions that marginalize less powerful, poorer role-players (Duraiappah 1998; Martinez-Alier 2002; Swinton et al. 2003). However, it would be naïve to think that poor people are archetypal 'environmental stewards'. Both poor and non-poor groups are responsible for unsustainable practices. Poor people may lack the means to invest significantly in protecting natural resources, but both poor and non-poor groups may lack incentives to invest in prudent resource management (Swinton et al. 2003). Hence, it is imperative to remove the disincentives and create incentives that foster ecological sustainability, alleviate poverty and eliminate inequity.

The prospect of securing 'win-win' poverty-environment outcomes has obvious appeal. But evidence in support of 'easy win-wins' is elusive, as portrayed by Adams et al. (2004):

> Although it is desirable to satisfy the goals of biodiversity and poverty reduction simultaneously, it may only be possible under specific institutional, ecological, and developmental conditions ... The links between biodiversity and livelihoods, and between conservation and poverty reduction, are dynamic and locally specific. In most cases, hard choices will be necessary between goals, with significant costs to one goal or the other. The acceptability of these costs will vary for different organizations and actors.

In practice, poverty–environment interactions are mediated by social and political institutions that extend from the local to global scale (Agrawal and Gibson 1999; Duraiappah 1998; Lambin et al. 2001; Leach et al. 1995, 1999). There are many different institutions that influence the intersection of poverty, inequity and sustainability. They may be formal and/or informal, and are often dynamic. Different people rely on different institutions to meet their needs. These institutions thus mediate how and by whom resources are accessed and used and, in the process, play a pivotal role in human wellbeing, environmental change and sustainability. Particular attention, therefore, needs to be focused on developing a nuanced understanding of these institutions and, particularly, the reality of political power (Gasper 1993; Gore 1993; Swift 1989). The practical steps that need to be taken to correct the institutional failures that prompt unsustainable and inequitable practices also need to be determined.

How, then, does ocean and coastal poverty and inequity manifest itself, and what challenges does this manifestation pose for sustainable ocean and coastal governance?

POVERTY, INEQUITY AND SUSTAINABILITY AT SEA

Sustainable Human Development in Oceans and Coasts

Notwithstanding decades of fisheries development efforts, fishing (small-scale fishing in particular) is held to be synonymous with poverty (Béné 2003). Poverty and inequity in fisheries-dependent communities, and coastal communities more generally, remain a pervasive and pernicious challenge (Béné 2003; Glavovic 2006a; Whittingham et al. 2003a). How, then, have these human development imperatives been addressed in ocean and coastal management efforts?

Human rights, poverty, equity and sustainability have been addressed in diverse ways over the last 4–5 decades of ocean and coastal governance endeavours. UNCLOS provides an important starting point by codifying State roles and responsibilities for managing marine resources within national jurisdictions, with a range of subsequent measures introduced to manage these resources on a sustainable basis (see Chapter 14). In developing the international ocean governance regime, increasing attention has been focused on the social sustainability dimension of marine governance. The role of oceans and coasts in promoting sustainable development gained international prominence at the 1992 United Nations Conference on Environment and Development (UNCED) held in Rio de Janeiro. The intersection of sustainability and poverty in the marine milieu, however, only gained prominence at the 2002 United Nations World Summit on Sustainable Development (WSSD) Conference held in Johannesburg. At this latter conference it was declared that 'eradicating poverty is the greatest global challenge facing the world today and an indispensable requirement for sustainable development' (Johannesburg Plan of Implementation 2002, para. 7).

Translating this rhetoric into practical reality is being addressed on a number of fronts. Notable examples include international agreements and efforts such as the development of FAO Guidelines on how to increase the contribution of small-scale fisheries to poverty alleviation and food security (FAO 2005); as well as diverse national and sub-national ocean and coastal management endeavours (Allison and Horemans 2006; Courtney and White 2000; Glavovic and Boonzaaier 2007; Moffat et al. 1998; Whittingham et al. 2003b). These developments have evolved in the context of broader international efforts to confront poverty and address inequity, including among others, the UN Millennium Development Goals, with the commitment to halve by 2015 the proportion of the world's population whose income is less than $US1 per day.

Fisheries and Sustainable Human Development

There is incontrovertible evidence that the impoverishment of fishers is often caused by, or related to, overexploitation or depletion of fish stocks. But, in reviewing the relationship between poverty and fisheries, Béné (2003) stresses, first, that preoccupation with the biophysical dimension of the poverty–fisheries relationship has resulted in other dimensions, particularly the socio-institutional drivers of poverty, being ignored. Second, the poverty literature has largely ignored fisheries-related poverty; and integration of the institutional dynamics of fisheries would contribute to better understanding of the poverty-environment nexus more generally.

Béné (2003) summarizes two contrasting interpretations of the poverty–fisheries relationship. The first interpretation posits that poverty is endemic in fisheries-dependent communities: 'they are poor because they are fishers' (World Bank 1992). Two arguments underpin this interpretation. First, fishers are poor because the open-access nature of the resource results in uncontrolled exploitation, and economic and possibly biological extinction. Second, because alternative incomes are low, fishers' incomes are kept low through mechanisms of labour transfer between sectors. In other words, economic circumstances outside fisheries – not overexploitation of the resource or rent dissipation – drive low incomes in fisheries, and hence poverty. Thus, regardless of what fishers might do, they are bound to remain poor. The second interpretation portrays fisheries as 'the employer of last resort' – a 'safety valve' for the poor – because their open access character provides livelihood options for poor people without alternatives (Baily and Jentoft 1990; Panayotou 1980; Townsley 1998). In other words, 'they are fishers because they are poor.' Béné (2003) argues that these two interpretations are the flip side of the same coin and represent the outdated paradigm of poverty–environment interactions: the two-dimensional 'vicious circle' rationale described previously. Béné goes on to emphasize the need to get to grips with the complex reality of fisheries-related poverty. Socio-institutional factors (such as health, education, social exclusion, vulnerability to shocks, political marginalization and powerlessness and so forth) play an even more important role in influencing the character of fisheries poverty than economic or biological factors. The inability of fishers to access fisheries resources and related commodities and services may be largely due to entitlement breakdowns – whereby institutional mechanisms hinder or exclude prospective ownership of and/or access to fisheries resources – and hence drive and determine the character of fisheries poverty.

Attention thus needs to be focused on the 'richness' of the socio-institutional reality of fisheries and, by extension, ocean and coastal communities. This will provide a better understanding of the role of collective action, decision-making processes, power relationships, local political dynamics, and so forth, which entrench and perpetuate poverty and inequality in fisheries-dependent communities. To alleviate poverty and improve food security:

> it is imperative that fisheries and other natural resources are not squandered, and that the benefits that flow from their use are equitably distributed. The biggest

single contribution to achieving this goal probably lies in the empowerment of small-scale fishers and fishworkers within a context of transparent and open engagement through legally enforceable rights to aquatic resources, and with improved access to capital, markets and know-how. (FAO 2005, p. 71)

However, sustainable human development in the fisheries sector cannot be realized by looking at this sector in isolation. Attention needs to be focused on the interconnections between fisheries and other ocean and coastal activities and livelihoods. Coastal management efforts over the last few decades have been developed to address these interconnections in pursuit of sustainable development.

Beyond a Biophysical Fixation?

Integrated coastal management (ICM) is widely considered to be the most appropriate approach to promote sustainable coastal development (Cicin-Sain and Knecht 1998). Increasing attention has been focused on poverty and equity issues in coastal management discourse in recent years (Bernal and Cicin-Sain 2002; Smith et al. 2004). Amongst other things, the WSSD underscored the key role ICM can play in securing essential environmental goods and services, and reducing the vulnerability of coastal communities to natural hazards. It provides a governance framework for reconciling contending coastal activities by bridging the horizontal (sectoral) and vertical (between spheres of Government) fragmentation that otherwise precludes holistic decision-making. It thus seeks to promote coast-dependent livelihoods that are ecologically, socially and economically sustainable (Bernal and Cicin-Sain 2002; Cicin-Sain et al. 2002). But ICM thinking and practice have tended to focus attention on the biophysical dimension of sustainability, somewhat to the neglect of the human dimension, and poverty and inequity issues (Glavovic 2006a).

A fundamental paradigm shift in prevailing ocean and coastal management thinking and practice is required to confront poverty and inequity. Much can be learned from fields such as Development Studies that have developed conceptual frameworks and practical tools to alleviate poverty and promote equity. The Sustainable Livelihoods (SL) approach is one such framework that could help to foster more people-centred, pro-poor ocean and coastal management. The SL approach has been applied to a range of coastal, lake and floodplain fisheries endeavours, especially small-scale fisheries (Allison 2005; Allison and Ellis 2001; Allison and Horemans 2006; Béné et al. 2003; Neiland and Béné 2004; Salmi 2005; Stirrat 2004; van Oostenbrugge et al. 2004). It has been less commonly used in, but has considerable applicability to, other marine sectors, such as coral reefs (Whittingham et al. 2003a, b) and ICM (Glavovic 2006a).

THE SUSTAINABLE LIVELIHOODS APPROACH

The SL approach was developed by Robert Chambers and colleagues (Chambers and Conway 1992) and has been refined and applied by a wide range of analysts and organizations. Its underpinning 'capabilities and capacities' rationale draws on Sen's (1985, 1992) work. It integrates this rationale with two other key dimensions of Development Studies, namely, the pivotal roles played by institutions in development processes (Leach et al. 1990); and the importance of authentic participation to ensure sustainable and equitable development (Mosse et al. 1998). It has close synergies with rights-based development approaches (Leach et al. 1999; Moser et al. 2001), which, in turn, draw on Sen's (1981) work on 'entitlements'.

Figure 11.1 portrays key elements of the SL approach. It highlights the vulnerability context in which poor households and communities live. These contexts are subject to an array of seasonal changes (for example, in the availability of certain coastal resources), trends (for example, changing coastal demographics) and shocks (for example, coastal hazards) that impact on the range of assets that can be drawn upon, which are portrayed in the 'asset pentagon'. These assets are represented by various 'capitals', including natural (for example, fish stocks), social (for example, kinship networks), physical (for example, boats and harbours), financial (for example, credit, savings and remittances) and human capital (for example, health, knowledge and fishing skills). Prevailing policies, institutions and processes (including markets, social relations and organizations) mediate access to these assets and how they might be combined to frame alternative livelihood strategies that can be pursued to achieve desired livelihood outcomes.

The SL approach is founded on the following principles: people-centredness; empowerment; responsiveness and participation; sustainability; holism, recognizing the linkages and interconnections between various scales and levels; partnerships; disaggregation, recognizing the heterogeneity and dynamic character of households and communities; and flexibility (Carney 2002). A variety of complementary methodologies are used to apply the SL approach, together with practical guidance (DFID 2000a, b).

The SL approach can enhance understanding of how people cope with and adapt to seasonal changes, trends and shocks. It can also highlight opportunities for policy and other interventions to improve poor people's coping and adaptive capacities, and hence their livelihood prospects. Such interventions may be specific to current livelihood strategies; for example, improving fishers' access to credit to purchase essential fishing gear. The SL approach may also highlight interventions seemingly unrelated to prevailing livelihoods; for example, improving fishers' access to education and healthcare, and/or access to land or non-fisheries resources so as to diversify livelihood options. It thus provides a useful perspective for better understanding the intersection of ecological sustainability, poverty and inequity, and the role of mediating institutions in pursuit of sustainable livelihoods.

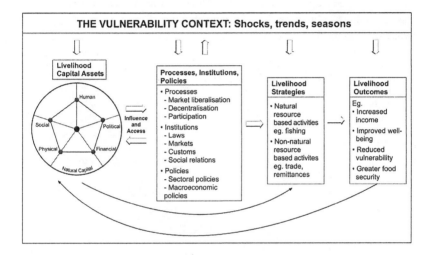

Figure 11.1 The sustainable livelihoods approach

There are three main ways in which the SL approach complements prevailing coastal management efforts (Glavovic 2006a). First, the SL approach is committed to sustainable development, but it shifts the nature-centred focus of prevailing efforts towards a people-centred focus. Second, it shifts the focus from barriers to development, to the capabilities and assets that poor people can draw upon to improve their livelihoods. The asset pentagon provides a diagnostic tool to better understand asset portfolios and identify opportunities for intervention. Third, it focuses attention on the pivotal mediating role played by policies, institutions and processes in determining access to these assets.

What then can be learned from 'real-world' efforts to promote sustainable human development in the marine context? The following South African case study attempts to provide some answers to this question.

OCEAN AND COASTAL POVERTY AND INEQUITY IN SOUTH AFRICA

The South African Coast and Fisheries in Context

There is a paucity of information about the character of coast-specific poverty and inequality in South Africa. Nonetheless, it is clear that poverty is concentrated geographically in former homeland areas and in remote rural areas, as well as in burgeoning informal settlements around coastal cities and towns (see Figures 11.2 and 11.3).

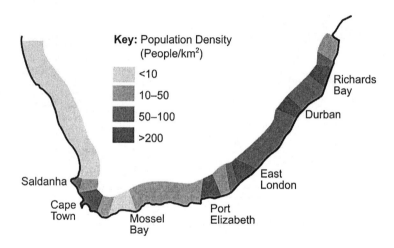

Figure 11.2 Population density on the South African coast, 1998 estimates

Furthermore, poverty is concentrated along racial lines, among black[1] South Africans and Africans in particular. In sharp contrast to the grinding poverty facing many rural coastal communities and those living in informal settlements, there is relentless intensive luxury development taking place along the coast, especially in and around coastal urban centres. The dynamic and vibrant economies of these centres constitute an increasingly important, but little appreciated, dimension of the overall economy. They are a driving force that offers distinctive opportunities for sustainable coastal development and for lifting poor people in historically marginalized regions out of the grip of poverty (McCarthy et al. 1998). This potential constitutes a core rationale of the White Paper on Sustainable Coastal Development (hereafter the White Paper) (CMPP 2000).

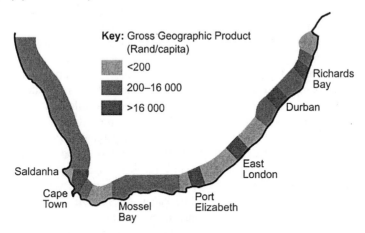

Figure 11.3 Gross Geographic Product along the South African coast, 1999 estimates

Note: $US1 = approximately 5 South African Rands (ZAR) in 1998.

How do poverty and inequity manifest in the fisheries sector? Before democracy, a small number of white-owned companies dominated the fishing industry (Raakjaer Nielsen and Hara 2006). Black South Africans were effectively excluded from commercial fisheries and were restricted to recreational and subsistence fishing in areas designated for 'non-whites'.

Since the transition to democracy in 1994, attention has been focused on confronting this legacy. The Constitution provides the key reference point for all Government action, including reforms to coastal management and the fisheries sector, reflected in the Fisheries Policy and Marine Living Resources Act (MLRA) (Witbooi 2006). The White Paper and the MLRA deliberately seek to incorporate constitutionally guaranteed environmental, socio-economic and procedural rights, amongst others, into the new ocean and coastal management dispensation. The practical implementation of these provisions, however, invariably brings sustainability, equity and economic efficiency, and associated rights, into contention. Reconciliation may not always be possible, and herein lies the challenge for promoting human development with ecological integrity in the ocean and coastal arena.

Towards Sustainable Coastal Livelihoods in South Africa

The White Paper seeks to confront the legacy of apartheid by creating opportunities to manage coastal resources to meet prevailing needs, while retaining options for future generations (Glavovic 2000). Implementation of the policy has brought an even sharper focus on alleviating poverty and improving equity, through a variety of initiatives dedicated to building sustainable coastal livelihoods and creating employment opportunities for chronically unemployed coastal dwellers (Glavovic 2006a, b). But the reality of coastal poverty and inequity presents enormous challenges (Glavovic 2006a; Glavovic and Boonzaaier 2007). First, prevailing development discourse and practice need to be critically questioned. Persistent and pervasive poverty contradicts the assertion that neo-liberal reforms and 'trickle down' economics will alleviate poverty. Second, a range of pragmatic governance challenges need to be confronted. For instance, six years have passed since Cabinet approved the White Paper. A Draft Bill has been issued for public comment. But questions must be asked about the extent to which the 'spirit' of the White Paper is reflected in this proposed law. Furthermore, aligning Governmental policies, laws and practices with the SL approach is challenging. Developing inclusive processes that embrace a more holistic and social science discourse is also a major challenge. Building the requisite institutional capacity to give practical effect to the policy rhetoric at the 'ground' level, especially in remote localities, presents a fundamental obstacle. Government–civil society partnerships at a strategic national level as well as at the community level are essential. Third, attention needs to be focused on project level challenges and opportunities, and lessons learned from past project experience.

Over the last decade, much has been achieved in transforming South Africa's coastal management approach from its roots in a conservation discourse to a sustainable development discourse. But converting the policy rhetoric into practical reality in poor and marginalized coastal communities is a 'field of struggle' (Glavovic 2006a). The economic imperative, driven by the prevailing market-oriented, growth-centred neo-liberal meta-narrative, supersedes the ecological and equity imperatives of sustainable development, notwithstanding rhetoric to the contrary. Reconciling these sustainability imperatives also lies at the heart of South Africa's efforts to reform the fisheries sector.

The Transformation of Fisheries: An Unfinished Agenda?

Since the mid-1990s, the Government has redistributed access rights and stimulated internal restructuring of existing companies to ensure that historically disadvantaged individuals (HDIs) and communities have more equitable access to fisheries. The needs of historically marginalized small-scale fishers have been addressed through the creation of a limited commercial sector. It gave legal recognition to subsistence fishers for the first time and declared areas for exclusive use by them. It has sought to achieve this equity imperative while maintaining the ecological sustainability of fish stocks, and the diversity, health and productivity of marine ecosystems. This is based on a renewed focus on marine biodiversity conservation together with a new focus on whole marine ecosystem protection and inter-generational sustainability. Simultaneously, it aimed to achieve economic viability, competitiveness and stability of the industry in the context of globalized markets. It sought to do this through 'optimal use', economic growth and job creation, chiefly by creating stability in the industry through allocation of long-term access rights and administrative cost-effectiveness based on a user-pays approach to fund fisheries management (Branch and Clark 2006; DEAT 2002; van Sittert et al. 2006). Achieving these, at times, conflicting economic, ecological and equity imperatives is central to the fisheries policy and MLRA (Cochrane 2000; Kleinschmidt et al. 2003), and has required fundamental changes in the approach and procedures traditionally used to govern fisheries in South Africa.

Significant changes have been brought about as a result of these reforms. There are, however, divergent views about the extent to which these reforms, first, truly foster equity in fisheries, and, second, appropriately reconcile contending sustainability imperatives. With regard to the former, remarkable gains have been made on the equity front: 'In short, changes in rights-ownership and management style over the short 10 years of democracy are an extraordinary, if unfinished, symphony' (Branch and Clark 2006, p. 15). However, HDI involvement in the fisheries reform process is generally deemed to have been 'weak' and bona fide fishers secured only marginal benefits. Isaacs (2006, p. 57) conclude that:

> the process for securing access rights was essentially geared towards those who were literate, credit-worthy and organized: poor fishers were poorly equipped on all accounts. In the absence of special provisions to empower HDIs, and poor bona fide fishers in particular, ... poor fishers have been doubly excluded, first by apartheid racism and now by post-apartheid neo-liberalism.

With regard to the latter, it is important to recognize that these fisheries reforms were fundamentally influenced by international trends and norms as South Africa sought re-entry into political and economic forums (Crosoer et

al. 2006; Witbooi 2006). All aspects of the fisheries reform process reflect the
Government's commitment to neo-liberal principles at the relative expense of
equity and ecological imperatives (Crosoer et al. 2006; Hersoug and Isaacs
2002a, b; Isaacs 2006; van Sittert et al. 2006).

In sum, in the struggle between reallocation (in interests of equity) and
stability (for economic security) the latter won the day because overall
Government processes place macroeconomic and business stability, and
entrepreneurship, ahead of fair and just allocation of resources, not to
mention ecological sustainability (Hersoug and Isaacs 2002a, b). The overall
ownership structure of the fisheries industry is fundamentally different, but
the control structure may be little changed. There are many new entrants but
their share of the total quota is limited. Many bona fide fishers still do not
have legitimate access and may resort to illegal fishing, which will generate a
host of ecological, social and economic impacts (Crosoer et al. 2006; Isaacs
2006; Raakjaer Nielsen and Hara 2006; Sowman 2006). For some, the
fisheries reform process has been little more than window dressing:
'Although a few HDIs have been enriched as part of the process, it is
important to distinguish between empowerment and enrichment.
Transformation was supposed to lead to a more equal distribution of wealth
within the broader society, and not just amongst a few individuals' (Raakjaer
Nielsen and Hara 2006, p. 50).

Even with the fundamental political changes in South Africa that
facilitated the sea-change in thinking about the nature of coastal management
and the role of fisheries in confronting poverty and inequity, making a
tangible difference to the lives of poor fishers and coastal communities has
proved to be a 'field of struggle'.

CONCLUSIONS

The South African experience underscores the obdurate challenge posed by
the pursuit of ocean and coastal sustainability. Even with genuine
Government commitment to this laudable goal, the reconciliation of
sustainability imperatives remains exceptionally fraught. Two key
interrelated challenges must be confronted. First, poverty and inequity will
remain a persistent reality, and sustainable human development will remain
an elusive ideal, as long as the dominant meta-narrative of economic growth
and 'trickle down' economics displaces ecological and social sustainability
imperatives (Fernando 2003; Rees 2002, 2003). Even when there is
Government commitment to foster sustainability, in practice, economic

interests undermine ecological and social sustainability – perpetuating and deepening poverty and injustice. The pursuit of sustainable development needs to be 'liberated' from the ideological and institutional 'clutches' of globalized capitalism. Second, persistent poverty and inequity are fundamentally political problems, legitimized in prevailing norms and discourse, and embedded in extant social and political institutions. The underlying power relationships that create and perpetuate the antithesis of unsustainable human development therefore need to be confronted. Inclusive, direct and deliberative processes are needed to build social consensus on a vision for sustaining global oceans and coasts, and for reconciling sustainability imperatives. There is a need to create opportunities for values-based dialogue about ocean and coastal issues of common concern. Participants need to work together to agree on process and substantive principles to guide such deliberations. Extreme caution needs to be exercised to ensure that such endeavours do not degenerate into superficial participatory processes captured by dominant interests.

The field of ecological economics faces four key challenges if it is to address more effectively the social sustainability imperative. Firstly, ecological economics can and should help to expose the consequences of prevailing ocean and coastal policies and practices, including inequity and poverty implications, and therefore contribute to better future policy- and decision-making. This is, however, a necessary but not sufficient role. A greater challenge is to develop and integrate into ecological economics a deeper understanding of the complex and multi-dimensional character of poverty and inequity, with particular attention focused on the social, psychological and political dimensions of poverty and inequity, especially from the perspective of poor and marginalized people themselves. Much can be learned from fields such as Development Studies. In essence, consideration needs to be given to ways in which the social sustainability imperative can be more effectively integrated into ecological economics thinking and practice. Secondly, more attention needs to be focused on the pivotal role of institutions in mediating access to resources and promoting sustainable human development. Recent developments in institutional economics (Rutherford 2001) offer valuable insights for ecological economics (see Chapter 14), and have considerable potential for the evolving agenda of ecological economics in developing and implementing more effective and sustainable governance solutions (Paavola and Adger 2005). However, more focused attention is needed on the role of politics (Faber et al. 2002) and power (Gale 1998) in perpetuating unsustainable development. Ecological economics can learn from work in 'political ecology', given its normative focus on social justice, equity and ecological sustainability, and its more radical approach to institutional change (Gray and Moseley 2005; Scoones 1999; Sneddon et al. 2006). Thirdly, ecological economic analysis needs to be extended by incorporating insights about place-based environmental histories to better understand complex and variable social–economic–ecological interactions and the associated spatial and temporal dynamics of context-specific poverty–inequity–environment interrelationships. Ecological economics can draw insights from fields such as ecological anthropology, environmental history and historical geography to develop such insights (Scoones 1999). Finally, ecological economics has a distinctive and important role to play in better understanding the 'value' and consequences of unsustainable human development. The valuation of environmental goods and services should be extended to, and integrated with, valuation of the 'costs' of poverty and inequity (or the 'benefits' of social sustainability).

In conclusion, ecological economics has a critical role to play in deepening understanding, exposing consequences and stimulating new practice with respect to the pursuit of ocean and coastal sustainability, and the alleviation of poverty and inequity at sea.

NOTE

1. The term 'black' is an inclusive term used in South Africa to include 'Africans', 'Indians' and 'Coloureds'. The term 'coloured' is commonly used to refer to people of 'mixed-race' descent. Even though these terms reflect apartheid classifications along racial and ethnic lines, they are still commonly used in contemporary democratic South Africa.

REFERENCES

Adams, W.M., R. Aveling, D. Brockington, B. Dickson, J. Elliott, J. Hutton, D. Roe, B. Vira and W. Wolmer (2004), 'Biodiversity conservation and the eradication of poverty', *Science*, **306**: 1146–1149.
Agrawal, A. and C.C. Gibson (1999), 'Enchantment and disenchantment: the role of community in natural resource conservation', *World Development*, **27**(4): 629–649.
Alkire, S. (2002), 'Dimensions of human development', *World Development*, **30**(2): 181–205.
Allison, E.H. (2005), 'The fisheries sector, livelihoods and poverty reduction in eastern and southern Africa', in F. Ellis and H.A. Freeman (eds), *Rural Livelihoods and Poverty Reduction Policies*, London: Routledge, pp. 256–273.
Allison, E.H. and F. Ellis (2001), 'The livelihoods approach and management of small-scale fisheries', *Marine Policy*, **25**(5): 377–388.

Allison, E.H. and B. Horemans (2006), 'Putting the principles of the Sustainable Livelihoods Approach into practice in fisheries development policy and practice', *Marine Policy*, **30**: 757–766.

Baily, C. and S. Jentoft (1990), 'Hard choices in fisheries development', *Marine Policy*, **14**(4): 333–344.

Baluch, B. (1996), 'The new poverty agenda: a disputed consensus', *IDS Bulletin*, **27**(1), Brighton: Institute of Development Studies, University of Sussex.

Béné, C. (2003), 'When fishery rhymes with poverty: a first step beyond the old paradigm on poverty in small-scale fisheries', *World Development*, **31**(6): 949–975.

Béné, C., A.E. Neiland, T. Jolley, S. Ovie, O. Sule, B. Ladu et al. (2003), 'Inland fisheries, poverty and rural livelihoods in the Lake Chad Basin', *Journal of Asian and African Studies*, **38**: 17–51.

Bernal, P., B. Cicin-Sain, with S. Belfiore and J. Barbière (2002), *Toward the 2002 World Summit on Sustainable Development Johannesburg: Ensuring Sustainable Development of Oceans and Coasts – A Call to Action*, Paris: Intergovernmental Oceanographic Commission, UNESCO; Newark, Delaware: Center for the Study of Marine Policy, University of Delaware.

Branch, G. and B. Clark (2006), 'Fish stocks and their management: the changing face of fisheries in South Africa', *Marine Policy*, **30**(1): 3–17.

Broad, R. (1994), 'The poor and the environment: friends or foes', *World Development*, **22**(6a): 811–822.

Carney, D. (ed.) (2002), *Sustainable Rural Livelihoods: What Contribution Can We Make?*, London: Department for International Development.

Cavendish, W. (2000), 'Empirical regularities in the poverty–environment relationship of rural households: evidence from Zimbabwe', *World Development*, **28**(11): 1979–2003.

Chambers, R. (1997), *Whose Reality Counts? Putting the First Last*, London: Intermediate Technology Publication.

Chambers, R. and Conway (1992), *Sustainable Rural Livelihoods: Practical Concepts for the 21st Century*, Discussion Paper 296, Brighton: Institute of Development Studies, University of Sussex.

Cicin-Sain, B., P. Bernal, V. Vandeweerd, S. Belfiore and K. Goldstein (2002), *Oceans, Coasts and Islands at the World Summit on Sustainable Development and Beyond: Integrated Management from Hilltops to Oceans*, Newark, Delaware: Center for the Study of Marine Policy, University of Delaware.

Cicin-Sain, B. and R.W. Knecht (1998), *Integrated Coastal and Ocean Management Concepts and Practices*, Washington, DC: Island Press (with the assistance of F. Fisk and D. Jang), Intergovernmental Oceanographic Commission, UNESCO, 517 pp.

Cling, J., D. Cogneau, J. Loup, J. Naudet, M. Razafindrakoto and F. Roubard (2006), 'Development, a question of opportunity? A critique of the 2006 World Development report: equity and development', *Development Policy Review*, **24**(4): 455–476.

Coastal Management Policy Programme (CMPP) (2000), *White Paper on Sustainable Coastal Development in South Africa*, Cape Town: The Department of Environmental Affairs and Tourism.

Cochrane, K.L. (2000), 'Reconciling sustainability, economic efficiency and equity in fisheries: the one that got away', *Fish and Fisheries*, **1**: 3–21.

Courtney, C.A. and A.T. White (2000), 'Integrated coastal management in the Philippines: testing new paradigms', *Coastal Management*, **28**: 39–53.

Crosoer, D., L. van Sittert and S. Ponte (2006), 'The integration of South African fisheries into the global economy: past, present and future', *Marine Policy*, **30**(1): 18–29.

DEAT (2002), *Where Have All the Fish Gone? Measuring Transformation in the South African Fishing Industry*, Cape Town: Department of Environmental Affairs and Tourism.

DFID (2000a), *Sustainable Livelihoods: Current Thinking and Practice*, London: DFID.

DFID (2000b), *Sustainable Livelihoods: Building on Current Strengths*, London: DFID.

Duraiappah, A.K. (1998), 'Poverty and environmental degradation: a review and analysis of the nexus', *World Development*, **26**(12): 2169–2179.

Faber, M., T. Petersen and J. Schiller (2002), 'Homo oeconomicus and homo politicus in ecological economics', *Ecological Economics*, **40**: 323–333.

FAO (2005), *Increasing the Contribution of Small-Scale Fisheries to Poverty Alleviation and Food Security*, FAO Technical Guidelines for Responsible Fisheries, No. 10, Rome: Food and Agricultural Organization.

Fernando, J.L. (2003), 'The power of unsustainable development: what is to be done?', *The Annals of the American Academy of Political and Social Science*, **590**: 6–34.

Gale, F.P. (1998), 'Theorizing power in ecological economics', *Ecological Economics*, **27**: 131–138.

Gasper, D. (1993), 'Entitlement analysis: relating concepts and contexts', *Development and Change*, **24**: 679–718.

Glavovic, B.C. (2000), 'A new coastal policy for South Africa', *Coastal Management*, **28**(3): 261–271.

Glavovic, B.C. (2006a), 'Coastal sustainability – an elusive pursuit? Reflections on South Africa's coastal policy experience', *Coastal Management*, **34**(1): 111–132.

Glavovic, B.C. (2006b), 'The evolution of coastal management in South Africa: why blood is thicker than water', *Journal of Ocean and Coastal Management*, **49**(12): 889–904.

Glavovic, B.C. and S. Boonzaaier (2007), 'Confronting coastal poverty: building sustainable coastal livelihoods in South Africa', *Journal of Ocean and Coastal Management*, **50**(1–2): 1–23.

Gore, C. (1993), 'Entitlement relations and 'unruly' social practices: a comment on the work of Amartya Sen', *Journal of Development Studies*, **29**(3): 429–460.

Gray, L.C. and W.G. Moseley (2005), 'A geographical perspective on poverty-environment interactions', *The Geographical Journal*, **171**(1): 9–23.

Gray, T. (ed.), *The Politics of Fishing*, London: Macmillan.

Hersoug, B. (ed.) (2002), *Fishing in a Sea of Sharks: Reconstruction and Development in the South African Fishing Industry*, Delft: Eburon, 224 pp.

Hersoug, B. and M. Isaacs (2002a), '"It's all about money!" – implementation of South Africa's new fisheries policy', in B. Hersoug (ed.), *Fishing in a Sea of Sharks: Reconstruction and Development in the South African Fishing Industry*, Delft: Eburon, pp. 137–172.

Hersoug, B. and M. Isaacs (2002b), 'The 2001/2002 allocations: a modus vivendi for the South African fishing industry?', in B. Hersoug (ed.), *Fishing in a Sea of Sharks: Reconstruction and Development in the South African Fishing Industry*, Delft: Eburon, pp. 201–224.

Isaacs, M. (2006), 'Small-scale fisheries reform: expectations, hopes and dreams of "a better life for all"', *Marine Policy*, **30**(1): 51–59.

Johannesburg Plan of Implementation (2002), para. 7, Available online at: http://www.un.org/esa/sustdev/documents/WSSD_POI_PD/English/POIToc.htm

Kleinschmidt, H., W.H.H. Sauer and P. Britz (2003), 'Commercial fishing rights allocation in post-apartheid South Africa: reconciling equity and stability', *South African Journal of Marine Science*, **23**: 25–35.

Lambin, E.F., B.L. Turner, H.L. Giest et al. (2001), 'The causes of land-use and land-cover change: moving beyond the myths', *Global Environmental Change*, **11**: 261–269.

Leach, M., R. Mearns and I. Scoones (1995), *Environmental Entitlements: A Framework for Understanding the Institutional Dynamics of Environmental Change*, Brighton: Institute of Development Studies, University of Sussex, 395 pp.

Leach, M., R. Mearns and I. Scoones (1999), 'Environmental entitlements: dynamics and institutions in community-based natural resource management', *World Development*, **27**(2): 225–247.

Lehtonen, M. (2004), 'The environmental–social interface of sustainable development: capabilities, social capital, institutions', *Ecological Economics*, **49**: 199-214.

Lele, S.M. (1991), 'Sustainable development: a critical review', *World Development*, **19**: 607–621.

Lipton, M. (1997), 'Editorial: poverty – are there holes in the consensus?', *World Development*, **25**(7): 1003–1007.

Lonergan, S.C. (1993), 'Impoverishment, population, and environmental degradation: the case for equity', *Environmental Conservation*, **20**(4): 328–334.

Martinez-Alier, J. (2002), *Environmentalism of the Poor*, Cheltenham, UK and Northampton, MA, USA: Edward Elgar.

Maxwell, S. (2001), 'WDR 2000: Is there a new "new poverty" agenda?', *Development Policy Review*, **19**(1): 143–149.

McCarthy, J., G. Baxter, J. Schroenn, M. McGrath, A. Forbes and S. Parnell (1998), *Coastal Economic Specialist Study*, Unpublished report for the Coastal Management Policy Programme, Cape Town.

Moffat, D., M.N. Ngoile, O. Linden and J. Francis (1998), 'The reality of the stomach: coastal management at the local level in Eastern Africa', *Ambio*, **27**(8): 590–598.

Moseley, W.G. (2001), 'African evidence on the relation of poverty, time preference and the environment', *Ecological Economics*, **38**: 317–326.

Moser, C. and A. Norton, with T. Conway, C. Ferguson and P. Vizard (2001), *To Claim our Rights: Livelihood Security, Human Rights and Sustainable Development*, Concept Paper, Overseas Development Institute, 67 pp.

Mosse, D., J. Farrington and A. Rew (eds) (1998), *Development as Process: Concepts and Methods for Working with Complexity*, London: Routledge.

Narayan, D., R. Chambers, M.K. Shah and P. Petersch (2001), *Voices of the Poor: Crying out for Change*, Oxford: Oxford University Press.

Neiland, A.E. and C. Béné (eds) (2004), *Poverty and Small-Scale Fisheries in West Africa*, Dordrecht, Netherlands: Kluwer; Rome, Italy: FAO.

Paavola, J. and W.N. Adger (2005), 'Institutional ecological economics', *Ecological Economics*, **53**: 353–368.

Panayotou, T. (1980), 'Economic conditions and prospects of small-scale fishermen in Thailand', *Marine Policy*, **4**(2): 142–146.

Raakjaer Nielsen, J. and M. Hara (2006), 'Transformation of South African industrial fisheries', *Marine Policy*, **30**(1): 43–50.

Reardon, R. and S.A. Vosti (1995), 'Links between rural poverty and the environment in developing countries: asset categories and investment poverty', *World Development*, **23**(9): 1495–1506.

Rees, W.E. (2002), 'An ecological economics perspective on sustainability and prospects for ending poverty', *Population and Environment*, **24**(1): 15–46.

Rees, W.E. (2003), 'Economic development and environmental protection: an ecological economics perspective', *Environmental Monitoring and Assessment*, **86**: 29–45.

Rutherford, M. (2001), 'Institutional economics: then and now', *Journal of Economic Perspectives*, **15**(3): 173–194.

Salmi, P. (2005), 'Rural pluriactivity as a coping strategy in small-scale fisheries', *Sociologia Ruralis*, **45**(1–2): 22–36.

Scherr, S.J. (2000), 'A downward spiral? Research evidence on the relationship between poverty and natural resource degradation', *Food Policy*, **25**: 479-498.

Scoones, I. (1999), 'New ecology and the social sciences: what prospects for a fruitful engagement?' *Annual Review of Anthropology*, **28**: 479–507.

Sen, A. (1981), *Poverty and Famines: An Essay on Entitlements and Deprivation*, Oxford: Clarendon Press.

Sen, A. (1985), *Commodities and Capabilities*, Amsterdam: North-Holland.

Sen, A. (1992), *Inequality Re-examined*, Cambridge, MA: Harvard University Press.

Sen, A. (1999), *Development as Freedom*, New York: Alfred A. Knoff.

Smith, T.F., D. Alcock, D.C. Thomsen and R. Chuenpagdee (2004), 'Improving the quality of life in coastal areas and future directions for the Asia-Pacific region', *Coastal Management*, **34**(3): 235–250.

Sneddon, C., R.B. Howarth and R.B. Norgaard (2006), 'Sustainable development in a post-Brundtland world', *Ecological Economics*, **57**: 253–268.

Sowman, M. (2006), 'Subsistence and small-scale fisheries in South Africa: a 10-year review', *Marine Policy*, **30**(1): 60–73.

Stirrat, R.L. (2004), 'Yet another "magic bullet": the case of social capital', *Aquatic Resources, Culture and Development*, **1**(1): 25–33.

Swift, J. (1989), 'Why are rural people vulnerable to famine? Vulnerability: how the poor cope', *IDS Bulletin*, **20**(2), Brighton: Institute of Development Studies, University of Sussex.

Swinton, S.M., G. Escobar and T. Reardon (2003), 'Poverty and environment in Latin America: Concepts, evidence and policy implications', *World Development*, **31**(11): 1865–1872.

Townsley, P. (1998), 'Aquatic resources and sustainable rural livelihoods', in D. Carney (ed.), *Sustainable Rural Livelihoods: What Contribution can We Make?*, London: Department for International Development, pp. 139–153.

UNDP (1997), *Human Development Report: Human Development to Eradicate Poverty*, New York: United Nations Development Programme.

UNDP (2005), *Human Development Report 2005: International Cooperation at a Crossroads*, New York: UNDP.

van Oostenbrugge, J.A.E., W.L.T. van Densen and M.A.M. Machiels (2004), 'How the uncertain outcomes associated with aquatic and land use affect livelihood strategies in coastal communities in the Central Moluccas, Indonesia', *Agricultural Systems*, **82**(1): 57–91.

van Sittert, L., G. Branch, M. Hauck and M. Sowman (2006), 'Benchmarking the first decade of post-apartheid fisheries reform in South Africa', *Marine Policy*, **30**: 96–110.

Wagel, U. (2002), 'Rethinking poverty: definition and measurement', *International Social Science Journal*, **54**(1): 155–165.

Whittingham, E., J. Campbell and P. Townsley (2003a), *Poverty and Reefs: Volume 1: A Global Overview*, Paris: DFID-IMM-IOC/UNESCO, 72 pp.

Whittingham, E., J. Campbell and P. Townsley (2003b), *Poverty and Reefs: Volume 2: Case Studies*, Paris: DFID-IMM-IOC/UNESCO, 231 pp.

Witbooi, E. (2006), 'Law and fisheries reform: legislative and policy development in South African fisheries over the decade 1994–2004', *Marine Policy*, **30**(1): 30–42.

World Bank (1992), *A Strategy for Fisheries Development*, Fisheries Series Discussion Papers No. 135. Washington, DC: World Bank.

World Bank (2000), *Attacking Poverty: World Development Report 2000/2001*, New York: Oxford University Press.

World Bank (2005), *World Development Report 2006: Equity and Development*, Oxford: Oxford University Press.

World Commission on Environment and Development (WCED) (1987), *Our Common Future*, Oxford: Oxford University Press.

PART IV

Implementing an Ecological Economics of the Oceans and Coasts

It is often asserted that ecological economics should have a 'practical problem solving' focus that 'makes a difference in the real world'. This implies that ecological economics must move beyond policy evaluation, to a concern for implementation and the associated requisite governance structures.

Chapter 12 deals with practical problems of 'uncertainty' and 'lack of information' that are encountered in the economic management of fisheries. As concluded in Chapter 4, it is the 'complex system properties' of marine ecosystems that gives rise to this uncertainty and consequently makes it 'difficult' to scientifically predict stock numbers in fisheries. It is therefore argued in this chapter that a practical way to deal with this problem is to use a Minimum Information Management (MIM) system – the MIM system and its rationale are explained in this chapter.

Chapter 13 focuses on the problem of designing property rights systems for achieving sustainable development of marine resources. A micro-economics approach is used to analyze property rights regimes that can be used to sustainably manage 'common property' marine resources. A case study of New Zealand's fisheries management regime demonstrates the operation of a tradable property rights system. Since its introduction in 1986, the system has achieved both sustainability outcomes and economic efficiency gains.

Chapter 14 outlines why prevailing ocean and coastal governance often fails to advance sustainability in the real world. It argues that such failure is because prevailing governance efforts remain fundamentally mismatched to the distinguishing ecological, economic and social characteristics of ocean and coastal systems. This gives rise to a number of governance challenges that are important in developing an ecological economics of the oceans and coasts that will have practical relevance and can be implemented.

12. Minimum Information Management: Harvesting the Harvesters' Assessment of Dynamic Fisheries Systems

Chris Batstone and Basil Sharp

A fisheries management regime must satisfy a number of social, economic and ecosystem requirements to enable sustainable utilization of natural resources. The information discovery process necessary to obtain dynamic solutions to optimal policy parameters is daunting from both capability and cost perspectives. Minimum Information Management (MIM) systems based in particular institutional arrangements – Individual Transferable Share Quota (ITSQ) – allow resource managers to take advantage of the market mechanism to resolve their management information problem.

THE MINIMUM INFORMATION MANAGEMENT (MIM) CONCEPT

Harvesters, through their frequent and often long-running interaction with the fishery system, develop tacit knowledge that enables effective harvesting operations. Their operations are informed by a process of discovery that incorporates understandings of the fishery system that coincide with fisheries managers' information requirements. Given liquidity constraints, harvesters' assessments of the system may be revealed through their investment decisions in ITSQ rights markets. On the assumption that harvesters act on rational expectations, fishery managers are able to achieve optimal solutions to establishing catches by adjusting harvest levels so that the value of quota prices is maximized. Derivative statistics such as implicit discount rates (IDR) allow managers to understand the economic consequences of alternate time paths of stock rebuilding and to monitor harvesters' assessments of the effects of policy interventions. Effectiveness relies on incentives created by the ITSQ specification in which rights are expressed as proportions of a total allowable catch, as opposed to an absolute definition. That specification aligns harvesters' incentives with managers' intentions by enabling harvest reduction (and expansion) without market intervention by management authorities.

Productivity in fisheries systems is determined by complex and often little understood ecosystem and oceanographic processes. The fundamental problem in coastal and oceans governance systems is one of information about complex systems characterized by non-linear processes that involve accumulation, feedback, reinforcement, and interaction between stimuli (see Chapter 4). Effective management requires discovery of state, pressure and response aspects of the fishery system. Knowledge and information generating techniques from the biological sciences, fishery science, computer science, mathematics, ecology and oceanography are required in this process. There is a tension in the scientific community between processes that generate information for policy decisions based in mathematical modelling and approaches based in adaptive management by way of feedback from system indicators. The inherent variability of such systems under a complex systems perspective may render modelling approaches ineffective. Multi-faceted interactions between pressure, state and response may act to confound model generated expectations. Scientific uncertainty compromises the ability of management agencies to control or manage single commercial species, let alone multi-species systems with scientific method based knowledge alone.

Definition of the scope of the system under consideration is critical. Fisheries management systems that focus solely on biophysical interactions tend to have been less successful than those that include the socio-economic domain. This is not uncontroversial. There are inherent conflicts between fishery management goals in biological/ecological and socio-economic domains. A further tension arises between centralized command and control and decentralized co-management approaches. A substantial contribution from the socioeconomic disciplines has been the understanding that it is open access to natural resources that underpins excess pressure and externalities of habitat degradation. Resolution of this aspect provides the avenue for generating sustainable utilization in fisheries systems. At the heart of the issue is the design of property rights, which influence the incentives that individual economic agents face, in turn conditioning their own responses. The MIM concept is based on the capacity of the market mechanism that underlies rights trading to mitigate scientific uncertainty by contributing an additional information discovery channel.

MIM is a concept that embraces the issues of property rights, incentives, information, and the tension between centralized and decentralized management regimes. MIM is about using information generated in rights markets to inform fisheries management decisions. It has the potential to contribute to natural resource management through generating additional information for the decision processes. It resolves a fundamental difficulty in respect of fishery management information – that of integrating knowledge formed through the scientific method with the experiential, tacit knowledge of the resource users themselves. MIM may contribute to defining the parameters of policy instruments around which interventions are designed. The information is also able to contribute in a feedback mode as an indicator to provide harvesters' assessments of the system's pressure, state and response attributes in adaptive management processes. A number of questions can be addressed such as: We think our allowable catches have changed the state of the system. What is the aggregate feedback from harvesters? Do they concur? The advantages of such a management system are attractive. A process is available that allows resource managers to discover in a cost-effective way information summarizing harvesters' assessments of the state of fishery system.

The Market Mechanism and MIM

The economic foundations of MIM lie in a combination of neoclassical and Austrian perspectives. The mathematical derivation of the theoretical underpinnings involves the invocation of enabling assumptions behind neoclassical use of constrained optimization mathematics.

The Austrian view of markets as economic institutions and their role in an economy underpins the idea of markets as information generators. A significant line of research has explored the relationship between the knowledge of individuals and how market outcomes are affected by the rules of the market (Smith 1982). Economists such as Von Mises, Hayek and later Kirzner held that the neoclassical view of perfect competition implied that economic agents have already discovered all there is to know about costs, prices, opportunities and preferences. The implication is that rivalry among market participants ceases and equilibrium occurs in the context of perfect knowledge (Hayek [1978] 1994). The corollary is a system in which optimal economic performance follows. In contrast, economists of the Austrian school perceived knowledge to be dispersed and incomplete. Their view of the market mechanism is one of a process of discovery as economic agents progressively move price/quantity combinations in market transactions from positions of greater to lesser disequilibrium (Hayek 1945).

The correspondence between ecosystem and economic system management is clear. If scientists and managers (economic agents) have discovered all there is to know that is relevant for dealing with the ecosystem or economic system under consideration, then allowable catches (quantities) may be prescribed and an optimal solution will emerge. Consistent with the so called economic calculation debate (Lange 1936; Mises [1920] 1935), ecologists, and often the experiences of fisheries managers, challenge this view. They cite the fluctuating nature of ecosystems as instances of complex dynamical systems that require a different approach to information acquisition to enable successful guidance (Ludwig et al. 1993; Massod 1997; Rose 1997; Walters and Maguire 1996).

The implication for fisheries management is significant. Harvesters reflect their own ongoing discovery and assessment of commercial and ecological systems through their investment and disinvestment decisions in markets for rights to allocations of proportions of total allowable catches (TAC). In the context of appropriately specified property rights of sufficient liquidity, rights markets may prove to be cost-effective generators of information that may contribute to reducing scientific uncertainty around assessments of state, pressure and response.

The Minimum Information Framework

Arnason (1990) proposed the fundamental framework for subsequent research applications, dealing with problems of optimal management of common-property fisheries and the potential contribution made possible by implementation of an ITSQ system. This rights specification makes possible market-based management systems requiring minimal information for their operation that may lead to enhanced effectiveness (and efficiency) in the management of common-property fisheries.

A fisheries management authority needs to satisfy multiple social and economic conditions associated with maximizing the present value of social economic profit. In contrast the goal of individual firms is maximizing the present value of private economic profit. For the fishery manager, specifying institutional structures and discovering the appropriate parameters for interventions that lead to coincidence of the shadow prices between social and private optimization processes are not trivial undertakings. Possible institutional alternatives to open-access harvest regimes are input controls on effort, taxes on catch, and output controls in the form of quotas.

For example, in order to discover the appropriate corrective output tax for an individual firm and its development over time, the manager must possess all the data relevant to the fishing firms at all times, under all conditions. In particular, the manager must have full knowledge of the resource growth function, the harvesting and cost functions of all the firms at all points in time. Further, the fishery manager must continuously monitor the state of the resource and the movement of the relevant economic prices for the optimal tax to be correctly continuously adjusted to new conditions. Clearly, these tasks would exceed the information capabilities of fishery managers and associated tax authorities.

An ITSQ system is an institutional setting that alleviates this information responsibility. Within the framework of a permanent share quota system, the prevailing quota market price reflects all relevant information about the current and future conditions in the fishery available to the fishing firms (Arnason 1990). It follows that the fishery manager only has to monitor the quota market price or derivatives to discover the same information. The time path of quotas contains the information that both individual firms require for efficient harvest and fishery management requires for efficient management.

In subsequent papers Arnason (1998, 2000) proposed the extension of the application of the ITSQ system in combination with the MIM procedure from single species to an ecosystem context. In those papers the analysis is extended from single fishery quota prices to show that a vector of multi-species prices may be used to establish an appropriate series of catches for optimal management of the system. Under the usual assumptions concerning market efficiency, the TAC vector that maximizes the aggregate value of all outstanding ITQ shares also maximizes the present value of expected profits from the fishery. An ITSQ system, coupled with the MIM procedure, offers a flexible and promising approach to deal with the problem of fisheries management. However, what the MIM procedure maximizes is expected rents in the fishing industry. Economic rents are not necessarily the same as profits. More importantly, the rents maximized are those according to the expectations of the fishing industry and other traders in the quota market.

Implementation of ITSQ systems

A limited literature has developed subsequent to Arnason's contribution and ITSQ systems have been implemented by only a handful of nations. Amongst the long established are those in Icelandic and New Zealand waters. Batstone and Sharp (2003, 2006) examined the potential application of Arnason's work in New Zealand ITSQ fisheries. The 2003 paper examines price formation in one quota market, the northern SNA1 snapper fishery. Markets are found to meet two of three of Fama's (1970) informational efficiency standards. Prices follow random walks and a demonstrable relationship exists between the quota's long-term asset price and underlying returns.

Evidence from time-series analysis of ITSQ prices supports Arnason's proposition that quota prices are functionally related to asset returns and perturbations to total allowable commercial catch (TACC). Relationships between asset prices, annual lease prices, and cost of capital are statistically significant and consistent with those expected in economic theory. These outcomes suggest that within this fishery quota markets meet the basic criteria for a fisheries management agency to use quota prices in management processes.

Newell et al. (2005) used a 15-year panel dataset from New Zealand that covers 33 species and more than 150 markets for fishing quotas to determine the fundamentals of quota lease prices and sale prices. They examined relationships in their data between quota lease and sale prices: (1) output and input prices, (2) ecological variability and (3) market interest rates to derive evidence of economically rational behaviour. Their results confirm that quota prices (1) increase with increasing prices for fish and increased quota demand, and (2) decrease with increasing costs and ecological uncertainty.

The authors indicate a substantial increase in quota prices since the rights-based system was established, which is consistent with an increase in the profitability of the fisheries. Quota price increases have been considerably greater for stocks that faced significant reductions in allowable catch levels. They found that quota sale prices have risen to a greater degree than quota lease prices. The greater increase in quota sale prices can be at least partly attributed to decreases in the market interest rate, which fell from about 11 per cent to 3 per cent in real terms over the relevant period. (The relationship between rates of increase in lease and asset prices is explored later in this chapter.) Increases in quota sale prices could also be driven in part by the perception of increased security of quota assets, although such an effect should not be important for quota lease prices.

One of the proposed advantages of rights-based management is that it reduces transaction costs through lower compliance and enforcement costs. Such management systems are supported by a regulatory apparatus that is enforced through a compliance function associated with the fishery management agency. Hatcher (2005) examined the effects of non-compliance, violations and ensuing penalties on quota demand and the equilibrium quota price in an ITSQ fishery. Noting that penalties are a function of violation size, lower quota prices are implied by expected penalties that decrease profitability. As violation dimensions increase, corresponding penalties are associated with decreased profitability, and in turn lower quota prices. However, under certain conditions expected penalties can produce higher quota prices. If there are both compliant and non-compliant firms in the fishery, there may be a shift in quota demand from compliant to non-compliant firms rather than the reverse.

The implications of these findings for fisheries management using ITQs are potentially significant. Absence of declining quota prices does not necessarily imply decline in non-compliance in the fishery. Similarly, increasing quota prices may not necessarily suggest increasing profitability in the fishery. They may, in part at least, be attributable to increased cheating. As a consequence, quota prices on their own may provide misleading signals and caution should therefore be exercised in their use in making fishery management decisions.

POLICY IMPLICATIONS: PUTTING MIM TO WORK

Given the insight that quota prices may reflect the information necessary to guide fishery managers, and noting the assumptions and caveats around the reliability of those price signals, the question arises: How can this information be harnessed?

There are three potential avenues that emerge that enable fisheries management authorities to utilize harvesters' revealed system knowledge:

- establishing estimates of optimal harvests through quota prices,
- monitoring stock rebuilds through implicit discount rates, and
- modelling the effects of policy parameter changes in bioeconomic models.

Establishing Estimates of Optimal Harvest with MIM

The original Arnason (1993, 1998, 2000) proposal was that fisheries managers set allowable catches to optimize the economic rent attributable to a fishery or fishery system by choosing allowable catches that optimized quota prices. On the assumption that all firms utilize similar technologies with comparable efficiency – there is a measure of homogeneity across firms – then on average profits should approximate resource rents. Quota prices multiplied by allowable catches represent the present value of total fishery rents. Ecosystem interdependencies across species are represented in vectors of future quota prices based on harvesters' understandings of the proportions of multi-species harvests. Arnason (1993) argued that the incentives faced by harvesters encouraged investment and dis-investment on the basis of expectations of future conditions. Accordingly, the time path of future prices tended toward the optimal one. It is not necessary for fishery managers to set the entire time path of quota, but to set initial catches for a given set of biological conditions that optimized quota price in the current period. This could be achieved through a Walrasian tatonnement process in a kind of quota exchange. Alternatively, Arnason suggested allowing harvesters to set optimal TACCs themselves in the context of procedural oversight by the fishery management authority. The implication is a co-management derivation of an optimal time path of quotas defined by the combined understandings of harvesters that integrates production and demand aspects of the fishery. This might address issues such as, 'if white fish prices are low presently and stock biomass is high, then we should refrain from harvest until output prices improve'.

Batstone and Sharp (2003) demonstrated, in the New Zealand SNA1 snapper fishery, that it was possible to obtain estimates of optimal TACCs from rights trading data that were reasonably consistent with the scientifically derived assessment. The SNA1 northern snapper fishery features many of the issues that are contentious in New Zealand's application of a rights-based approach to fisheries management. The allocation issue remains contentious in this fishery. There is a large urban population within close proximity to SNA1. The population of the adjacent Auckland, Waikato and Northland areas has grown to in excess of 1.5 million – and continues to grow – with implications for the magnitude of expected non-commercial catches. By the mid-1980s commercial catches had declined and stock showed signs of overfishing. Annual landings peaked in 1978 at 18 000 tonnes; catches declined to 8500 tonnes annually before the introduction of the Quota Management System (QMS). The stock showed signs of 'growth over-fishing' – fish not realizing their full growth potential before harvest. In 1986, when the QMS was introduced, the TACC for SNA1 was set at 4710 t, 55 per cent of the established catch history to allow for stock rebuilding (Annala et al. 1998). In 1992 the rights specification was modified from an absolute to a proportional specification. That is, harvesters' entitlements changed from an absolute tonnage specification to one that, while expressed in quantity terms, is defined as a percentage of the TACC.

A mathematically robust connection was established between quota asset prices and the level of allowable harvests. This allowed definition of a model of quota price formation. Readers with a mathematical inclination may follow the development of this analysis in the technical appendix at the conclusion of the chapter.

The level of allowable commercial harvest that maximizes this function was estimated to be 3982 tonnes, a figure that falls at the lower end of stock assessment recommendations in 1996 of 4150–7350 tonnes (Annala et al. 1998). The authors note a number of limitations for use of this estimate of an optimal harvest reflected by asset prices. First, that of the assumption of harvester homogeneity (Arnason 1998, 2000) and the relationship between average profitability and fishery economic rents. The second relates to the dynamic nature of fisheries ecosystems. This estimate has relevance only for the bioeconomic system and time period of the estimation. It is not a time invariant estimate of an optimal harvest in the fishery.

The analysis demonstrates the potential applicability of the MIM concept to establish and corroborate estimates of optimal harvests derived from other processes such as scientific stock assessment. The effectiveness of the technique in this implementation is limited by differential rights specifications across harvesting sectors. Commercial harvesters alone hold and trade proportional rights.

Monitoring Biomass Progress Toward Recovery: The Role for Implicit Discount Rates (IDR)

The key concept illustrated in this section is that transaction records can be used to establish 'revealed' discount rates that may be used to inform management decisions and to understand emergent issues in those processes. A deeper level of mathematical description is provided in the technical appendix at the conclusion of this chapter.

Theories of renewable resource use link optimal economic harvests outcomes to the cost of capital (Clark 1990). High discount rates imply more severe harvesting regimes that favour present consumption over the future. In contrast, low discount rates imply the opposite, a higher level of preference for the future over the present. Where natural systems management decisions are framed by the use of bioeconomic models, the choice of discount rates is crucial to modelling optimal outcomes. There are problems ascertaining the appropriate discount rates to adopt that reflect rates of preference that individuals hold. Rates may vary amongst individuals over time (Chichilnisky 1997) and they may also vary across gender, age cohorts and cultures.

Models for the economics of renewable resource use are defined in terms of the growth rate of stock biomass over time. The profit maximizing level of stock biomass is derived from the profit maximization objective function of the harvester that is expressed in terms of output price, the effect of stock biomass on costs, the discount rate, and the rate of growth of the stock. The solution to this optimization problem may be expressed in terms of the rate of stock growth and the 'own rate of interest' held by the harvester. In a surplus production fishery model, with stock biomass less than that which supports maximum sustainable yield, harvesters' 'own rate of interest' becomes smaller as the fish stock grows toward the stock biomass associated with maximum economic yield (B_{MEY}). At this point, the harvesters' own rate of interest is coincident with or tracks the economy-wide cost of capital represented by central bank wholesale interest rates. This occurs because the level of annual sustainable production is density dependent. The stock growth rate slows, and the flow on externality effect diminishes. Conversely, if the stock level declines, own rate of interest becomes larger and diverges from the cost of capital.

These aspects form the basis for the expectation that at point of introduction of a species to the QMS, the 'own rate of interest' of the harvest will be larger than the cost of capital for three reasons. First, the lower stock biomass supports a higher stock growth rate for reasons of density dependence. Second, the stock effect on costs will be larger due to stock externalities associated with the prior regime of an input-controlled, open-access fishery. Last, operations financing will require higher rates of return over and above the cost of capital to meet industry risk premiums.

Batstone and Sharp (2006) discuss the potential application of implicit discount rates (IDR) derived from Individual Transferable Quota (ITQ) trading data as indicators of fishery bioeconomic health. Quota trading generates price–quantity data that can be used to develop statistics that can reflect the state of the system through the process of revealed preferences. Short-run (annual) lease prices give an indication of immediate in-season profitability. Long-run asset prices are indicative of the future rents available in the fishery. Rights trading activity gives a view of the revealed preferences of the commercial sector in the New Zealand QMS.

There are biological data from the New Zealand rock lobster fisheries. These data show that a recovery of stock levels toward B_{msy} (biomass associated with the maximum sustainable yield) is underway since the introduction of the rights based output managed regime (Sullivan 2004). We expect decline in both the rate of stock biomass growth, and the marginal stock effect. This should be evidenced by data that show convergence of the 'own rate of interest' associated with harvest toward the cost of capital in the wider New Zealand economy.

Analytically, the central problem associated with demonstrating this is to be able to derive estimates for the harvesters' 'own rate of interest' associated with the various stock biomass levels. This problem can be resolved where stocks are managed under a traded rights regime with a proportional as opposed to absolute rights specification, and where financial information is collected systematically on rights trading. The time path of the quota price depends on optimal quota holdings for each firm, the marginal cost of effort, the initial biomass and two exogenous variables, the price of fish and the discount rate. In theory, the problem of discovering optimal holdings is resolved in the rights markets where asset prices represent the present value of future rents in the fishery and lease prices reflect annual profitability. The implicit discount rate at time t, $\hat{r}_t$ is defined as the ratio of lease price at t (LP_t) to asset price (AP_t) at time t.

$$\hat{r}_t = LP_t/AP_t \tag{12.1}$$

The behaviour of implicit discount rates derived from ITSQ trading data for one New Zealand rock Lobster Fishery designated CRA1 is considered for the period 1991 to 2001. The fishery was selected on the merit of commercial harvest by one method (potting) that creates a minimal technology externality. Figure 12.1 contrasts the growth in the New Zealand Rock Lobster *(jasus edwardsii)* stock following QMS implementation in 1991 with pre-QMS stock biomass decline through time series of annual biomass estimates for the CRA1 fishery.

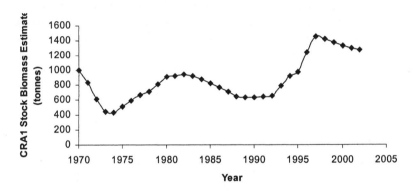

Figure 12.1 CRA1 estimated stock biomass 1970–2004
(Data source: NIWA 2005)

The use of price data from ITQ trading records in the CRA1 fishery is endorsed through demonstration of informational efficiency in those markets according to Fama's Efficient Markets Hypothesis criteria (Fama 1970). Fitting linear trends to time series of implicit discount rates from the CRA1 fishery and the cost of capital specified in terms of rates of return on NZ Treasury 90 Day Bills in real terms produces evidence of convergence. Asset title prices that reflect the long-run future of the fishery are growing at a faster rate than the lease title prices that represent the short-run. This outcome is consistent with the finding of Newell et al. (2005).

Further time series analytical techniques confirm relationships between

IDR and stock biomass. Estimation of a simple steady state model of the relationship between IDR and stock biomass generates evidence of a robust statistically significant relationship between the two. Time series tests of causality show a flow of causation (Granger Causation) from stock biomass to implicit discount rates. Granger Causality exists when lagged values of a variable x_t have explanatory power in a regression of a variable y_t on lagged values of y_t and x_t (Greene 1993).

In the CRA1 fishery the stock decline has been halted and the fishery is making steps toward recovery. As stock recovery strategies take effect, harvest costs decline and the value of ITQ rights should increase. Since stock abundance is increasing, the slope of the surplus production function decreases as stock biomass increases. In turn, we would expect the IDR to decline. ITQ trading data confirm this. Figure 12.2 describes CRA1 ITQ monthly average prices in NZ_{1990} terms for the period June 1990 to April 2001 for the months where trades in both lease and asset markets are evident.

Gathering further data on output prices enables estimation of the system elasticities through time series multivariate modelling. In this market system the elasticity between TACC and asset price is of the order of -1.4 per cent ($p < 0.05$) and lease prices (LP) and asset prices (AP) of the order of $+0.64$ per cent ($p < 0.05$) measured with asset price as the response variable.

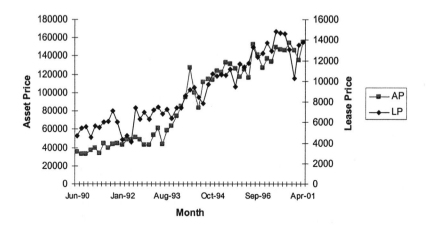

Figure 12.2   CRA1 ITQ monthly average prices in NZ_{1990} terms, June 1990 – April 2001
(*Data source:* NZ Ministry of Fisheries 2003)

Fitting linear trends to the data shows asset prices are growing at a faster rate than lease prices (Figure 12.2). Prices that reflect the long-term future of the fishery are growing at a faster rate than those that reflect short-term (annual) profitability. The implication is that the IDR will converge or track the cost of capital. The high-risk premium and required rates of return associated with open access fisheries are replaced by risk reduction enabled by stock recovery strategies derived and refined in multi-sector consultative processes of the NZ Rock Lobster Management Group.

Implicit discount rates (IDR) for the CRA1 fishery are described in Figure 12.3 along with real rates of return (R) on NZ Treasury 90-day bills. The long-run trend in both these series is for decline; with the fishery IDR declining at a rate faster than the return on 90-day bank bills.

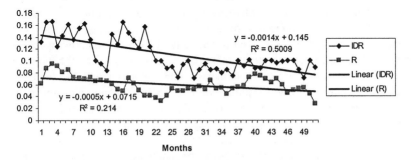

Figure 12.3 CRA1 IDR and real interest rates linear trends

The potential exists to monitor and compare the progress of fishery recovery using the IDR statistic or derivatives that reflect its time path to discount rate values associated with the stock management goal. An important reflection is that the IDR technique provides the opportunity to aggregate fishers' tacit knowledge with models of bioeconomic optima in understanding fishery ecosystem processes. Differential rates of change in IDRs across similar (technically, ecologically, geographically) fisheries may be indicative of differing progress toward management goals. IDRs are linked to stock biomass and are therefore an avenue for triangulation with other fisheries reference data in 'diagnostic' processes.

Modelling the Economic Effects of Policy Parameter Changes in Bioeconomic Models

Much fisheries literature concentrates on the problem of halting stock decline. Once this goal is achieved an ensuing set of problems emerges. How fast should stocks be rebuilt toward a management target? How are the dividends of stock rebuilding to be distributed? How can management agencies incorporate economic information in their decision-making processes? Sophisticated fishery bioeconomic models have been designed to answer these questions by incorporating one of a number of variants of biological stock models with an economic model. The economic sub-model usually combines catches, cost and output price data in a net present-value model to generate rent estimations. However, that treatment ignores the problems associated with applying such a model – for example, data fouling through strategic behaviour and harvesters' perceptions of a need for commercial confidentiality, and discount rate selection issues.

The catch limitation made possible under the QMS has halted stock decline in a number of New Zealand QMS fisheries. A number of management questions arise that focus on stock recovery strategies. What is the most appropriate duration of stock rebuilding, taking into account economic as well as biological considerations? How do managing agencies determine the duration of stock rebuilds? One view is that the optimal solution is to close the fishery to harvest until stocks reach the level of exploitable biomass that supports MSY – or the economic optimum maximum economic yield (MEY). However, other commentators, such as Boyce (1995), argue that this approach ignores the value of harvesting and processing assets and intellectual capital that would be lost due to fishery closure. At the heart of the issue is the notion that a large number of solutions to the problem exist, each with differing points of balance in terms of the duration of stock rebuilds and the temporal and cross-sectoral distribution of rebuild gains.

By specifying and applying a minimum information fishery bioeconomic model, managers may obtain the requisite information to take decisions that take account of economic consequences in a cost-effective way. The principal points of difference between this model and the customary bioeconomic model specification are that the parameters of the economic sub-model are derived from the time series analysis of transaction level data from harvesting-rights markets and the objective function is the rate of return (discount rate) to harvesting-rights holdings. Model inputs are interest rates (R), annual total allowable catch data (TAC), monthly rights lease price data (LP), asset price data (AP), fishery output prices (FOB), catch per unit effort (CPUE), and the associated elasticities. Figure 14.4 describes the model structure.

Time series analysis of rights markets data yields elasticities between quota prices and harvest levels (TACC) and in turn estimates of fishery economic rent. A fishery-specific surplus production model is fitted to CPUE data. Model outcomes are: (1) indicators of current biomass to reference points, (2) stock rebuilding times to biomass goals, (3) scenario specific lease and asset prices and (4) time series of implicit discount rates and estimates of economic rent.

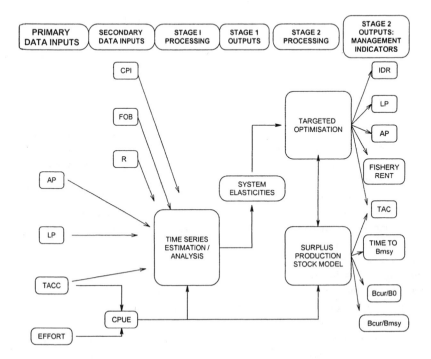

Figure 12.4 ITSQ minimum information bioeconomic model

Alternative scenarios of stock rebuilding are achieved by specifying alternative time paths of annual harvests (TACCs). From these flow descriptions of biological and economic parameters of management interest. Lower annual harvest regimes imply faster stock rebuilding, higher economic rent and low implicit discount rates. High tonnage harvest regimes imply slower stock rebuilding, higher discount rates and lower fishery economic rent. The information may be applied in decision processes to define the implications of alternate stock rebuilding strategies.

Harvesting-rights market transactions contain information about the commercial sector economic rent attributable to a fishery. This potentially removes the need to specify discount rates in rent calculations and to collect the revenue and cost information on which the net present value calculations are based. Managers are able to understand the economic implications of biologically determined catch levels and to select the level of the annual total allowable catch by nominating a preferred rate of return to the harvesting right. When combined with a surplus production model fitted to stock-specific data, economic information may be linked to conventional fishery management indicators such as changes in stock biomass, maximum sustainable yield and the duration of stock rebuilds to the stock biomass that supports maximum sustainable yield.

CONCLUSIONS

The requirement to take account of social and economic as well as ecological and oceanographic considerations exacerbates the information discovery problem facing fishery managers. The MIM concept offers an avenue to alleviate this information burden. It relies on understanding that harvesters develop tacit knowledge that enables effective harvesting operations and that knowledge incorporates understandings of the fishery system that coincide with fisheries managers' information requirements. This information is dispersed across a number of firms, each holding differing degrees of intuition as to the state of the fishery system. However, the knowledge behind those intuitions is aggregated in investment decisions in rights markets. The knowledge may be collected through monitoring and analysis of rights trading data where institutional arrangements are specified such that rights markets of sufficient liquidity exist.

The information may be used to determine optimal harvests through tatonnement or co-management processes. The time series analysis of ITSQ trading data may be incorporated in the fishery assessment process to complement scientific stock assessment in harvest setting processes. The implications of alternate scenarios for stock rebuilds may be assessed in terms of elasticities derived from rights trading data assessments of changes to economic rent and discount rates (rates of return). By linking rights trading data with models of fishery density dependence, a feedback mechanism is created for managers to evaluate the response of the fishery system to their interventions. At the core of this process is the information discovery attributes of the market mechanism.

TECHNICAL APPENDIX

Price Formation in ITQ Asset markets

In order to derive a fishery-specific connection between quota asset prices and the level of harvest (TACC) it is necessary to specify a model that adequately addresses two criteria. First, the model specification should explain a reasonable proportion of price variation. Second, it should be possible to test the relationship between quota prices and explanatory variables without violating the assumptions that underpin the validity of the modelling technique. In this case the data are time series and the relevant problem is that of 'spurious regression' – that is, relating non-stationary variables in time series regression models.

Since a number of the variables that are shown to influence asset price are non-stationary and co-integrated, it is not possible to adopt classical regression analysis to derive the relationships. To avoid this problem, price formation in asset title markets for SNA1 was specified in terms of the Autoregressive Distributed Lag Model (ADL) described by Wickens and Breusch (1988). The econometric convention used to describe this family of time-series model specifications is ADL (m, r) where m and r are terms used to indicate the order of the lag operator. The classical ordinary least squares (OLS) regression is specified in terms of ADL $(0, 0)$. Equations with lagged dependent variables may arise where there are adjustment costs such as transaction costs, search costs, or in situations where agents react slowly to changes in their environment due to factors such as uncertainty, inertia, or lags in the perception of change. Unobservable expectations about future conditions may appear as a function of prior prices (Hendry et al. 1984).

The ADL model adopted for this analysis is:

$$A_t = \kappa_0 + \sum_{i=1}^{m} \alpha_i A_{t-i} + \sum_{j=1}^{r} \beta j L_{t-j} + \sum_{j=1}^{r} \gamma_j Q_{t-j} + \sum_{j=1}^{r} \psi_j F_{t-j} + \sum_{j=1}^{r} \varphi_j R_{t-j} + \varepsilon_t$$

$$(12.2)$$

where A = asset price (\$); L = annual lease price (\$); Q = annual TACC (tonnes); F = FOB output price (\$); R = interest rates (per cent); κ_0 is a constant; $\alpha, \beta, \gamma, \psi, \phi$ are the estimated coefficients; and ϵ_t is the stochastic disturbance term.

A function for the total economic rent (QA), in the fishery based on the estimation results of the ADL $(1, 1)$ specified function above was derived:

$$QA = Q(116.119 - 14.48Q)$$

Derivation of IDR Concept

The starting point for the derivation of models for the economics of renewable resource use is defined in terms of the growth rate of stock biomass (B) over time (t) given by:

$$\frac{dB}{dt} = F(B) - H(t) \qquad (12.3)$$

where $F(B)$ is an expression for the stock biomass (often a logistic function) and $H(t)$ is the harvest in period t.

The profit-maximizing level of stock biomass is derived from the profit-maximization objective function of the harvester:

$$PV(\pi) = \int_0^\infty [P - C(B)]\left[F(B) - \dot{B}\right] e^{-\delta t} dt \qquad (12.4)$$

where $\dot{B}$ the rate of growth of the stock, P = output price, $C(B)$ is the effect of stock biomass on costs, and δ the discount rate.

The solution may be expressed in terms of the rate of stock growth and the 'own rate of interest' (δ) held by the harvester

$$\dot{B} - [C'(B)F(B)/P - C(B)] = \delta \qquad (12.5)$$

The first term on the left hand side of equation 12.5 is the rate of growth of the stock biomass. The numerator of the second term $C'(B) F(B)$ is the marginal stock effect or future effect of the stock on harvest profitability, and the denominator $P - C(B)$ is the net benefit from harvesting in the current period. As the rate of growth of the stock biomass tends to zero, $[C'(B)F(B)/P-C(B)]$ tends to the cost of capital, δ.

In a surplus production fishery model with stock biomass less than that which supports maximum sustainable yield, the left hand side of (12.5) becomes smaller as the fish stock grows toward the stock biomass associated with maximum economic yield (B_{MEY}). At this point, the harvesters' own rate of interest is coincident with (or tracks) the economy wide cost of capital (δ^*) represented by central bank wholesale interest rates (Figure 12.5).

This occurs because the level of annual sustainable production is density dependent. The stock growth rate slows, and the flow on externality effect diminishes. Conversely, if the stock level declines, the left ahnd side of (12.5) becomes larger and diverges from δ^*.

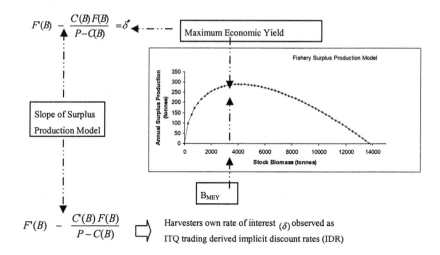

$$F'(B) - \frac{C(B)F(B)}{P-C(B)} = \delta$$

Maximum Economic Yield

Slope of Surplus Production Model

Fishery Surplus Production Model

B_MEY

$$F'(B) - \frac{C(B)F(B)}{P-C(B)}$$

Harvesters own rate of interest (δ) observed as ITQ trading derived implicit discount rates (IDR)

Figure 12.5 The surplus production context of the ITSQ revealed IDR concept

REFERENCES

Annala, J.H., K.J. Sullivan, C.J. O'Brien and S.D. Iball (1998), *Stock Assessments and Yield Estimates: Report from The Fishery Assessment Plenary*, May 1998, New Zealand Ministry of Fisheries.

Arnason, R. (1990), 'Minimum information management in fisheries', *Canadian Journal of Economics*, **23**: 630–653.

Arnason, R. (1993), 'ITQ based fisheries management', in S.J. Smith, J.J. Hunt and D. Rivard (eds), *Risk Evaluation and Biological Reference Points for Fisheries Management*, Canadian Special Publication Fisheries and Aquatic Science, pp. 345–356.

Arnason, R. (1998), 'Ecological fisheries management using individual transferable share quotas', *Ecological Applications*, **8**(1): S151–S159.

Arnason, R. (2000), 'Economic instruments for achieving ecosystem objectives in fisheries management', *ICES Journal of Marine Science*, **57**: 742–751.

Batstone, C.J. and B.M.H. Sharp (2003), 'Minimum information management systems and ITQ fisheries management', *Journal of Environmental Economics and Management*, **45**: 492–504.

Batstone, C.J. and B.M.H. Sharp (2006), 'Observing recovery: the role of implicit discount rates in ITQ fisheries', *Proceedings of the 13th Biennial Conference of the International Institute of Fisheries Economics and Trade*, University of Portsmouth, UK, 11–14 July.

Boyce, J.R. (1995), 'Optimal capital accumulation in a fishery: a nonlinear irreversible investment model', *Journal of Environmental Economics and Management*, **28**: 324–339.

Chichilnisky, G. (1997), 'What is sustainable development?', *Land Economics*, **73**(4): 467–491.

Clark C.W. (1990), *Mathematical Bioeconomics: The Optimal Management of Renewable Resources* (2nd edn), New York: Wiley, 383 pp.

Fama, E.F. (1970), 'Efficient capital markets: a review of theory and empirical evidence', *Journal of Finance*, **25**: 383–417.

Greene, W.H. (1993), *Econometric Analysis* (2nd edn), New York: Macmillan, 791 pp.

Hatcher, A. (2005), 'Non-compliance and the quota price in an ITQ fishery', *Journal of Environmental Economics and Management*, **49**(3): 427–436.

Hendry, D.F., A.R. Pagan and J.D. Sargan (1984), 'Dynamic specification', in Z. Griliches and M.D. Intriligator (eds), *Handbook of Econometrics*, Vol. 2, Amsterdam: North-Holland, pp. 1023–1100.

Hayek, F.A. (1945), 'The use of knowledge in society', *American Economic Review*, **35**(4): 519–530.

Hayek, F.A. ([1978], 1984), 'Competition as a discovery procedure', in C. Nishiyama and K. Leube (eds), *The Essence of Hayek*, Stanford: Hoover Institution Press.

Lange, O. (1936), 'On the economic theory of socialism: part I', *Review of Economic Studies*, **4**(1): 53–71.

Ludwig, D., R. Hilborn and C. Walters (1993), 'Uncertainty, resource exploitation, and conservation: lessons from history', *Science*, **260**(17): 36.

Massod, E. (1997), 'Fisheries science: all at sea when it comes to politics?', *Nature*, **386**: 105–106.

Mises, L. ([1920] 1935), 'Economic calculation in the socialist commonwealth', in F. Hayek (ed.), *Collectivist Economic Planning*, London: Routledge.

Newell, R.G., J.N. Sanchirico and S. Kerr (2005), 'Fishing quota markets', *Journal of Environmental Economics and Management*, **49**: 437–462.

NIWA (2005), *Data Source CRA1 Biomass Estimate Series*, personal communication.

NZ Ministry of Fisheries (2003), *Data Source CRA1 Asset and Lease Data*, [FishServe], Wellington, NZ: NZ MAF.

Rose, G.A. (1997), 'The trouble with fisheries science!', *Reviews in Fish Biology and Fisheries*, **7**: 365–370.

Sullivan, K. (2004), *Stock Assessments and Yield Estimates*, Report from the Mid-Year Fishery Assessment Plenary, Science Group, November 2004, New Zealand Ministry of Fisheries.

Smith, V.L. (1982), 'Markets as economizers of information: experimental examination of the "Hayek" hypothesis', *Economic Enquirer*, **20**: 165–179.

Walters C. and J. Maguire (1996), 'Lessons for stock assessment from the northern cod collapse', *Reviews in Fish Biology and Fisheries*, **6**: 125–138.

Wickens, M.R. and T.S. Breusch (1988), 'Dynamic specification: the long run and the estimation of transformed regression models', *Economic Journal*, **98**(Supplement): 189–205.

13. Designing Property Rights for Achieving Sustainable Development of the Oceans

Basil Sharp

This chapter focuses on the design of property rights for achieving sustainable development of the oceans. Particular emphasis is given to the economic characteristics of property rights while recognizing the significance of sustaining natural systems such as fish stocks. How people use ocean resources is *inter alia* a product of the institutions governing economic activity. For example, the depletion of offshore oil deposits occurs within a set of rules that govern access and use rates. In this context property rights can be considered as factors of production (Coase 1960). Rules also limit land-based activities that produce contaminants that enter harbours and the marine ecosystem, and govern non-commercial use and enjoyment of ocean resources, such as boating, swimming and recreational fishing. A property right is a socially recognized right to selected uses of an economic good or service. The usual definition of property rights is quite broad and includes both formal and informal rules that guide and govern the allocation of resources and distribution of welfare within society.

The chapter is organized as follows. The first section uses the tools of microeconomics to provide a framework for analysing the wide array of property right regimes that exist within, and are potentially available to, society (Bromley 1989). The second section discusses common property as a distinct arrangement of property rights. The third section sets property rights within a broader context, providing a background for institutional change and the evolution of property rights. A case study of New Zealand's fisheries management regime, which is based on tradable rights, is used to demonstrate the operation of tradable property rights within sustainability constraints and the efficiency gains that have followed since their introduction in 1986.

PROPERTY RIGHTS AND EFFICIENCY

Property rights are instrumental in mapping resource allocation decisions onto outcomes and wellbeing. Given competitive conditions and zero transaction costs, efficiency will be achieved provided property rights are non-attenuated (Cheung 1970; Furubotn and Pejovich 1972). Randall (1975), an early contributor to the property rights literature, defines non-attenuated rights as having the following characteristics:

- The set of rights is completely specified. Complete specification reduces ignorance and uncertainty.
- Rights are exclusive so that all costs and benefits are internalized and private costs equal social costs.
- Rights are enforced.
- Rights are transferable so that, like any other input, they may gravitate to their most highly valued use.

In theory, a competitive economy with non-attenuated property rights will be Pareto optimal for some distribution of endowments. In this state it is not possible to improve the wellbeing of one individual without reducing the wellbeing of another individual. This result is, of course, the first theorem of welfare economics. Initial endowments, as we shall see below, are important in the design of property rights because there will be distributions of welfare that the competitive market cannot achieve, given initial endowments. The second theorem of welfare economics tells us that any Pareto optimal allocation can be achieved at a competitive equilibrium if appropriate lump-sum transfers are made (Mas-Colell et al. 1995). Within the context of property rights a practical application of this theorem would be in assigning space for aquaculture, as an initial endowment, to a particular group within society in order to create an opportunity for them to improve their wellbeing.

The assumption of zero transaction costs is commonly used as an analytical convenience. In most modern economies, significant resources are used to coordinate the activities of individuals, firms and units of government. According to Arrow (1969), coordination costs are simply the costs of running the economic system. Transaction costs, within the context of the above discussion, are the costs associated with contracting and are usually associated with gathering information, negotiation, monitoring and enforcing agreements. Crocker (1971) usefully describes these as informational, contractual and policing costs. Although transaction costs are positive in the real world this does not necessarily indicate inefficiencies. If the transaction industry (comprised, for example, of rights brokers and buyers) is competitive, then there is no *a priori* reason why efficiency should be compromised. However, we will show how relatively high transaction costs could work to favour the use of non-market arrangements.

Economic Rent

Economists use the term 'rent' to describe payment for use of a resource regardless of whether it is land, labour or equipment (Alchian 1998). The concept of rent has occupied a prominent place in economics. In the 19th century, land was considered fixed in supply and its use was seen as generating rents. The concept of rent also applies to resources embodied in oceans. Users of space, such as marine farmers, combine coastal space with inputs, such as labour and other intermediate factors of production purchased at market prices. Profits arise from the difference between revenue and the total cost of market priced inputs. Thus, in the case of marine farming, the demand for coastal space is based on the contribution of coastal space to profit.

In the 20th century, resource economists (for example, Hotelling 1931) – working with models of non-renewable (for example, minerals) and renewable resources (for example, fish) – recognized the significance of use rates over time vis-à-vis optimal resource extraction. They used the term resource rent to describe the marginal value of the resource at a given point in time. Setting aside complicating factors – such as stock size, uncertainty and market power – resource rent is the difference between the market price of the commodity and the marginal cost of extraction (Field 2001). Resource-extracting firms must be offered at least this amount to supply the market. Because time is involved, total resource rent associated with the use of a natural resource would be the present value of rents over the period of use.

The concept of economic rent applies to ocean resources. It is reasonable to assume that the supply function for products derived from the ocean (minerals, fish, energy) is upward sloping (Clark 1990). If use of the ocean's resources is profitable, then resource rents should be non-negative (Arnason 2002). Regardless of whether we are dealing with non-renewable or renewable resources, the system of property rights used to govern access and control use will have a significant impact on resource rent. Positive rents will attract new entrants and, unless controlled, economic rent will be dissipated and the value that attaches to the resource will be driven to zero.

Before leaving this section it is worthwhile clarifying the idea of quasi-rent, which is closely related to economic rent. The notion of quasi-rent was defined by Marshall (1920) to denote a return to short-run fixed inputs. For example, uncertainty over the impacts of aquaculture on the marine environment might lead government to limit access to coastal space. If this becomes a binding constraint on aquaculture development then, in the short-run, the economic return to coastal space is determined by fixity as opposed to the value of marginal productivity of coastal space. In this case imputing an economic surplus to coastal space may not be consistent with the long-run equilibrium rental price of coastal space.

In summary, rent arises from the profitable use of market-priced factors of production in combination with scarce ocean resources. Rent is the marginal value of the resource. At any point in time resource rent is contingent on market conditions and expectations. A fall in demand for the commodity *ceteris paribus* would result in resource rent trending down. In the absence of tradable rights that attach to the resource, identifying and measuring resource rent is not straightforward. On the other hand, if rights to the resource are well-defined then price – value of the right – will be revealed in the market.

Economic Value of Rights

Looked at another way, economic rent represents what a profit-seeking firm would pay for the right to extract a resource. We also noted that, in theory, if the right is non-attenuated, then the competitive market mechanism will result in Pareto optimality. When we step away from the theoretical construct of non-attenuation and examine the positive attributes of real-world property rights, it becomes obvious that there is a multitude of different systems of property rights in the economy. If existing rights to ocean resources lead resource users to behave in an unsustainable way then a once-off restructuring of rights might result in efficiency gains. Regular restructuring, however, could result in so much investment uncertainty that no gains are realized. This section uses standard microeconomics to describe important elements in a system of property rights as well as providing a basis for empirically testable hypotheses.

We assume that firm A uses ocean space, input i, and derives profit π which is a function of output price p and vector of input prices w. If the profit function is well-behaved (Chambers, 1988) and differentiable, then the firm's derived demand for input i is given by:

$$x_i^A = -\frac{\partial \pi^A(p,w)}{\partial w_i} \qquad (13.1)$$

and the derived demand function for space is non-decreasing in the price (w_i) of the input:

$$\frac{\partial x_i^A(p,w)}{\partial w_i} \leq 0 \tag{13.2}$$

To illustrate the significance of transferability, let us assume that ocean space is not priced, is allocated on a first-come–first-served basis, and that the right to occupy space is not transferable. Firm A occupies a quantity of space and the value of the right to occupy is:

$$v^A = \int_0^q x_i^A dq > 0 \tag{13.3}$$

If ocean space is scarce and another firm, say B, has access to more profitable technology, say $v^B > v^A$, then the economy is foregoing rent. But if the right is divisible and transferable then A and B can negotiate. Either B can buy all of A's entitlement to space or they can negotiate a price w_i^* such that:

$$x_i^A \Big|_{w_i^*} = x_i^B \Big|_{w_i^*} \tag{13.4}$$

Transferability enables property rights to gravitate to their most profitable use. The ability to transform a right ties in with the notion of transferability. Transformability enables the rightholder to create a derivative right. For example, a fishing firm owning tradable harvesting rights to a species may choose not to exercise the right in a given fishing season and lease the right out to another fisher. Transformability creates flexibility.

Exclusion defines the right to exclude others from competing for the resource and/or free riding on investment. Non-exclusion is an attribute of pure public goods. Initially, we assume that the objective is to maximize the value of rent and that many profit-seeking firms harvest a resource from the ocean. Each firm is assumed to maximize profit π_i, by recovering q, using a composite input e that costs w per unit and sells output for p per unit. The economic outcome associated with two extreme property rights regimes (α) is shown in Figure 13.1. Under open access $(\alpha = 0)$ the right to exclude others from entering and harvesting the resource does not exist. With open access the prospect of positive profit $v^i > 0$ encourages entry to the point where individual profit is zero $v^i > 0$; and, therefore, total rent is zero.

This equilibrium is described by average revenue being equal to average cost. If one firm had sole rights to harvest the resource and it had the right to exclude $(\alpha = 1)$ then it will balance marginal revenue against marginal cost and economic rent will be positive. Thus the right to exclude prevents dissipation of value.

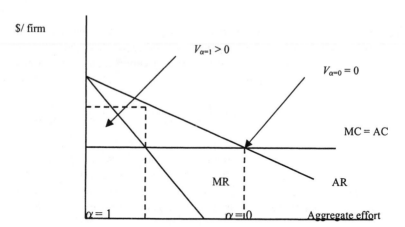

Figure 13.1 Open access and sole ownership

The above model can be generalized by making the degree of exclusion a continuous variable $\alpha \in [0,1]$, where open access and perfect exclusion are the lower and upper bounds, respectively (Witt 1987). Out of recognition that the right to exclude requires monitoring and enforcement, we specify transaction costs as $C(\alpha)$ and assume

$$\frac{\partial C(\alpha)}{\partial \alpha} > 0 \qquad (13.5)$$

The objective function

$$V(\alpha) = \sum_{i=1}^{n} v^i(\alpha)$$

comprises the sum of individual profit, which is a function of the degree of exclusion. Within the context of policy, the design of property rights can be considered in terms of maximizing net benefits $NB(\alpha) = V(\alpha) - C(\alpha)$. Three outcomes can be readily identified:

No exclusion $\alpha = 0$: $C(\alpha) > V(\alpha)$

Some exclusion $\qquad \alpha \in (0,1): \dfrac{\partial C(\alpha)}{\partial \alpha} = \dfrac{\partial V(\alpha)}{\partial \alpha}$

Perfect exclusion $\qquad \alpha = 1: \dfrac{\partial C(\alpha)}{\partial \alpha} < \dfrac{\partial V(\alpha)}{\partial \alpha}$

Duration is the third important dimension of a property right. Assuming $\alpha = 1$, if we let $v^i(\alpha,t)$ represent the claim that firm i has over profits in each year t, then the present value of the right to profit is:

$$v^i(\alpha, t, r) = \int_{t=0}^{T} v^i(\alpha,t)\, e^{-rt} dt \cdot$$

Two additional parameters must now be considered. First, the discount rate r is an opportunity cost. Other things being equal, higher discount rates lower the present value. Second, duration works in the opposite direction, longer duration *ceteris paribus* increases of present value of the right. The market value of a right in perpetuity is greater than the value of a right of more limited duration:

$$V^i(\alpha,t,r) = \int_{t=0}^{\infty} v^i(\alpha, t)\, e^{-rt}\, dt = \frac{v^i}{r} > \int_{t=0}^{T} v^i(\alpha, t)\, e^{-rt}\, dt \qquad (13.6)$$

Duration also has an impact on the choice of investment and therefore value of the right. For example, when the duration of the property right is limited then an investor will want at least to recover capital and a return within that period. Let us assume that project A yields a positive net present value over t_1 years. Within the set of feasible projects, there could be an alternative B that produces positive net returns which if discounted over a longer period $T > t_1$ will yield a higher net present value:

$$V^i_B(T) > V^i_A(t_1) \qquad (13.7)$$

Property rights that are secure against appropriation by others are relatively more valuable. Developers of offshore oil fields would look for secure title before making asset-specific investments. The higher the probability of government nationalizing oil fields, the lower the level of security. Similarly, investors in aquaculture would require a right to space that could survive challenges from other competing interests.

We now map the above dimensions of a property right into value (Arnason 2000). The metric used on the axes in Figure 13.2 ranks quality between 0 and 1. For example, if the right is defined in perpetuity then it receives a score of 1. If the right was not tradable then it would receive a score of 0. Property rights A scores higher in all dimensions than property rights B and we expect these scores to be reflected in the value of the rights, namely $V^A > V^B$.

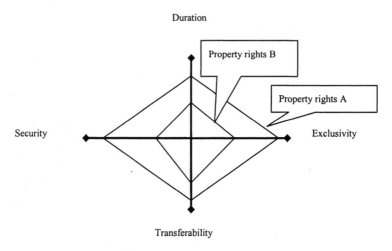

Figure 13.2 Mapping rights into value

Initial Entitlements

Ronald Coase, writing in the 1960s on the problem of 'social cost', suggested efficient outcomes could be achieved simply by establishing a set of non-attenuated property rights. One popular version of the Coase theorem states that in the absence of transaction costs it does not matter who gets the initial entitlement, efficiency will be achieved provided the rights are well-defined and, of course, tradable. Using earlier notation, let us assume that firm A's demand for ocean space is given by x^A, and being first-in-time firm A is able to gain access to all space – say Z hectares – available for aquaculture. Firm B, on the other hand, can not get access. Initial entitlements in this instance are shown in Figure 13.3 as Z_A. Clearly this initial allocation is not efficient, firm B could offer an amount sufficient enough to convince A to give up some space. Provided the rights are tradable they would bargain out to Z^*. If we were to reverse the initial allocation so that firm B gets the rights and A cannot get access, the initial entitlement is now Z_B. Similar logic applies – the firms will bargain out to Z^*. Thus the above version of the Coase theorem tells us that the outcome of bargaining is efficient and invariant with respect to both the initial entitlements if, and only if, transaction costs are zero.

Transaction costs can destroy this invariance. To illustrate, let us assume that firm A gets the initial entitlement and that rights are tradable. However, if firm B wants to buy rights it must hire a broker ($c > 0$) to negotiate a deal with A; thus B's input demand function is $x^B(z, c > 0)$.

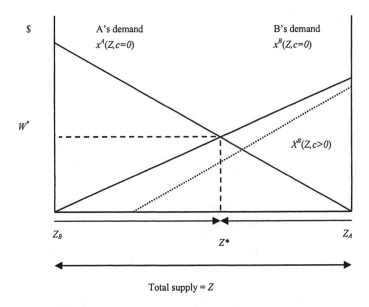

Figure 13.3 Initial entitlements, bargaining and transaction costs

Figure 13.3 shows B's demand shifting down. Exactly how transaction costs affect B's demand function for space is an empirical issue. Transaction costs could fall differently but the invariance of the outcome to initial entitlements is unlikely to be preserved. Griffen (1991) has shown that transaction costs convey inertia to initial entitlements. The difference between pre-trade and post-trade allocations decreases with increasing transaction costs. Transaction costs also impact on market liquidity, a term used to describe the ability to quickly buy or sell a right. The essential feature of a liquid rights market is that there are numerous buyers and sellers. Relatively low transaction costs, *inter alia*, are a feature of a liquid asset. The frequency with which rights are bought and sold provides an empirical measure of liquidity. Thus, transaction costs can affect both post-trade allocations and the liquidity of the rights market. In Figure 13.3 transaction costs are shown to lower B's gains from trade, thus drawing the post-trade allocation closer to the pre-trade entitlement Z_A.

COMMON PROPERTY

The property rights outlined above could be described as systems of private property rights. The ability to exclude others from deriving benefit from the flow of services associated with investment and the opportunity to transfer the right are essential to the operation of the market mechanism. As we will see later in this chapter, private ownership of a natural resource is not necessary. For example, fish in the wild are typically *res nullius*, nobody owns them. As sovereign entities, governments might claim the right to manage the stocks using a system of transferable harvesting rights. In contrast, fish stocks farmed in the marine environment are privately owned. The term 'common property resource' is often used to describe situations where government owns the resource; no one individual owns the resource (*res nullius*); or the resource is owned by a community of resource users (*res communs*). Unfortunately, the term 'open access' has come to be used interchangeably with common property when describing common pool resources, typically fish stocks (Schlager and Ostrom 1992). Common property resources are resources in which property rights exist and the property rights are exercised by members of a group. There is rivalry in consumption within the group and membership of the group is limited to legally recognized and enforceable rights (Seabright 1993). Clearly open access does not fit within the set of possible common property arrangements.

If we limit discussion to a local commons, such as an area of coastal space set aside for the supply of seafood to a community, then the members of the community are known to each other, some of their actions are observable, and they have the ability, and sometimes the incentive, to build reputations (Seabright 1993). Property rights exercised by the community include: (1) management: the right to invest in projects that enhance the flow of services from the resource and the right to regulate use; (2) exclusion: the right to determine who will have access and how that right might be transferred; (3) alienation: the right to sell interest in the rights (Schlager and Ostrom 1992). These characteristics of a local commons make generalizations about objectives, structure and functions difficult. For example, a local commons may decide that its management objective is to harvest fish for local consumption that are of a size greater than that associated with a strictly market-rent-maximizing policy. Or, the local community may decide to maximize the flow of non-market values – for example, recreation values – associated with coastal space.

Continuing with the seafood example, conflicts of interest might well arise over what size of fish to harvest. Attitudes to risk and rates of time preference are relevant here. Community members with higher rates of time preference and risk neutral preferences might argue for increasing harvest – smaller fish – while those with lower rates of time preference and risk-averse preferences might prefer to harvest larger fish. Given heterogeneity of preferences in the community, the central problem is one of devising incentives, informal and formal, for cooperation that advances community interests and the interests of the fleet.

Let us deal with informal incentives first. Figure 13.4 shows the well-known prisoners' dilemma. The two players can't communicate and only play the game once. The numbers in brackets represent the payoff to each player; the total payoff is simply the sum of individual payoffs. Therefore, if player 1 decides to defect and player 2's strategy is to cooperate, then the combined payoff is –5. Both players will reason that defection is the best strategy. Thus aggregate utility is zero. If, on the other hand, the prisoners could communicate and they agreed to cooperate, then aggregate utility would be 8. If the game is repeated, say at the beginning of the next fishing season, then the two players may see the benefits of not defecting and decide to cooperate. Two conditions are necessary for sustaining cooperation. First, the expected individual utility of future benefits from cooperation must outweigh the immediate gains from defection. Second, retaliation must be sufficiently credible so that if defection occurs other members of the commons will invoke sanctions. Trust-building activities, such as contributing to community wellbeing and the sense of community reputation, can also underpin cooperative behaviour.

| | | Player 2: | |
		Cooperate	Defect
Player 1:	Cooperate	(4,4) = 8	(–10,5) = –5
	Defect	(5, –10) = –5	(0,0) = 0

Figure 13.4 Prisoners' dilemma

Formal mechanisms for cooperation in the management of a common property resource would involve combining elements of property rights as described above. This does not necessarily imply privatization (White and Runge 1994). For example, the creation of private rights to harvest from a community-owned fishery may fail to account for externalities. In this particular instance, the community might set an aggregate harvest limit for the season, lease annual share harvesting rights to members and allow individuals to transfer these rights. The community could undertake monitoring and enforcement activities. Clearly, defining harvesting rights is only part of the common property arrangement. Participation in management decisions and the distribution of benefits to the community might also feature in the common property arrangement (Townsend 2005). An example of a devolved, commercially focused, fisheries management organization that also provides recreational harvesting opportunities is described by Sharp (2005).

The above discussion suggests that common property arrangements are likely to comprise rights explicitly granted (*de jure*) to resource users. For example, legislation could be the source of the right of access, management, exclusion and alienation. Rights (*de facto*) can also originate among resource users. The community might, for example, define the set of allowable harvesting methods and the harvest period to coincide with cultural norms. Thus a mixture of *de jure* and *de facto* rights could underpin a common property arrangement. Different bundles of property rights affect the incentives that individuals face, the actions they take, and the outcomes achieved (Schlager and Ostrom 1992). We should take heed of Demsetz's (1969) advice to avoid comparing the ideal institutions implicit in economic theory with actual institutions. The performance of alternative common property arrangements is a topic for empirical analysis where the comparative performance of different arrangements, working in similar situations, can be assessed (Stevenson 1991).

EVOLUTION OF PROPERTY RIGHTS

At any point in time we can observe a huge array of property arrangements, including private property and common property. This array could be likened to an asset that provides a flow of transaction services over time. Continuing with the stock-flow analogy, transaction costs could be viewed as the cost of sustaining the flow of services within society. Over time, the stock of property arrangements, and indeed the flow of services from any given stock, will change.

For example, a particular mineral extracted from the seabed might become relatively more valuable, leading to a need for property rights better aligned with public policy objectives. The design of new systems of property rights is akin to an investment that offers the potential to enhance net benefits to society or groups within society. Or, technical change could lower monitoring costs adding value to the existing property rights regime, and possibly, enabling new rights to evolve.

At the most fundamental level, institutions can be thought of as sets of rules that apply to the community that influence and provide sanctions for breaches of the rules (North 1990; Ostrom 1990). These rules can be the product of the legislature, governments, the courts, and social convention. In a narrow sense, institutions provide a set of rules that govern market exchange, the supply of services from government and the distribution of goods and services in the economy (Davis and North 1971). Philosophers such as John Locke and Friedrich Hayek emphasized that the structure of politically determined institutions had to rest on other institutions such as conventions about behaviour, custom and manners. In their view, government-made rules are not necessarily the primary source of society's institutional framework.

The notion of external institutions is useful when analyzing reforms and the evolution of property rights. External institutions, such as procedural rules that instruct agents of government on approaches to resource allocation and income distribution, are the product of political action (Kasper and Streit 1998). Because they are prescriptive, external institutions place a high requirement on information and knowledge. For example, in the context of the fisheries case study described below, government officials are required to set an allowable harvest that moves the stock of fish towards maximum sustainable yield. This external rule is part of a broader framework within which rights to fish can be traded. In other words, decisions as to who will fish, and when, are decided in a decentralized market – the aggregate quantity of harvest is decided by external rules administered by government officials. Typically, legal sanctions exist for violating external rules.

A slightly modified version of Anderson and Hill's (1975) model is used to illustrate the evolution of property rights. Establishing and protecting property rights is an economic activity which is summarized by the variable x. The net benefits associated with x are given by: $NB(\alpha(x)) = v(\alpha(x)) - C(\alpha(x))$. On the benefit side the activity x results in a degree of exclusion, which we defined earlier as α. The cost of producing property rights increases because of the opportunity cost of resources used in property rights activity. Optimal property-right-producing activity is given by:

$$\frac{\partial NB(\alpha(x))}{\partial x} = 0 \qquad (13.8)$$

Comparative static analysis follows in a straightforward way. For example, the marginal benefit function would shift outwards if the asset's value increased because of increased relative scarcity. A fall in the price of property right producing inputs, as might come about through advances in surveillance monitoring systems, would contribute to lowering marginal cost.

If we step outside the assumptions of microeconomic models into the so-called real world it is not possible to specify an optimal institutional design within the context of sustainable development. However, we can check whether the attributes of institutional structure and decision-making are consistent with the general notions of sustainable development. Property rights as a primary institution for facilitating economic growth should contribute to the following outcomes (Sharp 2002):

- In the case of renewable resources, the flow of rents, in real terms, should be non-declining.
- The mechanism should unleash a dynamic that enables parties to exploit commercial opportunities for mutual gain.
- Users should be confronted with the real, and dynamic, opportunity cost of use.
- The allocation mechanism should have the flexibility to adapt to changes in the profile of opportunity costs over time.
- The mechanism should make anticipation and strategic planning feasible for users and present low cost opportunities to reassign property rights.

What tends to be neglected in most arguments for and against market-based reforms is the fact that all instruments generate effects. The inescapable conclusion is that market-based instruments provide a least-cost option for achieving an environmental target because they provide flexibility in the firm's response, whether through investment, changing input mixes, changing production, and so on. Furthermore, transparency tends to be greater with market-based instruments relative to the less-visible costs associated with regulations (Sharp 2002).

NEW ZEALAND'S QUOTA MANAGEMENT SYSTEM

The aim of this section is provide a real-world illustration of how tradable property rights can be designed to provide a basis for sustainable and profitable utilization of oceanic resources. Before the 1980s, the Government used financial incentives, coupled with relatively open access, to encourage development of New Zealand's fisheries. Under these conditions the simple model illustrated in Figure 13.1 would predict fisheries characterized by a high level of effort and low economic rent. Data show that by the early 1980s many important fisheries exhibited the biological and economic effects of over-fishing. In short, too many boats were chasing diminished stocks. Fisheries managers were faced with the twin problem of removing harvesting in excess of sustainable yield, and reducing effort. Effort reduction was achieved in two stages. First, part-timers and those not exercizing their right to fish had their permit revoked. Second, the Government operated a buy-back mechanism involving sealed tenders where fishers stated their willingness to accept compensation to permanently withdraw their historical harvest entitlement (Sharp 1997).

Legislation in 1986 introduced the quota management system (QMS) into a number of New Zealand's commercial fisheries. The QMS has two structural pillars: an annual total allowable catch (TAC); and individual transferable quota (ITQ) rights. The initial allocation of quota, to those choosing to remain in the industry, was based on the average of harvests taken in any two out of the three fishing years 1982–84. Fish stocks outside the QMS are managed by a system of non-transferable permits and administrative allocations.

Total Allowable Catch

Legislation imposes a duty on the Minister of Fisheries to set a TAC that moves a stock towards its Maximum Sustainable Yield (MSY). In deep water fisheries, such as orange roughy, there is no recreational interest to recognize and the total allowable commercial catch (TACC) is set equal to the TAC. However, in shared fisheries, such as rock lobster, the Minister is required to make allowances for non-commercial harvest. If we summarize the latter allowances as a total allowable non-commercial catch (TANC), then the following equality holds: TAC = TACC + TANC. Commercial fishers exercise their ITQ rights when harvesting their share of the TACC; non-commercial harvesters are regulated by daily catch limits. Two conditions are necessary for efficient allocation in a shared fishery: (1) the TAC is set at the optimal level; and (2) the allocation of the TAC across the sectors is such that the present value of net marginal benefits is equal. If the right to harvest is tradable across sectors, then provided the TAC is set at the optimal level, use of the right for commercial or recreational fishing is immaterial to achieving efficiency.

Efficiency is beyond the reach of New Zealand's QMS for at least two reasons. First, the TAC is set according to a legislative mandate that requires the Minister of Fisheries to move stocks toward their MSY, not their maximum economic yield. Second, the QMS sits within a broader institutional structure where the non-commercial allowance is set after consultation with stakeholders. Recreational fishers are not licenced and harvest is limited by daily bag limits. This asymmetry in management makes it impossible to conclude that the outcome of the TAC setting process satisfies the net-benefit maximizing criterion. This shortcoming was noted by the Court of Appeal during a case involving a proposed decrease in the north eastern snapper fishery TACC.

When the QMS was introduced, future changes in the TAC were to be effected through buying and selling activities of government. By 1989 the cost of effecting reductions to the TACC was considered unmanageable and legislation redefined quota rights as a percentage of the TACC. Any changes to the TACC are now pro-rated across ITQ owners. The change to proportional ITQ shifts the distribution of stock assessment risk from Government to industry. The Minister sets the TACC and the net benefits of this decision fall on industry. Re-establishing incentive compatibility into the TACC adjustment mechanism hinges to a large degree on the involvement of industry in future catches through stock assessment research and cooperative behaviour within industry (Pearse 1991). Evidence of cooperation is found in New Zealand's hoki fishery, where a majority have argued that the TACC should be reduced for a number of years in order to grow the harvestable biomass.

Individual Transferable Quota Rights

Quota rights are an essential input into commercial fishing. Let us assume that we are considering rights to a single species in a given fishing management area. We can summarize the demand for rights as $D_i(w,p) = \frac{\partial \pi(p,w)}{\partial w_q}$.

Diminishing returns to quota ownership is assumed and market demand for quota is simply the sum of individual firm demand. This definition lends itself to standard microeconomic analysis. A commercial fisher's willingness to pay (w_q) for the right will depend on the quality of the right, stock abundance, the price of other rights, the market price of fish, harvesting technology and so on. Figure 13.4 provides a static framework for comparative analysis.

As is the case with private goods in the economy, aggregate demand for

ITQ is arrived at by horizontally adding the demand of individual firms at a given market price. Returning to Figure 13.4, the TACC constrains harvest; firm 2 is willing to pay more per unit of harvest than firm 1; thus firm 2 will harvest a greater share of the TACC. This decentralized outcome may change. For example, firm 1 might invest in a more efficient vessel, effectively shifting its demand curve out beyond firm 2. Given the binding nature of the TACC, firm 1 would have to pay firm 2 for the additional rights required. Trading ensures that rights gravitate to their most highly valued commercial use. The economic impact of adjusting the TACC is also evident in Figure 13.4. Increasing the TACC *ceteris paribus* will result in the market price of ITQ falling, and the opposite applies for reducing the TACC. Batstone and Sharp (2003) provide empirical evidence of a functional relationship between the quota price for snapper, and a set of explanatory variables including the TACC, interest rates and export prices.

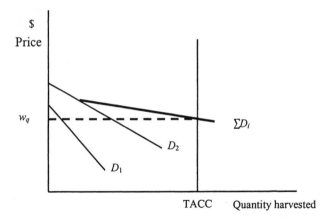

Figure 13.4 Simple model of New Zealand's quota management system

Annual catch entitlements (ACE) were introduced in 2001 (Peacey 2004). Quota rights continue to be expressed as shares of the TACC whereas ACE are expressed in kilograms, based upon the shares held and the TACC set at the start of that year. ACE are generated each year from ITQ and can be traded separately from ITQ. However, ITQ cannot be used to balance catch, only the ACE it generates. Fishers without sufficient ACE to cover catch by the 15th of the month following catch get a deemed value invoice that must be paid within 20 days. If, after 20 days, the amount owing for deemed value is in excess of $1000 then their permit is suspended, and any further fishing will be a criminal offence. There are two rates of deemed values – interim and annual. The interim rate is designed to act as a bond to encourage fishers to get ACE into their account. The annual rate is designed to be a major disincentive to have any stocks out of balance at the end of the year.

Coverage of Species

Transferable rights to harvest 27 species were introduced in 1986 and, at that time, Government signalled its intention to introduce more species in the near term. Each species received a three-letter species code and a suffix code that identified the area. The extent to the right to harvest is broken down into areas, is variable, and reflects *inter alia* the number of stocks, their biological characteristics and knowledge of the species. In 1996, 32 species or groups of species were controlled by the QMS. At that time, over 130 species were not covered under the QMS. In his review of fisheries management, Pearse (1991) noted that there was an incentive to harvest non-ITQ stocks because catch history was used to establish initial allocations when these species are incorporated into the QMS. In 1992, government closed entry to non-ITQ fisheries in an attempt to limit fishing pressure. In 2006, 92 species were controlled by the QMS.

Rights of Māori

Traditional fishing interests of Māori were guaranteed under the Treaty of Waitangi 1840 and have been acknowledged in fisheries legislation since 1877. In 1983, the Fisheries Act stated that 'nothing in this Act shall affect any Māori fishing right'. When the QMS was introduced, the strength of this provision was tested in the High Court, which found that the Fisheries Act did not affect the exercise of customary rights. Although Māori agreed with the conservation functions of the QMS, they saw the allocation of quota as inconsistent with the Treaty and the section in the Fisheries Act protecting their rights. The High Court found that the QMS had been developed without taking into account Māori rights in fisheries and that it was possible that the system may breach these rights.

After extensive negotiations between the Crown and Māori, the Crown offered a package on the basis that it formed the full and final settlement of Māori claims to sea fisheries. The settlement transferred 10 per cent of all existing ITQs to Māori and allocated 20 per cent of the TACC for any additional fish stock brought into the QMS to them. Funding was also provided to assist Māori into commercial fishing. The Deed did not, however, extinguish the right of Māori to have their customary non-commercial claims considered. Taiapure provisions of the Fisheries Act 1983, and the maitaitai reserves of the Treaty of Waitangi (Fisheries Claims) Settlement Act 1992, together seek to provide Māori with a management role in customary fishing and to recognize Māori food gathering interests.

Monitoring and Compliance

The ability to monitor catch levels accurately and balance these against quota holdings is critical to the success of the QMS. According to Clement and Associates (2002), the Ministry has established procedures to monitor and enforce the QMS based on a system that tracks the flow of fish and fish products from the catcher to the purchaser and then to reconcile these catches with quota holdings. Fishing permit holders are required to provide detailed catch reports, along with additional information on effort. Permit holders are required to complete a report at the end of each fishing trip to record catch details (including vessel, location, species and quantities), what quota the catches are to be counted against, and to whom the fish is sold. Commercial fishers are restricted to selling fish to licensed wholesalers and processors. Licensed receivers are also required to provide monthly reports. These sources of information enable the Ministry to monitor catches against quota holdings and audit records. The opportunity exists for quota owner associations to participate in monitoring and compliance activities.

Bycatch

The integrity of an ITQ system of management relies on commercial fishers exercising their harvesting rights only for those fish covered by their entitlement. Any fisher who willfuly targets species, without harvesting rights, is committing an offence. Willful intent may be difficult to prove. Dumping species is also illegal. In a multi-species fishery it is likely that individual harvest will not conform exactly with quota holding. Depending on the technology used, and species targeted, other species will be caught. The structure of property rights therefore needs to make allowance for the likelihood of accidental over-fishing, especially bycatch that are not the primary target species. The problem of bycatch has characteristics of a moral hazard (Jensen and Vestergaard 2002) in that fishers make unobservable decisions that have spill-over effects. Addressing this problem is an issue of incentive design.

From 1986 until 2001, the primary unit of the catch-balancing regime was ITQ. The 'catch-balancing regime' is the term used to describe the system by which a fisher's catch is reconciled with the catching rights that s/he holds. According to Peacey (2004), four options were available to those who accidentally exceed their quota entitlement: surrender fish; acquire quota; bycatch tradeoff; and pay deemed value. A new catch-balancing regime was implemented in October 2001: ITQ remains the in-perpetuity right to receive a share of the TACC each year. At the start of each fishing year, the ITQ generates ACE based on the share of the TACC. This ACE is allocated to the owner of the ITQ who can either use the ACE to cover catch of the relevant fish stock or sell it to other fishers. ACE is now the only currency for covering catch. In most fisheries, the only requirement before fishing is that a fisher holds a fishing permit. Permit holders are required to obtain ACE to cover their catch or pay the appropriate Deemed Value. Most fishers obtain ACE before they go fishing; some obtain it after they have taken the catch. Both approaches are acceptable (Peacey 2004).

Resource Rentals

When Government implemented the quota management system it stated that resource rentals were to be levied. Until 1994 resource rentals were one of the most contentious elements of the government's fisheries policy. Regardless of whether fish were harvested, a resource rental on ITQ was payable to Government on a per tonne basis. The rental varied across species and was not paid on quota held by Government. The Minister had the right to vary resource rentals each year. The maximum increase was 20 per cent in any one year. In setting the rental, the Minister was required to have regard to the value of the ITQ, the impact on net commercial returns, and relevant changes to TACC. From the outset Government made it clear that it intended to increase resource rentals until the value of annual traded quota approached zero. Resource rentals were to be paid into the Fisheries Fund, which was to be used to finance management and research activities. The fund was never established and rentals were paid into Government's consolidated fund.

Industry vigorously opposed resource rentals. Stock ownership is unclear. Even if tradable rights create an economic surplus in the fishery, the problem of determining Government's share of the surplus is not straightforward. Property legislation produces rents elsewhere in the economy and it is not clear why rents in the fishery should be singled out for taxation. Each year significant resources were allocated – by industry and Government – to present convincing arguments for and against changes to resource rentals. Resource rentals contributed to the overall level of commercial uncertainty in the fishery. In 1994, resource rentals were removed as part of Government's policy to recover management costs from commercial fishers.

Sustainable Development Outcomes for the Rock Lobster Fishery

Within the context of fisheries, management mechanism design can be assessed according to the changes in economic rent and biomass over time. The outcomes associated with fisheries management before 1986 were not sustainable. Achieving the twin goals of sustainability required at least two policy instruments – tradable rights working within the constraints of a sustainable harvest. We use the rock lobster fishery to illustrate the gains associated with the QMS.

Before the 1980s, commercial rock lobster fishing in New Zealand was characterized by low profitability and unsustainable harvest levels. A moratorium limiting further entry into the fishery was implemented in the early 1980s. Rock lobster was introduced into the QMS in 1990, constraining commercial harvest to a TACC directed towards MSY and, importantly, enabling fishers to trade in the market for quota. In general, biological models show the vulnerable biomass of rock lobster increasing since 1990. Sustained increases in catch per unit effort support independent evidence that the overall biological state of the fishery has improved quite markedly over the period. Summary statistics for the rock lobster fishery show average landings, and landings per labour unit, increasing over time. Overall, the rate of technical progress, measured in terms of cost reduction over the period 1990–2000, has shown steady improvement (Sharp and Jeffs 2004). In terms of profitability, positive quota prices indicate positive rents. Econometric estimates of the rate of profit return as a function of the opportunity cost of capital and changes in the vulnerable biomass provide evidence of an optimal fishery (Zhang et al. 2006).

CONCLUSIONS

Pearce et al. (1989) define sustainable development in terms of devising a social and economic system that ensures a set of desirable goals or objectives for society are sustained. Institutional reform is one of the most powerful instruments that governments can use to achieve sustainable development of oceans. This chapter has provided a microeconomic framework that can be used to analyze the detail and structure of alternative systems of property rights that might be used to achieve sustainable development of the oceans.

Obviously, legal and political considerations will work to shape the feasible set of alternatives. However, in general, oceans policy will be better served by aligning property rights, incentives and outcomes. The New

Zealand fisheries management system is a practical world-leading example of how rights-based fishing can deliver both profitable and sustainable use of ocean resources.

REFERENCES

Alchian, A.A. (1998), 'Rent', in J. Eatwell, M. Milgate and P. Newman (eds), *The New Palgrave: A Dictionary of Economics*, vol. 4, London: Macmillan Reference Ltd, pp. 141–143.

Anderson, T.L. and P.J. Hill (1975), 'The evolution of property rights: a study of the American West', *Journal of Law and Economics*, **18**: 163–79.

Arnason, R. (2000), 'Property rights as a means of economic organization', in R. Shotton (ed.), *Use of Property Rights in Fisheries Management*, FAO Fisheries Technical Paper 404/1, Rome: FAO, pp.15–25.

Arnason, R. (2002), 'Resource rent taxation: is it really non-distortive?', Paper presented at *2nd World Congress of Environmental and Resource Economists*, Monterey, 24–27 June, 16 pp.

Arrow, K. (1969), 'The organization of economic activity: issues pertinent to the choice of market versus non-market allocation', in *The Analysis and Evaluation of Public Expenditure: The PPB System*, vol. 1, US Joint Economic Committee, 91st Congress, session 1, Washington, DC: US Government Printing Office, pp. 59–73.

Batstone, C.J. and B.M.H. Sharp (2003), 'Minimum information systems and ITQ fisheries management', *Journal of Environmental Economics and Management*, **45**: 492–504.

Bromley, D.W. (1989), *Economic Interests and Institutions*, New York: Basil Blackwell.

Chambers, R.G. (1988), *Applied Production Analysis: A Dual Approach*, New York: Cambridge University Press.

Cheung, S. (1970), 'The structure of a contract and the theory of a non-exclusive resource', *Journal of Law and Economics*, **13**: 49–70.

Clark, C.W. (1990), *Mathematical Bioeconomics: The Optimal Use of Renewable Resources* (2nd edn), New York: J Wiley.

Clement and Associates (2002), *The Quota Management System*, http://www.fishinfo.co.nz/clement/qms/content.html#anchor451525.

Coase, R. (1960), 'The problem of social cost', *Journal of Law and Economics*, **3**: 1–44.

Crocker, T. (1971), 'Externalities, property rights and transactions costs: an empirical study', *Journal of Law and Economics*, **14**(2): 451–464.

Davis, L.E. and D.C. North (1971), *Institutional Change and American Economic Growth*, Cambridge: Cambridge University Press.

Demsetz, H. (1969), 'Information and efficiency: another viewpoint', *Journal of Law and Economics*, **12**: 1–22.

Field, B.C. (2001), *Natural Resource Economics: An Introduction* (2nd edn), New York: McGraw-Hill.

Furubotn, E.G. and S. Pejovich (1972), 'Property rights and economic theory: a survey of recent literature', *Journal of Economic Literature*, **10**(4): 1137–1162.

Griffen, R.C. (1991), 'The welfare analytics of transaction costs, externalities, and institutional choice', *American Journal of Agricultural Economics*, **73**: 601–614.

Hotelling, H. (1931), 'The economics of exhaustible resources', *Journal of Political Economy*, **39**(2): 137–175.

Jensen, F. and N. Vestergaard (2002), 'Moral hazard problems in fisheries regulation: the case of illegal landings and discard', *Resource and Energy Economics*, **24**: 281–299.

Kasper, W. and M.E. Streit (1998), *Institutional Economics, Social Order and Public Policy*, Cheltenham, UK and Lyme, USA: Edward Elgar.

Marshall, A. (1920), *The Principles of Economics* (8th edn), London: Macmillan.

Mas-Colell, A., M.D. Whinston and J.R. Green (1995), *Microeconomic Theory*, New York: Oxford University Press.

North, D.C. (1990), *Institutions, Institutional Change and Economic Performance*, Cambridge and New York: Cambridge University Press.

Ostrom, E. (1990), *Governing the Commons: The Evolution of Institutions for Collective Action*, Cambridge and New York: Cambridge University Press.

Peacey, J. (2004), 'Managing catching limits in multi-species: ITQ fisheries', *Proceedings of the International Institute of Fisheries Economics and Trade (IIFET) Conference*, Tokyo, July.

Pearce, D., A. Markandya and E.B. Barbier (1989), *Blueprint for a Green Economy*, London: Earthscan Publications Ltd.

Pearse, P.H. (1991), *Building on Progress, Fisheries Policy Development in New Zealand*, a report prepared for the Minister of Fisheries, Wellington: Ministry of Fisheries.

Randall, A. (1975), 'Property rights and social microeconomics', *Natural Resources Journal*, **15**: 729–747.

Schlager, E. and E. Ostrom (1992), 'Property-rights regimes and natural resources: a conceptual analysis', *Land Economics*, **68**(3): 249–262.

Seabright, P. (1993), 'Managing local commons: theoretical issues in incentive design', *Journal of Economic Perspectives*, **7**(4): 113–134.

Sharp, B.M.H. (1997), 'From regulated access to transferable harvesting rights: policy insights from New Zealand', *Marine Policy*, **21**(6): 501–517.

Sharp, B.M.H. (2002), *Institutions and Decision Making for Sustainable Development*, New Zealand Treasury Working Paper 02/20, Wellington: New Zealand Treasury.

Sharp, B.M.H. (2005), 'ITQs and beyond in New Zealand fisheries', in D. Leal (ed.), *Evolving Property Rights in Marine Fisheries*, Lanham: Rowman and Littlefield, pp. 193–211.

Sharp, B. and A. Jeffs (2004), 'Growing the seafood sector: technical change and innovation', *Proceedings of the 2004 International Institute of Fisheries Economics and Trade (IIFET) Conference*, Tokyo, July 2004.

Stevenson, G. (1991), *Common Property Economics: A General Theory and Land Use Applications*, Cambridge, UK: Cambridge University Press.

Townsend, R.E. (2005), 'Producer organizations and agreements in fisheries: integrating regulation and coasian bargaining', in D. Leal (ed.), *Evolving Property Rights in Marine Fisheries*, Lanham: Rowman and Littlefield, pp. 127–148.

White, T.A. and C.F. Runge (1994), 'Common property and collective action: lessons from cooperative watershed management in Haiti', *Economic Development and Cultural Change*, **43**(1): 1–41.

Witt, U. (1987), 'The Demsetz–hypothesis on the emergence of property rights reconsidered', in R. Pethig and U. Schlieper (eds), *Efficiency, Institutions and Economic Policy*, Berlin: Springer-Verlag, pp. 83–93.

Zhang, M., C. Batstone and B. Sharp (2006), Rate of Profit Return with ITQs: Fishing for Optimality – Research Report, Auckland: Department of Economics, The University of Auckland, 20 pp.

14. Ocean and Coastal Governance for Sustainability: Imperatives for Integrating Ecology and Economics

Bruce Glavovic

This chapter aims to develop a conceptual foundation for integrating economics and ecology in order to govern oceans and coasts for sustainable development. It starts by providing an overview of New Zealand's experience in conserving Fiordland (New Zealand) marine resources. This experience reveals the complex and evolving challenges and opportunities that characterize ocean and coastal governance – reinforcing the need for an integrated ecological economics approach that transcends traditional disciplinary analysis. The chapter goes on to explore the distinctive characteristics of ocean and coastal systems – including ecological, economic, social, political and other considerations. It highlights key shortcomings of prevailing international marine governance efforts, and suggests imperatives and priority actions for achieving ocean and coastal sustainability.

CONSERVING THE MARINE RESOURCES OF NEW ZEALAND'S FIORDLAND

Fiordland (located on the south-west corner of New Zealand's South Island) is a unique and globally significant marine environment. Its stunning landscapes and remote and rugged setting draw about one-third of all New Zealand's overseas tourists to Fiordland every year. These features and the region's incredible biological diversity have prompted calls for preserving Fiordland as part of our global heritage. The region has long supported important commercial and recreational fisheries. It is also a place of special significance to the indigenous Māori people of the region – Ngai Tahu. Such divergent and conflicting interests are commonplace and lie at the heart of global oceans and coastal governance.

Local stakeholders were prompted to work together to develop a long-term solution in the face of mounting evidence about the negative impacts of fishing, dramatically increasing tourism pressures, and the prospect of Government-imposed preservation measures that could end fishing. In 1995, local fishers, charter boat and tourism operators, scientists, environmentalists, community members, and representatives of Ngai Tahu met to explore opportunities. Initial suspicion and mistrust were overcome by facilitated discussions that led to the establishment of the Guardians of Fiordland's Fisheries and Marine Environment Incorporated (the Guardians). The Guardians developed a shared vision for the region: 'That the quality of Fiordland's marine environment and fishery's experience, be maintained or improved for future generations to use and enjoy' (Tierney 2003). For four years, the Guardians focused on improving their knowledge and understanding about the Fiordland fisheries and marine environment – integrating scientific research and local knowledge from current users and 'old codgers'.

From 2000 to 2003, the Guardians worked on a strategy for managing the wider region. Many meetings and discussions were held. It was not an easy process, with many differences exposed and heated moments. But, notwithstanding their different interests, participants were 'down to earth' locals who shared an intense love for Fiordland. Their passion and commitment to the region transcended their selfish interests. They developed a distinctive 'gifts and gains' philosophy, in which Guardian representatives made a 'sacrifice' that benefited other representatives and helped to achieve their shared vision. For instance, commercial fishers agreed to stop fishing within the fiords in return for recreational fishers committing to reducing bag limits at fiord entrances and on the outer coast.

After eight years of deliberation and hard work, the Guardians submitted their Fiordland Marine Conservation Strategy to the Minister of Fisheries and Minister of Environment. The Ministers committed to implementing the Strategy as far as possible within two years. Government established an investigative group to advise on how best to implement the strategy. These efforts culminated in the passage of the Fiordland (Te Moana o Atawhenua) Marine Management Act on 21 April 2005, together with fisheries regulations. Among other things, the Act established eight new marine reserves, set a 5–7 year moratorium on establishing new marine reserves, and made changes to the Regional Coastal Plan to control anchoring in fragile habitats and impose biosecurity measures. Significantly, the Act established a statutory Guardian's Committee to continue the catalytic role played by local stakeholders. In addition, non-statutory measures are being implemented by central and regional Government agencies in close collaboration with the Guardian's Committee. These measures include a marine resource monitoring plan, a compliance and enforcement plan, an information and education programme, and a plan to manage bio-invasion risks (see Carey 2004; http://www.fmg.org.nz/index.php?p=home).

According to Challis and McCrone (2005), the key ingredients for the success of the Guardian process include:

- The process was *community-driven* as opposed to being led by Government – local people defined the scope, vision and pace of the process.
- Guardians defined a *shared vision* for the region – their common values and love for the region overcame sectoral interests.
- Information was shared and a *common knowledge base* was jointly developed – scientific research and local knowledge were integrated, building trusting relationships.
- Guardian representatives were *passionate* about the region and *committed* to the process – respected by their peers, they were able to negotiate with the support of their constituencies.
- A *creative and independent facilitator* played a pivotal role in overcoming differences and in securing agreements.
- The process was *supported by Government funding and technical expertise* – enabling the Guardians to shape the process without being pressured by inadequate resources or dominant interests.
- There was *adequate time* to develop trust in the process and each other – enabling the Guardians to negotiate in good faith and work towards mutually beneficial outcomes.
- *Political support* by local politicians and key Ministers was essential for implementing the strategy quickly and without significant revision.
- *Professional support* by the Southland Regional Council eased the burden on the Guardians – among other things, the Council provided venues for meetings, compiled meeting minutes and records, collected and collated public submissions, and maintained a transparent record of community consultation efforts.

Does the Fiordland experience offer a model for ocean and coastal governance more generally? Simply trying to replicate this experience elsewhere is bound to fail – the process is unique even in a New Zealand context. The region is isolated, with less intense population and development pressures compared with more built-up regions in the country. Local people are especially passionate about their region. There are relatively few interest groups, and the circumstances that emerged in the mid-1990s compelled local people to work together or likely face Government intervention and the imposition of 'top-down' solutions. The partnership that has been established between local stakeholders and Government, and the resultant combination of statutory and non-statutory measures, is essential to achieving the Guardian's vision for Fiordland.

However, the proliferation of piecemeal laws for different marine environments would be problematical if the Fiordland experience were uncritically replicated elsewhere in New Zealand. Attention clearly needs to be focused on improving and better integrating existing planning, fisheries and environmental policies, laws and related institutions (Challis and McCrone 2005). Importantly, not everyone agrees with the outcome of this process. Some environmentalists, for example, lament the missed opportunity to establish more extensive protected areas. Others perceive missed opportunities to improve their livelihoods. But, in general, critics are inclined to acknowledge the achievements of the Guardians rather than dwell on what has not been achieved. In conclusion, much can be gained by reflecting on this experience, and lessons can be learned and perhaps applied elsewhere based on the key ingredients outlined above. This experience offers a useful point of reference for developing a conceptual foundation for integrating ecology and economics for sustainable oceans and coastal governance.

THE DISTINGUISHING CHARACTERISTICS OF OCEANS AND COASTS

An ecological economics perspective on ocean and coastal governance recognizes 'the value of natural capital and ecosystem services, the large uncertainty inherent in ocean science and governance, the importance of the problem of scale mismatches between ecosystems and human governance institutions, and the limitations of current property rights regimes in addressing ocean governance issues' (Costanza et al. 1999, pp. 172–173). From an ecological economics perspective, the key governance challenge is to design and build institutions that can take into account the distinguishing characteristics of ocean and coastal systems, and foster sustainable use and development of marine resources.

Figure 14.1 highlights the central role that governance institutions play in mediating access to oceanic and coastal resources. As explained in Chapter 1, social and economic sub-systems are embedded in the natural system. This figure elaborates on the socio-economic sub-systems, drawing on insights from work on sustainable livelihoods (see Chapter 11). Marine stakeholders make choices in a particular vulnerability context (influenced by natural, political, social and economic trends, shocks and impacts). They draw upon various livelihood assets (for example, natural capital such as fish for food; human capital such as knowledge, skills and experience in fishing, and so on) in seeking desired livelihood outcomes (such as food security and/or improved income). Prevailing policies, institutions and processes (including markets, social relations and organizations) play a critical role in mediating access to these assets and how they might be combined to frame alternative livelihood strategies that can be pursued to achieve desired livelihood outcomes. This, in turn, impinges on the source and sink functions of marine ecosystems, and the portfolio of livelihood assets. The Fiordland experience corroborates the interdependencies between marine biophysical, social and economic systems. Moreover, it demonstrates the pivotal role that governance institutions play in mediating access to livelihood assets, and the consequential livelihood strategies and outcomes.

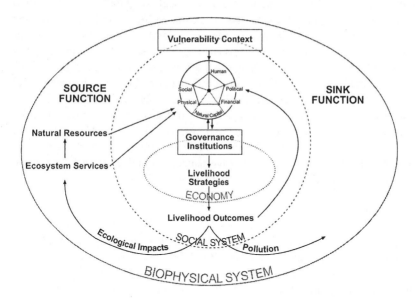

Figure 14.1 The role of governance institutions in mediating access to livelihood assets, including natural capital

What, then, are the distinctive characteristics of the marine environment that are important in establishing an ecological economics of the oceans and coasts? These are identified and discussed below, and form the root foundation to conceptual framework developed in this chapter.

Diversity

Ocean and coastal systems are remarkably diverse. Biophysical heterogeneity is reflected in differences that extend from the poles to the tropics, from the sea-shore to the ocean depths, and from discrete local systems to interconnected global systems. The human realm also varies remarkably. Even in relatively close proximity, maritime communities are often remarkably diverse, invoking quite different governance arrangements to manage marine resources.

Interactions Within and Between Multiple Scales and Levels

Biogeochemical cycles link the oceanic, terrestrial and atmospheric realms; and marine interchanges extend from the local to global level. The fluid environment and porous boundaries of marine systems facilitate strong and rapid connectivity. Moreover, oceans and coasts are coupled 'human-in-nature' systems – ecological systems sustain humans, with economic systems embedded in social systems. The globalization of ocean and coastal activities has expanded rapidly in recent decades, making the links between local coastal communities and global processes, such as international trade and economic trends, more tightly coupled than in the recent past. Consequently, there are multiple-scale, cross-scale and cross-level links and interactions in ocean and coastal systems. Therefore, there is a range of interlinked scales pertinent to ocean and coastal governance, including spatial, temporal, jurisdictional, institutional and management scales.

Dynamism

The marine environment is characterized by the seemingly contradictory notions of constancy and dynamism. It exhibits relatively stable or constant characteristics like temperature, ionic composition, and so on. But it is also characterized by perpetual movement, from constant fluxes to daily tidal exchanges to seasonal and longer-term changes, such as glacial and inter-glacial cycles. This dynamism is reinforced by the relatively rapid and significant institutional changes in marine governance that have taken place over the last four decades, together with significant ongoing technological changes and economic globalization.

Uncertainty

Our knowledge about how these systems function, their interactions and our impacts on them is surprisingly limited. Even in the fisheries sector, with its long history and intensive scientific effort, knowledge about fish life histories, distribution and ecological roles is limited. Catch statistics are not entirely reliable. Knowledge about the human realm of fisheries, for example, employment, livelihoods and income in fish capture and farming, is also limited. Superimposed on the foregoing are the uncertainties associated with climate change impacts.

Complexity

The combined effect of the above distinctive features is best described in terms of 'complex systems' (see Chapter 4). The behaviour of complex, coupled human-in-nature marine systems is typified by unpredictability, non-linearity and evolutionary behaviour, with critical feedback loops between and within scales and levels. Such systems have emergent properties that cannot be discerned readily by isolating system components and then re-aggregating them. In essence, the whole is greater than the sum of its parts. Globalization and the lengthening of chains between marine exploitation, production, trade, and so on, have significantly increased complexity of ocean and coastal governance.

Resilient but Finite and Vulnerable

Contrary to popular perception, the vast oceans are finite and vulnerable to human-induced impacts (see Chapter 9). There is growing evidence that human-induced climate change is evoking significant changes in the ocean realm that have not been experienced for millennia. Given lag- and scale-effects, these changes are likely to persist for considerable time into the future. Ocean and coastal systems are resilient. But beyond critical thresholds, systemic changes occur that profoundly affect their structure and function, health and integrity; resulting in potentially irreversible changes. Irreversible impacts make the consequence of environmentally damaging interventions risky and potentially catastrophic.

Public Interest – Our Global Heritage

Oceans and coasts play a fundamental role in maintaining the health and integrity of the planet's life support systems and meet many of the livelihood needs of the majority of the world's population. Moreover, these assets and resources constitute a fundamental part of our shared global heritage. Coasts are typically held in trust by the State on behalf of citizens, and the oceans have traditionally been considered the quintessential 'global commons'. International law has been promulgated to keep key ocean ecosystems, such as Antarctica, intact in perpetuity as a fundamental part of our global heritage.

THE NATURE, STATUS AND SHORTCOMINGS OF PREVAILING OCEAN AND COASTAL GOVERNANCE EFFORTS

What is Ocean and Coastal Governance?

Historically, ocean and coastal resources have been managed in an ad hoc, fragmented and sector-specific manner. Moreover, ocean and coastal management approaches have evolved as parallel discourses, despite calls for integration (Cicin-Sain and Knecht 1998). Given the above distinguishing characteristics, these traditional, compartmentalized management approaches need to be reconceptualized and integrated to form a broader, more inclusive and holistic notion of marine governance (Kooiman et al. 2005).

Governance transcends government to include other role players, such as business organizations, communities and non-governmental organizations (NGOs), whose interactions facilitate (and/or hinder) sharing of power, social coordination and collective action. According to Kooiman (2003, p. 4):

> *Governing* can be considered as the totality of interactions, in which public as well as private actors participate, aimed at solving societal problems or creating societal opportunities; attending to the institutions as contexts for those governing interactions; and establishing a normative foundation for all those activities. *Governance* can be seen as the totality of theoretical conceptions on governing.

Given the distinguishing characteristics of marine systems, and the multitude of interacting actors and structures involved in marine affairs, ocean and coastal governance ought to be conceived of as 'interaction' – actors interact and are enabled and/or constrained by prevailing institutions and processes. 'Governance therefore is not merely something governors do, but a quality in the totality of the interactions between those governing and those governed – it is itself an interaction' (Kooiman and Bavinck 2005, p. 19). This view of governance as being principled, interactive and stakeholder-driven, stands in stark contrast to more traditional views in which governance is portrayed as unitary, authoritarian and instrumental – with the former view being reinforced by the Fiordland experience.

Institutions are the means by which governance is affected – providing the structure, order and predictability that people need to manage public affairs – mediating access to livelihood assets, and influencing livelihood strategies and outcomes. Institutions need to be seen to be relevant and legitimate by those whose interactions, rights, roles, responsibilities, routines and general practices are to be guided by them – to ensure that appropriate choices can be made between what is 'right' and what is 'wrong', what is appropriate or inappropriate. Institutions are thus embedded in their social milieus; they have history. They are social constructs that are created and changeable, even if there is resistance to change. Their appropriateness, effectiveness and legitimacy vary widely. Institutions therefore need to be critically evaluated and, where appropriate, modified to facilitate better marine governance (Jentoft 2004). This broad view of institutions extends beyond 'rules'. It encompasses norms and even cognitive attributes as well as their social and cultural foundations. This is especially appropriate given the diversity, multiple interacting scales and levels, dynamism, complexity, uncertainty, vulnerability and public interest character of ocean and coastal systems.

Consideration needs to be given to the roles played by and interactions between the State, market and civil society (and community in particular) institutions, because not one of them on their own can govern oceans and coasts for sustainability. For example, only the State can provide the requisite supporting legislation; the market provides the setting in which coastal livelihoods can flourish; and civil society enables the norms and relationships of trust and reciprocity that facilitate social engagement and cooperation. The functional roles and interactions of these institutions will vary depending on different situations, and will need to be 'tailor-made' for them. Interacting governance institutions are therefore needed to address the distinguishing characteristics of ocean and coastal systems on relevant scales and levels. This imperative is borne out by the Fiordland experience.

There is no one size fits all: decentralization might work well when the issues and challenges at the local level can be addressed effectively at that level. But there are marine issues that transcend local capabilities and influence, and therefore require higher levels of intervention. These issues could be fundamentally ecological in nature – when ecosystem boundaries transcend local boundaries and require governance mechanisms to foster cooperation across local and even regional scales (for example, migratory fish). These issues could be social or political in nature – when attention needs to be focused on fundamental human rights that require a trans-local governance intervention, or when political and economic interests transcend the nation-state (for example, Antarctica). The factors influencing a particular issue may have their roots beyond that sector. For example, overfishing may have multiple drivers, including external factors such as unemployment and limited livelihood options in other sectors, inadequate enforcement of prevailing regulations because of systemic corruption or weak enforcement capacity, and/or a failure in traditional management systems. Improving ocean and coastal governance may therefore require reforms to sectors and institutions external to the particular sector under consideration.

In essence, the pursuit of ocean and coastal sustainability demands reforms to the State, market and civil society institutions that structure the relationships between, and practices of, marine stakeholders and actors. Our understanding of the associated challenges, and requisite governance imperatives and actions, has been significantly advanced by recent scholarship on 'environmental governance'.

Environmental Governance: Adaptive Governance of Social–Ecological Systems

Ocean and coastal governance can be subsumed under 'environmental governance', which describes the various regulatory processes, mechanisms and organizations through which political actors influence environmental actions in pursuit of desired outcomes (Lemos and Agrawal 2006). State-centred international regimes have failed to address pressing global environmental problems. Consequently, innovative hybrid environmental governance strategies are being explored, including a mix of State, market and civil society-based governance arrangements, offering hope through expanded and more inclusive governance.

Significant advances are being made in understanding the nature of and imperatives for environmental governance through complementary research streams, including environmental governance (Hempel 1996; Lemos and Agrawal 2006), governance of the 'commons' (Dietz et al. 2003; Ostrom 1990, 2005), institutional ecological economics (Paavola and Adger 2005), adaptive comanagement (Olsson et al. 2004), and adaptive governance (Dietz et al. 2003; Folke et al. 2005). Ecosystem complexity renders redundant the prevailing static, equilibrium-centred and control-oriented approach to resource management. An adaptive management approach offers greater potential for enabling resilient responses to changing circumstances based on testing and improving knowledge about ecosystem dynamics through experimental learning-by-doing (Holling 1978; Gunderson et al. 1995).

Comanagement is essentially concerned with sharing management power to resolve resource problems that transcend sectors and government spheres (Carlsson and Berkes 2005; Jentoft 1998). Adaptive comanagement refers to flexible community-based systems of resource management that are customized to specific places and situations and are supported by, and involve collaboration between, diverse organizations and actors at different levels. Adaptive comanagement integrates the dynamic learning feature of adaptive management with the 'working together' characteristic of cooperative (Jentoft 2000; Pinkerton 1989) and collaborative (Wondolleck and Yaffee 2000) management.

The concept of adaptive governance expands the focus beyond ecosystem management to encompass the wider socio–political context of ecosystem-based management. Environmental governance institutions play a pivotal role in building the resilience of social–ecological systems (Berkes et al. 2003; Gunderson and Holling 2002); enabling adaptation to perturbations so that key system characteristics relating to function, structure, identity and feedback are retained; and, where appropriate, even transforming the system to achieve improved outcomes. Interaction between institutions can facilitate diverse and more appropriate responses to uncertainty, change and perturbations. Adaptive governance is characterized by polycentric institutional arrangements – essentially nested quasi-autonomous decision-making entities that operate at different scales to reconcile centralized and decentralized control (Imperial 1999; McGinnis 2000; Ostrom 1996).

Insights from these diverse but related fields of scholarship provide an increasingly coherent picture of the governance challenges that entrench unsustainable practices, and the consequential imperatives and actions necessary for promoting sustainable development. The following sections draw on insights from this body of knowledge and experience to outline shortcomings of prevailing efforts, and imperatives and actions for sustainable ocean and coastal governance. But, first, what is the status of international ocean and coastal governance?

A 'Stock-Take' of International Ocean and Coastal Governance Efforts

Ocean governance
During the third United Nations Conference on the Law of the Sea (UNCLOS), which took place from 1973 to 1982, it became clear that international efforts to govern oceans were failing and that a new approach was needed. This led to vesting responsibility in coastal States as the entities most dependent on them and most likely to steward their use. Hence, the extension of coastal State jurisdiction, and the widespread establishment of 200 nautical mile Exclusive Economic Zones (EEZs), emerged as perhaps the

most far-reaching institutional change of the 20th century (Hoel et al. 2005). UNCLOS confers rights and responsibilities with respect to the degree of control States can exercise in different maritime zones (see Figure 14.2). In essence, a coastal State's rights of control diminish with increasing distance from the shore, with all States having 'freedom of the high seas' from 200 nautical miles offshore.

UNCLOS is an evolving process of ocean governance institutions and instruments, as opposed to a once-off passage of international law. It is the core around which the following key interconnected oceans issues are governed: Fisheries management; resource conservation; global processes; the UN Regional Seas Programme; pollution prevention; anti-dumping and hazardous waste management; shipping regulation; arms control; and criminal law. States interact with each other, and with the international institutions and processes associated with UNCLOS, in a complex and dynamic web of norms, principles, regulations, rules and guidance that frames appropriate ocean uses and activities. UNCLOS has been supplemented by a diversity of binding and non-binding provisions with environmental concerns dominating fisheries governance, and within which coastal States are defining their oceans policies and developing sustainable ocean management regimes.

For example, the 1992 UN Conference on Environment and Development (UNCED) focused attention on sustainable ocean and coastal governance, addressing problems associated with among other things: integrated management; fisheries (including unregulated fishing, fishing 'vessel reflagging', overcapitalization of the fishing industry, inadequate enforcement, and insufficient cooperation); small island states; pollution; biodiversity; and freshwater–oceans linkages.

The Convention on Biological Diversity (CBD) provides an international framework for conservation and ecologically sustainable development. It was reinforced by the Jakarta Ministerial Statement that reaffirmed the CBD goals and established global consensus on the importance of marine and coastal biodiversity, and the need to focus on integrated management, marine protected areas, sustainable use of living resources, mariculture, and alien species.

Key initiatives relating to fisheries governance include the UN Agreement on Straddling Fish Stocks and Highly Migratory Fish Stocks (UNFSA), which aims to ensure the long-term conservation and sustainable use of these stocks through UNCLOS provisions. It obliges Parties to protect the marine environment and requires States to ensure stock sustainability. It also requires States to apply the Precautionary Principle and adopt conservation measures for species that are part of the same ecosystem. The FAO Compliance

Agreement calls on States to control vessels flying their flag (especially 'reflagging' of vessels to avoid compliance with UNCLOS provisions) and to join Regional Fisheries Management Organisations (RFMOs). The non-binding FAO Code of Conduct for Responsible Fishing urges States to use the precautionary approach to reduce waste, discards and catch of non-target species, ghost fishing (lost or abandoned gear that continues to catch fish), bycatch, and the negative impacts of fishing on associated or dependent species. Other provisions include data collection and information exchange.

The 2002 World Summit on Sustainable Development sharpened international focus on oceans governance. Among other things, it encouraged application of an ecosystem approach to fisheries management by 2010; completion of an effectively managed, ecologically representative network of marine protected areas by 2012; maintaining or restoring fish stocks to sustainable yield levels by 2015; and putting into effect FAO plans of action regarding illegal, unreported and unregulated fishing by 2004.

Thus recent ocean governance efforts have, among other things, increased roles for coastal States, strengthened regional and sub-regional mechanisms, and introduced codes of conduct and compulsory standards applicable to fisheries in regulated areas.

In February 2006, 149 countries were parties to UNCLOS. EEZs now cover most continental shelf resources and the majority of the world's fisheries. The role of NGOs in international affairs has changed fundamentally since the adoption of UNCLOS – reflected, for example, in their inclusion as an integral part of most aspects of the UN system – to the point at which one can argue that 'global civil society' has emerged (Borgese 1999). At the same time, privatization and reliance on 'the market', underpinnings of neoliberalism, have become a dominant feature of post-modern ocean governance (Mansfield 2004a, b).

Complementing the proliferation of international agreements, conventions and so forth, a variety of regional, national and local instruments have been developed to govern ocean resources. There are literally hundreds of interrelated multi- and bi-lateral, regional, and sub-regional treaties, codes of conduct and recommendations by diverse expert bodies. Remarkably, this complex regime of international law has developed in a little over three decades. Joyner (2000, p. 200) draws two main conclusions about the evolution of ocean law: it developed in an ad hoc manner in response to perceived crises; and provisions to protect and manage the marine environment have evolved in a piecemeal fashion. 'The available law has come more as patchwork obligations, rather than as a carefully premeditated, internationally coordinated effort aimed at constructing a coherent legal regime for conserving and protecting biological diversity in the world's

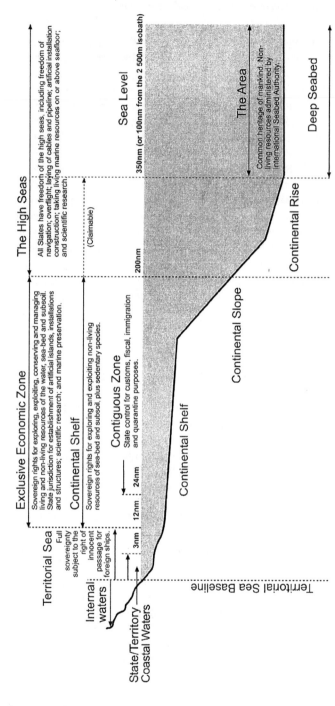

Figure 14.2 Maritime zones associated with the provisions of UNCLOS

(*Source:* Adapted from Gorina-Ysern et al. 2004, p. 199; Kimball 2003, p. 8)

oceans'. The regime has a long way to go to foster sustainable ocean governance (Miles 1999; Joyner 2000; Lodge 2004; Vicuña 2001). Among other things, the challenge is to get about 150 nations to cooperate to manage global marine resources on a sustainable basis.

The limitations of many UNCLOS-related provisions arise because not all States are party to these conventions, agreements, and other instruments. Moreover, many provisions in these instruments are ambiguous or vague with respect to marine conservation. In addition, effective monitoring, compliance and enforcement are extremely difficult to achieve, given the vastness of the oceans. Furthermore, in many cases, it is difficult for parties to secure and allocate the necessary resources to give effect to the provisions outlined in these instruments. Notwithstanding the rights, responsibilities and restrictions outlined in the associated body of international ocean law, the open-access nature and freedom of the high seas means that associated living and biogenetic resources are often viewed as 'economic resources' that can be used without restraint. In short, the enclosure of the oceans through the introduction of EEZs does not avert the 'tragedy of the commons' inherent in high seas freedoms – it just lessens and pushes the problem further out to sea (Stokke 2001).

What then is the prognosis for ocean governance? Johnston and Van der Zwaag (2000) described ocean law at the turn of the millennium as 'treading water' and 'sinking'. They pose seven challenges (a 'hard swim') for international law: coping with the proliferation of negotiated instruments; overcoming political opposition to environmental commitments; clarifying the jurisprudential underpinnings of international environmental law; resolving the relationship between environmental ethics, science and the rule of law; elaborating the principles of sustainable development; addressing practicalities in implementing international responsibilities; and visioning the future of ocean governance. According to Friedheim (2000), there is no shortage of international governmental organizations involved in oceans governance. To be effective, however, they need to be empowered with: action mandates; authority to make their decisions 'stick'; commitment to achieving sustainable development; shared norms to reduce compliance problems; effective internal decision-making mechanisms; appropriate expertise; adequate resources; effective dispute resolution mechanisms; and open and transparent participation. Ocean governance institutions will have to be reformed to contend with these challenges. In particular, there is an urgent need to focus on: addressing the root causes of fishing, namely excessive fishing capacity and effort (Parsons 2005); securing international agreement on currently unregulated high seas fisheries (High Seas Task Group 2006); securing a UN General Assembly moratorium on high seas bottom trawling;

reforming RFMOs (Gjerde and Breide 2003); improving high seas area conservation management; and promoting ocean exploration for the benefit of humankind.

Coastal governance

Over the last four decades, coastal nations around the world have focused increasing attention on coastal governance (Cicin-Sain and Knecht 1998). Integrated Coastal Management (ICM) has become accepted international practice since the 1990s, and the number of ICM initiatives has increased dramatically in recent times. An estimated 75 countries and organizations were involved in about 217 ICM initiatives in 1993. By 2002, some 145 countries and organizations were involved in 698 such initiatives (Sorensen 1993, 2002). But coastal activities continue to be managed in a largely ad hoc, sector-specific and compartmentalized fashion, with system-wide and long-term consequences generally ignored by decision-makers. ICM presents a paradigm shift in thinking and practice. It focuses explicit attention on the interconnections that characterize coastal systems. ICM is a holistic perspective that takes into account the links between inland catchments, the coastal zone and the marine environment. It develops and maintains governance institutions and processes that are inclusive, and that foster cooperation, coordination and integration between and among the array of coastal sectors, agencies and actors. It seeks to reconcile divergent interests and promote sustainability through vertical and horizontal integration, and build bridges across sectoral, administrative, spatial and temporal boundaries that otherwise bedevil integration. Attention is focused on issues of strategic concern to coastal stakeholders. ICM draws on available scientific and technical knowledge, as well as local and traditional knowledge, to better understand coastal systems. ICM demands critical thinking, context-specific application and reflective practice based upon monitoring and lesson-learning. Obviously, achieving such a paradigm shift in such a complex governance arena is a difficult and time-consuming undertaking – it takes decades.

A variety of functional activities need to be carried out in ICM including: coastal area planning, economic development, stewardship of coastal resources, conflict resolution, securing public safety, and proprietorship of public coastal land and waters. These functions take place within a typical policy cycle and draw on a variety of policy, planning and impact assessment techniques (Olsen 2002, 2003). Figure 14.3 presents a modified version of this ICM policy cycle to emphasize the pivotal role authentic public participation should play at each stage of the cycle. Such participation ought to be inclusive and founded on effective capacity-building efforts that are informed by 'civic science', which links traditional science, social values, and local and traditional knowledge (Lee 1993). Policy cycles unfold over time and take on a wider set of issues, cover more extensive geographic areas, or even evolve in more fundamental and philosophical ways. Importantly, however, this evolving process is neither linear nor predictable – it is significantly influenced by the prevailing political and institutional milieu (see Chapter 11).

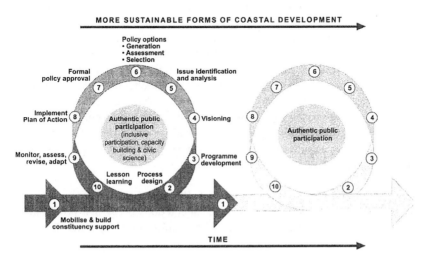

Figure 14.3 A people-centred integrated coastal management policy cycle

Note: The policy cycle is dynamic and must be adapted to the local context. It is seldom a simple progression from one step to another.

Key Shortcomings of Prevailing Ocean and Coastal Governance Efforts

Fundamental challenges for developing an ecological economics of the oceans and coasts arise because of the disconnection between prevailing governance approaches and the distinctive characteristics of the ocean and coastal systems they are supposed to govern. These are identified and discussed below, and form part of conceptual framework developed in this chapter.

Uni-dimensional and universal solutions
While ocean and coastal systems are diverse, governance approaches tend to be dominated by one-dimensional management responses. The bioeconomic

fisheries model, for example, dominates fisheries management. But this approach is limited and fisheries management has been ineffective because it focuses on maximizing the catch of a single target species, ignoring impacts on the habitat, predators and prey of the target species, and other ecosystem components and interactions. The indirect social and economic costs of this narrow focus are substantial (Pikitch et al. 2004). More generally, there is over-reliance on a single governance institution. For example, efforts to resolve the oceans commons dilemma have been virtually confined to the specification of private property rights or government sanctions *per se* (see section on 'collective action problems' below). Another more recent panacea is devolving management responsibilities to the lowest possible tier of government. As appropriate as this may be, given the countervailing tendency to rely on centralized and often far-removed institutional responses, there are circumstances in which management at a local level is inappropriate or becomes problematical – for example, when local management faces trans-local issues or when prevailing capacity is inadequate. In short, the diversity of ocean and coastal systems demands more than a 'one size fits all', universally applicable governance response.

Ignorance, incongruous boundaries, plurality and externalities
At least three cross-scale and cross-level interactions occur that profoundly affect the sustainability and resilience of human-in-nature systems (Cash et al. 2006):

- Ignorance: when scale and level interactions are simply not recognized – for example, when well-intentioned national initiatives hamper local management efforts, or when short-term solutions become long-term problems.
- Mismatch: when institutional boundaries are incongruent with the ecological systems they are supposed to govern – for example, transboundary pollution or migratory fisheries.
- Plurality: when it is incorrectly assumed that a problem is best characterized and addressed at only one scale and level, failing to recognize the diverse ways in which different role players view scales and levels – for example, when an issue, such as public access, is defined as solely 'local' or 'national' rather than considering scale- or level-appropriate institutional responses.

All natural resource management challenges involve cross-scale and cross-level dynamics and consequently demand multiple levels of management simultaneously. The connectivity of marine systems makes these cross-scale and -level interactions especially significant. Furthermore, notwithstanding efforts to internalize externalities, reconciling private and local interests with broader public and even global interests remains problematical in practice.

Inertia and inflexibility
While ocean and coastal systems are dynamic, governance approaches are characterized by inertia and inflexibility. Resistance to change occurs, at least in part, because of the politics of vested interests, and also because of bureaucratic inertia and inflexibility. Consider, for example, the hegemony of the bioeconomic fisheries model despite the collapse of many local and regional fish stocks and the dire state of the world's fisheries (see Chapter 9).

Discounting the future
Ocean and coastal systems are characterized by profound uncertainty, but short-term political time frames and the supremacy of economic rationality result in the future being significantly discounted. As a consequence, greater risks relating to long-term social and ecological concerns are taken than would otherwise be the case.

Reductionism
Ocean and coastal systems are complex, but governance approaches seek to break complex problems down into component parts, each of which is then confronted in isolation, with the expectation that the whole problem will be solved as each mini-solution is re-aggregated. This rationale is fundamentally flawed when it comes to dealing with ocean and coastal management issues as characterized above. Yet reductionism is entrenched in prevailing efforts, at least in part because it is expedient and serves vested interests; and there is little incentive to get to grips with complexity.

A frontier mentality
Ocean and coastal systems are resilient, but beyond certain thresholds they become vulnerable and prone to sudden and even catastrophic collapse. Yet, a frontier mentality characterizes the 'no holds barred' race to exploit marine resources. This mentality is rooted in ignorance and arrogance – as if there are no limits to the marine realm, or that somehow one can simply substitute depleted resources or secure alternatives through human ingenuity.

Collective action problems
Ocean and coastal systems are archetypal assets of public interest and even global heritage. But they embody the 'tragedy of the commons' and 'public good' characteristics of 'non-excludability' (excluding 'outsiders' by

physical or institutional mechanisms is difficult and/or costly), and 'subtractability' (each user is able to detract from the benefits of others). A critical challenge is to construct governance systems that facilitate self-regulation and control of 'outsiders'. The usual prescription to avert the tragedy is to assign private property rights or to impose strict State sanctions. But there is also a wide range of social and community institutions that have been used to manage commons over many centuries. Drawing insights from this experience and the associated literatures is essential for building a robust ecological economics of the oceans and coasts.

As pointed out by McCay and Jentoft (1998), 'community' is an important but neglected concept in understanding commons governance. Users are invariably members of communities (notwithstanding the problems of defining communities) that convey norms, duties and responsibilities that transcend aggregates of the utility-maximizing individuals portrayed in Hardin's (1968) tragedy of the commons. One therefore needs to understand the historical, political and social context and relationships within which individual commons users are embedded – their 'communities'. The Fiordland experience demonstrates the pivotal role that community relationships play in overcoming collective action problems.

It is not just market failure that can lead to the tragedy of the commons. 'Community failure' can also lead to such an outcome – social norms, duties and responsibilities become frayed and dysfunctional to the point where these community influences no longer have a bearing on individual choices. This is a process of 'dis-embedding' that is not always due to internal factors. Context-specific analysis is needed to discern the root causes and drivers of such 'failure' – the State, market or community, or exogenous factors. Ironically, prescriptions to avert the tragedy, either State or market intervention, can both cause community failure. Intervention by the State can create a self-fulfilling prophecy in which the very conditions necessary for communal resource management – namely solidarity, trust and cooperation – are transformed into competitive relationships dependent on the State rather than communal relationships. Markets, through commercialization and monetization, can transform and break down traditional subsistence systems as money transactions dominate social relationships and traditional norms. Community failure can also result from internal dysfunction, by way of limited information and understanding, internal conflict, disorganization, and so on. Community failure can thus be both the *cause* and *result* of government intervention or marketization.

The challenge is to better understand the root causes of commons failure, which, in turn, require more textured understanding of what property rights mean to different stakeholders in different settings and how this understanding can be translated into norms, customs, law and practice. It demands context-specific understanding of the internal and external drivers and dynamics that give rise to the tragedy of the commons.

IMPERATIVES FOR AN ECOLOGICAL ECONOMICS APPROACH TO MARINE GOVERNANCE

Given the distinctive 'system characteristics' of oceans and coasts, and prevailing 'governance shortcomings', what then are the imperatives for developing an ecological economics approach to ocean and coastal governance? These imperatives are considered below and form part of the conceptual framework described by Figure 14.4.

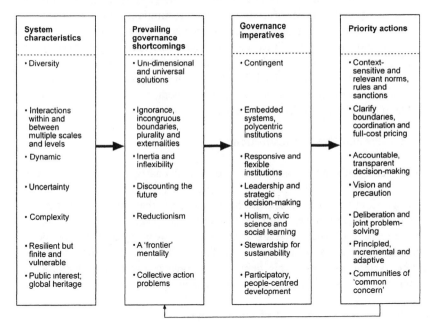

Figure 14.4 System characteristics, prevailing governance shortcomings, imperatives and priority actions for an ecological economics approach to marine governance

Need for Contingent Reponses

To deal with the diversity of ocean and coastal systems, governance systems and responses need to be contingent – that is, tailored to take into account the variability and distinctive characteristics of different settings. Furthermore, contingent responses are essential in the face of inevitable change and surprise.

Need for Embedded Systems; Polycentric Institutions

If governance is to be sustainable, more textured understanding is required of multiple- and cross-scale and cross-level dynamics. Governance responses need to transcend uni-dimensional and universal responses – oceans and coasts are fundamentally embedded human-in-nature systems that need to be governed by polycentric institutions. Such institutions exist on multiple levels, have some autonomy, and are complemented by modest overlaps in authority and capability. Whilst these arrangements may be perceived to be inefficient, the associated diversity and redundancy, with overlapping functions across organizational levels, can be essential for adapting to changing circumstances and spreading risks. Interaction between institutions will help to address cumulative and synergistic impacts.

Responsive and Flexible Institutions

To contend with the dynamism of oceans and coasts, and the inertia and inflexibility of prevailing governance systems, there is a need to build more responsive institutions. This will help to ensure that context-specific but changing circumstances are effectively addressed. The ecological characteristics of marine systems are given. But governing systems are social constructs that can and must be adjusted and tailored to what the human-in-nature system requires – this demands responsive governance institutions, which also need to be flexible to adjust to changing circumstances.

Leadership and Strategic Decision-Making

Leadership and strategic decision-making are essential for confronting uncertainty and myopic decision-making. Leadership provides vision and builds trust. It facilitates collaboration, manages conflict, and secures support for new initiatives and adaptation to novel circumstances. Leaders recognize constraints and barriers, unlock opportunities, empower others, and mobilize support to overcome conflicting values and interests to forge greater resilience.

Need for Holism, Civic Science and Social Learning

Reductionism needs to be replaced by holism, 'civic science' and social learning if we are to begin to understand and deal with the complexity of ocean and coastal systems. Holism focuses on the whole system, acknowledging that system characteristics transcend the simple aggregration of component parts. Civic science integrates and complements scientific research with local and traditional knowledge, and is informed by social values. Social learning processes encourage sharing of knowledge and joint learning, providing better prospects for understanding the different dimensions, perceptions and challenges of ocean and coastal sustainability. Holism, civic science and social learning are essential for developing reflective, responsive and flexible institutions: to learn from past experience to make incremental improvements for the future.

Stewardship for Sustainability

Sustainability is widely recognized in ecological economics as a core imperative to guide human action. It requires, among other things, a focus on timescales that are attuned to ecosystem and intergenerational processes rather than the short-term time frames that govern typical business, political and project cycles. At root, it is an ethical imperative. To avoid exceeding biophysical limits and thresholds, the prevailing frontier mentality needs to be replaced by an environmental ethic that is more in tune with the foregoing imperatives. Environmental values extend from narrow anthropocentric views to more radical eco-centric views. An ethic of 'caring for nature' is inherent in all major religions and most traditional cultures. A 'stewardship' ethic is the minimum ethical requirement for sustainability. This does not, however, mean that a deeper, more radical environmental ethic might not be even more appropriate.

Participatory, People-Centred Development

To ensure that the public interest and global heritage character of oceans and coasts is secured, and to overcome collective action problems, governance needs to be people-centred and empowering – that is, it needs to be driven by human development imperatives. To do so requires inclusive and authentic participation in both the formulation and implementation of ocean and coastal governance. Such participation helps to build credible and enduring governance institutions that are more likely to promote sustainability. Moreover, it is rooted in an ethic of 'caring for people'. Together with the preceding imperative, an ethic of caring for nature and people, governance institutions will be more fundamentally oriented towards sustainability.

PRIORITY ACTIONS

What, then, are the priority actions that need to be taken to translate these 'imperatives' into 'practical reality'? Seven priority actions are identified and discussed below, which are not only important for the ecological economics of the oceans and coasts, but also for the broader field of oceans and coastal governance.

Context-Sensitive and -Relevant Norms, Rules and Sanctions

Effective compliance and enforcement are essential to achieve sustainable ocean and coastal governance. Reliance on 'command and control' *per se* is inadequate. Translating a disaggregated and contingent governance response into practice demands context-sensitive and -relevant norms, rules and sanctions. This context-sensitivity and -relevance must be both ecological and social – that is, contextualized to specific marine social–ecological systems. It demands sensitivity in attitude, approach and action (Jentoft in press).

Clarify Boundaries, Coordination and Full-Cost Accounting

To build embedded, polycentric governance institutions that address multiple- and cross-scale and cross-level interactions, it is imperative to understand better the boundaries of marine ecosystems, resources and user groups and their interconnections, and to adopt measures that are scale and level relevant. Securing governor-relevant information about the marine system, at the appropriate scale, is essential. The appropriate scales and levels of governance intervention will be those that have the necessary information and capacity, are best able to respond quickly and effectively, take into account all internal and external costs and benefits, and integrate across boundaries. Progressing from awareness to communication and ultimately coordination is the pathway to cross-scale and -level integration.

Accountable and Transparent Decision-Making

Accountability and transparency are essential if governance is to be responsive and flexible, and compliance and enforcement prospects are to be enhanced.

Vision and Precaution

Leadership stimulates visionary thinking and practice to counteract the negative consequences generated by uncertainty and preoccupation with immediate concerns. A desired future, at least decades from now, needs to be envisioned. Action should then be taken to work towards this ideal. The need to apply the Precautionary Principle in the face of uncertainty is becoming a widely recognized cornerstone of environmental governance. In essence, in the face of uncertainty and in the absence of compelling evidence, decisions should be risk-averse to avoid irreversible impacts. Moreover, the burden of proof should be borne by those whose activities may be potentially harmful.

Deliberation and Joint Problem-Solving

Putting holism, civic science and social learning into practice requires a fundamentally different way of doing things – inclusive dialogue and deliberation are needed. By bringing key stakeholders and those with knowledge and insight together (including scientists and those with local and traditional knowledge) a more complete picture of the complexity of ocean and coastal systems is fostered. Such processes can draw upon 'social memory', whereby previous experience can be mobilized for coping with novel circumstances. By tackling governance issues in an inclusive and joint problem-solving manner, outcomes are more likely to be fair, efficient, wise and enduring (Susskind and Cruikshank 1987). In so doing, however, disputes will inevitably arise as power differentials and contending values and interests come to the fore. A 'principled negotiation' approach is needed for constructive conflict management and dispute resolution (Fisher and Ury 1980).

Principled, Incremental and Adaptive

To overcome the prevailing frontier mentality, and to build more resilient maritime communities, ocean and coastal governance efforts need to be founded on the minimum ethical standard of stewardship. Furthermore, information about marine social–ecological systems needs to be gathered and critically analyzed, on an ongoing and collaborative basis, to facilitate incremental adaptations that foster sustainability and resilience. Ocean and coastal governance is a long-term process that evolves iteratively as key roleplayers learn to work together to adapt to changing and even surprising circumstances.

Communities of 'Common Concern'

Ocean and coastal governance needs to be 'by and for people', as opposed to meeting project, programme and process requirements. It needs to be empowering and inclusive, taking into account the diversity within and between different kinds of community. It needs to look beyond actors and institutions to 'communities of common concern'. Trust is the basis of all social institutions. As people work together and begin to develop and extend their networks, shared understanding and norms can evolve – 'community spirit' develops. Investment in social relationships creates social capital that facilitates cooperation and adaptive governance (Adger 2003; Folke et al. 2005; Pretty 2003; Pretty and Ward 2001), with the prospect of building more sustainable and resilient maritime 'communities of common concern'.

CONCLUSION

Governance institutions play a pivotal role in shaping the sustainability of marine resource use and development. In a remarkably short period of time, a complex web of governance institutions has been developed to promote global marine sustainability. But much remains to be done to realize this elusive ideal. The Fiordland experience demonstrates that unsustainable practices can be reversed by innovation, dedication and collaboration. Drawing on this experience and other sources, a conceptual framework was developed for providing insights on how to design governance systems that promote the sustainable development of our oceans and coasts; particularly by integrating ecological and economic dimensions. This framework shows that at the root, prevailing governance efforts are fundamentally mismatched in relation to the distinguishing 'system characteristics' of marine systems. The 'governance shortcomings', 'governance imperatives' and 'priority actions' that stem from these system characteristics are outlined by the framework.

REFERENCES

Adger, W.N. (2003), 'Social capital, collective action and adaptation to climate change', *Economic Geography*, **79**: 387–404.
Berkes, F., J. Colding and C. Folke (eds) (2003), *Navigating Social–Ecological Systems: Building Resilinece for Complexity and Change*, Cambridge, UK: Cambridge University Press.
Borgese, E.M. (1999), 'Global civil society: lessons from ocean governance', *Futures*, **31**: 983–991.
Carey, P. (2004), 'Guardian angels', *North and South*, July: 70–78.
Carlsson, L. and F. Berkes (2005), 'Comanagement: concepts and methodological implications', *Journal of Environmental Management*, **75**: 65–76.
Cash, D.W., W.N. Adger, F. Berkes, P. Garden, L. Lebel, P. Olsson, L. Pritchard and O. Young (2006), 'Scale and cross-scale dynamics: governance and information in a multilevel world', *Ecology and Society*, **11**(2): 8.
Challis, J. and A. McCrone (2005), 'Fiordland: a model for future integrated marine management?', Seachange 05: Managing our coastal waters and oceans conference proceedings, accessed 23 April 2007 from: http://www.eds.org.nz/content/documents/seachange_papers/Ann%20McCrone.pdf.
Cicin-Sain, B. and R.W. Knecht (1998), *Integrated Coastal and Ocean Management*, Washington, DC: Island Press.
Costanza, R., F. Andrade, P. Antunes, M. van den Belt, D. Boesch, D. Boersma, F. Catarino, S. Hanna, K. Limburg, B. Low, M. Molitor, J.G. Pereira, S. Rayner, R. Santos, J. Wilson and M. Young (1999), 'Commentary: Ecological economics and sustainable governance of the oceans', *Ecological Economics*, **31**: 171–187.
Dietz, T., Ostrom, E. and P.C. Stern (2003), 'The struggle to govern the commons', *Science*, **302**: 1902–1912.
Fisher, R. and W. Ury (1980), *Getting to Yes: Negotiating Agreement without Giving In*, New York: Penguin Books.
Folke, C., T. Hahn, P. Olsson and J. Norberg (2005), 'Adaptive governance of social–ecological systems', *Annual Review of Environmental Resources*, **30**: 441–473.
Friedheim, R. (2000), 'Designing the ocean policy future: an essay on how I am going to do that', *Ocean Development and International Law*, **31**: 183–195.
Gjerde, K.M. and C. Breide (2003), *Towards a Strategy for High Seas Marine Protected Areas*, Proceedings of the IUCN, WCPA and WWF Experts Workshop on High Seas Marine Protected Areas, 15–17 January 2003, Malaga, Spain, Gland: IUCN.
Gorina-Ysern, M., K. Gjerde and M. Orbach (2004), 'Ocean governance: a new ethos through a world ocean public trust', in L.D. Glover and S.A. Earle (eds), *Defying Ocean's End: An Agenda for Action*, Washington, DC: Island Press, pp. 197–212.
Gunderson, L. and C.S. Holling (eds) (2002), *Panarchy: Understanding Transformations in Human and Natural Systems*, Washington, DC: Island Press.
Gunderson, L., C.S. Holling and S. Light (eds) (1995), *Barriers and Bridges to the Renewal of Ecosystems and Institutions*, New York: Columbia University Press.
Hardin, G. (1968), 'The Tragedy of the Commons', *Science*, **162**(3859): 1243–1248.
Hempel, L.C. (1996), *Environmental Governance: The Global Challenge*, Washington, DC: Island Press.

High Seas Task Group (2006), *Closing the Net: Stopping Illegal Fishing on the High Seas*, Governments of Australia, Canada, Chile, Namibia, New Zealand, and the United Kingdom, WWF, IUCN and the Earth Institute at Columbia University.

Hoel, A.H., A.K. Sydnes and S.A. Ebbin (2005), 'Ocean governance and institutional change', in S.A. Ebbin, A.J. Hoel and A.K. Sydnes (eds), *A Sea Change: The Exclusive Economic Zone and Governance Institutions for Living Marine Resources*, Dordrecht: Springer, pp. 3–16.

Holling, C.S. (1978), *Adaptive Environmental Assessment*, New York: Wiley.

Imperial, M.T. (1999), 'Institutional analysis and ecosystem-based management: the institutional analysis and development framework', *Environmental Management*, 24: 449–465.

Jentoft, S. (1998), 'Fisheries co-management: delegating government responsibility to fishermen's organisations', *Marine Policy*, 13(2): 137–154.

Jentoft, S. (2000), 'Co-managing the coastal zone: is the task too complex?', *Ocean and Coastal Management*, 43: 527–535.

Jentoft, S. (2004), 'Institutions in fisheries: what they are, what they do, and how they change', *Marine Policy*, 28: 137–149.

Jentoft, S. (in press), 'Limits of governability: institutional implications for fisheries and coastal governance', *Marine Policy*.

Johnston, D.M. and D.L. Van der Zwaag (2000), 'The ocean and international environmental law: swimming, sinking, and treading water at the millennium', *Ocean and Coastal Management*, 43: 141–161.

Joyner, C.C. (2000), 'The international ocean regime at the new millennium: a survey of the contemporary legal order', *Ocean and Coastal Management*, 43: 163–203.

Kimball, L.A. (2003), *International Ocean Governance: Using International Law and Organisations to Manage Resources Sustainably*, Gland: IUCN.

Kooiman, J. (2003), *Governing as Governance*, London: Sage Publications.

Kooiman, J. and M. Bavinck (2005), 'The governance perspective', in J. Kooiman, M. Bavinck, S. Jentoft and R. Pullin (eds) (2005), *Fish for Life: Interactive Governance for Fisheries*, Amsterdam: Amsterdam University Press, pp. 11–24.

Kooiman, J., M. Bavinck, S. Jentoft and R. Pullin (eds) (2005), *Fish for Life: Interactive Governance for Fisheries*, Amsterdam: Amsterdam University Press.

Lee, K.N. (1993), *Compass and Gyroscope: Integrating Science and Politics for the Environment*, Washington, DC: Island Press.

Lemos, M.C. and A. Agrawal (2006), 'Environmental governance', *Annual Review of Environmental Resources*, 31: 297–325.

Lodge, M.W. (2004), 'Improving international governance in the deep sea', *The International Journal of Marine and Coastal Law*, 19(3): 299–316.

Mansfield, B. (2004a), 'Neoliberalism in the oceans: "rationalization", property rights, and the commons question', *Geoforum*, 35: 313–326.

Mansfield (2004b), 'Rules of privatization: contradictions in neoliberal regulation of North Pacific fisheries', *Annals of the Association of American Geographers*, 94(3): 565–584.

McGinnis, M. (2000), *Polycentric Governance and Development*, Ann Arbor, MI: University of Michigan Press.

McCay, B.J. and S. Jentoft (1998), 'Market or community failure? Critical perspectives on common property research', *Human Organization*, 57(1): 21–29.

Miles, E.L. (1999), 'The concept of ocean governance: evolution toward the 21st century and the principle of sustainable ocean use', *Coastal Management*, **27**: 1–30.

Olsen, S.B. (2002), 'Assessing progress towards the goals of coastal management', *Coastal Management*, **30**: 325–345.

Olsen, S.B. (2003), 'Frameworks and indicators for assessing progress in integrated coastal management initiatives', *Ocean and Coastal Management*, **46**: 347–361.

Olsson, P., C. Folke and F. Berkes (2004), 'Adaptive comanagement for building resilience in social-ecological systems', *Environmental Management*, **34**(1): 75–90.

Ostrom, E. (1990), *Governing the Commons: The Evolution of Institutions for Collective Action*, Cambridge: Cambridge University Press.

Ostrom, E. (1996), 'Crossing the great divide: coproduction, synergy, and development', *World Development*, **24**(6): 1073–1087.

Ostrom, E. (2005), *Understanding Institutional Diversity*, Princeton, NJ: Princeton University Press.

Paavola, J. and W.N. Adger (2005), 'Institutional ecological economics', *Ecological Economics*, **53**: 353–368.

Parsons, S. (2005), 'Ecosystem considerations in fisheries management: theory and practice', *The International Journal of Marine and Coastal Law*, **20**(3–4): 381–422.

Pikitch, E.K., C. Santora, E.A. Babcock, A. Bakun, R. Bonfil, D.O. Conover, P. Dayton, P. Doukakis, D. Fluharty, B. Heneman, E.D. Houde, J. Link, P.A. Livingston, M. Mangel, M.K. McAllister, J. Pope and K.J. Sainsbury (2004), 'Ecosystem-based fishery management', *Science*, **305**(5682): 346–347.

Pinkerton, E. (1989), *Cooperative Management of Local Fisheries: New Directions for Improved Management and Community Development*, Vancouver: University of British Columbia Press.

Pretty, J. (2003), 'Social capital and the collective management of resources', *Science*, **302**: 1912–1914.

Pretty, J. and H. Ward (2001), 'Social capital and the environment', *World Development*, **29**: 209–227.

Sorensen, J. (1993), 'The international proliferation of integrated coastal zone management efforts', *Ocean and Coastal Management*, **21**(1–3): 45–80.

Sorensen, J. (2002), *Baseline 2000 Background Report: The Status of Integrated Coastal Management as an International Practice*, Second Iteration, 26 August 2002, Urban Harbors Institute: University of Massachusetts, Massachusetts, USA.

Stokke, O.S. (ed.) (2001), *Governing High Seas Fisheries: The Interplay of Global and Regional Regimes*, Oxford: Oxford University Press.

Susskind, L. and J. Cruikshank (1987), *Breaking the Impasse: Consensual Approaches to Resolving Public Disputes*, New York: Basic Books.

Tierney, L. (2003), *Fiordland Marine Conservation Strategy*, Te Kaupapa Atawhai o Te Moana o Atawhenua, Guardians of Fiordland's Fisheries and Marine Environment Inc., 138 pp.

Vicuña, F.O. (2001), 'The international law of high seas fisheries: from freedom of fishing to sustainable use', in O.S. Stokke (ed.), *Governing High Seas Fisheries: The Interplay of Global and Regional Regimes*, Oxford: Oxford University Press, pp. 23–52.

Wondolleck, J.M. and S.L. Yaffee (2000), *Making Collaboration Work: Lessons from Innovation in Natural Resource Management*, Washington, DC: Island Press.

15. Summary and Future Challenges for an Ecological Economics of the Oceans and Coasts

Murray Patterson and Bruce Glavovic

OCEANS AND COASTS AS CRITICAL NATURAL CAPITAL

Our first and most important conclusion is that the oceans and coasts are coming under unprecedented pressure from economic development. Intensifying economic activity on the coastal margins, as well as the expanding global economy, are having a fundamental impact on the marine environment. We agree with the *Millennium Ecosystem Assessment* that 'marine and coastal ecosystems are being degraded and used unsustainably and are therefore deteriorating faster than other ecosystems' (Brown et al. 2006). In short, the 'natural capital' embodied in oceanic and coastal and ecosystems is being degraded, often irreversibly.

Sink Functions

Oceanic and coastal ecosystems perform 'sink' functions. That is, they process and purify emissions that are produced by the global economy. This ability of oceanic and coastal ecosystems to process and purify emissions is not limitless. There are critical thresholds and limits beyond which these ecosystems cannot continue to process and purify emissions, without some significant change to the environmental quality of the receptor environment. For the oceanic and coastal environment, there are a range of such impacts already occurring as a result of the growth of the global economy:

- nutrient enrichment of marine ecosystems from terrestrial pollutants (mainly agricultural run off) resulting in increasing occurrence of: (1) hypoxic or so called 'dead zones'; and (2) the modification and

simplification of coastal–marine ecosystems as the nutrient status of the ecosystem supports a narrower range of species;
- ecological impacts from persistent and toxic pollutants, oil/oil byproducts and nuclear wastes from the terrestrial economy. These 'non-nutrient' pollutants have a variety of unintended impacts including, for example, significant concentration of organochlorine pesticides found in food chains in places (such as the Arctic) far away from the place and time they first entered the environment;
- significant impact on coastal zone geomorphology and ecosystems, due to decreased sediment loads (resulting from sediment interception by dams and other engineering works);
- climate change (resulting from greenhouse gas emissions from the economy) having a number of impacts: (1) greater CO_2 absorption by seas and oceans, which *inter alia* contributes to coral bleaching; (2) losses in biological productivity due to less nutrient supply in the upper ocean, caused by less mixing of warmer waters; (3) potential loss of coastal ecosystems (wetlands, salt marshes, mangroves) and low-lying land due to sea level rise.

The inevitable conclusion is that the oceans and coasts are not a 'vast limitless sink' for emissions and waste products from the expanding global economy. The evidence shows that many of the thresholds (for the oceans and coasts to continue to absorb and process wastes/emissions) have already been reached.

Source Functions

The same 'frontier economics' that characterizes our thinking about the 'sink functions' of the oceans and coasts is prevalent in our thinking of their 'source functions'. Marine ecosystems and resources (food, fossil fuels, minerals) are the 'source' of critical inputs into the global economy, all of which have quantitative limits to their exploitation, whether they be a 'renewable' or so-called 'non-renewable' resource. Most importantly, for example, although the oceans are a rich source of food, providing 16 per cent of the protein for the global population, there is conclusive evidence that we have 'overshot' the sustainable yield of many of the world's fisheries, with 24 per cent collapsing in the last 50 years primarily due to over-fishing. Fishing practices such as bottom trawling (loss of benthos habitat) and drift nets (catching non-target species) also have significant direct negative environmental impacts.

The oceans currently provide 30 per cent of the world's oil and 50 per cent of the world's natural gas. A frontier economics also drives much of our thinking concerning the future level of exploitation of energy and minerals, as the oceans become the 'last frontier' for development. From an ecological economic perspective, this is an over-optimistic view – there is an urgent need to analyze the ecological and thermodynamic viability of such proposed developments by using methods such as net energy analysis. For example, it could be possible that some marine energy development proposals do not have positive net energy yields – that is, more embodied energy goes into extracting the energy resource than is contained in the extracted resource (Cleveland 1992).

The coasts also provide 'space' for economic activities such as urban development, port development, tourism, marinas, and so forth. Due to these developments, considerable loss of habitat in marine ecosystems (particularly mangroves, estuaries, coral reefs) has been recorded worldwide. For example, for countries for which there are available data, it is estimated that globally 35 per cent of mangroves have disappeared in the last two decades (Brown et al. 2006).

Challenges for Future Ecological Economics Research

In general terms, there is a poor and underdeveloped appreciation of the oceans and coasts as critical natural capital. In Chapter 2, Ben McNeil reviewed the fundamental ecological processes and functions of the oceans and coasts (namely, the 'critical natural capital' embodied in the oceans and coasts) in supporting human and non-human life. Chapter 6 has shown how these processes and functions could be valued using non-market valuation methods, building on earlier work by Costanza et al. (1997). We need to build on these insights so that we can better understand the role of oceans and coasts as critical natural capital. The focus of the research thus far has been on the benefit/value that can be derived from marine natural capital and ecosystem services, with little attention given to the risk and cost of irreversibly degrading these ecosystems services and natural capital. There is also a need to investigate exactly where the critical thresholds lie in degrading the natural capital of the oceans and coasts, and where the boundary lies between critical natural capital and natural capital that can be substituted with man-made capital.

There is also a need for better understanding of the 'dynamics of economic drivers of change' that impact on marine ecosystems (natural capital). That is, we need to know about: (1) dynamics that drive growth in coastal economies, coastal tourism and coastal urban development; and (2) the dynamics that drive the demand for marine products such as fish and energy resources.

Furthermore, we need to know about the sometimes complex causal chains that eventually connect these 'economic drivers of change' to 'impacts on marine ecosystems'. Without this knowledge, it will be far more difficult to formulate integrated policy responses that can reduce these impacts of the economy on marine natural capital.

IRREDUCIBLE COMPLEXITY, UNCERTAINTY AND THE UNKNOWABLE

A recurrent theme in this book has been the problem of uncertainty and lack of information when it comes to our knowledge and understanding of the oceans and coasts, particularly relative to our knowledge of the terrestrial environment. This presents an uncomfortable problem for conventional economic analysis as it is often based on a Cartesian view of the world that assumes perfect information and predictable behaviour. There is therefore a fundamental need to develop approaches in ecological economics that can deal with (and even expect) uncertainty and indeterminacy in difficult-to-manage complex systems such as the oceans and coasts.

This uncertainty occurs at a number of levels, all of which need to be addressed in an ecological economics enquiry into the oceans and coasts. The first type of uncertainty is 'risk' where we can statistically calculate the probability of an event occurring – for example, we may be able statistically to estimate the probability of a storm event occurring at a specific coastal location. However, in most cases in the marine environment, the uncertainty is more deep-seated than just measuring risk in a statistical way. That is, we are dealing with pure uncertainty where *we cannot calculate probabilities* because either we do not know all the variables that have cause–effect relationships in the system, and/or we are dealing with a system that is so intrinsically non-linear that statistical probabilities cannot reliably be calculated. Wilson et al. (1996) would argue this is the case with fisheries, the dynamics of which are impossible to model with any reliability and certainty.

The third type of uncertainty is 'ignorance' of the system of processes that *we should, but do not, know about.*[1] This type of uncertainty is very prevalent in the coasts and particularly the oceanic environment. Even at a very macro-level, our understanding of oceanic processes and biodiversity is in most cases very poor if not completely lacking. In spite of recent advances, for example by Worm et al. (2006), our understanding about the possible links between biodiversity and ecosystem services is woefully limited by our ignorance – refer to Chapter 3.

A fourth level of uncertainty is 'indeterminacy' – that is, the systems' behaviour is inherently impossible to predict due to circularities, incongruities, recursion and other such properties of the system. For some time, ecological economists such as O'Connor (1994) have appreciated that ecological–economic systems often have 'indeterminate behaviour', with these ecological economists drawing their insight from fields such as mathematics, system theory and non-equilibrium thermodynamics. It could be argued that many marine systems are characterized by indeterminacy, particularly when the problem is framed in broad terms and over longer time frames and diverse spatial scales. In Chapter 8, Charlotte Šunde rightfully drew our attention to that which is unknowable and immeasurable, at least in a rational Western-science sense. Much of our 'knowing' of the sea can fall outside the realm of intellectual endeavours, belonging more to the spiritual dimension – this is particularly so of cultures that still maintain a close connection with the marine environment.

Awareness of these categories of uncertainty is critical in framing a research agenda for an ecological economics of the oceans and coasts – even more so than in terrestrial contexts. As ecological economists, we need to develop methods that can deal with these different categories of uncertainty and learn from other disciplines (such as the policy and planning sciences) that have a longer history in dealing with such issues. This is not to say that we should abandon traditional economic methods of dealing with risk and uncertainty in economics, but that we should move beyond them to embrace processes such as adaptive management (from the ecologist, Holling) and mixed scanning (from the sociologist-planner, Etzioni). We also need to develop more market-orientated methods for dealing with the lack of information in the marine environment, such as the 'Minimum Information Management' (MIM) advocated by Chris Batstone and Basil Sharp in Chapter 12. The movement to a wider range of methods and broader appreciation of uncertainty, away from the simplistic Cartesian approaches often used in economics, is vital, particularly in relation to the uncertain world of oceans and coasts. All too often we over-simplify so that we can solve what Cartwright (1973) refers to as 'simple problems' when we are in fact dealing with 'messy' or 'metaproblems'.

VALUE CONFLICTS AND VALUATION

The issues of *value conflicts* and the way in which *we go about valuing marine resources* are both recurrent and related themes to emerge from this book. This is important because value has been a central concept in economics and, as Cole et al. (1991) point out, tensions between schools of economic thought often come down to fundamental differences over theories of value. Schumpeter (1954), in *History of Economic Analysis*, also recognized that 'the problem of value must always hold the pivotal position as the chief tool of analysis in any pure theory that works with a rational schema'. In fact, the neoclassical theory of value (price)[2] is absolutely central to the theoretical framework of neoclassical economics and indeed is probably the main reason for the unquestionable success of neoclassical economics. From this theory of value (price) come powerful implications concerning the definition of equilibrium conditions and what this means for efficient resource allocation. In Chapter 5, Sharp and Batstone used this neoclassical framework to derive conclusions about the optimization of value derived from both renewable and non-renewable marine resources.

Ecological economists, however, have not come to any theoretical consensus on how to deal with the issue of value in ecological economics, which presents the discipline with a significant challenge. Instead, a range of valuation methods and approaches is used in contemporary ecological economics, including: neoclassical methods (as used by Wilson and Liu in Chapter 6); group-based methods that are often extensions of neoclassical methods (for example, Blamey et al. 2000; Wilson and Howarth 2002); multi-criteria methods (Martinez-Alier et al. 1998; Munda et al. 1994); discursive–ethical approaches (O'Hara 1996; Sagoff 1998); conjoint analysis (Stevens et al. 2000); energy-based methods (Costanza and Hannon 1989); and ecological pricing (as used by Patterson in Chapter 7, for example).

Valuation is critical in enabling us to make rational decisions about the oceans and coasts, so that we can get a true appreciation of both the costs and benefits. All too often, however, in the frontier economics of the oceans and coasts where economic externalities such as degradation of ecosystems services prevail, not all the costs are taken into account, which results in biased decision-making. Spatial discounting (Not in My Back Yard syndrome) is also very prevalent in situations where inland industries can negatively affect the marine environment but the cost of their external effects is ignored. In this respect, the type of valuation data collected by Wilson and Lui in Chapter 6 can be helpful as it enables the true cost of these externalities to be measured in readily understood dollar terms. But the valuation challenge for the oceans and coasts needs to go beyond anthropocentric methods of neoclassical economics to include more biocentric methods such as the ecological pricing approach advocated by Patterson in Chapter 7. Some would argue for more multi-criteria methods and some would argue for a total abandonment of formal valuation methods and movement towards more 'process-based methods' of decision-making to resolve value conflicts. In Chapter 8, Charlotte Šunde issued an even broader challenge to ecological economists to look beyond concepts of 'externalities' and 'ecosystem services' and to include non-rational and spiritual ways of valuing oceans and coasts.

The valuation debate in ecological economics, unlike that in neoclassical economics, remains unresolved, with no signs of an enduring consensus. The preliminary research by Costanza et al. (1997), using standard neoclassical methods of valuation, showed that marine ecosystem services are far more valuable ($US22.6 trillion in 1994) than terrestrial ecosystem services ($US10.7 trillion). Ecological economists, however, need to move beyond this preliminary work to truly understand the value of marine systems from a multiplicity of perspectives and methods – such a manifestation of methodological pluralism should be seen as a sign of strength, not as a sign of indecision and weakness.

NEED FOR A SPATIAL DIMENSION

Neoclassical models of economic behaviour and growth are 'aspatial'. Blaug (1997), a renowned historian of economic thought, comments that there has been a 'curious disdain of location theory on the part of mainstream theory, and asserts that 'this neglect largely continues to this day'. Ecological economists such as Robert Costanza have, however, attempted to introduce a spatial dimension into their analyses, particularly in relation to tracking the environmental impacts of economic activity (Costanza and Greer 1997).

We argue that an 'ecological economics of the oceans and coasts' must have a strong spatial dimension, because many of the environmental impacts, and the associated activities that cause them, have a critical spatial dimension that cannot be ignored or simply assumed away. First, we argue that the spatial analysis of the ecological impacts is a necessary requirement of 'integrative management' when it comes to the oceans and coasts. When there is spatial dislocation of the cause (for example, inland farming) and the effect (for example, nutrient 'over-enrichment' of the coastal zone), spatial analysis is unavoidable if you are going to arrive at a 'whole–system' understanding of the problem. In situations like this, in order to arrive at integrative planning and policy solutions, we need spatial analyses that show exactly how, where and at what rate nutrients move across space from inland areas and eventually to the coast, using methods such as cellular automata systems for simulating the spatial dynamics. Such spatial analyses should recognize the spatial heterogeneity of the terrestrial environment as well as the recipient marine environment and the differential effects that nutrients (or other pollutants) have on biota within these environments. All too often, ecological economists tend to measure the output of pollutants into the 'sink' environment, without appreciating that is a highly ecologically and spatially differentiated environment – for example, the effect of one tonne of nitrogen will have a markedly different impact depending on where it is disposed (for example, a mangrove swamp compared with an outfall three miles from the coast) and where it eventually ends up.

Second, the drivers of change of economic activity have an unavoidable spatial dimension that is not captured by mainstream growth theories such as those developed by Solow (1956) or more recently Romer (1990). The fact that neither of these mainstream models have a spatial dimension is unsatisfactory when it comes to explaining the patterns and drivers of economic change on the coastal margins. Our analysis in Chapter 9 demonstrated that the forces of 'economic agglomeration' in coastal regions are strong determinants of growth, with industries tending to co-locate on the coast due to self-reinforcing advantages to do with: market access, close proximity of other growth industries, as well as access to finance, innovators and entrepreneurs. In short, we are dealing with the idea of 'circular and cumulative causation' as originally put forward by Myrdal (1944) – because when (coastal) regions experience initially higher growth, the flow of the factors of production from slowly growing regions reinforces the initial advantage many times over. It seems to us that this type of 'economic geography' model has greater explanatory power and is of more use than the aspatial neoclassical models, when analyzing the economic growth of coastal economies. Furthermore, it provides a spatial dimension that can be directly integrated into the ecological–spatial analysis discussed above. Fujita et al. (1999) provide a useful summary of modern-day economic geography theories and methods that could be used in such an analysis of the 'ecological economics of the oceans and coasts'.

NEED FOR INTEGRATION TO ACHIEVE SUSTAINABLE DEVELOPMENT

The ecological economics agenda can be seen as narrow, focusing only on the interactions between the economy and the environment. An emergent theme from this book is that such an approach is necessary but not sufficient to achieve the sustainable development of the ocean and coasts. In Chapter

11, Bruce Glavovic showed that, in our efforts to improve both economic and ecological outcomes in the coast, equity and poverty issues are often overlooked, resulting in undesirable outcomes. In Chapter 8, Charlotte Šunde also demonstrated that the cultural and spiritual values of indigenous peoples are often compromised or ignored. Although ecological economists have engaged in debates about poverty and inequity (for example, Goodland and Daly 1993; Martinez-Alier 2002), the level of coverage of such issues in the ecological economics literature is low, as evidenced by Costanza and King's (1999) citation analysis. To our knowledge, when it comes to the oceans and coasts, such issues have received no literature attention by ecological economists. Thus, there is a need to take up Bruce Glavovic's (see Chapters 11 and 14) and Charlotte Šunde's (Chapter 8) challenges for ecological economics. If the goal of sustainable oceans and coastal development is to be progressed, these and other social dimensions need to be considered alongside ecological and economic dimensions in a connected fashion.

Whether ecological economics necessarily needs to integrate these social dimensions into its theoretical frameworks is, however, more debatable. Probably more to the point, ecological economists (whose expertise lies at the economy–ecology nexus) need to work with other researchers and practitioners in an integrative way to define viable and preferred policy options to make progress towards sustainable development. Achieving an overall integrative economics that includes 'economic + ecological + social' dimensions is a more ambitious agenda; and probably not necessary so long as ecological economists can work with social scientists and others and be cognizant of their concerns with dimensions such as poverty, equity, spirituality, traditional knowledge and indigenous peoples.

Another area that requires an integrated approach is the ability to analyze and integrate marine environmental impacts that occur across space and time. All too often in the marine area, environmental impacts are considered in a compartmentalized way – for instance:

- one-species models instead of whole community or whole ecosystem models;
- considering only one spatial location when we know the cause (for example, inland farming) can be located far away from the effect (for example, oceanic nutrient enrichment);
- using one-pollutant studies that have one impact when in the coastal or marine environment we know there is often a cascade of impacts that are interrelated (nutrient enrichment and climate change); and
- considering only first-order effects when we know the effects are cumulative across both space and time (for example, bio-accumulation of

persistent pesticides in marine food chains).

Not only are these environmental impacts interrelated, but layered on top of them are interactions with the economy and communities. Integrated Coastal Management and ecosystem-based management regimes are steps in the right direction. Ecological economists need to support such initiatives by providing good quality information, particularly on the connectivity between the economy and the marine environment. Integrative Economy–Environment Modelling tools, such as those outlined by Mathias Ruth in Chapter 10, are useful steps in this direction as they enable the interactions and tradeoffs between the economy and the environment to be simulated and tested. Integrative marine management also requires a good integration of governance and policy processes that are appropriately mapped onto temporal and spatial scales. Although governance, *per se*, is not the domain of ecological economists, we can assist in this process by providing information, insights, and critiques from an ecological economics perspective, concerning the appropriateness of governance and policy structure and processes.

POOR GOVERANCE AND POLICY IMPLEMENTATION

A final and important theme to emerge is the conclusion that, generally speaking, oceanic and coastal governance is failing worldwide. Although there are a few so-called success stories, such as the management of New Zealand fisheries using a quota management system as reported by Basil Sharp in Chapter 13, these 'success stories' are the exceptions rather than the rule. Marine ecosystems worldwide are deteriorating, as was shown in Chapters 3 and 9, often with economic benefits that are uncertain and/or outweighed by greater equity and poverty dis-benefits.

Due to a multiplicity of factors, governance structures and processes in the marine environment are arguably poorly developed, compared with the terrestrial situation. In this regard Bruce Glavovic (in Chapter 14) has listed seven challenges for marine governance that have come as a result of the disconnection between prevailing governance approaches and the distinctive characteristics of marine systems. These challenges include dealing with:

- Inappropriate one-dimensional and universal solutions; 'one size does not fit all' in the marine environment, given the multi-faceted and complex nature of these ecosystems and their connections with the economy and communities.

- Inability to deal with cross-scale and cross-level interactions due to ignorance, lack of information or scale mismatch.
- Inertia and Inflexibility: Oceans and coasts are dynamic complex systems that require an adaptive approach, rather than traditional command and control bureaucratic responses.
- Inappropriate Discounting of Time: Short-term thinking and timeframes often prevail, working against the long-term viability and welfare of the system.
- Inappropriate Reductionism: Whereby complex problems are dealt with by breaking down the problem into its component parts. Such a reductionist approach is unrealistic, given the complex nature of coastal and marine systems.
- Frontier Mentality: Which either assumes there are few foreseeable ecological, thermodynamic and economic constraints to developing marine resources, or assumes these constraints are not relevant.
- Collective Action Problem: Many marine systems are open-access common property resources that transcend national and regional jurisdictional boundaries. This presents particular governance issues when applying property right systems that have been developed for terrestrial contexts where *inter alia* property rights are more 'private' in character.

Many of these governance challenges raised by Glavovic have a strong ecological economics dimension to them concerning issues such as: intergenerational equity, sustainability, property rights design, economy–environment interactions, economic efficiency dimensions, value commensurability, and tradeoff analysis. Hence, there is an obligation by ecological economists to inform the governance debate by offering their particular set of expertise and insights.

FINAL COMMENT: FROM FRONTIER ECONOMICS TO ECOLOGICAL ECONOMICS

To date, a frontier economics has prevailed in the management of our coasts and oceans. There has been acceleration of pressures on the coasts and oceans over the last 30–40 years, including: greatest population growth occurring in coastal locations; unprecedented coastal urbanization; rapidly growing coastal tourism; intensifying of agricultural impacts on the oceans; and heavy demand for fish and offshore energy resources. Under a frontier economics, many of these pressures are expected to continue unchecked, if not to accelerate, in spite of their well-known ecological impacts that are already occurring at an unsustainable rate. Ecological economics, working with other disciplines, needs to seriously address these issues by specifically:

- developing and applying new and existing tools of analysis, such as systems modelling, that can evaluate oceanic–coastal policy options in an integrative manner;
- undertaking more in-depth analyses of the role that oceans and coasts play as critical natural capital;
- obtaining a clearer picture of the value conflicts and valuation issues underlying oceanic–coastal resource management problems;
- developing new ways of understanding and dealing with the inherent complexity and uncertainty in marine systems;
- applying integrative approaches of analysis that track effects occurring across temporal and spatial scales;
- critically analyzing the connections between poverty, environment and economy in the marine context;
- through incisive analysis, helping inform the ongoing debate concerning governance structures and processes in the oceans and coasts.

In short, there is an urgent need to develop an ecological economics of the oceans and coasts that is holistic, realistic, useful and one that, above all, ultimately serves the needs of both current and future generations.

NOTES

1. In Chapter 7, Patterson presented a method for making visible the contributory value of species and processes that exist in nature, but are not picked up by neoclassical valuation methods due to the lack of knowledge (ignorance) of either the survey respondents and/or survey designers.
2. Alfred Marshall (1842–1924) first formalized the *neoclassical theory of value (price)* in terms of a 'partial equilibrium framework'. That is, he constructed the now well-known 'Marshallian scissors', consisting of a supply curve (marginal costs) and a demand curve (marginal utility). The equilibrium price was found to be the point where the two curves intersected (that is, marginal utility = marginal cost). At this equilibrium price, the maximum net economic benefit is generated. This became the standard theory of value (price) that has dominated neoclassical economics to this day. It has become the orthodox approach – rarely challenged and widely applied to a whole range of public policy issues, including ecological problems.

REFERENCES

Blamey, R.K., P. McCarthy and R. Smith (2000), *Citizens, Juries and Small Group Decision-Making*, Canberra: The Australian National University.

Blaug, M. (1997), *Economic Theory in Retrospect*, Cambridge: Cambridge University Press.

Brown, C., E. Corcoran, P. Hekerenrath and J. Thonell (eds) (2006), *Marine and Coastal Ecosystems and Human Wellbeing: A Synthesis Report Based on the Findings of the Millennium Ecosystem Assessment*, New York: United Nations Environment Programme, 76 pp.

Cartwright, T.J. (1973), 'Problems, solutions and strategies: a contribution to the theory and practice of planning', *Journal of the American Institute of Planners*, **39**: 179–187.

Cleveland, C.J. (1992), 'Energy quality and energy surplus in the extraction of fossil fuels in the U.S.', *Ecological Economics*, **6**: 139–162.

Cole, K., J. Cameron and C. Edwards (1991), *Why Economists Disagree: The Political Economy of Economics*, Harlow: Longman.

Costanza, R. and J. Greer (1997), 'The Chesapeake Bay and its watershed: a model for sustainable ecosystem management', in R. Costanza, *Frontiers in Ecological Economics: Transdisciplinary Essays by Robert Costanza*, Cheltenham, UK and Lyme, USA: Edward Elgar, pp. 427–472

Costanza, R. and B. Hannon (1989), 'Dealing with the mixed units problem in ecosystem network analysis', in F. Wulff, J.G. Field and K.H. Mann (eds), *Network Analysis in Marine Ecology: Methods and Applications*, Berlin: Springer, pp. 90–115.

Costanza, R. and J. King (1999), 'The first decade of ecological economics', *Ecological Economics*, **28**: 1–9.

Costanza, R., R. d'Arge, R. De Groot, S. Farber, M. Grasso, B. Hannon, K. Limburg, S. Naeem, R.V. O'Neil, J. Paruelo, R.G. Raskin, P. Sutton and M. van den Belt (1997), 'The value of the world's ecosystem services and natural capital', *Nature*, **387**: 253–260.

Fujita, M., P. Krugman and A.J. Venables (1999), *The Spatial Economy: Cities, Regions and International Trade*, Cambridge: MIT Press.

Goodland, R. and M.E. Daly (1993), 'Why northern income growth is not the solution to southern poverty', *Ecological Economics*, **8**: 85–101.

Martinez-Alier, J. (2002), *Environmentalism of the Poor*, Cheltenham, UK: Edward Elgar.

Martinez-Alier, J., G. Munda and J. O'Neill (1998), 'Weak comparability of values as a foundation for ecological economics', *Ecological Economics*, **26**: 277–286.

Munda, G., P. NijKamp and P. Rietreld (1994), 'Qualitative multicriteria evaluation for environmental management', *Ecological Economics*, **26**: 97–112.

Myrdal, G. (1944), *An American Dilemma*, New York: Harper and Brothers.

O'Connor, M. (1994), 'Complexity and co-evolution: methodology for a positive treatment of indeterminacy', *Futures*, **26**(6): 610–615.

O'Hara, S.U. (1996), 'Discursive ethics in ecosystem valuation and environmental policy', *Ecological Economics*, **16**: 95–97.

Romer, P.M. (1990), 'Endogenous technological change', *Journal of Political Economy*, **98**: S71–S102.

Sagoff, M. (1998), 'Aggregation and deliberation in valuing environmental public goods: a look beyond contingent pricing', *Ecological Economics*, **24**: 213–230.

Schumpeter, J.A. (1954), *History of Economic Analysis*, London: Allen and Unwin.

Solow, R.M. (1956), 'A contribution to the theory of economic growth', *Quarterly Journal of Economics*, **70**: 65–94.

Stevens, T.M., R. Belkier, D. Dennis, D. Kittredge and C. Wills (2000), 'Comparison of contingent valuation and conjoint analysis in ecosystem management', *Ecological Economics*, **32**: 63–74.

Wilson, J.A., J. Acheson and P. Kleban (1996), 'Chaos and parametric management', *Marine Policy*, **20**(5): 429–438.

Wilson, M.A. and R.B. Howarth (2002), 'Discourse based valuation of ecosystem services: establishing fair outcomes through group deliberation', *Ecological Economics*, **41**: 431–433.

Worm, B., E.B. Barbier, N. Beaumont, J.E. Duffy, C. Folke, B.S. Halpern, J.B.C. Jackson, H.K. Lotze, F. Micheli, S.R. Palumbi, E. Sola, K.A. Silkoe, J.J. Stachowiscz and R. Watson (2006), 'Impacts of biodiversity loss of ocean ecosystem services', *Science*, **314**: 787–790.

Index

biomes 35
biophysical approach 9–12
biophysical interdependencies 140
see also contributory value
Bird's Head seascape, Indonesia 58
Black Sea 66, 208
Blaug, M. 349
blue crab fishery 133
bluefin tuna *see* tuna fishing
Bockstael, N.E. 134
Borges, A.V. 47
bottom trawling 64, 204
bottom-up responses 85–6
Boulding, K.E. 7, 8, 168–9
boundaries
clarifying 336
incongruous 330
Boyd, P.W. 36
'breaks' in transportation 188–9
Breitbart, M. 59
Brown, C. *see* Millennium Ecosystem
Assessment
bycatch 204–6, 307–8

Canada 56, 64
capabilities 245–6
capital assets 252, 253, 317
see also natural capital
capital investment 105
capital theory 95
Capone, D.G. 54
carbon cycle 2, 43–4, 45, 53–4
carbon dioxide
anthropogenic global carbon budget
44–5
contributory value in global marine
system 161
emissions and global economic
growth 191
future climate change 44–7
past climate variations 41–3
processes controlling atmospheric
concentrations 43–4, 45
carbon export 44, 45
carnivores 33, 34
Cartesian duality 167
Cash, D.W. 330
catch-balancing regime 307–8
cellular respiration 34

Census of Marine Life 70
Challis, J. 315
Chambers, R. 252
chaotic behaviour 87
charismatic megafauna 2, 17, 53, 161
Chesapeake Bay 134
Chiesura, A. 9
Chisholm, S.W. 51
chlorophyll 34
chrematistics 178–9
circular and cumulative causation
189–90, 350
circulation, oceanic 2, 28–30, 48
Ciriacy-Wantrup, S.V. 96
civic science 328–9, 335
civil society 321, 332
global civil society 325
Clark, C.W. 95, 109
climate change 5, 12, 41–9, 66, 191, 344
ENSO 37
future climate change 44–7
impacts on ocean ecology 47–9
global economic growth 191
impacts on coastal ecosystems 201
impacts on oceanic ecosystems 208–9
oceanic influence 41–7
past climate variations 41–3
closure
of fisheries 282
of marine sanctuary 234–9
Coase, R. 289, 296
Coase theorem 296–7
coastal agglomeration 189–90, 350
coastal economies
growth 3–4, 188–90, 350
uneven development 190
coastal ecosystems 2, 38–9
impacts on 196–202
coastal oceans 38–9
global carbon budget 47
coastal zone ocean 28
role in climate change 47
coasts 15, 19, 27–50
biological characterization 30–41
distinguishing characteristics 316–20,
333
ecological and economic importance
1–3
increasing economic pressures 3–5

fish landings 63–5
trophic pyramid 33–4
Trujillo, A.P. 30
trust 338
tuna fishing 229, 232, 235
  impacts of sanctuary closure 236–9
Tydemers, D.H. 206

uncertainty 319, 346–7
UNEP Global Programme of Action for
  Protection of the Marine
  Environment from Land-Based
  Activities 6
uneven development 190
United Nations Agreement on Straddling
  Fish Stocks and Highly Migratory
  Fish Stocks (UNFSA) 324
United Nations Conference on
  Environment and Development
  (UNCED) (1992) 6, 51, 66, 249,
  324
United Nations Convention on the Law
  of the Sea (UNCLOS) 6, 67, 249,
  323–5, 326, 327
United Nations Millennium
  Development Goals 249
United States of America (USA) 208
  Chesapeake Bay 134
  Delaware Bay economy–ecology
    model 220–28
  Florida salt marsh 133
  Louisiana 2, 132–3, 133
  Stellwagen Bank National Marine
    Sanctuary 228–40
universal solutions 329–30, 352
universalism 14, 173
upwelling zones 37, 38, 39
urban runoff 200
use values 97
UV-B radiation 66

Vachon, R. 180
value 16–17
  conflicts and valuation 347–9
  contributory *see* contributory value
  economic value of rights 292–6
  intrinsic value of biodiversity 56
  neoclassical analysis 16, 95–118
  non-market value *see* non-market

value
  non-rational approach *see* non-rational
    approach to value
  total economic value 3, 96–8, 127–8
Van der Zwaag, D.L. 327
vicious circle 247, 250
vision 337
Vitousek, P.M. 10
vulnerability context 252, 253, 317

Wackernagel, M. 62–3
Waitangi, Treaty of 306
Walker, B. 90
Ward, B. 168
wastes 206–8
  see also pollution
water 29
water quality 134–5
water regulation 123, 130
water supply 123, 130
Waterhouse, J.C. 13
way-finders 174, 182
weak comparability 166
weather forecasting 87
whales 230
  movement of 232, 233
    impact of sanctuary closure on
      234–6, 237, 239
  watching 229–30, 232, 234
    impact of sanctuary closure 234–6,
      237, 238, 239
*White Paper on Sustainable Coastal
  Development in South Africa* 255,
  256
willingness to accept compensation
  (WAC or WTA) 124, 126, 127
willingness to pay (WTP) 124–5, 126,
  127, 133–4, 140
Wilson, E.O. 51
Wilson, J.A. 13
wind damage 133
World Bank 4, 170
World Conservation Union 197
  'Red List' 62
World Summit on Sustainable
  Development (WSSD) (2002) 6,
  249, 251, 325
Worm, B. 2, 4
WWF 68